Rationalization in Religions

This volume was published with the support of the Berlin-Brandenburg Academy of Sciences and Humanities and the Israel Academy of Sciences and Humanities.

berlin-brandenburgische
AKADEMIE DER WISSENSCHAFTEN

האקדמיה הלאומית הישראלית למדעים
المجمع الوطني الإسرائيلي للعلوم والآداب
THE ISRAEL ACADEMY OF SCIENCES AND HUMANITIES

Rationalization in Religions

Judaism, Christianity and Islam

Edited by Yohanan Friedmann
and Christoph Markschies

DE GRUYTER

ISBN 978-3-11-073659-5
e-ISBN (PDF) 978-3-11-044639-5
e-ISBN (EPUB) 978-3-11-043734-8

Library of Congress Control Number: 2018951297

Bibliografical information published by the Deutsche Nationalbibliothek
The Deutsche Nationalbibliothek lists this publication in the Deutsche Nationalbibliografie; detailed bibliografical data are available at http://dnb.dnb.de.

This volume is text- and page-identical with the hardback published in 2019.
Cover image: Game of Chess between a Crusader and a Saracen. From a Spanish manuscript of the *Libro de los Juegos*, commissioned by Alfonso X, the Wise (1221–1284), king of Castile and Leon from 1252. 13th century. akg-images / WHA / World History Archive
Typesetting: Dörlemann Satz GmbH & Co. KG, Lemförde
Printing and binding: CPI books GmbH, Leck

www.degruyter.com

Table of Contents

Foreword —— VI

Christoph Markschies
Introduction: Rationalization in Religions —— 1

Shaul Shaked
Dualists against Monotheists: Zoroastrian Debates with Other Religions —— 5

Maren R. Niehoff
Philo's Rationalization of Judaism —— 21

Moshe Idel
Forms of Rationalization in Medieval Jewish Thought —— 45

Christoph Markschies
Origen of Alexandria: The Bible and Philosophical Rationality, or: Problems of Traditional Dualisms —— 63

Aryeh Kofsky and Serge Ruzer
Theodore of Mopsuestia: Rationalizing Hermeneutics and Theology —— 74

Yonatan Moss
"I Trapped You with Guile": Rationalizing Theology in Late Antiquity —— 103

Moshe Sluhovsky
Rationalizing Visions in Early Modern Catholicism —— 127

Simon Gerber
"They Shall Be All Taught of God": Schleiermacher on Christianity and Protestantism —— 146

Johannes Zachhuber
Christian Theology as a Rationalization of Religion: The Case of the Nineteenth-Century Research University —— 156

Volker Gerhardt
Die Rationalität des Glaubens
Über die wechselseitige Angewiesenheit von Glauben und Wissen — 178

Sarah Stroumsa
Early Muslim and Jewish *Kalām*: The Enterprise of Reasoned Discourse — 202

Livnat Holtzman and Miriam Ovadia
On Divine Aboveness (*al-Fawqiyya*):
The Development of Rationalized Ḥadīth-Based Argumentations
in Islamic Theology — 224

Binyamin Abrahamov
Rationality and Rationalism in Islamic Mysticism:
The Case of Ibn al-ʿArabī — 270

Yohanan Friedmann
Quasi-Rational and Anti-Rational Elements in Radical Muslim Thought:
The Case of Abū al-Aʿlā Mawdūdī — 289

Contributors to This Volume — 301

Index
Places — **303**
Names — **304**

Foreword

The present volume is based on the conference on "Rationalization in Religions" convened jointly by the Berlin-Brandenburgische Akademie der Wissenschaften and the Israel Academy of Sciences and Humanities in Berlin on December 16–18, 2013. The conference was the first in a series of workshops on religion and modernity arranged on the basis of the collaboration agreement concluded in 2000 between the two academies. We are grateful to the Fritz Thyssen Foundation in Cologne for its part in funding the conference; to Mark Bergermann for organizing the conference in Berlin; and to the leadership and staff of our respective academies for their support.

Our thanks are due to Simon Cook for his initial round of copy-editing of most of the articles in this volume, and particularly to Deborah Greniman, Senior Editor of English-language publications in the Publications Department of the Israel Academy, who revised all the material and prepared it for press with her customary professionalism and efficacy. We are grateful as well to Dr. Sophie Wagenhofer of De Gruyter in Berlin for arranging the volume's publication and to Janine Brückner of Humboldt University Berlin for her assistance.

Yohanan Friedmann, The Israel Academy of Sciences and Humanities
Christoph Markschies, Berlin-Brandenburgische Akademie der Wissenschaften

Jerusalem and Berlin, 2018

https://doi.org/10.1515/9783110446395-001

Christoph Markschies

Introduction: Rationalization in Religions

Philosopher Carl Friedrich Gethmann, a member of the Berlin-Brandenburg Academy, has described rationalization as the "targeted, structured and reproducible operation of optimization."[1] Gethmann's broad definition covers rationalization across a range of very different areas – in the economy, in society, even in the mind of the individual. In our own field of religious studies, the first scholar who comes to mind in this context is the philosopher and sociologist Max Weber, who introduced the term "rationalization" to the field.[2] Maintaining that religious rationalization preceded social rationalization, Weber identified rationalization structures within the Judeo-Christian tradition that, as Gethmann puts it, "encouraged the establishment of rational conceptions of the world and the emergence of a modern consciousness."[3] In his studies of the "economic ethics of the world religions," Weber developed the notion of a universal historical process of "disenchantment" (*Entzauberung*[4]) of the religious-metaphysical conceptions of the world and argued for a "unidirectional rationalization of all world religions." According to Weber, all paths of religious rationalization lead towards an understanding of the world that is purified of magical notions. Only the occidental path of development, however, leads to a fully decentralized understanding of the world.[5]

It is not my intention, at this juncture, to provide a full recapitulation of Weber's view of the rationalization that is inherent in all world religions. His basic assumptions concerning an occidental rationalism, and thus a particularly marked rationalism in the occidental religions, which he set against the Orient and its religions,[6] appear highly problematic to us today. In view of the obvious problems in Weber's conceptualization, I believe it makes more sense, in talking about "rationalization in religions," to stick with Gethmann's definition of rationalization and to speak of an optimization of the "rationality" of religion. But what is rationality? I turn again to Gethmann, who defines "rationality" as "developing processes for the discursive upholding of claims to validity, to follow these and to

1 Gethmann 1995a:463. The following introductory remarks are based on the greetings I delivered as Vice President of the Berlin-Brandenburg Academy to the participants in the Berlin conference on "Rationalization in Religions" on which this volume is based.
2 Schluchter 2016:22–42, 127–261.
3 Gethmann 1995a:463.
4 Weber 1994:22 and 2001:273; cf. also Joas 2017:201–277 and Schluchter 2009:1–17.
5 Habermas1981.
6 Weber 1984:9–11; cf. Schluchter 2016:192–196.

https://doi.org/10.1515/9783110446395-002

avail of them."[7] A religion becomes rationalized when its exponents argue discursively – that is, in line with contemporary standards of rationality – in favor of its claims to validity, and when those claims to validity can be asserted in this way, instead of authoritatively and using instruments of power.

Notwithstanding our criticism of Weber, we are left with the question of whether such a tendency is actually inherent in all world religions, and whether this development intensifies over time. The conference on which the present volume is based set out to address this question, focusing mainly on Judaism, Christianity and Islam, aside from Shaul Shaked's treatment of Zoroastrianism. Many of the papers focus specifically on the formative periods in which these three religions (sometimes referred to as "Abrahamic") came into contact with the "cultures of rationality" that surrounded them, leading them to develop independent philosophies, theologies or at least argumentations with the pagan culture of rationality on the basis of their respective Holy Scriptures.

To an extent, Berlin can be described as a hot spot for this kind of research into the formative periods of the Abrahamic faiths. In the area of Judaism, for example, one could mention the studies of Peter Schäfer of Berlin (and Princeton), who convened several conferences, the results of which have since been published, to examine the relationships between the Greco-Roman culture of rationality and the large corpuses of rabbinic literature.[8] Regarding Islam, we might point to the Berlin research of Islamic studies scholar Sabine Schmidtke, also of (Berlin and) Princeton, whose paper "Rediscovering Theological Rationalism in the Medieval World of Islam"[9] was part of a larger project funded by the European Research Council – the groundwork for which, however, was laid down by several research groups at the Israel Institute for Advanced Studies, to which our Jerusalem colleagues, such as Sarah Stroumsa, made a considerable contribution.[10] In the area of Early Christianity, we may note the studies of the reception of the Alexandrian culture of knowledge, and especially of (neo)Platonic philosophy, among Alexandrian Christians such as Clement of Alexandria and Origen; this work, too, has taken place in Berlin, within the circle surrounding the edition of the works of these Early Christian thinkers, in particular at the Berlin-Brandenburg Academy, but of course not only there.[11]

7 Gethmann 1995b:468. For a different way of understanding the term, see Schluchter 2015:519–525.

8 Schäfer 1998–2002.

9 For details and a bibliography (including open-access publications) see: https://cordis.europa.eu/project/rcn/88937_en.html (accessed May 5, 2018).

10 See Schmidtke et al. 2007.

11 See Markschies 2007.

A number of efforts have recently been made to analyze and compare these attempts – facilitated by the continued existence in Late Antiquity of a culture of knowledge with shared standards of rationality – to integrate a culture of knowledge and rationality into the respective religions; worth mentioning here, for example, are the publications of Guy Stroumsa.[12] These comparative approaches are, of course, still in their nascent stages, with studies of "rationalization in religions" generally limited to one of the three – Judaism, Christianity or Islam – not to mention certain limitations in their perspectives (for example, because of the way reception has developed in modern times, the significance of Platonism has been afforded more attention than that of the Stoic tradition).

An earlier collaborative effort to examine "Religion and Rationality" was undertaken at a conference with that title held in Berlin in 2009.[13] That conference took a closer look at the relationship between scripture and rationalization – that is, between normative texts and efforts to adapt reflective work on them to contemporary standards of rationality. The colloquium's thesis was that interpretation, particularly in the form of scientific commentaries, is a literary medium and institutional method for approaching holy texts that makes it possible to arrive at rationalizations in accord with a methodically controlled procedure. The colloquium took a very broad comparative approach, classifying Marxist texts alongside ancient oriental ones as "Scriptures" in the terms of a phenomenological approach to religion. The question already arose there as to whether a phenomenological comparison of the possibly differing potentials of religions to rationalize their traditions, and of their possibly differing strategies, would have to look not only at interpreting Holy Scriptures but also at theological reflections that are not presented in the form of commentary.

While we might tremble today to sketch broad outlines and model clear structures like those proposed by Weber, perhaps we can nevertheless create a list of criteria to outline how rationalization might be practiced by those actively involved in religions (such as religious experts or theologians). I would like to mention a few questions that might be helpful in this regard:

- What factors promote/impede rationalization?
- From where are the criteria for rationalization drawn, and how are they applied?
- In what institutions does rationalization take place, and where is it critiqued?

---

12 See G. Stroumsa 2013.

13 For the papers presented there, see Kablitz and Markschies 2013. We are indebted to the Fritz Thyssen Foundation for its part in funding both that conference and the one on which this volume is based.

- What circles of proponents propagate, support and utilize rationalization?
- Does the friction between clergy and other theologians that is so characteristic of Christianity exist in other religions as well?

The papers presented herein offer a historical perspective on these and other questions, along with some answers.

References

Gethmann, Carl Friedrich. 1995a. "Rationalisierung." In Jürgen Mittelstraß (ed.), *Enzyklopädie Philosophie und Wissenschaftstheorie*, III. Stuttgart: Metzler. 463 f.

—. 1995b. "Rationalität. *Ibid.* 468–481.

Habermas, Jürgen. 1981. "Max Webers Theorie der Rationalisierung." In idem, *Theorie des kommunikativen Handelns*, I. Frankfurt am Main: Suhrkamp. 225–365.

Joas, Hans. 2017. *Die Macht des Heiligen: Eine Alternative zur Geschichte von der Entzauberung*. Frankfurt am Main: Suhrkamp.

Kablitz, Andreas, and Christoph Markschies (eds.). 2013. *Religion und Rationalität* (Geisteswissenschaftliches Colloquium, 1). Berlin–New York: De Gruyter.

Markschies, Christoph. 2007. *Origenes und sein Erbe: Gesammelte Studien* (Texte und Untersuchungen zur Geschichte der altchristlichen Literatur, 160). Berlin–New York: De Gruyter.

Schäfer, Peter (ed.). 1998–2002. *The Talmud Yerushalmi and Graeco-Roman Culture*, I–III (Texts and Studies in Ancient Judaism, 71, 79, 93). Tübingen: Mohr Siebeck.

Schluchter, Wolfgang. 2009. *Die Entzauberung der Welt: Sechs Studien zu Max Weber.* Tübingen: Mohr Siebeck.

—. 2015. *Grundlegungen der Soziologie: Eine Theoriegeschichte in systematischer Absicht* (Universitätstaschenbücher, 4263). 2nd edition, Tübingen: Mohr Siebeck.

—. 2016. *Religion und Lebensführung*, II: *Studien zu Max Webers Religions- und Herrschaftssoziologie* (Suhrkamp Taschenbücher Wissenschaft, 962). 2nd edition, Frankfurt am Main: Suhrkamp.

Schmidtke, Sabine, Camilla Adang and David Sklare (eds.). 2007. *Common Rationality: Mu'tazilism in Islam and Judaism* (Istanbuler Texte und Studien, 15). Würzburg: Ergon.

Stroumsa, Guy. 2013. "Athens, Jerusalem, Mecca: The Patristic Crucible of the Abrahamic Religions." In M. Vinzent (ed.), *Studia Patristica 62: Papers Presented at the Sixteenth International Conference on Patristic Studies Held in Oxford 2011*. Leuven: Peeters. 153–168.

Weber, Max. 1984 [1920]. *Die Protestantische Ethik*, I: *Eine Aufsatzsammlung*, ed. Johannes Winckelmann (Gütersloher Taschenbücher Siebenstern, 53). 7th edition, Gütersloh: Gütersloher Verlagshaus.

—. 2001 [1914/1921/1922]. *Wirtschaft und Gesellschaft: Die Wirtschaft und die gesellschaftlichen Ordnungen und Mächte*, II: *Religiöse Gemeinschaften*, ed. Hans G. Kippenberg (Max-Weber-Gesamtausgabe, I/22–2). Tübingen: Mohr Siebeck.

—. 1994 [1917/1919]. *Wissenschaft als Beruf, 1917/1919: Politik als Beruf, 1919*, eds. Wolfgang J. Mommsen and Wolfgang Schluchter (Max-Weber-Gesamtausgabe, I/17). Tübingen: Mohr Siebeck.

Shaul Shaked

Dualists against Monotheists: Zoroastrian Debates with Other Religions

Zoroastrianism is regarded as a dualistic religion, perhaps even as the dualistic religion *par excellence*. It is, however, not entirely certain that this was the self-description of Zoroastrians in antiquity. A label is meant to distinguish the group that carries it from other groups. If no groups in the vicinity are designated "monotheistic," the banner of dualism is superfluous. There is no indication that these terms were known in Old or Middle Iranian, and Zoroastrians do not appear to have used the dualist label until late in their history, perhaps not earlier than the early Islamic period.[1]

In antiquity the religion is regularly described by its adherents as Mazdayasnian, that is, relating to the worship of Mazda (an abbreviation of the full name of the deity Ahura Mazda). It may be surmised that followers of the Avestan religion would have been surprised to learn that they were "dualists," i.e., worshippers of two entities (which they were not). Members of the ancient Israelite federation of tribes might have been no less appalled to learn that their worshipping the God of Israel and rejecting the enemies of this deity, whether in the form of the primordial snake, of a Satan, or of the gods of the other peoples around them, marked them as dualists.

When did the Zoroastrian community or its leaders come to the awareness that they were "dualists"? The parallel question could well be pursued regarding the Jewish community: When did they affirm themselves as monotheists? This second question is not part of the present investigation, and I shall not enter into it in any detail. There seem, however, to be indications in the biblical texts that YHWH, the God of Israel, was often regarded, not as a unique deity, but as the

1 The earliest secure attestation of the term *dōīh*, "dualism," seems to be in the ninth-century literature, most likely echoing the Arabic term *thanawiyya*; cf., e.g., *ŠGV* 10:1: *han dar awar xuaškār i yakī-xuaškārą kəš vīnārašnica i duī ažaš padāihəṭ*, "Another chapter. Concerning the theory of the monotheists, of which [chapter] will also be manifest the [right] management of dualism." The term *dōīh* is also used in the sense of the contrast of two opposing notions; cf. *GBd* 4:27: *ānōh kū gannāg-mēnōg zamīg suft padeš andar dwārist čiyōn hamāg xīr ī gētīg pad dōīh wardišnīh hamēmāl ud ham-kōxšišn ud ul ud frōd gumēzišnīh paydāg būd*, "in the place where the Evil Spirit entered, having pierced the Earth, just as all the things of the material world appeared by changing into duality [as] a mixture of adversary and fellow-combatant, [of] up and down."

https://doi.org/10.1515/9783110446395-003

mightiest of deities, more powerful and more deserving of worship than the gods of the peoples surrounding the early Israelites.

Coming back to the Zoroastrians, or rather to the Mazda-worshippers, the question as to the nature of the change from being simply Mazdaeans to becoming upholders of a theology of dualism is quite pertinent. We have no documentary evidence for a decision to switch from one form of belief to another, and indeed it is unlikely that such a switch ever took place. It may be assumed that this change was not abrupt or deliberate, but the outcome of a long period of contact with religious groups that perceived themselves as worshippers of a single god, to the exclusion of the other gods venerated by ethnic or religious communities in their environment. This, of course, is what distinguished the Jews of Late Antiquity (or the Christians, who were initially affiliated with them) from most other peoples of the Near East.

We have indirect evidence for this assumption in the Christian martyrologies of the Sasanian period. In that literature Christian devotees are brought to trial and accept severe torture and execution, sometimes following a theological debate with a *mōbadh*, in which the Christian (who grew up as a Zoroastrian) is accused of betraying the religion of his forefathers. He retorts by demonstrating the inanity of the Zoroastrian faith and its practice. We may take it for granted that the sermons delivered by the Christian martyrs, and indeed the whole legal discourse presented in these narratives, is not historically accurate. But the setting and the underlying assumptions of the Christian authors of these narratives certainly reflect their perceptions of their own faith and that of their Zoroastrian adversaries.

In these accounts, the Christians do not attack their opponents as dualists but tend rather to dwell upon features that display the *polytheism* of the Zoroastrians. Most of the time, the Christians standing trial and then martyred are faced with the demand that they worship the sun, the moon and fire; sometimes the requirement of the authorities is that, in addition, they offer sacrifices "to the great god Zeus, to Nanai the greatest goddess and to the gods Bel and Nebo."[2] This seems to indicate that in the fourth and fifth centuries, the main point of the theological debate was not to demand of the renegade who had converted to Christianity that he adopt dualism, but that he worship gods other than the Christian deity. This was the Christians' understanding of the situation, and we have no serious reason to suppose that they misunderstood the Zoroastrian demands, although they may have had a distorted understanding of the subtleties of the Zoroastrian religion. Many Zoroastrian laymen presumably had the same view of the practice of Zoroastrian worship as reflected in this list of deities.

2 For example, Hoffmann 1880:29, in the martyrology of Mu'ain.

At any rate, there is little evidence to show that the debate ran along the lines of monotheism versus dualism; it was really an argument of Christian monotheists against what they regarded as Zoroastrian polytheism. This comes up very forcefully, for example, in the account of the martyrdom of Qardagh.[3] The arguments of ˁAbdišōˁ, a Christian hermit who conducted a theological debate with Qardagh (then still a Sasanian functionary, a *marzbān*) and managed to convert him to Christianity, are very clearly of the type addressed to people who belong to a religion where various natural objects are worshipped, such as the sun, the moon, earth, water and fire, and who may be criticized for worshipping non-living beings. Qardagh is swayed by these arguments, embraces Christianity and becomes a martyr.

In the case of Qardagh, the Christian missionary shows no understanding of the meaning of Zoroastrian worship, and the dualism that may have been a theme of this theological debate is never mentioned. Qardagh himself may have had no more than a faint understanding of his own religion, or at least no firm notion of the dualistic basis of its theology – as viewed through the lens of the Christian narrator. The notion of dualism becomes prominent only much later, and it flourishes in the early Islamic period, in the ninth and tenth centuries of the Common Era, when the Muslim theologians, who show great interest in tabulating the different religions of the world by using distinct labels for each, take delight in attacking the dualistic views of the Persians, to whom they usually apply the term *majūs*[4] and sometimes, more vaguely, *thanawiyya*, "dualists."

An abundance of literature was produced in the early Islamic period in Middle Persian, debating with the three monotheistic religions and with Manichaeism, and defending the idea of Zoroastrian dualism as the only rational explanation of the problems of the universe, its origin, its purpose, and in particular the status of evil in the world. In the debate with the Manichaeans, the thrust of the argument is to establish the claim that only the Zoroastrian version of how the world was created can be regarded as acceptable and intellectually satisfying. From the Muslim point of view, the core of the anti-Zoroastrian argument is the allegation that dualism deviates from the principle of a single deity by depicting the world as the outcome of a battle between two divine powers.[5]

3 Bedjan 1891:452–456.

4 Reflecting *maguš*, the Old Iranian term designating a Zoroastrian priest. It was in all likelihood borrowed into Arabic via Aramaic *magušа*.

5 This is apparent in the polemic of al-Qāsim b. Ibrāhīm against (supposedly) Ibn al-Muqaffaʿ; see, e. g., Guidi 1927:31. Guidi himself wavers on the issue of whether Ibn al-Muqaffaʿ is indeed the author of the book attacked by al-Qāsim b. Ibrāhīm. As I have discussed elsewhere (Shaked 1984), this seems unlikely. A fairly large body of Ibn al-Muqaffaʿ's writings is extant, and none shows a

This line of argument may have started somewhat earlier than the Muslim conquest of Iran. The great assemblage of short theological treatises included in the third book of the *Dēnkard*, compiled, as second editor, by Ādurbād ī Ēmēdān in the ninth century CE, contains chapters of debates with Jews and Christians.[6] Some of these chapters may have been composed in the late Sasanian period, but there is generally no way of establishing a precise date for these sections of the text.

The arguments used by the Mazdaean theologians against their monotheistic adversaries mostly belong to the stock-in-trade claims and counter-claims that are so common in theological polemics between Jews, Christians and Muslims. We shall come back to some of the detailed arguments further on, but it is interesting to look first at some of the basic postulates of the Mazdaean theologians, as formulated by Mardān-Farrox (ninth century CE), author of the polemical *Škand-gumānīg-wizār* (henceforth: *ŠGV*), a title that may be translated as "The Doubt-Smashing Expounder."

Mardān-Farrox establishes at the outset that "Ohrmazd is a *mēnōg* even among the [other] *mēnōg* entities."[7] This is a paradoxical statement. *Mēnōg* and *gētīg* refer, respectively, to the non-material form of existence and the form of existence obtaining in the material world, the world of creation. *Gētīg* can be apprehended by the senses, while a *mēnōg* entity can only be grasped mentally or intellectually, not sensually.[8] This distinction might seem somehow to parallel the hierarchical division of existence into material and spiritual, widespread in late Judaism, Christianity and Islam, and shared with the Gnostic systems. This, however, is a false impression.[9] While the gnostic schools, whose influence on

---

Manichaean tendency. Ibn al-Muqaffaʿ's compositions include several translations from Middle Persian literature, as well as writings that carry his name as author. Both groups (including those that he signed as his own compositions, e.g., *al-adab al-ṣaghīr* or *al-risāla fī l-ṣaḥāba*) contain passages that can clearly be identified as deriving from extant Zoroastrian books. In none of these texts do we come across Manichaean tendencies or quotations from Manichaean literature. In addition, the style of the book attacked by al-Qāsim b. Ibrāhīm shows marked differences from that of Ibn al-Muqaffaʿ's elegant prose.

6 These Zoroastrian debates have been translated and discussed more than once. See, e.g., Darmesteter 1889; Gray 1906; Shaked 1990. On the *Dēnkard* in general, see Menasce 1958.

7 *Andar-ez mēnōgān mēnōg* (*ŠGV* 1:2). Skjærvø (2002:30, n. 7; also 2014:col. 272, n. 35) argues in favor of transcribing *mēnōy* as a reflection of *maniiauua* and *gētīy* as a reflection of *gaēθiia*. However, the spellings **mynwg** and **gytyg** are attested in Manichaean Middle Persian (see Durkin-Meisterernst 2004:170, 236), and I see no reason to reject them.

8 For a discussion of these terms, see Shaked 1971.

9 The Islamic paired contrasting notions of *bāṭin*, "internal" (or "invisible"), and *ẓāhir*, "exterior" (or "apparent"), have also – erroneously, I believe – been compared to the Zoroastrian

late Judaism, Christianity and Islam was profound, present evil as identical with matter, Zoroastrianism does not equate the ontological dichotomy of spiritual versus material with the ethical split between good and evil.

The Zoroastrian way of thinking does not assign a moral or religious supremacy to the non-material aspect of the universe and does not regard the material aspect as morally debased. On the contrary, *gētīg*, the world that can be grasped by the senses, is essentially a creation of Ohrmazd, the supreme god, while *mēnōg*, the non-material world, is not a monopoly of Ohrmazd. Ohrmazd and the divine entourage are indeed *mēnōg* entities, but so also are Ahreman and the demonic world, embodying the principle of evil. The two principles, good and evil, are non-material. The material world is also divided between these two, but the good creation is the work of Ohrmazd, while the Ahremanian evil presence, which infiltrated the material world with the aim of destroying it, is in a sense alien to it. The evil element in the world is not perceived as an actual creation. It is a distortion, a corruption, and does not constitute a legitimate part of the material world. As long as the present world lasts, Ahreman is active within it and is capable of causing damage and destruction, but in the eschatological dimension Ahreman is eliminated from the material creation.[10]

The meaning of the remarkable phrase "He [= Ohrmazd] is a *mēnōg* even among the *mēnōg* entities" is based on a semantic play on the term *mēnōg*, which has two different usages in this phrase. In the first occurrence it is used in the sense of "imperceivable by the senses," hence "exalted," while in the second it denotes the ontological mode of existence of those belonging to the sphere of non-visible entities. The phrase seeks to convey the idea that if all the deities (as well as all the demons) are *mēnōg*, i. e., invisible, Ohrmazd holds a special position among them as the most refined and least easily apprehended.

The *ŠGV*[11] begins its series of refutations of what it regards as the false religions by giving several basic postulates. Among them is the statement that contraries can never collaborate; hence, the possibility that the deity could change

---

pair *mēnōg* and *gētīg*, according to the "Addenda and Corrigenda" attached to Menasce 1945, which mentions an oral suggestion by Fritz Meier. However, notwithstanding the apparent partial overlap, the Arabic pair of notions belongs to a different semantic sphere. In the usage of Sufis, Ismāʿīlis, jurisprudents and others, *bāṭin* denotes something that has a deeper (hidden) meaning or aspect that is not readily evident, while *ẓāhir* stands for something that is visible and often regarded as superficial, conventional or of lesser value. The Zoroastrian dichotomy deals with an ontological difference and does not introduce a distinction of value between the two.

10 Shaked 1971.

11 For more on the *ŠGV*, see Menasce 1945 and Cereti 2004.

the essence of evil to good is logically excluded. Good and evil are autonomous principles that are essentially immutable (*ŠGV* 3:29–37).

Elsewhere, the author explains the structure of the universe through a metaphor. God, the creator of the universe, is like a gardener who plants a garden and takes care of it. He acts against the destructive beasts whose aim is to cause damage. Ohrmazd is the gardener, Ahreman the harmful beasts. The traps that the gardener sets in order to prevent the animals from causing damage are represented in the universe by the sky. The means of inhibiting the destruction caused by the beasts is Time. There are also treasurers who examine the merits and faults of the various creatures; these are the good and evil agents, who create the right reward for a person's actions. In this way Ohrmazd saves and protects the good creatures (*ŠGV* 4:63–101).

A brief account of the main Sasanian creation narrative may be in order.[12] In the beginning there were two spirits, unlimited by time and space. Ohrmazd was on high, Ahreman below. Ohrmazd was omniscient (knowing future events in addition to those that have already taken place), while Ahreman's knowledge was deficient (of the type that comes after the act). Ohrmazd was luminous; Ahreman resided in darkness. Both were equally powerful. Ohrmazd was bent on doing good, while Ahreman's nature led him to cause damage, destruction and strife.

The action starts with Ahreman looking upward, perceiving the luminosity of Ohrmazd and experiencing an urge to get hold of it and destroy it. Ohrmazd, by virtue of his omniscience, knows that a war will break out between them and that neither will win as long as the battle takes place in *mēnōg* (the only form of being before the creation of the world). He offers peace to Ahreman, but his offer is rejected. He proposes to his adversary that the duration of the battle be limited to nine thousand years. Ahreman agrees and thus signs his own ultimate defeat. Their agreement means that the fighting will take place not in *mēnōg*, where no time limits exist and the fighting can continue forever, but in *gētīg*, the material world, where time and space are delimited.

The material world is a creation of Ohrmazd. Ahreman, in his destructive zeal, invades it and causes enormous devastation. At the same time, however, Ahreman finds himself entrapped. The sky, in the shape of an egg, encloses the created world and makes it impossible for Ahreman to escape. Their initial agreement ensures ultimate victory to Ohrmazd, but it leaves Ahreman in the created world with enormous power to do evil.

---

12 In the following paragraphs I offer a concise paraphrase put together from the two main textual sources for the Zoroastrian creation story, found in *GBd* and *WZ*.

This, in a nutshell, is the frame story of the creation, leading to the salvation of the world. It certainly possesses a coherent and logical structure, and its potential appeal to people in antiquity and, indeed, to some thoughtful people in modern times, is understandable.[13]

When we return from the mythological narrative to the philosophical arguments of the *ŠGV*, we come across such statements as: "Although there are innumerable pairs of opposites, it is impossible to talk about innumerable separate entities. All of them fall under the basic distinction between good and evil" (*ŠGV* 8:92–102). There are ontologically only two entities, and the apparent multitude of beings is reducible to the two categories of good and evil.

Other postulates occurring in the *ŠGV* may be mentioned. It is impossible for evil to be derived from something that is perfectly good (*ŠGV* 8:104). If God is perfect in goodness and knowledge, it is manifest that ignorance and evil cannot derive from Him. Were it possible for those negative attributes to derive from Him, it would mean that He is not perfect (*ŠGV* 8:108–109). If someone says: "I see that both good and evil (sometimes) proceed from a single substance, like a man," this is because man is not perfect in something. Lack of perfection in goodness causes evil to issue from that person; lack of perfection in health causes him to get sick, and for this reason he dies (*ŠGV* 8:117–119). There is a complementary relationship between the physiological and the moral sphere.

The integration of the moral sphere of action with religious or mythological language is best exemplified by the following saying: "When a man becomes angry, this is because Wahman[14] is far from him, and when Wahman holds his place (in him), there is no Xešm[15] there" (*ŠGV* 8:128–129). Similar things apply to uttering truth or lying: Each of the actions that affect the religious and moral integrity of a person can be tied to the presence of the corresponding good or evil entity in man. That man is capable of uttering words of truth as well as lies demonstrates that men, or at least most men, are not perfectly attuned with one of the spirits recognized by the Zoroastrian religion. A certain mode of behavior, according to the Zoroastrian doctrine, demonstrates that the person who behaves in this manner is inhabited by a spirit that represents the corresponding quality, whether good or evil. The radical separation of the two poles requires that each action be classified as one or the other. It follows that man, prone as he is to con-

---

13 Among them the great Iranist W.B. Henning (see Henning 1951:45–47).

14 Wahman, literally "good thinking," is one of the powers in the retinue of Ohrmazd and stands for harmony, balance and tranquility.

15 Xešm, "anger, fury," the direct antagonist of Wahman and a member of the retinue of Ahreman, stands for uncontrolled and irrational behavior.

tradictory behavior, can hardly be described as a perfect example of one of the two modes of being. In other words, he can seldom be absolutely good or absolutely evil.

The most conspicuous logical weakness of the monotheists, according to the Zoroastrian arguments, is that they indirectly impute to God both good and evil. God is said to be omniscient and omnipotent, and yet the world created by Him contains so much evil that the question arises: Is God responsible for the evil in the world? If the answer is positive, God is not good. If God is not responsible for evil, He cannot be called omnipotent. Should we rather say – thus goes the Zoroastrian argument – that God does not know that evil exists? In that case He is not omniscient.

Here are some extracts from the *ŠGV*, illustrating the polemical style of the Zoroastrian author in his attacks on the Islamic doctrines:

> Ask them [the Muslims] now: The God who is always benevolent, forgiving, doer of good deeds, upholder of the law, one who knows all that is, was and will be, and whose will is carried out in everything that He desires – is (His action) only (according to) justice and arbitration,[16] or is it once thus and once otherwise? For if He is benevolent, doer of good deeds and forgiving, why did He, through His benevolence, good deeds and forgiveness, hurl at His own creatures Ahreman, the *dēvs*, hell (and) all those evil sparks of lightning(?)?[17] If He did not know that, where is His wisdom and omniscience? If He did not wish to prevent wickedness and evil from reaching the creatures, and to give good things to every single person, where are His acts of justice and arbitration? (*ŠGV* 11:6–10)
> Whenever they [the Muslims] say that all good and evil came from God – unless they deny Him these four capacities that are necessary in a divinity, namely omniscience, omnipotence, goodness and forbearance – they inevitably take away from Him one of these capacities, (and) He is not perfect in His divinity. For if God is [by definition] omniscient, omnipotent, good and forbearing, then one who is not omniscient, omnipotent, good and forbearing, is not God.[18] (*ŠGV* 11:13–16)
> Further. If He is a Lord who imposes His will on every person and every thing, why did He not keep His kingdom and His royal domain, which are the product of His action, free from

16 The two terms, in Pazand, are *dāēstąnī* and *miiąnžaī*. The suggested distinction of meaning between them, viz. "the office of a judge in a court of law" as opposed to "an arbiter-judge," is conjectural. On the use of the term *miyānzīg/miyānjīg* as a general term for "judge," see Shaked 1980.

17 The original, in Pazand, has *vat vīrōšaa*, which may correspond to *wad-warrawišn(ag)* in Pahlavi (this seems to be de Menasce's understanding), but may possibly be associated with Parthian **wrwc** (cf. Durkin-Meisterernst 2004:345), "lightning," which might have been borrowed from Parthian in the form *wirōš(ag)*.

18 My translation here and in the following passage is somewhat different from that of de Menasce (1945).

> all enemy and adversary, so that no person in His royal domain should (be subject to) any violence, tyranny, injustice, or complaint? (*ŠGV* 11:17)
> Further. If He is victorious, conqueror and mighty, His victory, conquest and might – over whom are they? For victory and conquest are over enemies [and] rivals, but it is not appropriate for someone to be a rival and enemy to himself. As long as one does not have a rival and an enemy over whom one can become triumphant and victorious, no triumph and victory can be attributed to him. For [in that case] even cattle and sheep by themselves, who have no adversaries and attackers, are victorious and triumphant. (*ŠGV* 11:20–26)
> Further. Is everything that He says truthful [and] trustworthy or not? Is what He says truthful and trustworthy when he says: "I am a friend of virtue and an enemy of evil"? If He constantly creates evildoers more than virtuous creatures, where is His truthfulness? (*ŠGV* 11:30–33)
> Further. Is His desire good or evil? If His desire is evil, from where does His divinity derive? If His desire is good, why are evildoers and evil more plentiful than virtuous people and virtue? (*ŠGV* 11:34–36)
> Further. Is everything that He does done with reason, or not? If He acts without reason, this is a vain action, and it is not proper to praise vain action in a wise deity. If He acts with reason, what is the aim of creating all those creatures such as demons (or) disobedient and contrary people who strive against His will, and countless unworthy creatures? (*ŠGV* 11:88–92)
> If it wasn't He himself who gave sinful thoughts to man, who is it who gives sinful thoughts without His order and without His will? If it was He himself who gave people sinful thoughts, and who now blames them for that, where does His justice and arbitration come from? (*ŠGV* 11:109–110)
> If He created [evil things] as a test, as they say that He brought bad tests upon [His] creatures, how come He did not know man and the [other] creatures beforehand? For one who is a master of testing cannot be called omniscient. (*ŠGV* 11:115–117)

This selection of arguments from the debate against the Muslims illustrates one facet of the Zoroastrian confrontation with the monotheistic religions. Zoroastrian theologians also conducted a verbal contest with Jews and Christians. Some excerpts from the argument with Judaism, concerned principally with the account of the creation in the Book of Genesis, may give a taste of this further debate. Through what channels Zoroastrians became acquainted with the biblical text remains unclear. Aramaic versions of the Bible were available, and some of them may have been accessible to the Zoroastrian theologians; it is also possible that Standard Persian or Judeo-Persian renderings were within their reach. Alternatively, they may have relied on oral transmission through personal contact with Jews or through Muslim mediation.

How the author of the *ŠGV* became acquainted with the faith of different religions he explains himself, although his is not an account that can be accepted at face value. He uses a literary device frequently employed in the Sasanian period – that of a quasi-autobiographical account of a prolonged religious quest in which the author claims to have inspected all religions and creeds and to have reached his firm conviction at the end of a process of trial and reflection.[19] This particular quest story begins as follows:

> I have looked into all the creeds of the theologians of the world. There are two foundations to the faith that they hold: one that says that all good and evil that exist in the world are from God; and one that says that all good in the world and the hope of saving the soul are from God, and the cause of all the evil of the body and the fear of the soul are from Ahreman. (*ŠGV* 10:38–41)
>
> Now I became a seeker, everywhere and with fervent mind, in pursuit of the knowledge of God, as I wrote above. [I did this] by questioning and searching God's *dēn* and His desire. For this same pursuit I set out to a far-off country and to the land of the Indians and that of many diverse peoples. For what I loved was not the *dēn* that is [followed] by heritage;[20] I desired, on the contrary, that [*dēn*] which is most firmly established and most acceptable by wisdom and by [theological] discourse [*gōwāgīh*[21]]. (*ŠGV* 10:43–46)
>
> I also went to the assemblies[22] of numerous deviant groups,[23] until all at once, through the bounty of the deities and the power, splendor and force of the Good Religion, I was delivered from many abysses of darkness and from doubting [that leads to] wrong explanations. [...] I was saved from the multifarious uncertainties, errors, deceits and wickedness of the [false] sects, especially from those of the greatest deceiver, the mightiest evil teacher, the chief of the intoxicated[?], Mani,[24] whose doctrine is sorcery, whose *dēn* is deceit, whose teaching is wickedness,[25] and whose manner is secretiveness. (*ŠGV* 10:47–49, 58–60)
>
> I came to profess [the Zoroastrian faith] with full knowledge, through the power of wisdom and the strength of acquaintance with the scripture, not by rigid faith, but by the pure *dēn* of separation from the *dēws*,[26] which is the law of Ohrmazd, taught by the Creator Ohrmazd to the righteous Zardušt.[27] (*ŠGV* 10:61–63)

The debate with the Jews begins with a passage that obviously takes aim at the narrative of creation in the Book of Genesis, but with some puzzling deviations:[28]

---

19 On this common theme in Middle Persian literature, see Shaked 1994:104–106.

20 This looks like a borrowing of the concept of *taqlīd*, used in the theological discourse of Islam to designate religious faith based on blindly following the transmitted lore.

21 A calque of Arabic *kalām*, which designates theological discourse.

22 Pazend *āwāgī*, literally "get-together," as it would seem.

23 Pazend *jaṯ sardagą*.

24 The name is written *mānāē*.

25 The text has *dōšī*, which may be a corruption of *dušīh*.

26 The demons or evil entities. The expression *jaṯ dēw dīn* alludes to the section of the Avesta usually referred to in Middle Persian as *jud-dēw-dād*, "the law of separation from the demons," an imitation of the Avestan *vi-daēva-dāta* (*Widēwdād*).

27 Zardušt is the Middle Persian form of Zoroaster.

28 In the following translated passages, the pronoun referring to God is capitalized, partly because this is the (old-fashioned) convention in English, but also to enable the reader to differentiate references to the deity from those referring to humans.

> Now I shall say a little concerning that which lies inside their chatter and their fraudulent speech. That land which is an island[?],[29] and darkness and obscurity, God and His spirit, and the black water:[30] Where were they, and within what borders were they? God Himself, what was His manner? (*ŠGV* 13:48–50)
> It is manifest that He was not luminous, for when He saw the light, it seemed to Him good, because He had not seen it [earlier].[31] (*ŠGV* 13:51–53)
> Further, that One whose place and abode was within darkness and the black water, and who had never seen the light, how could He see light? And what is the source of His divinity? For even now, no one dwelling in darkness has the capacity to see the light. For it is well known that darkness cannot keep its ground facing light, for light pushes it away and destroys it. (*ŠGV* 13:59–63)
> Further. The earth that is an island[?] and obscurity, was it limited or unlimited? If it was limited, what was outside it? If unlimited, where did its infinity go? (*ŠGV* 13:64–67)
> That which Adīnō[32] said: Let there be light, and there was. Now one should note that Adīnō was before there was light. When He desired to make light, and He gave an order that it should be, He thought: what shape does light have, is it pretty or ugly? If light existed with its quality in the knowledge and thought of Adīnō, [it follows that] light was there both within and outside the knowledge and thinking of Adīnō. For it is impossible to know and find anything unless it is existent and manifest. If light always existed, it is not[33] the creation of Adīnō. And if they [the Jews] say that light did not exist by its qualities in the knowledge [of Adīnō], that [means that] He sought light without knowing its qualities. [This is] great ignorance. Or [else], how is it possible that He would have in His mind and thought something that He had never pondered about or known? (*ŠGV* 13:68–77)

The Zoroastrian polemicist thus finds contradictions in the story of the creation of light as it is presented in the Book of Genesis. Whether we assume that light preceded God or the other way round, something is at fault with the logic and con-

29 The Pazand text has *āw xūn*. The meaning of the equivalent Persian compound *āb-xūn*, according to *Borhān-e qāṭe'* (Borhān 1342/1923), is "island"; Dehxodā's *Loghat-nāme* (1973/4) has the same definition, equating it with *ābx(w)ast*. However, no supporting citations are given. In Ṣādeqī, *Farhang-e jāme'* (Ṣādeghi 2013:264b), the compound is defined as the equivalent of *xūnābe*, "tears of blood," with quotations from Ferdowsī and Moxtārī. De Menasce (1945) regards this word as a rendering of the biblical Hebrew expression *tohu vabohu*, without explaining how.
30 Darmesteter (1889:6, n. 1) rightly mentions, on the authority of Israël Lévi, that this is a familiar concept in Mandaic. The expression *mia siawia* in Mandaean literature indicates a component of the universe. It is hard to escape the feeling that the occurrence of this expression in the *ŠGV* is not unrelated to the Mandaic usage, and yet it is not clear how to interpret its appearance in the Jewish context of this chapter. On this element and its relation to others in the Mandaean description of the universe see Drower 1937:253–256.
31 Cf. Gen. 1:4.
32 The text consistently has Adīnō for Hebrew Adonay. This form may be consistent with an auditory reception of the Hebrew text.
33 The text has *rā*, which de Menasce emends to *nē*, a small change graphically. Left to stand as written, the syntax would make no sense, and I therefore follow de Menasce's emendation.

sistency of the biblical narrative. This line of argument is continued relentlessly in the following passages:

> This too. The command for light to be, was it given to something or to nothing? This is certain: A command can properly be given only to [someone who] can carry it out. If He addressed it to an existent luminous being, the luminous being was itself [already] there; if He addressed it to a non-existent [being], how did [that which is] nothing hear the command of Adīnō? Or how did he know: "Adīnō's desire is that I should become light"? For the non-existent did not hear the command of Adīnō, just as if it had not been given, since that which does not exist cannot even think in any way. That which is nothing, it was decreed that it is nothing, but there was [in] the existence[34] of the sage a prevision [according to which] he knew: "In what manner does Adīnō want me to come into being?" He [in effect] became that manner [of entity] which [Adīnō] wanted him to be. (*ŠGV* 13:78–85)
> If they [the Jews] claim that light came into being from Adīnō's speech, who said: "Be!" and it did come into being. [All this] while Adīnō and his selfness were dark, and He had never seen the light. In what manner can light be formed from speech? For it is well known that the birth of speech is from thought! (*ŠGV* 13:86–88)
> If they claim that His word became light, this is very strange, because it follows that light is the product of darkness, and darkness the seed the [manifest] mark of which is light. A command can only be given to something that receives it; hence it follows that light existed before the command was given. (*ŠGV* 13:89–91)

These arguments are designed to make the biblical story look unsubstantial, in that it obviously cannot be reconciled with the sophisticated logical postulates that Mardān-Farrox is applying. A further topic raised in this polemic is the inconsistency in the story of the Garden of Eden. God asks Adam "Where are you?" showing His lack of omniscience. Other failings in the depiction of the deity in the Jewish scriptures are also pointed out:

> From this speech, too, it is manifest that He had not the slightest knowledge. For if He came forth to the Garden and raised His voice and called Adam by name, saying: "Where are you?"[35] [He acted] in such a way as if He did not know where [Adam] was. Had He been left without an answer, He would have been ignorant of the whereabouts of Adam. (*ŠGV* 13:135–137)
> Even if He had a voice, He did not have prescience as to [whether Adam] had or had not eaten from the tree. Nor indeed did He have knowledge as to whom and how: who had eaten, and who was the deceiver. If He had known, He would never have [asked]: "Did you eat of the tree concerning which I ordered, Do not eat [of it]?" [Gen. 3:17] What is the reason for the question? (*ŠGV* 13:140)

34 Read *bə: hast [pa mīnišn] i dānā.*
35 Gen. 3:9.

> His deceitfulness is manifest from the fact that He said: “When you eat of this tree, you will die” [Gen. 2:17], and they ate and did not die, but became knowledgeable and distinguished good from evil. (*ŠGV* 13:143–144)

These are some of the forceful arguments in the *ŠGV*. The monotheistic adversaries would presumably be hard put to find ways of justifying their position. The aim of this exercise is to locate contradictions or, worse still, passages that go against the logical postulates of the author.

Can we conclude that these arguments constitute a victory of the dualists over the monotheists? Two points can be made in response to this question. First, most of these arguments can be turned around and used with equal force against the Zoroastrian position. Thus, if Ohrmazd is omnipotent, how can he be restricted in his power by the existence and activity of his adversary? If he is without limit, how can he be accommodated together with Ahreman in the same boundless space? If he is benevolent, how can he tolerate the wicked activity of Ahreman? The riddles of the universe are not really solved if we disburden evil from the deity. The question as to the origin of evil is not made more easily digestible by giving evil perfect independence.

The only point at which the dualistic position has a certain intellectual, or rather emotional, advantage is that of the promise of the ultimate victory of good over evil in the eschatological era. This promise is the logical outcome of the Zoroastrian story of creation; it makes sense of the creation right from the start and endows the toil of mankind and of the rest of the good creation, in the intermediate period between creation and the eschatological era, with meaning and purpose. However, as much as it makes sense to conceive of a perfect creation, corrupted by evil but bravely fighting for a final predetermined victory of good, this notion can be maintained only by faith prevailing in an internal struggle over doubt. One is reminded of modern-day secular faiths that maintain that the inevitable progress of history will solve the deep problems of mankind. The only mainstay of such hopes seems to be the need to cling to some solid comfort in a harsh world.

The second point is that the pugnacious position of the Zoroastrians is almost certainly part of their defense system against the attacks launched on them by holders of the monotheistic position. These attacks were also addressed by the other major dualistic religion of Late Antiquity, that of the Manichaeans.

The main argument against the dualistic position is that it undermines monotheism. The idea of a single divine power was felt to be the great achievement of the emerging new world of Late Antiquity. The new religion of the Manichaeans, but also the ancient religion of the Zoroastrians, constituted a menace to the monotheistic point of view and threatened to pull the faithful back toward an old-fashioned polytheism, under the guise of dualism. However, Zoroastrian dualism has little in common with polytheism, and it makes better sense to classify it as a variant of monotheism.[36]

It is obvious that the polemics of the *ŠGV* cannot be viewed separately from the religious history of the environment in which it was composed. As several scholars have pointed out, there are indications of contact between its author's style and method and the prevailing types of apologetic arguments known from Jewish, Christian and Islamic sources.[37]

The ethical dualism of good and evil of the type represented by Mazdaism and Manichaeism, emerging from this debate as an intellectual system capable of giving hope and strength in the face of adversity, is *not* based on faith in two deities. Its recognition of one omnipotent and omniscient deity, absolved from responsibility for all that is ugly and impure in the world, makes it a variant of the monotheistic mode of faith. Monotheism cannot provide a satisfactory solution to the problem of evil, but it grapples with it valiantly by allowing it to hide beneath the robe of the deity. Evil in the monotheistic formulations is either a mutation of the deity or a rebel power. None of these definitions of evil can entirely absolve the deity from responsibility for the imperfections of the world, leaving the door open to the Zoroastrian apologist, who asks: Does God have no knowledge of the existence of evil? Is He incapable of putting it to a stop? If the answer to such questions is positive, what kind of a god is this who is neither omniscient nor omnipotent? The debate runs on in endless circles. The counterargument against the Zoroastrian position, as we have seen, is that it seriously limits the capacity and the actual sustainability of God.

Both approaches, that of the dualists as well as the faith of the monotheists, represent attempts at offering a solution to a keenly felt problem that is in essence insoluble. Both reveal disturbing fallacies in the theological positions of their rivals, but neither appears to overcome the counterarguments. Rational-

36 Shaked 1994:22–26, and the literature cited there.

37 See most importantly Menasce 1945, in the introductions to the chapters and the notes following most chapters. Several noted scholars of the work of Ḥiwi (or perhaps rather Ḥayyoy, as suggested by Poznanski 1916:6) Habalkhi (ninth century CE), likely a native of Balkh, who sharply criticizes the Hebrew Bible and points out inconsistencies and illogical statements in it, believe that he may have borrowed some of his points from the *ŠGV* (Davidson 1915:20, 29, 80–82; Poznanski 1916:13; Neusner 1963:283, n. c). The text of Ḥiwi's book has not been preserved, and its content is mostly known from a polemical poem written by Saadya Gaon (fl. in Baghdad in the ninth–tenth centuries CE). It is, however, equally possible to assume that both Mardān-Farrox and Ḥiwi used material that was current in the speculative literature of the time and was available in Khorasan in the early Islamic period.

ity and logic may not be the best tools for achieving a measure of confidence in the field of religion, but the great prestige that scientific investigation enjoyed in the theological discourses of Late Antiquity and the early Islamic period pushed theologians and missionaries to construct ever more elaborate and sophisticated edifices of rational debate.

References

Dēnkard – see Ādurbād ī Ēmēdān 1874–1928, 1911 and 1966; and de Menasce 1958 and 1973.
GBd = *Greater Bundahišn* – see Anklesaria 1956.
ŠGV = *Škand gumānīg wizār*, by Mardān-Farrox ī Ohrmazddādān – see de Menasce 1945.
WZ = *Wīzīdagīhā ī Zādspram* – see Gignoux and Tafazzoli 1993.

Ādurbād ī Ēmēdān. 1874–1928. *The Dinkard.* Edited by P.B. Sanjana and D.P. Sanjana (Sunjana). 19 vols. Bombay: Duftur Ashkara Press.

—. 1911. *The Complete Text of the Pahlavi Dinkard.* Edited by D.M. Madan. Bombay.

—. 1966. *Dēnkart – Pahlavi text.* Edited by M.J. Dresden. Facsimile edition of manuscript B of the K.R. Cama Oriental Institute Bombay. Wiesbaden: Harrassowitz.

Anklesaria, Behramgore Tehmuras. 1956. *Zand-ākāsīh: Iranian or Greater Bundahišn – Transliteration and Translation in English.* Bombay: Rahnumae Mazdaysnan Sabha.

[Bedjan, Paul]. 1891. *Acta martyrum et sanctorum*, II. Paris–Leipzig: Otto Harrassowitz.

Borhān, Moḥammad Ḥusayn b. Khalaf Tabrizi. 1342 AH (1923). *Borhān-e Qāṭeʿ* (2nd edition). 5 vols. Tehran.

—. 2004. "*Škand Gumānīg Wizār.*" *Encyclopædia Iranica.* At: www.iranicaonline.org/articles/shkand-gumanig-wizar (accessed June 13, 2015).

Darmesteter, James. 1889. "Textes pehlvis relatifs au Judaïsme." *Revue des Études Juives*, 18:1–15; 19:41–56.

Davidson, Israel. 1915. *Saadia's Polemic against Ḥiwi al-Balkhi: A Fragment Edited from a Genizah MS* (Texts and Studies of the Jewish Theological Seminary of America, 5). New York: Jewish Theological Seminary of America.

Dehxodā, ʿAlī Akbar. 1973/4 (1352 H.). *Loghat-nāme.* Tehran: University of Tehran–Dehxodā Institute.

Drower, E.S. 1937. *The Mandaeans of Iran and Iraq: Their Cults, Customs, Magic Legends, and Folklore.* Oxford: Oxford University Press. (Reprint: Piscataway, NJ: Gorgias Press, 2002.)

Durkin-Meisterernst, Desmond. 2004. *Dictionary of Manichaean Middle Persian and Parthian* (Corpus Fontium Manichaeorum: Subsidia – Dictionary of Manichaean Texts, 3:1). Turnhout: Brepols.

Gignoux, Philippe, and Ahmad Tafazzoli. 1993. *Anthologie de Zādspram.* Édition critique du texte pehlevi, traduit et commenté par Ph. Gignoux et A. Tafazzoli (Studia Iranica, 13). Paris: Association pour l'Avancement des Études Iraniennes.

Gray, Louis H. 1906. "The Jews in Pahlavi literature." In *Actes du XIVe Congrès International des Orientalistes.* Paris: Ernest Leroux. 177–192.

Guidi, Michelangelo. 1927. *La lotta tra l'Islam e il Manicheismo: Un libro di Ibn al-Muqaffaʿ contro il Corano confutato da al-Qâsim b. Ibrâhîm, testo arabo pubblicato con*

introduzione, versione italiana e note (Fondazione Caetani per gli Studi Musulmani). Rome: R. Accademia Nazionale dei Lincei.
Henning, Walter Bruno. 1951. *Zoroaster: Politician or Witch-doctor?* (Ratanbai Katrak Lectures, 1949). London: Oxford University Press.
Hoffmann, Georg. 1880. *Auszüge aus syrischen Akten persischer Märtyrer* (Abhandlungen für die Kunde des Morgenlandes, 7:3). Leipzig: F.A. Brockhaus.
de Menasce, Jean Pierre. 1945. *Une apologétique mazdéenne du IXe siècle, Škand-gumânîk vicâr: La solution décisive des doutes* (Collectanea Friburgensia, NS 30). Freiburg: Librairie de l'université.
—. 1958. *Une encyclopédie mazdéenne: Le Dēnkart – Quatre conférences données à l'Université de Paris sous les auspices de la Fondation Ratanbai Katrak* (Bibliothèque de l'école des Hautes études, Section des Sciences Religieuses, 69). Paris: Presses Universitaires de France.
—. 1973. *Le troisième livre du Dēnkart, Traduit du pehlevi* (Bibliothèque des Oeuvres Classiques Persanes, 3:5). Paris: Travaux de l'Institut d'Etudes Iraniennes de l'Université de Paris.
Neusner, Jacob. 1963. "A Zoroastrian Critique of Judaism." *Journal of the American Oriental Society*, 83:283–294.
Poznanski, Samuel (שמואל אברהם פאזנאנסקי). 1916. *Ein Fragment der polemischen Schrift Saadja Gaons gegen Chiwi al-Balchi* (תשובות רב סעדיה גאון על שאלות חיוי הבלכי). Warsaw: Hatsefira.
Ṣādeghi, ʻAli Ašraf. 2013. *A Comprehensive Dictionary of the Persian language* – فرهنگ جامع زبان فارسی, I. Tehran: Academy of Persian Language and Literature.
Shaked, Shaul. 1971. "The Notions *mēnōg* and *gētīg* in the Pahlavi Texts and Their Relation to Eschatology." *Acta Orientalia*, 33:59–107. (Reprinted in Shaked 1995.)
—. 1980. "Mihr the Judge." *Jerusalem Studies in Arabic and Islam*, 2:1–31. (Reprinted in Shaked 1995.)
—. 1984. "From Iran to Islam: Notes on Some Themes in Transmission." *Jerusalem Studies in Arabic and Islam*, 4:34–67. (Reprinted in Shaked 1995.)
—. 1990. "Zoroastrian Polemics against Jews in the Sasanian and Early Islamic Period." In S. Shaked and A. Netzer (eds.), *Irano-Judaica*. Jerusalem: Ben-Zvi Institute. 85–104.
—. 1994. *Dualism in Transformation: Varieties of Religion in Sasanian Iran* (Jordan Lectures in Comparative Religion). London: School of Oriental and African Studies.
—. 1995. *From Zoroastrian Iran to Islam: Studies in Religious History and Intercultural Contacts* (Collected Studies Series, 505). Aldershot: Variorum.
Skjærvø, Prods Oktor. 2002. "Praise and Blame in the Avesta: The Poet-Sacrificer and His Duties." *Jerusalem Studies in Arabic and Islam*, 26:29–67.
—. 2014. Review of G. König, *Geschlechtsmoral und Gleichgeschlechtlichkeit im Zoroastrismus*. *Bibliotheca Orientalis*, 71:264–274.

Maren R. Niehoff

Philo's Rationalization of Judaism

The term rationalization presupposes something irrational, which inherently opposes the laws of logic and reason. Such irrational elements may pertain to a variety of fields, such as personal emotions, traditional beliefs and mythological stories. Common to all is a lack of reflection: One feels or believes the way one does without rendering account to people who do not share the basic assumption that such emotions or beliefs are acceptable. Irrational patterns are not examined with regard to their efficiency or contribution to society. The process of rationalization, by contrast, involves reflection, accountability and the use of universal language. It is prompted by critical questions about apparently given traditions and realities. Rationalization often occurs in moments of history when inherited structures are challenged by new scientific discoveries, political changes or acquaintance with new cultures. Rationalists, who usually pertain to the elite of society, attempt to account for such clashes of values and examine which traditions can be identified as rational and thus acceptable in a new context of discourse. As Sigmund Freud alerted us, such efforts at rationalization often amount to apologetics and even self-deceit, which barely cover the irrational impulses that continue to be active beneath the surface.

Religions are special test cases for rationalists, because they tend to be based on canonical texts, such as Homer's epics or the Bible, whose truth value is assumed to be beyond examination. Religions often constitute themselves around exceptional experiences, such as revelation or miracle. Each religious tradition creates social structures, such as priesthoods or caste systems, which in turn reinforce the beliefs of that religion. The history of Western religions is characterized by the intermittent rise and fall of rationalizing movements. In our current state of affairs, with many Western monotheists celebrating a return to irrational forms of religion that defy considerations of personal, political and social benefit, it is important to think about the dynamics of rationalization processes in the past.[1]

In the West, Greek philosophers were the first to discuss religion critically. Prompted by a new confidence in the human mind, following breathtaking scientific discoveries, philosophers questioned the veracity of Homer's stories about the gods. Already in the sixth century BCE, Xenophanes rejected the anthro-

1 On the emergence and role of canonical texts, see Halbertal 1997; Finkelberg and Stroumsa 2003; Ehrman 2003:229–246; Brakke 2011; Niehoff 2012. On the intricate connection in modernity between personal religiosity and the academic study of religion, see G. Stroumsa 2010.

https://doi.org/10.1515/9783110446395-004

pomorphic character of Homer's gods, suggesting that Homer ascribes to them "all deeds that among men are a reproach and disgrace" (fr. 11). While men have a tendency to create gods in their own image – "the Ethiopians imagine their gods as black" (fr. 16) – Xenophanes claimed that the true nature of the divine can be deduced by reason. Following this approach, one must recognize that there is but one god "in no way like mortals either in body or in mind" (fr. 230).

Heraclitus and Plato continued this criticism of the Homeric gods, demanding a more philosophical form of religion. Heraclitus judged everything by reference to the all-pervading Logos and warned his readers not only of anthropomorphic conceptions of the gods, but also of their material worship. Plato unmasked Homer as an unreliable narrator, whose gods must be excluded from the educational program of future statesmen and philosophers. The proper way of thinking about the divine is to acknowledge the gods' utter transcendence from the material realm. Like the Ideal Forms, Plato argued, the gods do not change and assume different forms, but rather present the ultimate good, which man should strive to imitate (*Rep.* 377B–379B).[2] Rationalist approaches in ancient Greece thus questioned the authority of the canonical text, which presented anthropomorphic stories about the gods. It was moreover assumed that the divine provides an authentic standard beyond momentary conventions and corruptions, one that guides men as individuals toward their moral improvement. While Xenophanes, Heraclitus and Plato each developed his own arguments, they shared the conviction that the worship of a god must not be an end in itself, but should rather serve broader philosophical aims. The satisfaction of a god's idiosyncratic desires was certainly not to be given serious consideration.

Rome added an important new dimension to these Greek discourses of rationalization. At the end of the Republic, the Roman scholar Varro offered a rational approach to religion that emphasized the historical and social dimensions of religion. He studied the development of religious phenomena, tracing contemporaneous institutions and rituals to their roots. Varro concluded that men regularly turn great benefactors into gods. Such human origins of religion were presented in a positive light, as part of the fabric of a creative and well-functioning society.[3] In comparison to Greek approaches, especially that of Plato, Varro and other Roman thinkers were more inclined toward contextualizing religion and appreciating its contribution to society. Not the individual and his relationship to the gods of the

2 See also Guthrie 1962:370–380, 419–482; Burkert 1985:305–337; Männlein-Robert 2010.

3 Varro's work has not survived, but is quoted by Augustine (*Civ. Dei* 6.2–6, 4.22–24, 4.27, 4.31–32); and similar arguments are mentioned by Cicero's Stoic spokesman (Cic., *N.D.* 2.60–62). On Varro see also Van Nuffelen 2010; Cancick 2001; Rüpke 2012, 2014.

fathers, but rather the functioning of society with appropriate institutions were at the center of their discussion. The issue of anthropomorphism remains marginal in Rome, certainly in comparison to Athens. Since Varro spoke about religion as such, rather than a particular form of it, his approach was potentially relevant for any *homo religious*. His criticism was profoundly challenging because it could hardly be reduced to an internal critique of a specific tradition.

Christianity from its very beginning was imbedded in Greek language and culture. Already Paul and the authors of the Gospels used well-established literary genres, namely epistles and biography, to explain the story of Jesus in easily accessible Greek, using images understandable to broader pagan audiences. Not surprisingly, Christian authors were soon concerned to inscribe their religion into Greek discourses of rationality. In the second century CE, only a few decades after the composition of the Gospel of Matthew, Justin Martyr presented the Christian creed as "the only certain and efficient philosophy." Upon conversion, he declared himself a "philosopher" (*Dial.* 8.1–2). Justin uses the term philosophy in the rather narrow sense of philosophical theology. He highlights Plato's contribution without addressing his opposition to traditional forms of religion. Justin moreover introduces the biblical prophets as philosophers who had reached a higher degree of truth than the Classical thinkers because they acknowledged man's need for epistemological help from God and Jesus Christ. Justin thus affirmed sources of religious authority that the Greek rationalists wished to abolish, while at the same time identifying the prophets as uncompromising searchers for absolute truth (*Dial.* 2.1–8.4). On Justin's account, Christianity follows "right reason," assumes an unchanging deity and inculcates rational ethics in accordance with nature. In all of these respects it is far more philosophical than Judaism, which in his view clings to outdated laws and silly anthropomorphisms (*Dial.* 8.2–4. 10.1, 19.3).[4]

Clement of Alexandria similarly inscribed Christianity into Greek discourses of rationality. He quoted Greek critiques of religion, not in order to advocate their philosophical approach as such, but rather to attack Greek polytheism. Like Justin Martyr, Clement postulated a special congeniality between Plato and Christianity, while Homer's gods and Greek ritual were dismissed as deceitful, dead and silly. Clement is more positive than Justin about the role of Judaism in the Christian narrative. Rather than excluding Jewish law from the category of the rational, Clement focuses on the beneficial influences, not only of the biblical prophets,

4 On Paul's use of epistolary style, see Stowers 1989. On the adoption of the biographical genre in the Gospels, esp. the Gospel of Luke, see Hägg 2012:148–186; and Burridge 2004. On Justin's complex identity, see Chadwick 1966:9–23; and Norris 2004:38–40; and Niehoff, forthcoming.

but also of Moses himself. He praises them as fighters against idolatry and teachers of a virtuous life style.[5]

Early Christian authors thus emerge as highly aware of Greek discourses on religion, which they used as a paradigm for evaluating their own tradition. They did not reflect critically on their religion, perhaps because it was so young, but rather used Greek notions to defend it against external criticism. Varro's approach, which puts religion into historical perspective and relativizes it, was denounced by Christian authors, especially Tertullian and Augustine. On the whole, Christian authors were concerned to show enlightened pagan readers that Christianity conforms to Greek norms of rationality and inculcates a universal code of ethics. Judaism was partly integrated into this narrative and partly left out in order to highlight Christianity's uniqueness. Jewish law turned out to be especially controversial.

Judaism enjoyed a long and rich history before its encounter with Greek culture. Its foundational language is Hebrew rather than Greek, and, in comparison to Christianity, its engagement with Greek culture came at a relatively late stage, after centuries of consolidating Jewish identity in alternative ways. The outcome of the encounter between Judaism and Hellenism is therefore especially complex and deserves our close attention. When, indeed, did Jewish authors begin to rationalize their religion, and how did they go about it? Did they engage Greek or perhaps even Roman discourses, and if so, did their engagement resemble that of the Christians?

The first thorough processes of rationalization in Judaism are connected to the encounter with Hellenism in Alexandria. Jews in the Hellenistic Diaspora self-consciously immersed themselves in a lively encounter with Greek culture, while proudly preserving their Jewish heritage. Alexandria, where the Hebrew Scriptures were quickly translated into Greek, was the metropolis of Jewish Hellenistic culture. Already in the second century BCE, Alexandrian Jews took significant steps toward a philosophy of Judaism. Aristobulus is the earliest such author known to us, through some fragments preserved by the Church Father Eusebius. He questioned the anthropomorphic images of the biblical God, rejecting their literal sense and urging his readers "to receive the interpretations in their natural sense and to get hold of suitable notions about God and not to lapse into a mythical and human way of thinking" (τὸ μυθῶδες καὶ ἀνθρώπινον κατάστημα; fr. 2). The extant fragments of Aristobulus's work shed no light on the details of his thought and do not allow us to judge whether he consciously engaged Greek

5 Clem., *Exh.* chaps. 2, 6, 8–9; see also Heine 2004:117–120; G. Stroumsa 1999, 2009; and Markschies 1997, 1999.

philosophers who had expressed similar concerns about the anthropomorphic images of their gods. Yet it is clear that he shared their rationalistic approach and reflected critically on the canonical texts of his religion. He identified problems in these texts and seems to have addressed fellow Jews, whose reading of them did not in his view conform to philosophical standards. It is moreover significant that Aristobulus, unlike Justin Martyr, includes Jewish law in the category of the rational, stressing that it was "set up with a view to piety, justice, self-control and other qualities that are truly good" (fr. 4.8).[6]

Aristeas was another Alexandrian Jewish author of the mid-second century BCE who adopted a rationalistic approach to Judaism. He composed the so-called *Letter of Aristeas*, which explains the translation of the Hebrew Bible into Greek as a broad process of acculturation. Aristeas expresses the view that all men worship the same creator God, but under different names, some calling him Zeus, while others recognize him as the God of Israel (Ar. 16). Rejecting both Greek mythology and Egyptian animal worship, Aristeas pleads for a philosophical conception of God. He asks his readers not to fall into inferior ways of thinking and instead to consider God as one and omniscient, setting up laws "for the sake of righteousness." Indeed, "to live well means to keep the customs," each law having "a profound reason for it" (Ar. 127, 143). Wild birds, for example, are excluded from the kitchen so as to teach the Jews to refrain from violence and rather pursue a life of righteousness. Like Aristobulus, Aristeas is acutely aware of the mythological dimension of his religious tradition and uses Greek notions for its broader philosophical interpretation. His efforts to rationalize Judaism are clearly prompted by a wish to render his tradition universally valid and communicable.[7]

Philo enters the stage of these discussions in the early first century CE, on reaching maturity in Alexandria. He is not only the best preserved Jewish Alexandrian author, but also the most learned, complex and creative. Very little is known about his personal life, except that he served as the head of the Jewish embassy to the Roman emperor Gaius Caligula following the pogrom in 38 CE in Alexandria. His oeuvre includes a striking variety of genres, ranging from systematic Bible commentary to philosophical and historical treatises, as well as biographies of the biblical forefathers and works on Jewish law. A chronology of his works can be established by starting with his explicit references to datable events in the historical writings and working our way back on internal grounds to his early

---

6 On Alexandria as a cultural metropolis, see Fraser 1972; Clauss 2003; Georges et al. 2013; Hadas-Lebel 2012:1–68. Regarding the translation of the Bible into Greek and its cultural ramifications, see Gutman 1969:115–131; Rösel 1994. On Aristobulus, see Walter 1964; Holladay 1995.
7 On Aristeas, see also Collins 2000:97–103; Barclay 1996:138–150.

treatises.[8] Following this approach, we can identify Philo as a thinker who began his career in Alexandria as an interpreter of the Jewish Scriptures. At that stage he engaged the work of Jewish colleagues who had adopted the critical methods of Homeric scholarship and investigated the Bible as a literary work. Philo opposed such readings and instead offered allegorical interpretations in a Platonic vein.

Later on, Philo travelled to Rome as an ambassador and became familiar with the particular intellectual climate there. This journey had profound implications for his intellectual development, which we are only beginning to estimate. Thus far, it has already become clear that Philo radically changed his style of writing upon arrival in Rome and adopted new literary genres that were popular among Romans and suitable to their discourses. He now mainly addressed non-Jews, presenting a more general picture of Judaism and engaging numerous notions of Stoic philosophy, which flourished in contemporary Rome. Philo was a remarkably flexible thinker, who quickly perceived the new intellectual opportunities in Rome and developed creative ideas that are vital to a proper understanding of early Christianity as well as of Greek culture in the Roman Empire (the so-called "Second Sophistic").[9] His efforts to rationalize Judaism are of special interest in this context and need to be discussed with a view to the dramatic changes in his life and outlook. I shall focus my discussion on two themes that we have already encountered as foci of previous debates, namely, the nature of God and biblical law.

Philo's Rationalizations of the Biblical God

In his early writings from the Alexandrian period, Philo confronted Jewish interpreters who read the Scriptures in light of Homer's epics. These interpreters concluded that the Scriptures, too, contain myths. Comparing the biblical story of the Tower of Babel to a similar Homeric tale about men wishing to reach heaven, they posed the following critical question to Philo:

> Now do you still speak solemnly about the ordinances as if they contain the canons of truth herself? For behold, the books called holy by you contain also myths about which you regularly laugh whenever you hear others relating them. (*Conf.* 3)

---

8 For details, see Niehoff 2018:1–22.

9 On the historical events, see Tcherikover and Fuks 1960; Van der Horst 2003. On Philo's increasing engagement with Roman discourses, see Niehoff 2011a:133–151, 2011b and 2018:passim.

These anonymous Alexandrian Jews were concerned about biblical anthropomorphisms, especially the notion that God feels threatened by man. They were not willing to allegorize such biblical stories, insisting that they be taken literally and the issue of God's apparent irrationality confronted. They adopted a strikingly critical and historical approach, suggesting that mythological stories about the God of Israel are remnants of the literary sources that Moses had used when composing the Bible.[10]

Philo emphatically rejects such interpretations and admonishes his audience: "such fables [about an anthropomorphic deity] may never enter our mind" (*All.* 1.43). He offers instead a philosophical interpretation of the Book of Genesis and rationalizes the image of God in his own way. Already in Gen. 2.7, Philo encounters a grave problem of anthropomorphism, which gives him an opportunity to develop his own approach:

> "And God formed man by taking clay from the earth, and breathed into his face a breath of life, and the man became a living soul." (LXX Gen. 2.7) ... "Breathed into," we note, is equivalent to "inspired" or "besouled" the soulless. Let us not be infected with such absurdity as to think that God uses for inbreathing organs, such as mouth or nostrils. For God is not only non-anthropomorphic, but belongs to no class or kind [ἄποιος γὰρ ὁ θεός, οὐ μόνον οὐκ ἀνθρωπόμορφος]. Yet the [biblical] expression indicates something most natural [φυσικώτερον]. It implies necessarily three things: that which inbreathes, that which receives and that which is inbreathed. That which inbreathes is God, that which receives is the mind, and that which is inbreathed is the spirit. ... For how could the soul have conceived of God, had He not inbreathed it and grasped it as far as possible? The human mind would not have dared to soar so high as to grasp the nature of God [θεοῦ φυσίς], had not God Himself drawn it up to Himself, as far as it was possible that the human mind should be drawn up, and stamped it with the impress of the powers that are accessible to being understood. (*All.* 1.35–38, after Colson)

Philo is obviously disturbed by the anthropomorphic notion of God breathing into man's face, which he rejects as an "absurdity." He immediately translates the notion of physical breathing into a spiritual activity, which requires no human organs. While Philo's emphasis on the non-anthropomorphic nature of God is shared by a variety of philosophical schools, including the Stoa (D.L. 7.147), his decision to place God above the material realm rather than within it engages Platonic ideas. Philo admired Plato and explicitly quotes from his works, adopting his distinction between a negative material realm and a positive spiritual one. Philo also assumes with Plato that the perceiving agent and the perceived object

10 See also *Deus* 21, *All.* 3.4. For further details on the anonymous Jewish interpreters, see Niehoff 2011a:77–92.

must be congenial, so that only the soul, man's most spiritual part, can hope to rise above the material realm and understand God.[11]

Plato's philosophical theology proved very useful for Philo. As we have already seen, Plato was appalled by the anthropomorphic images of Homer's gods (*Rep.* 377B–378D). A close reader of the canonical text, he took issue with specific passages that present the gods as going to war, showing human weaknesses and expressing everyday emotions. In light of such passages, Plato set out to define the "patterns of right speech about the gods" (οἱ τύποι περί θεολογίας). His theology amounts to a comprehensive assertion that God is "of course good in reality [ἀγαθὸς ὅ γε θεὸς τῷ ὄντι] and always to be spoken of as such," doing nothing harmful (*Rep.* 379A–B). Insisting on the gods' perfect goodness, Plato demands that they not be depicted in human fashion, because that would compromise their character and amount to a lie. The gods should only be held responsible for the good aspects of the world, while any shortcomings or evil must be attributed to other factors (*Rep.* 380C). The perfectly good character of the gods moreover requires that they do not change, because that would imply deterioration. Plato's discussion ends with a remarkable statement, which had considerable implications for subsequent readers, including Philo:

> It is impossible then, I said, even for a god to wish to alter himself, but, as it appears, each of them being the fairest and best possible abides for ever simply in his own form [μένει ἀεὶ ἁπλῶς ἐν τῇ αὑτοῦ μορφῇ]. (*Rep.* 381C)

Rejecting anthropomorphic conceptions of the gods, Plato develops a positive theology that posits the divine as a perfect model of ethics to be imitated by human beings. He stresses that the gods are "fairest and best possible" in character, enjoying an eternal, unchanging and non-composed existence. They resemble, in other words, the Ideal Types.

Philo shares Plato's transcendental theology and stresses the unchanging Oneness of God. A whole treatise of his *Allegorical Commentary* is devoted to the subject of the "Unchangeableness of God," in which he repeatedly criticizes literal readers of the Bible who suppose that God regrets man's creation, has human emotions and angrily threatens punishment for the transgression of His laws. Such passages, Philo explains, were written only for simple-minded people, who need concrete images of a personal God to guide them in their lives because they are unable to grasp His ethereal nature and perform moral actions without a penal

11 On Philo as a Platonist, see Dillon 1977; Runia 1986, 2001; Niehoff 2010.

system. Like Plato, Philo speaks of God as a refuge from the material world, to which the good soul escapes in order to attain virtue.[12]

In several important respects, however, Philo departs from Plato. To begin with, he retains the canonical text of his religion as an authoritative and truthful guide for life. While Plato absolved future philosophers and statesmen from the study of Homer, Philo insists on the centrality of the Scriptures for Jewish education. Secondly, where Plato rejected allegorical interpretations of his canonical text, fearing that even such guided readings may lead to wrong conceptions of the gods, Philo offers allegorical interpretations and pleads for the rationality of the Jewish tradition by interpreting the text in a philosophical mode. Philo also differs from Plato in his abovementioned description of God as "belonging to no class or kind" (ἄποιος γὰρ ὁ θεός). While Plato systematically stressed the unconditional goodness of the gods, Philo occasionally reserves the right to withhold judgment about the ultimate nature of God, suggesting that one can only know that He exists, not what He is like.

How can we explain Philo's assertion of God's absolute transcendence beyond all categories of human perception, even beyond notions of virtue and the good? Philo's approach must be appreciated in the context of Alexandrian Platonism, which had a strong tendency toward Pythagorean ideas. John Whittaker drew attention to significant connections between Philo and the negative theology of the Neopythagorean Platonists in Alexandria. He pointed to an important fragment of the Alexandrian Platonist Eudorus, who speaks about the deity as "the god who is above" (ὁ ὑπεράνω θεός).[13] Whittaker also stressed that Philo quotes the Pythagorean Philolaus, who speaks about God as "a supreme ruler of all things, ever One abiding, stable and without motion, Himself alone like unto Himself, different from all others" (*Opif.* 100). Whittaker's argument prompts us to identify further Philonic statements in the *Allegorical Commentary* as engagements with his Alexandrian environment. His assertions that God is "Himself One and whole," "unoriginate and incorruptible," incorporeal and "above His Potencies" (ὑπεράνω τῶν δυνάμενων), certainly belong to this context of Pythagorizing Platonism in Alexandria.[14] Philo refers rather explicitly to such circles:

---

12 *Deus* 20–22, 60–69, *Fug.* 53–70, *Husb.* 129; see also Dillon 1983.
13 Eud. apud Simpl., *In Phys.* 181.17; Whittaker 1973; on Philo's negative theology, see also Calabi 2008 and 2013:77–79; and Ben Sasson and Halbertal 2012 (who compare Philo's notions to those of the rabbis).
14 *All.* 1.44, 1.51, *Deus* 55, *Conf.* 137.

> [They] maintain that the Unoriginate resembles nothing among created things, but so completely transcends them [τοῖς ὅλοις ὑπερβάλλον], that even the swiftest understanding falls far short of apprehending Him and acknowledges its failure. (*Somn.* 1.184)

This passage shows, as Whittaker suggested, that Philo was indeed aware of Pythagorean Platonism in his intellectual environment.[15]

It is time now to advance further and ask what precise role Philo played in these Alexandrian discourses. Was he merely a mirror of contemporary discussions, or did he make his own contribution? In the most radical passages of the *Allegorical Commentary*, Philo offers novel views that take the Alexandrian debates a significant step further. Philo insists here that literally nothing can be known about God:

> Nothing that can give assurance can give positive assurance touching God, for to none has He shown His nature [οὐδενὶ γὰρ ἔδεξεν αὐτοῦ φύσιν], but He has rendered it invisible to our whole race. Who can assert of the First Cause either that it is without body or that it is a body, that it is of such a kind or that it is of no kind? In a word, who can make any positive assertion concerning His essence or quality or state or movement? (*All.* 3.206)

In this passage, Philo's theology is so radically negative that he cannot even know whether God is corporeal or not. The deity transcends the most basic distinction of Platonic ontology and collapses the borderline between an inferior material and a superior spiritual realm. While the Alexandrian Platonists had already stressed that God cannot be known, Philo explores the implications of this principle further and draws a conclusion of total negation. He is ahead of his time and anticipates the anonymous commentator on Plato's *Parmenides*, who paid much attention to the problem of God's transcendence, asking whether such a notion amounts to postulating nothingness for the deity.[16]

Philo's radically negative theology raises questions about his commitment to rationality, which looks to the human mind as the ultimate judge of religion. His interpretations of the Book of Genesis start with the assumption that the biblical God cannot be perceived in terms of human weakness. Philo stresses instead God's transcendental Oneness as well as His benevolence. In these passages the human mind is the judge of God's qualities, and Philo rejects those that do not suit his overall conception of the deity. In other passages, however, where Philo insists on man's inherent inability to comprehend God, he introduces skepticism with

---

15 Whittaker 1973; similarly, Bonazzi 2008.

16 See *Conf.* 97, *Mut.* 15, *Fug.* 94, 97; on the anonymous commentator, see Lernould 2010.

regard to overall standards of judgment. While certainly more abstract than the gods of mythology, Philo's wholly negative image of God may be no more rational.

Philo himself attenuates the consequences of his negative theology by developing an innovative theory of God's Logos that restores the role of the human mind. He speaks about the Logos almost exclusively in his early Alexandrian writings and hardly ever mentions this notion in the *Exposition of the Law*, from the later Roman stage of his career. The Logos responds to Philo's urgent sense that God cannot be known; it builds a bridge between the utterly transcendent deity and man, providing the latter with a picture of God's workings in the world.

Philo developed his new approach on the basis provided by the Pythagorean Platonism of Alexandria.[17] He introduces the Logos in the context of a discussion of the powers represented by numbers, where he mentions "the Pythagoreans" and suggests that the Logos has the same kind of force in the cosmos as do numbers. Philo then describes the Logos as God's instrument in the creation of an Ideal world, which preceded the material world.[18] The Logos is that aspect of God that comes into contact with the lower realms. It is transparent and can be addressed by man, providing a more predictable structure for human experience. At the same time, however, it is clear that God's essence remains unknown, thus generating a sense of mysticism in Philo's early writings.

This extreme form of transcendentalism undergoes dramatic changes in Philo's later writings, from his Roman period. Adopting a strikingly different approach, he no longer addresses fellow Jews but rather a general audience, to whom he explains the very basics of Judaism.[19] More importantly, in this late context Philo is no longer concerned with negative theology. In the works written in connection with the embassy to Rome, he does not dwell on man's inability to know God and is little concerned with anthropomorphic images. He even affirms that one may gain "knowledge of Him that truly is, Who is the primal and most perfect good" (*Dec.* 81). Philo now stresses the positive image of God as a fatherly, providential creator and devotes a whole treatise to the creation of the world, a theme that played only a minor role in his early writings. Thus, near the beginning *On the Creation of the World*, he writes:

---

17 Contra Bréhier 1950:83–111; Reydams-Schils 1995; and Dillon 1977, who all argue for the Stoic origins of Philo's Logos. See also Wolfson 1947:226–240, who argues for a classical Platonic background without considering more recent Alexandrian developments; and Winston 1985:9–25, who considers some aspects of Alexandrian Platonism while also pleading for Stoic influences.
18 *All.* 1.2; Philo relies here on LXX Gen. 2:4–5, which differs significantly from the Masoretic text and introduces a dimension of Plato's Ideal patterns; on LXX Gen. 2:4–5 see also Rösel 1994:59.
19 See also Birnbaum 1996.

> Reason demands [αἱρεῖ λόγος] that the Father and Maker exercise care for that which has come into being. After all, a father aims at the safety of his children and a craftsman aims at the preservation of what has been constructed, repelling by every means all that is injurious and harmful, while keenly desiring to provide in every way that which is advantageous and profitable. (*Opif.* 10, transl. Runia, with changes)

Philo concludes this treatise with an emphatic confirmation of divine providence:

> God also takes care of the cosmos. For it is required by the laws of nature and the ordinances [φύσεως νόμοις καὶ θεσμοῖς] that the maker always cares about the thing made; in accordance with these [laws] parents also take care of their children. (*Opif.* 171–2)

In contrast to his early Alexandrian period, Philo is now wholeheartedly committed to universal standards of rationality, which he also applies to God. He stresses that God acts according to reason and the laws of nature. He is a predictable and reliable deity, who conforms to norms that are also followed by man. Philo's presentation of these rational qualities, as well as his comparison of God to human parents, suggest that he was inspired by the Stoic theology that was then dominant in Rome. The Stoics are known to have made nature and her laws the standard of ethics and theology. They developed a monotheistic approach to religion, assigning to Zeus, and later, in Rome, to Jupiter, an exclusive role in the creation of the world. Cicero, in the first century BCE, says that the Stoics address Jupiter as the helper and "father of gods and men" (Cic., *N.D.* 2.64).

The Stoics moreover emphasized providence more than any other Hellenistic school, producing numerous treatises on the subject. Philo assumes with them that God takes personal care of the world, especially of man, who is "the being dearest and closest" to God. Philo is eager to expand the biblical creation story, according to which man is created in the "image" and "likeness" of God. He stresses that this resemblance pertains only to man's mind, which distinguishes him from all other creatures. Man, created last, was thus provided with all the necessaries, thereby being able to enjoy a "means of living and living well." The elements of the world were destined for man and his needs. The Stoics similarly viewed the world from an anthropocentric perspective. Chrysippus compared the world to a handsome mansion "built for its masters, not for mice."[20]

Philo's dramatic change of orientation, from transcendentalism, bordering on negative theology, to immanentism, with a fatherly image of God, reflects his acute awareness of Roman discourses. The latter inspired him to approach the

20 *Opif.* 69–77; *D.L.* 7.138–139; Cic., *N.D.* 1.3, 2.58, 2.154–163, 3.26; *Ac.* 1:6; see also D. Frede 2002; M. Frede 2010.

Jewish Scriptures in a new way and to integrate Judaism into contemporary discourses. While the young Philo was concerned in a typically Greek fashion with biblical anthropomorphisms and the question of how individual men can imitate God, the mature Philo appreciates God in Roman terms as the benefactor of the world and of human society at large. This intellectual development points to broader changes in contemporary culture. Rome was not only the political center of the world, but increasingly also its cultural standard. Philo thus indicates the profound changes that different groups in the Roman Empire would undergo. Not surprisingly, Philo's later form of rationalizing the Jewish God also became dominant among the Rabbis, known for their many father–son parables and their image of a fatherly creator God.[21]

Philo's Rationalization of Jewish Law

Philo is the first Jewish author to develop a philosophy of law and provide an overall rational framework for interpreting particular commandments. Philo's achievement in this area is unparalleled in Judaism until the Middle Ages, when Saadya Gaon and Maimonides developed a similar approach independently.[22] Philo's treatises on the *Decalogue* and the *Special Laws* belong to the later stage of his career and come as a surprise, because he had shown little interest in Jewish law in his earlier Alexandrian period. In his early writings he deals with narrative materials in Genesis and Exodus, which he reads in a Platonic mode as allegories of the soul's ascent from the material realm to God. Nevertheless, he does once address the issue of Jewish law observance in Alexandria, reacting to a group of Jews who argue that literal observance is no longer necessary if the allegorical meaning is taken seriously. In this internal Jewish context, Philo stresses that "the Holy Word teaches us to consider good repute and abandon nothing of the customs fixed by divinely inspired men greater than those of our time" (*Migr.* 90). This position is rather traditional and withdraws from the rationalistic approach visible in Alexandria already in the second century BCE. Philo relies here on the authority of God and divinely inspired men. What prompted him, in the *Exposition*

---

21 On transformations of Hellenistic culture in the Roman Empire, see Whitmarsh 2001; and Swain 1996. On the Rabbis' parables and notion of a fatherly God, see Ziegler 1903; Urbach 1983:29–52.

22 On Saadya Gaon and Maimonides, see Halbertal 2009 and S. Stroumsa 2009. On the beginnings of medieval Jewish philosophy in the writings of Al-Muqammis, see S. Stroumsa 1989.

of the Law, to move beyond these brief remarks and formulate a highly innovative philosophy of law?

Political developments played a central role. In the third book of *On the Special Laws*, Philo says that he was plunged "into the ocean of state affairs" and "civil turmoil," which radically changed his hitherto contemplative mode of life. He must be referring here to the events connected to the pogrom in Alexandria and the subsequent Jewish embassy to Rome. In this context Philo began to deal with political issues revolving around the civil status of the Jews and their particular customs. Some of the views he encountered among his interlocutors were so negative that he began his treatment of the commandments with "that ridiculed among many," namely, circumcision. Philo justifies circumcision by invoking the Egyptians, who also practice it, and he invites his readers to appreciate that the Jews are not the only ones "mutilating the bodies of themselves and their nearest." Such concern to defend Jewish custom must have been directed to a Roman rather than an Alexandrian audience, because the Egyptians were familiar with the practice. It was in Rome that circumcision not only became a well-known marker of the Jews but also a special focus of scorn. Tacitus, Horace and Petronius did not hide their disdain. Philo's contemporary Apion, who served as the head of the parallel Egyptian embassy to Gaius, engaged such sentiments in Rome and "scoffed at circumcision." When, a generation later, Josephus addressed these issues in Rome, he would note significantly that Apion's rhetoric did not accord with his Alexandrian background.[23]

Philo develops his philosophy of Jewish law as an author who is actively involved in politics, and he works hard to maintain a balance between his public responsibilities and the leisure required for intellectual pursuits. Unlike the Rabbis and authors in the Land of Israel during the Second Temple period, he neither sets out to judge particular cases of Jewish law nor discusses applications of biblical law to contemporary issues. He is concerned not with the minutiae of observance, but rather with the overall meaning and ethical rationale of traditional Jewish life. His main argument is that Jewish law is a perfect guide to ethical life, appealing to each individual to fashion himself in accordance with virtue. How does Philo transform biblical law, which is mostly based on God's authority, into a guidebook for individual moral development?

Philo initially considers the nature of biblical law by comparing it to other legal codes. He rejects the approach of those legislators who draw up "without

23 *Spec.* 3.3–5, 1:3; Tac., *Hist.* 5:5, 2; Hor., *Serm.* 1:9, 70; Petr., *Satyr.* 102:13–14; Jos., *C.A.* 2:137–144; see also Stern 1980:41 (re Tacitus), 1974:324–326 (re Horace), 443–444 (re Petronius); Schäfer 1997:98–100; Isaac 2004:472–474.

embellishment and nakedly the things held righteous among their people," because such practice is "unreflecting and careless and not philosophical." Philo assumes an intrinsic connection between laws and wider philosophical principles. The laws cannot be reduced to a list of specific actions, singled out for either reward or punishment. Their overall intellectual purpose must instead be given proper attention. Philo praises Moses for introducing his law code with the creation account, thereby "not stating at once what should be practiced or avoided, because it was necessary to mold beforehand the minds of those who will use the laws."[24] According to Philo, Mosaic law is concerned with the shaping of man's mind. The aim of the law is beyond its literal fulfillment. This immediately raises questions about the relationship between philosophical principles or advice, which are voluntarily adopted for the purpose of individual improvement, and commands, which rely on obedience to authority.

Philo does not accidentally raise these issues. They were being discussed in contemporary Rome. Thus, Seneca rejects the approach of his predecessor, Posidonius, who argued that "the law should be brief so that it can be easily grasped by the ignorant." According to Posidonius, it was a mistake on the part of Plato to add introductions to his treatises on the laws. Seneca, by contrast, thinks that such introductions are vital because they set the mind in the right philosophical direction and enable men to perform the particular precepts with full intention. While he regards philosophy as a "law of life" (*vitae lex*), Seneca insists on the importance of specific admonitions. Such precepts constantly remind the wavering mind of its moral duties and prevent relapse into sin. He remarks, with a psychological insight that sounds rather modern, that we "sometimes know, but pay no attention" and thus need regularly to be reminded to behave properly. For Seneca, the only difference between "philosophical principles and precepts" is that the former are "general precepts, while the latter are specific." Both, however, lead man in the same direction of moral improvement, one by providing insights, which are freely implemented, the other by giving specific instructions for particular circumstances of life. This discussion, which is rooted already in Cicero's works, illuminates Philo's introductory remarks in the *Exposition*; clearly, he interprets Jewish law from the perspective of wider Roman discourses that had no parallel in the extant sources from contemporary Alexandria.[25]

In his treatise *On the Decalogue*, Philo develops a highly innovative notion of Jewish law that has been recognized as an important breakthrough in ancient

24 ἄσκεπτον καὶ ἀταλαίπωρον καὶ ἀφιλόσοφον ... ἐπειδὴ προτυπῶσαι τὰς διανοίας τῶν χρησομένων τοῖς νόμοις ἀναγκαῖον ἦν ... (*Opif.* 1–2).

25 Sen., *Ep.* 94.1–21, 25, 31, 38; Cic., *Rep.* 2.1–3.

Judaism. While the Ten Commandments had probably been used in liturgical contexts already by the first century BCE, Philo is the first to identify them as central principles that serve as "heads" for the rest of the Mosaic legislation. In Philo's words, "those [laws] revealed in His own person and by Himself alone are both laws and heads [κεφάλαια] of the particular laws, while those given through the prophet all belong to the former category." Philo's special emphasis on the Decalogue may well have been a response to its unique nature and place within the Bible. It constitutes the covenant between God and Israel and contains timeless instructions for every Israelite, without reference to particular circumstances. Moreover, the number ten is typological, as Philo enthusiastically points out, and the Tenth Commandment is unique in biblical law. It describes things not to be desired and thus addresses the subject of intention, an area by definition beyond the realm of legislation, which deals with action, or the practical consequences of intention. All of these special characteristics of the Decalogue point to fundamental questions of human conduct.[26]

Philo is the first known reader of the Decalogue to use it as a basis for a philosophy of Jewish law. He argues that the Ten Commandments constitute the overall ethical principles on which the other laws are based. He speaks of the "ten words" or "exhortations" as "generic laws" that "allude" to a variety of congenial precepts. The particular laws, in his view, are "dependent species" that are "contained" or "implied" in the leading principles. Philo's interpretation is not only new but in fact contrary to earlier approaches, such as that of the Book of Jubilees, where general injunctions are often connected to specific events in Israelite history and thus transformed into more particularistic precepts than they originally were.[27]

Philo's idea of the Decalogue as "heads of laws" introduces overall rational categories to the interpretation of Mosaic law. In his view, God gave the Ten Commandments as the underlying principles of all the particular laws. By saying that the Ten Commandments "run through the whole of the legislation," Philo suggests that even the most minute or ritual regulations are anchored in overall philosophical principles, opening "broad highroads leading to one end, namely, the undisturbed journey of the soul ever desiring the best." Connecting the particular

---

26 *Dec.* 19, 175. Philo's innovation is treated appreciatively by both Amir 1985 and Termini 2004, contra Wolfson 1947:200–202, who mistakenly identifies some rabbinic passages as sources of Philo. On the liturgical use of the Decalogue, see Urbach 1985.

27 *Spec.* 1.1 (δέκα λόγοι); *Dec.* 82 (παραίνεσις); *Dec.* 165 (ὑπαινίττεται); *Spec.* 4.132 (ὑποστέλλοντα εἴδη, according to Colson's textual correction *ad. loc.*); *Dec.* 162 (ἐμφέρονται), 168, 171 (ὑποτέτακται).

laws to the Decalogue, Philo provides them with an ethical basis. This dimension of the law is stressed by his insistence, against the Scriptures themselves, that no punishment is envisaged for the transgression of the Ten Commandments. According to Philo, God purposely refrained from threats of punishment "so that people will choose the best, not involuntarily, but out of a willing consciousness [καθ' ἑκούσιον γνώμην], not using fear as their senseless counselor, but the good sense of reason." By implication, the particular laws, too, are provided with an aspect of philosophical choice, which transforms them from commandments based on obedience into rational advice, chosen for its intrinsic good. Characteristically, Philo argues that intention must seriously be taken into account when judging particular transgressions.[28]

The background to Philo's revolutionary interpretation of the Decalogue is again the Stoic philosophy then dominant in Rome. Cicero already describes Stoic ethics as a system that attributes utmost importance to free choice. The morally good is chosen for its own sake, without consideration for either punishment or reward. The ultimate aim of Stoic ethics is to live in accordance with nature and free of external as well as internal constraints. The wise man achieves this end, enjoying happiness and a "perfect and fortunate life, free from all hindrance." Moreover, for the Stoics, the law, even in its most specific form, is rooted in philosophy and reflects universal right reason. Cicero even formulates the ethical function of the law in terms almost identical to those of Philo: "The law ought to be a reformer of vice and an incentive to virtue; the doctrine of living may be derived from it."[29]

Seneca devotes an important epistle to the Stoic dispute about whether precepts are necessary. Some adherents of the school argued that precepts amount to old wives' advice and are therefore useless. By contrast, Cleanthes, former head of the Stoic school, considered particular precepts useful as long as they are grounded in general philosophical principles or "heads" (*capita*). Seneca follows Cleanthes in affirming the importance of precepts, stressing that nature does not teach us our duty in each particular case. Man thus requires specific instructions, derived from nature, in order to see what he or she should do in particular situations. Seneca justifies precepts by grounding them in general philosophical principles. He pleads for a deep connection between the two realms, suggesting that they are like two sides of the same coin. Precepts do not coerce "but plead," and

---

28 *Dec.* 37–39, 50, 154, 177, 17, 13–14; *Spec.* 1.86–87, 3.104–107.

29 Cic., *Fin.* 3:11–12, 26, 31–32; *Leg.* 1.16–17, 32–35, 58. While Philo briefly mentions the idea of the Ten Commandments as heads of the particular laws in the *Allegorical Commentary* (*Congr.* 120) he characteristically refrains there from discussing the philosophical implications of this idea.

are effective if they are “often with you.”[30] To be sure, Seneca indicates that the Stoics discussed the tension between philosophical principles and particular precepts at least from Cleanthes’ time onwards. Philo could thus have read his work in Greek in Alexandria. Yet in his early Alexandrian writings there is no sign of an interest in these issues. Philo applies himself to a detailed study of the Decalogue and its philosophical significance only in his later writings, after he has arrived in Rome. The intellectual climate he encountered there seems to have stimulated him to think about the Jewish tradition in new ways.

Philo’s rationalization of biblical law has significant implications for early Christianity. Paul, in his Letter to the Romans, written a few years after Philo’s *Exposition*, expresses a strikingly similar idea of the law. He uses the same notion of particular laws being “summed up” in an overarching principle, using the verb ἀνακεφαλαιόομαι, derived from the root meaning “head” that Philo had already used. In Paul’s view, the four ethical commands of the Decalogue are summed up in the law “love your neighbor as yourself.”

In contrast to Philo, however, Paul no longer includes the wealth of specific laws under the rubric of philosophical principles. He has clearly moved to a far more general plane, leaving behind traditional Jewish customs. Paul is not concerned to justify Jewish practices by endowing them with philosophical value, but instead gives absolute priority to ethical principles, reducing four relatively specific commandments of the Decalogue to an even more general principle. In his words, “love does no wrong to a neighbor [as such specified in the Decalogue]; therefore love is the fulfillment of the law.” In light of his harsh criticism of traditional Jewish observance elsewhere in the Letter to the Romans, it is clear that Paul offers a substitute model for the relationship between particulars and general principles: As the principles sum up the specific, the faithful Christian no longer has to be concerned with the particulars.[31] Philo may have provided Paul with a model for thinking about the connection between philosophy and law. If so, and if he had lived a few years longer to see the Letter to the Romans, he would surely have been surprised by the use to which his ideas had been put.

---

30 Sen., *Ep.* 94.4, 19–27, 31, 37, 42; *Ep.* 81.19–21; *Ben.* 1.6.1.

31 Rom. 13.8–10. Paul’s attitude toward Jewish law observance remains a controversial issue in modern scholarship; see esp. Barclay 1998; Watson 2007; and Hayes 2015; cf. Boyarin 1994.

Conclusion

Philo addresses two important issues, both of which had previously been discussed by Jewish rationalists in Alexandria: biblical anthropomorphism and biblical law. In both areas Philo perceived a clash of values, which prompted him to interpret his tradition in rational and universal terms. Early in his career in Alexandria, he confronted the criticism of Jewish colleagues who compared biblical stories about God to similar tales in Homer's epics and concluded that the Jewish Scriptures also include myths. Philo countered this approach by applying Plato's transcendental notions to the biblical God. In this way he both defended the validity of the Jewish Scriptures and inscribed Judaism into Greek discourses of rationality. In some passages, however, Philo reached a stage of totally negative theology and denied any quality to God, thus reverting to a more mystical position.

At a later stage of his career, after coming to Rome as an ambassador, Philo encountered new challenges of a philosophical and political nature. The dominant school of philosophy in Rome at that time was not Platonism but the Stoa. The Stoics' approach to theology was more immanentist than that of Platonism and prompted Philo to emphasize the creation of the world as well as God's fatherly involvement in it. He now stressed that God functions according to the same rational criteria that guide men in their ethics. In Rome, moreover, Philo encountered critical views of Jewish law, with circumcision especially ridiculed. He resolved this clash of values by arguing for the underlying philosophical rationale of Jewish law. According to Philo's highly innovative interpretation, all particular laws are anchored in the Ten Commandments, which present philosophical principles to be chosen for their intrinsic value rather than out of obedience to a deity.

Philo's different ways of rationalizing Judaism illustrate the dynamics of such processes. He responded creatively to diverse challenges to his religion, both from within and from without. Especially in Rome, rationalizing one's religion meant rendering it transparent to outsiders and relevant to contemporary discourses. In a way, Philo's rational interpretation of Judaism submitted his religion to Rome's political hegemony. At the same time, however, he thus ensured its acceptance, and his innovations updated it for many generations to come.

References

Classical Works

Ar. = Aristeas, *Letter of Aristeas*, Greek text with French translation by A. Pelletier. 2007. Paris: Edition du Cerf.

Aristobulus, fr. = fragments, in Holladay 1995.

Augustine, *Civ. Dei* = Augustine, *The City of God*, Latin text with English translation by G.E. MacCracken. 1957. Cambridge MA: Harvard University Press.

Cic., *Fin.* = Cicero, *De Finibus Bonorum et Malorum*, Latin text with English translation by H. Rackham, 1967. London: W. Heinemann.

–, *Leg.* = *De Legibus*, in *On the Commonwealth and On the Laws*, Latin text with English translation, edited by James E. G. Zetzel, 2017. Cambridge, U.K.–New York: Cambridge University Press.

–, *N.D.* = *On the Nature of the Gods*, Latin text with English translation by H. Rackham. Cambridge, MA: Harvard University Press, 1979).

–, *Rep.* = *De Republica*, in *On the Commonwealth and On the Laws*, Latin text with English translation, edited by James E. G. Zetzel, 2017. Cambridge, U.K.–New York: Cambridge University Press.

Clem., *Exh.* = Clement, *Exhortation to the Greeks*, Greek text with English translation by G.W. Butterworth. 1982. Cambridge, *MA*: Harvard University Press.

D.L. = Diogenes Laertius, *Lives of Eminent Philosophers*, II: *Books 6–10*, Greek text with English translation by R.D. Hicks, 1925. Cambridge, MA: Harvard University Press

Hor., *Serm.* = *Sermones*, in *Horace: Satires, Epistles, The Art of Poetry*, Latin text with English translation by H. Rushton Fairclough, 1926. Cambridge, MA: Harvard University Press.

Jos., *C.A.* = Flavius Josephus, *Against Apion*, Greek text with English translation and commentary by John M.G. Barclay, 2013. Leiden: Brill.

Justin Martyr, *Dial.* = *Justini Martyris Dialogus cum Tryphone*, Greek text edited by M. Marchovich. 1997. Berlin: De Gruyter.

Petr., *Satyr.* = Petronius, *The Satyricon*, Latin text with English translation, introduction and notes by P.G. Walsh, 1997. Oxford: Oxford University Press.

Philo, *Works*, Greek text with English translation by F.H. Colson. 1981. Cambridge, MA: Harvard University Press.

–, *All.*= *Legum allegoriae* (*Allegorical Interpretion*)

–, *Conf.* = *De confusione linguarum* (*On the Confusion of Tongues*)

–, *Congr.* = *De congressueru ditionis gratia* (*On the Preliminary Studies*)

–, *Dec.* = *De decalogo* (*On the Decalogue*)

–, *Deus* = *Quod Deus sit immutabilis* (*On the Unchangeableness of God*)

–, *Fug.* = *De fuga et inventione* (*On Flight and Finding*)

–, *Husb.* = *De agricultura* (*On Husbandry*)

–, *Migr.* = *De migratione Abrahami* (*On the Migration of Abraham*)

–, *Mut.* = *De mutatione nominum* (*On the Change of Names*)

–, *Opif.* = *De opificio mundi* (*On the Creation*)

–, *Somn.* = *De somniis* (*On Dreams*)

–, *Spec.* = *De specialibus legibus* (*On the Special Laws*)

Plato, *Rep.* = *Republic*, Greek text with English translation by P. Shorey. 1982. Cambridge, MA: Harvard University Press.
Sen., *Ben.* = Seneca, *Beneficiis*: *On Benefits*, Latin text with English translation by Miriam Griffin and Brad Inwood, 2011. Chicago: University of Chicago Press.
—, *Ep.* = *Epistulae: Letters on Ethics: To Lucilius*, Latin text with English translation, introduction and commentary by Margaret Graver and A.A. Long, 2015. Chicago: University of Chicago Press.
Sinpl., *In Phys.* = Simplicius, *On Aristotle Physics 1.3–4*, Latin text with English translation by Pamela Huby and C.C.W. Taylor, 2011. London: Bristol Classical Press.
Tac., *Hist.* = *Tacitus: Histories, Books 4–5; Annals, Books 1–3*, Latin text with English translation by Clifford H. Moore and John Jackson, 1931. Cambridge, MA: Harvard University Press.
Xenophanes, fr. = fragments, in *Die Fragmente der Vorsokratiker*, ed. H. Diels. 1954 (7th ed.). Berlin: Weidmann.

Secondary Works

Amir, Yehoshua. 1985. "The Decalogue According to the Teachings of Philo of Alexandria." In Benzion Segal (ed.), *The Ten Commandments as Reflected in Tradition and Literature Throughout the Ages*. Jerusalem: Magnes Press. 95–125. Hebrew.
Barclay, John M.G. 1996. *Jews in the Mediterranean Diaspora*. Berkeley, CA: University of California Press.
—. 1998. "Paul and Philo on Circumcision: Romans 2:25–9 in the Social and Cultural Context." *New Testament Studies*, 44:536–556.
Ben Sasson, Hillel, and Moshe Halbertal. 2012. "The Divine Name YHWH and the Measure of Mercy." In Maren R. Niehoff, Ronit Meroz and Jonathan Garb (eds.), *And This Is for Yehuda: Studies Presented to our Colleague, Professor Yehuda Liebes, on the Occasion of His Sixty-Fifth Birthday*. Jerusalem: Mandel Institute of Jewish Studies–Bialik Institute. 53–69. Hebrew.
Birnbaum, Ellen. 1996. *The Place of Judaism in Philo's Thought*. Atlanta: Scholars Press.
Bonazzi, Mauro. 2008. "Towards Transcendence: Philo and the Renewal of Platonism in the Early Imperial Age." In Francesca Alesse (ed.), *Philo of Alexandria and Post-Aristotelian Philosophy*. Leiden: Brill. 233–252.
Boyarin, Daniel. 1994. *Paul: A Radical Jew*. Berkeley: University of California Press.
Bréhier, Emile. 1950. *Les Idées Philosophiques et Religieuses de Philon d'Alexandrie*. Paris: Librairie Philosophique J. Vrin.
Brakke, David. 2011. "Scriptural Practices in Early Christianity: Towards a New History of the New Testament Canon." In Anders-Christian Jacobsen and Jörg Ulrich (eds.), *Invention, Rewriting, Usurpation: Discursive Fights over Religious Traditions in Antiquity* (Early Christianity in the Context of Antiquity, 11). Frankfurt: Peter Lang. 263–280.
Burkert, Walter. 1985. *Greek Religion* (English transl. by John Raffan). Oxford: Basil Blackwell.
Burridge, Richard. 2004. *What Are the Gospels? A Comparison with Graeco-Roman Biography*. Grand Rapids–Dearborn, MI: Eerdmans–Dove Booksellers.
Calabi, Francesca. 2008. *God's Acting, Man's Acting*. Leiden: Brill.
—. 2013. *Filone di Allessandria*. Rome: Carocci editore.

Cancick, Hubert. 2001. "Historisierung von Religion: Religionsgeschichtsschreibung in der Antike (Varro – Tacitus – Walahfrid Strabo)." In Glenn W. Most (ed.), *Historicization – Historisierung*. Göttingen: Vandenhoeck und Ruprecht. 1–13.

Chadwick, Henry. 1966. *Early Christian Thought and the Classical Tradition*. Oxford: Oxford University Press.

Clauss, Manfred. 2003. *Alexandria: Eine antike Weltstadt*. Stuttgart: Klett-Cotta.

Collins, John. 2000. *Between Athens and Jerusalem: Jewish Identity in the Hellenistic Diaspora*. Grand Rapids: Eerdmans.

Dillon, John. 1977. *The Middle Platonists*. London: Duckworth.

—. 1983. "The Nature of God in the Quod Deus." In David Winston and John Dillon (eds.), *Two Treatises of Philo of Alexandria*. Chico: Scholars Press. 217–227.

Ehrman, Bart. 2003. *Lost Christianities*. Oxford: Oxford University Press.

Finkelberg, Margalit, and Guy G. Stroumsa (eds.). 2003. *Homer, the Bible and Beyond: Religious Canons in the Ancient World* (Jerusalem Studies in Religion and Culture, 2). Leiden–Boston: Brill.

Fraser, Peter M. 1972. *Ptolemaic Alexandria*. Oxford: Clarendon Press.

Frede, Dorothea. 2002. "Theodicy and Providential Care in Stoicism." In eadem and André Laks (eds.), *Traditions of Theology*. Leiden: Brill. 95–108.

Frede, Michael. 2010. "The Case for Pagan Monotheism in Greek and Greco-Roman Antiquity." In Steven Mitchell and Peter van Nuffelen (eds.), *One God: Pagan Monotheism in the Roman Empire*. Cambridge: Cambridge University Press. 53–81.

Georges, Tobias, Felix Albrecht and Reinhard Feldmeier (eds.). 2013. *Alexandria*. Tübingen: Mohr Siebeck.

Guthrie, William Keith Chambers. 1962. *The Earlier Presocratics and the Pythagoreans* (= *A History of Greek Philosophy*, I). Cambridge: Cambridge University Press.

Gutman, Yehoshua. 1969. *The Beginnings of Jewish-Hellenistic Literature*. Jerusalem: Bialik Institute.

Hadas-Lebel, Mireille. 2012. *Philo of Alexandria: A Thinker in the Jewish Diaspora* (English transl. by Robyn Frechet). Leiden: Brill.

Hägg, Tomas. 2012. *The Art of Biography in Antiquity*. Cambridge: Cambridge University Press.

Halbertal, Moshe. 1997. *People of the Book: Canon, Meaning, and Authority*. Cambridge MA: Harvard University Press.

—. 2009. *Maimonides*. Jerusalem: Zalman Shazar Center.

Hayes, Christine. 2015. *What's Divine about Divine Law? Early Perspectives*. Princeton: Princeton University Press.

Heine, Ronald E. 2004. "The Alexandrians." In Frances Young, Lewis Ayres and Andrew Louth (eds.), *The Cambridge History of Early Christian Literature*. Cambridge: Cambridge University Press. 117–130.

Holladay, Carl. 1995. *Aristobulus* (= *Fragments from Hellenistic Jewish Authors*, III). Atlanta: Scholars Press.

Isaac, Benjamin. 2004. *The Invention of Racism in Classical Antiquity*. Princeton: Princeton University Press.

Lernould, Alain. 2010. "Negative Theology and Radical Conceptual Purification in the *Anonymous Commentary on Plato's Parmenides*." In John D. Turner and Kevin Corrigan (eds.), *Plato's Parmenides and Its Heritage: History and Interpretation from the Old Academy to Later Platonism and Gnosticism*. Atlanta: Society of Biblical Literature. 257–274.

Männlein-Robert, Irmgard. 2010. "Umrisse des Göttlichen: Zur Typologie des idealen Gottes in Platons Politeia II." In Dietmar Koch, Irmgard Männlein-Robert and Niels Weidtmann (eds.), *Platon und das Göttliche* (Antike-Studien, 1), Tübingen: Attempto. 112–138.
Markschies, Christoph. 1997. *Das antike Christentum: Frömmigkeit, Lebensformen, Institutionen*. Munich: Beck.
—. 1999. *Between the Two Worlds: Structures of Early Christianity*. London: SCM Press.
Niehoff, Maren R. 2010. "Philo's Role as a Platonist in Alexandria." *Études Platoniciennes*, 7:35–62.
—. 2011a. *Jewish Exegesis and Homeric Scholarship in Alexandria*. Cambridge: Cambridge University Press.
—. 2011b. "The Roman Context of Philo's *Exposition*." *Studia Philonica Annual*, 23:1–21.
—. (ed.). 2012. *Homer and the Bible in the Eyes of Ancient Interpreters*. Leiden: Brill.
—. 2018. *Philo of Alexandria: An Intellectual Biography*, New Haven, CT: Yale University Press. Hebrew translation: Tel Aviv: Hakibbutz Hameuchad, 2019 (forthcoming); German translation: Tübingen: Mohr Siebeck, 2019 (forthcoming).
—. Forthcoming. "A Jew for Roman Tastes: 'The Parting of the Ways' in Justin Martyr's Dialogue with Tryphon." *Journal of Early Christian Studies*.
Norris, Richard A. Jr. 2004. "The Apologists." In Frances Young, Lewis Ayres and Andrew Louth (eds.), *The Cambridge History of Early Christian Literature*. Cambridge: Cambridge University Press. 36–44.
Reydams-Schils, Gretchen. 1995. "Stoicizing Readings of Plato's *Timaeus* in Philo of Alexandria." *The Studia Philonica Annual*, 7:85–102.
Runia, David T. 1986. *Philo of Alexandria and the Timaeus of Plato*. Leiden: Brill.
—. 2001. *Philo of Alexandria: On the Creation of the Cosmos according to Moses – Introduction, Translation and Commentary*. Leiden: Brill.
Rösel, Martin. 1994. *Übersetzung als Vollendung der Auslegung*. Berlin–New York: De Gruyter.
Rüpke, Jörg. 2012. *Religion in Republican Rome: Rationalization and Ritual Change*. Philadelphia: Pennsylvania University Press.
—. 2014. "Historicizing Religion: Varro's *Antiquitates* and History of Religion in the Late Roman Republic." *History of Religions*, 53:246–268.
Schäfer, Peter. 1997. *Judeophobia: Attitudes Toward the Jews in the Ancient World*. Cambridge, MA: Harvard University Press.
Stern, Menahem. 1974. *Greek and Latin Authors on Jews and Judaism*, I: *From Tacitus to Simplicius*. Jerusalem: Israel Academy of Sciences and Humanities.
—. 1980. *Greek and Latin Authors on Jews and Judaism*, II: *From Herodotus to Plutarch*. Jerusalem: Israel Academy of Sciences and Humanities.
Stowers, Stanley K. 1989. *Letter Writing in Greco-Roman Antiquity*. Philadelphia: Westminster Press.
Stroumsa, Guy. 1999. *Barbarian Philosophy: The Religious Revolution of Early Christianity*. Tübingen: Mohr Siebeck.
—. 2009. *The End of Sacrifice: Religious Transformation in Late Antiquity*. Chicago: Chicago University Press.
—. 2010. *A New Science: The Discovery of Reason in the Age of Reason*. Cambridge: Harvard University Press.
Stroumsa, Sarah. 1989. *Dawid Ibn Marwan Al-Muqamma's Twenty Chapters*. Leiden: Brill.
—. 2009. Mai*monides in His World*. Princeton: Princeton University Press.
Swain, Simon. 1996. *Hellenism and Empire*. Oxford: Clarendon Press.

Tcherikover, Victor A., and Alexander Fuks. 1960. *Corpus Papyrorum Judaicarum*, II. Cambridge MA: Harvard University Press.

Termini, Cristina. 2004. "Taxonomy of Biblical Law and φιλοτεχνία in Philo of Alexandria: A Comparison with Josephus and Cicero." *Studia Philonica Annual*, 16:1–29.

Urbach, Efraim E. 1983. *The Sages*. Jerusalem: Magnes Press. Hebrew.

—. 1985. "The Place of the Ten Commandments in Ritual and Prayer." In Benzion Segal (ed.), *The Ten Commandments as Reflected in Tradition and Literature throughout the Ages*. Jerusalem: Magnes Press. 127–146. Hebrew.

Van der Horst, Pieter W. 2003. *Philo of Alexandria: Philo's Flaccus, The First Pogrom – Introduction, Translation and Commentary*. Leiden: Brill.

Van Nuffelen, Peter. 2010. "Varro's *Divine Antiquities*: Roman Religion as an Image of Truth." *Classical Philology*, 105:162–188.

Walter, Nicolaus. 1964. *Der Toraausleger Aristobulus: Untersuchungen zu seinen Fragmenten und zu den pseudepigraphischen Resten der jüdisch-hellenistischen Literatur*. Berlin: Texte und Untersuchungen zur Geschichte altchristlicher Literatur.

Watson, Francis. 2007. *Paul, Judaism, and the Gentiles*. Grand Rapids: Eerdmans.

Whitmarsh, Tim. 2001. *Greek Literature and the Roman Empire*. Oxford: Oxford University Press.

Whittaker, John. 1973. "Neopythagoreanism and the Transcendent Absolute." *Symbolae Osloenses*, 48:77–86.

Winston, David. 1985. *Logos and Mystical Theology in Philo of Alexandria*. Cincinnati: Hebrew Union College Press.

Wolfson, Harry A. 1947. *Philo: Foundations of Religious Philosophy in Judaism, Christianity and Islam*. Cambridge MA: Harvard University Press.

Ziegler, Ignaz. 1903. *Die Königsgleichnisse des Midrasch beleuchtet durch die römische Kaiserzeit*. Breslau: S. Schottlaender.

Moshe Idel

Forms of Rationalization in Medieval Jewish Thought

On Pre-Kabbalistic Forms of Judaism

Judaism in its biblical and rabbinic forms are what I call a religion without a constellated theological universe, one that operates without a sustained systematic theology. In both these forms of classical Judaism, the will of God and the deeds it mandates constitute the major religious factors, in reality and as to what should be known by a religious person. The most one can find in the way of theological notions in rabbinic literature in the first century CE is mention of divine attributes, two or more, especially those of mercy and of judgment, envisioned as governing this world.[1] Angels, for example, play only a minor role in Rabbinism, though they surge, contemporaneously with the development of rabbinic literature, in the so-called Hekhalot literature and in Jewish magic.[2] The few mentions of distinct feminine powers within the divine world, *Shekhina* and *Keneset Yisra'el*, sometimes related sexually or erotically to the masculine divinity, did not coalesce into a systematic theology.[3] From the point of view of the history of religion, these two layers of Judaism are performative types of religion at their core, concerned with the details of the divine imperatives, the commandments.

The much more systematic and elaborate thought of Philo of Alexandria, written in Greek, reflects the deep impact of Greek philosophy, and it turned into a theology that was then ignored or rejected by rabbinic authorities, although Philo's synthesis of scripture and Greek philosophy left an indelible imprint on Christian theology, on the one hand, and on Western philosophy, on the other.[4] This does not mean that the Rabbis did not have their personal theologies, each his own, but there is no systematic discussion or presentation of them in the classical rabbinic literatures: the Mishna and the two Talmuds, the various forms of midrash and the vast poetic literature known as *piyut*. These were concerned with shaping a way of life much more than a way of thought; the synchronicity of per-

---

1 See e.g., Urbach 1979:37–65; Naeh 1997; Liebes 2008:135–157; and also Ben-Sasson and Halbertal 2012.

2 See Urbach 1979:135–183; Idel 2008a.

3 See, e.g., Idel 2011a.

4 H. Wolfson 1982.

https://doi.org/10.1515/9783110446395-005

formance that they espoused made them a social glue, which is why I have characterized their anthropology as a matter of the "performing body."[5] The actions of the body and the study of the texts were both intended to shape a certain concrete way of life for individuals as part of a religious community. Both Rabbis and ordinary Jews shared this emphasis on performance, and even the preoccupation of the former with studying was intended to extract details of precise behavior, conceived as constituting the content of Halakha. The basic assumption of the Rabbis was that the commandments, understood as the divine will, include religious, ethical and social values, and no rationales need be offered for them. To define this literature in terms of what is absent: No book on science or nature was written by the Rabbis in the first millennium of Rabbinism, which means that no treatise on astronomy or mathematics, or on psychology, grammar or poetics is extant in Hebrew.

In the Middle Ages, however, some elite Jewish thinkers adopted a variety of theological thought, of primarily Greek and Hellenistic extraction, mediated and adapted by Islamic translations and by various original thinkers. They contributed to the emergence of different theological views that systematized the religious life and constitute rationalizations of the performative and historical aspects of Judaism – though by this I mean that they offer some form of explanation, not necessarily "rational," a term that I find suspicious, since it assumes a superior type of reasoning.[6]

In addition, the scientific approach to nature was adopted and adapted. This theological turn, accomplished by a few rabbinic figures, is one of the most drastic changes in the religious history of Rabbinic Judaism. It consists in a new emphasis on the correct way of thinking or believing, especially in connection to the deity, implicitly relegating the performative aspects of earlier forms of Judaism to a secondary status. This means that one is now judged more by what he thinks, believes or imagines, than by what he does.

The Sociology of Rationalization

Let me start with a simple sociological observation: Religion is a sum of processes that develop continually in different directions, like rays. Each of the various social strata found in any major religion has its own specific variants of the "same" religion, and each develops differently from the other strata. This is why a history of

5 Idel 2009:251–271.
6 See the interesting remarks in Atlan 1986.

any particular religion should take into consideration not only what one stratum has to say, but as many other strata of believers as possible.

The difference between common people and elite is one of the principal distinctions that may be discerned within the bosom of the same religion. Naturally, the elites are more conservative than the common people in some cases, as it is the priestly elites who are connected to the performance and preservation of rituals; but they can also be more open to changes, as they interact with other elites on elitist issues. When part of a majority religious phenomenon, elites tend more to preserve than to innovate; when part of a minority, however, they are more prone to adapt the views of the majority elites.

When dealing with Kabbalah, I distinguish between primary and secondary elites, the former more conservative, the latter more open.[7] Elites, like the common people, vary with time and certainly with place, an observation that is particularly cogent for a cosmopolitan religion like Diaspora Judaism. Dispersion created various amalgams, which were determined to a certain extent by the nature of the majority culture surrounding any particular Jewish community. That is why differing Jewish rituals and liturgies emerged, such as Sefardi, Ashkenazi, Romaniot and so on.

It is in this context that rationalizations should be understood. A variety of new and elaborate interpretations were offered by various elites to different forms of Judaism, while the inertia was much greater among the common people, though forms of syncretism, especially related to popular magic, can be discerned. Let me illustrate this generalization by surveying some developments within a rather limited area in a particular period: southern Spain, Al-Andalus, under Muslim governance, circa 1050–1150. This is the period when several forms of philosophy and science were adopted and adapted by the Muslim elite from earlier Arabic sources, which mediated between the Greek and Hellenistic literary corpora of antiquity and late antiquity, written in Greek, and medieval thought, written in Arabic and Hebrew. From the conceptual point of view, we may distinguish between two main approaches: the occultist and syncretistic, on the one hand, and the more purist, systemic approach, on the other. The first reached southern Europe especially in the form of anthologies and doxographies that combined astrology, astronomy, magic, Hermeticism, Pythagoreanism and Neoplatonism in various proportions.[8] The latter was prominently represented by Aristotelian and Neoaristotelian treatises, along with some shorter Platonic and Neoplatonic ones.

---

7 Idel 1994a, 1998.

8 See, e.g., Stroumsa and Sviri 2009; Netton 1982; Stern 1971; Pines 1955; Zimmermann 1986; Fenton 1992.

The former trend is more evident in contemporary Jewish thinkers like Abraham ibn Ezra, Moshe ibn Ezra and to a certain extent also Yehuda Halevi. The latter approach had an impact on Shlomo ibn Gabirol (Abicebrol), a fully-fledged Neoplatonic thinker, and on Moses ben Maimon (Maimonides) and Abraham ibn Dawud, who were both deeply immersed in Arabic Neoaristotelianism.

These two trends were often presented by Jewish thinkers as providing the clues for decoding authentic Judaism from the canonical Jewish texts; in other words, they provided forms of rationalization for a small elite. From Al-Andalus, they were disseminated to other Jewish centers, mainly in Egypt, Provence and Christian Spain. The elitist nature of these interpretations is evident in the language used: Arabic, signifying that they were intended solely for a particular segment of Jewry. Some treatises, such as Maimonides' *Guide for the Perplexed*, were cast in a peculiar esoteric mode of writing that defied attempts at decoding the secrets contained in them by all but a very few.

Maimonides' critique of writings related to the occultist wave was clear,[9] and it succeeded for a while in limiting the impact of that wave. But from the early fourteenth century occultist elements returned and assumed a more significant role in Judaism, inter alia because of the earlier interest in these elements displayed in the court of Alfonso Sabio (r. 1252–1284), which facilitated the reception, translation and dissemination of additional occult material, the best-known treatise being the twelfth-century *Ghayat al-Hakhim*, known in Latin as the *Picatrix*.

Both major types of rationalization constitute adoptions and adaptations of modes of thought already in vogue among non-Jewish elites. They were elements in what may be called an apologetic strategy, undertaken, so it seems, *bona fides*, with the intention, inter alia, of defending Judaism, and sometimes, though not always, of recasting it in more universalistic terms. This rationalization was accomplished by using allegories, more often than not quite artificial, to project onto Jewish texts the contexts of corpora articulated outside the classical forms of Judaism, in a process of what I call inter-corporal exegesis.[10]

So far I have discussed philosophical forms of order – modes of organizing the universe – that were taken up by Jewish elites in Spain and then elsewhere. Let me turn now to a later development in European Judaism: the schools known under the umbrella term of Kabbalah, which developed somewhat later then the Andalusian schools but benefited from some of their speculative elements, though often by way of critical dialogue with them.[11] Early Kabbalists organized

---

9 See Marx 1935:378–380; Sonne 1939. For more on Mamonides's letter, see Harvey 1992.
10 On this phenomenon see Idel 2002.
11 See Farber 1996; Idel 1990, 1993a, 2004a.

earlier mythological and theological elements into wider structures, in answer to the challenges presented by the philosophical arcanizations of Judaism, either in the astral form found in the writings of Abraham ibn Ezra or in the Maimonidean one.[12]

Three Conceptual Rationalizations in Kabbalah

The working hypothesis informing my approach to this literature is that diverse speculative models informed the thought, the praxis and subsequently also the writings of various Kabbalists and, later on, hasidic masters.[13] Far from representing a unified or monochromatic line of thought that allegedly has changed throughout history, the diverse kabbalistic literary genres, and to a lesser extent also the various hasidic schools, have focused around at least three major models: theosophical-theurgical, ecstatic and talismanic. It is the developments within these models and the interplay and interactions between them that give many important moments of kabbalistic creativity their character. In the words of Alexander Pope, we should "observe how system into system runs." I shall not elaborate on the three models but only mention very briefly the most important characteristics of each, and their relevance for understanding linguistic operations related to performances of important aspects of Jewish ritual, preserving an approach that can be described as pre-axial in comparison to the much more axial approaches mentioned in the previous section.

The theosophical-theurgical model, which informs many of the discussions in the Provencal and Spanish forms of Kabbalah and flourished even more vigorously in sixteenth-century Safed, assumes the importance of the commandments, as evinced by the emergence of commentaries on their rationales – *ta'ame hamitsvot* – a specifically kabbalistic genre.[14] This model refers to the dynamic relationship between a complex divinity, constituted by many divine powers or configurations, and human religious deeds – namely, the rabbinic commandments – an effect that I call theurgy. It assumes as well that language reflects the inner structure of the divine realm, the sefirotic system of divine powers; at the same time, language is also conceived as influencing this structure by means of theurgical activities, which aim to restore harmony within the divine realm.

12 See Liebes 1993:1–64; for arcanization see Idel 2002.
13 Idel 1995a:45–145; 2005:213–233, 238–246; 2007:616–621.
14 See Idel 1988:xiv–xv; 1993b; E. Wolfson 1988.

Both in its symbolic role of reflecting the theosophical structure and in its theurgical function of affecting that structure, language is conceived by this type of Kabbalah as hypersemantic. That is, language is not only semantic in the ordinary sense of serving for communication, a characteristic well-known to Kabbalists, who wrote mainly in Hebrew, but its basic function in the kabbalistic enterprise is due to a surplus of meaning, which adds semantic fields to those designated by the ordinary meaning. The two aspects, the symbolic or referential and the theurgical or performative, different as they may be from each other, should not be conceived as totally independent: The symbolic role of language in reflecting the structure of the divine powers is often just one side of the coin, whose other side is the use of that symbolic knowledge to affect processes taking place within the divine realm.[15] Deeply immersed in issues related to the rationales for the commandments, this is the most particularistic model, and we shall have more to say about it in the next section.

The ecstatic model is palpably different. It assumes that the Kabbalist can use language to induce a mystical experience by means of manipulating linguistic elements, together with other mystical techniques.[16] This approach is much less concerned with divine inner structures, focusing as it does upon the restructuring of the human psyche in order to prepare it for an encounter with the divine. The ecstatic theory of language is less mimetic, and thus less symbolic and theurgical, than the view espoused by the theosophical Kabbalah. While the theosophical-theurgical approach to language assumes the paramount importance of information that is either absorbed by the human mind or transmitted, in energetic form, by the soul to the divine, the ecstatic view of language encourages the effacement of knowledge as part of the opening toward the divine. Practitioners of ecstatic Kabbalah cleanse their consciousness by using mystical techniques to break words into non-semantic units. While the theosophical Kabbalah emphasizes the given, structured aspects of language as manifested in the canonic writings, ecstatic Kabbalah employs the deconstruction of canonic texts, and of ordinary language as well, is an important mystical tool for restructuring the human psyche.[17]

Most kabbalistic writings belonging to this type of literature conceive of the universe as constellated by the ten separate cosmic intellects, while the meaningful relationship is that between the human intellect and the last and lowest of those intellects, the Active or Agent Intellect, as it was understood in the Arabic

15 See Elkayam 1990.

16 See Idel 1987:13–71.

17 See Idel 2002:314–389.

and Jewish medieval Neoaristotelian tradition. According to a view expressed by R. Isaac of Acre in his mystical diary, a later book belonging to the tradition of ecstatic Kabbalah, the holy language is tantamount to the efflux originated by the divine presence, the *Shekhina*.

> The holy language comes to the souls of the mystics of Israel from the radiance of the glory of the *Shekhina*.[18] And before the generation of the Tower of Babel, there was only the holy language alone, as it is said: "And all the earth was [speaking] one language and the same words" [Gen. 11:1]. And understand that "language" is the secret of *Shekhina*, and "words" allude to the divine name formed of seventy-two [units] whose letters are 216.[19]

The secrets hinted at in this text devolve from the equivalence of the words *safa* (שפה), language, and *Shekhina* (שכינה); the letters of both, used as numbers, have the numerical value of 385. Thus, the linguistic material of the Hebrew language is tantamount to the intellectual forms that flow from the divine presence. Speaking Hebrew is, accordingly, the corporeal articulation of the divine overflow. Not so much a creation of the human vocal organs, Hebrew emanates from above.[20] This Kabbalist seems to have in mind a dictum whose earlier sources are rather obscure, according to which "the *Shekhina* spoke from the throat of Moses."[21] This conception differs from the regular understanding of Hebrew as divine because of its origin as a creation of God. It is divine, according to this Kabbalist, because it flows from the divine realm onto the mystic, so that the very act of speaking of this language may perhaps be understood also as an experiencing of the presence of the divine. We witness here an attempt to ontologize the language by comparing and even identifying it with the Neoplatonic emanation that descends upon the mundane realm. Indeed, Jewish Neoplatonic thinkers like Solomon ibn Gabirol and Isaac ibn Latif, and some theosophical Kabbalists like Jacob ben Sheshet, had already compared the emanative process to the emission of speech.[22] However, for them this comparison seems to have been only a simile, whereas Isaac of Acre describes the language itself as an overflow descending upon the souls of the mystics of Israel. No wonder that ecstatic Kabbalists regarded knowledge

---

18 On this radiance, see also Isaac of Acre, *Otsar ḥayim*, fol. 160a; Idel 1987:141.

19 Isaac of Acre, *Otsar ḥayim*, fol. 79a.

20 See Idel 2003:xlv–xlix, where I deal with ontological conceptualizations of language as found in the supernal worlds. Unlike the different orders I discuss in this article, which deal with supernal structures in themselves, the three models discussed here have to do with the connections between the constellating structures and human activities and experiences.

21 See Werblowsky 1977:269–270.

22 See Heller-Wilensky 1967:208–209, and the numerous sources referenced in her footnotes.

of the principles of kabbalistic linguistics as the core of Kabbalah. According to Abraham Abulafia:

> Whoever does not know [the wisdom of] the combinations of letters and is not a very 'examined' and experienced[23] person in this lore, and in the counting of letters and their division and the changing of their order and permutations according to what is written in the *Book of Creation*, does not know the Lord, according to our way.[24]

The Kabbalist distills the contents of the language, which reaches him from on high, using exegetical principles of the linguistic Kabbalah, which are seen as ensuring knowledge of God. Just as the philosophers gain their knowledge by receiving the intellectual overflow from above and transforming into distinct statements with metaphysical significance, so the Kabbalist uses his 'superlogical' exegetical techniques to attain another, experiential type of connection with God, achieved through the permutation of letters; and so he achieves a knowledge of God that seems to escape the philosophers.[25]

Last but not least is the talismanic model, which assumes the importance of the astral order: celestial bodies, planets and stars, imagined as having an impact on what happens in this world. Knowledge of the qualities of these astral bodies, and the interactions between them, is capable of bringing down the spiritual powers found within those bodies, the *pneumata*, *ruḥaniyat* or *ruḥaniyut*, in Greek, Arabic and Hebrew respectively.[26] This bringing down is related in many magical texts to the practice of talismans. In this model, language is conceived as one of the primary means of attracting supernal – divine or celestial – powers down upon the magician or the mystic, who may become a vehicle of extraordinary forces that can be described as magical. Originally a type of pagan worship practiced to acquire magical powers, talismanic magic has its rituals, which include prayers, clothing, food, etc., associated with a certain heavenly body. The Kabbalists appropriated this structure and applied it to the divine powers, on the one hand, and to the meaning of the commandments, on the other. In general, the talismanic approach can be described as hyposemantic: Language is conceived

---

23 *Baḥun umenuse*. This phrase occurs in many magical recipes and points to the "fact" that the recipe has been tested and found efficacious. See also Abulafia, *Sheva' netivot haTora*, ed. Gross 2000:129.

24 Abulafia, *Sefer sitre Torah*, ed. Gross 2002:161, Ms. Paris, fol. 163a.

25 Idel 2002:90.

26 On the history of this seminal term in talismanic magic see Pines 1980, 1988. See also Idel 1995a:427, index, s. v. *ruḥaniyyut*.

as magically effective irrespective of its semantic aspects.[27] This model is strongly anthropocentric, in that it envisages enhancing the spiritual and material well-being of an individual, or of the whole religious group, as an important core of religion.

The theosophical-theurgical and talismanic models assume that language, in addition to its semantic aspect, has an energetic aspect that works either by affecting the supernal world or by attracting it from below. In ecstatic Kabbalah, by contrast, though these two aspects are sometimes present, they play a relatively marginal role. Ecstatic Kabbalah recognizes the magical powers of language but conceives of them as exercising an influence on a lower, inferior level of existence, as compared to the cathartic role played by language in purifying the soul or the intellect in order to prepare them to receive the supernal efflux.

By and large, the talismanic model in Kabbalah, as exemplified by linguistic magic, is a synthesis between the particularistic tendency characteristic of the theurgical model, which mainly deals basically with halakhic behavior, and the more universalistic tendency of the Hermetic sources. Focused as they are on Hebrew words as their principal tools, the linguistic talismanics, and sometimes also the ecstatic Kabbalists, assume that not only the words, but also Hebrew letters and, especially, what they called "Hebrew" sounds may serve as talismanic means. At least on the level of the monadic linguistic elements, this gives them a more universalistic potential, in that, given the need to deconstruct conventional languages, including Hebrew, into their elementary units on the level of phonetics, the notion of a resemblance between the different languages is plausible. From several points of view, the ecstatic model as represented by Abraham Abulafia is dependent not on the rabbinic commandments but on the new techniques he contrived; it is close to Maimonidean philosophy and reflects a universalistic approach, perhaps even more than that found in Maimonides himself.[28]

The theosophical-theurgical and ecstatic models are amply represented by distinct kabbalistic schools and literary corpora, which can be described as embodying the above-mentioned speculative assumptions insofar as language is concerned. Thus, the theosophical-theurgical Kabbalah and the ecstatic Kabbalah are known from largely independent bodies of writings; the talismanic model, however, was borrowed by both theosophical-theurgical and ecstatic kabbalists, who adapted the astro-magical sources to their specific spiritual purposes. That is one reasons why this last model has been neglected by modern scholarship of Kabbalah. Scholarly concern to present a unified picture of the development of

---

27 See Idel 2017.
28 See, for the time being, Idel 2012, 2013.

kabbalistic lore has produced a rather monochromatic view of its phenomenology, pushing the magical schemes, and to an extent also the ecstatic literature, into a corner, while emphasizing – in my opinion, overemphasizing – the centrality of the theosophical kabbalistic model.

To formulate the three models from the point of view of their objectives, the ecstatic model is concerned with the changes that a certain mystical technique, based mainly – though not exclusively – on language, may induce in a person, and its meaningful constellations are the cosmic intellects; the talismanic model emphasizes the effects one's linguistic acts may have on the external world and operates in a universe dominated by astral bodies; and the theosophical-theurgical model is concerned with inducing harmony within the divine realm, which is governed by the ten *sefirot*. These, then, are the three types of constellations that emerge from the different sources, but there are also important examples of combinations or syntheses between the models.[29]

A Combination of Two Models

Interesting as these models may be, they have only rarely been expounded as completely separate approaches. For example, the ecstatic model was sometimes combined with the talismanic one, so that the talismanic operator was described as needing to make contact with the divine realm before being able to draw down the supernal power. Likewise, the theurgical operation, which ensures the continuing pulsation of energy within the divine realm, has often been combined with the magical or talismanic approaches, so that kabbalist's act of drawing the emanation down from the higher *sefirot* to the lower ones was followed by one of causing the descent of this emanation into the extra-divine world. Common to all these models is the view that language, at least as represented by the canonic texts, involves a strong type of "speech act," to use the phrase coined by John Searle, while the recitations of letters are performative utterances par excellence in the sense defined by J.L. Austin.[30] However, the efficacy of the kabbalistic approaches to language depends much more on the parasemantic than on the semantic qualities of language.

29 See, e.g., the views of R. Abraham Abulafia and R. Joseph ben Shalom Ashkenazi, analyzed in Idel 2011b:12–29, or those of R. Yohanan Alemanno, who also adopted elements from Neoaristotelian and Neoplatonic ways of thinking, as discussed in Idel 1983.
30 Searle 1969; Austin 1962.

Let me adduce one example of the theosophical-theurgical model being combined with the talismanic-magical one. The following passage is taken from *Tefila leMoshe*, a commentary on the prayer-book by the renowned sixteenth-century kabbalist R. Moses Cordovero, a who was active in Safed:

> The significance of the blessing [*berakha*] is attested by its name, which means drawing down, and this denotes the drawing down of spirituality and effluence from the highest echelon[31] to [the *sefira* of] *Malkhut*, which is the pool [*bereikha*][32] where the effluence comes together, and that is why She [*Malkhut*] is called *Keneset Yisra'el*, because She brings together and collects all the effluence of *Yisra'el*, which is [the *sefira* of] *Tif'eret*, and afterwards it is drawn down to the lower [entities], and we are obliged to draw it down solely through Her. It is She who gives "food to her household and portion to Her maidens" [Proverbs 31:15] in Her way. And lo, that blessing will act on high to draw down the effluence to *Malkhut* when it is fitting, that is, when it is not [pronounced] in vain. And the reason for it is that when the blessing is upon a commandment or an action that is one of the [obligatory] actions, that action becomes a vessel or bucket by which the waters of the effluence are drawn from "the wells of salvation" [Is. 12:3]. And since there is a vessel, which is *Malkhut*, within which the emanated blessing is received, so that blessing is not in vain; that is, that seed is not sown in vain – namely, to the external powers,[33] God forbid – but *Malkhut*, which is the soul, comes close to the place of that action, and She receives the effluence, and the seed is inseminated into the "womb of Her that is with child" [Eccles. 11:5].[34]

The interpretation of the term *berakha*, blessing, as drawing down and as spirituality (*ruḥaniyut*)[35] is part and parcel of the talismanic model. By the act of bless-

---

31 *Merom hamadregot*, i. e., from the highest of the *sefirot*, plausibly *Keter*. This has to do with the descent of the seed from the brain, envisioned as the highest aspect of the theosophical system, in accordance with Galen's physiology, which was accepted in Kabbalah from the outset. See, e. g., Scholem 1989:154–155, and Cordovero 1892:140a.

32 Scholem 1989:69–70, 380 n. 36.

33 See also Cordovero 1985, XIII:128.

34 *Tefila leMoshe* (Cordovero 1892), f. 4a; for another instance of combining an astral and a theosophical order, see Idel 2003:lv–lvii. On the womb as a symbol of *Malkhut*, cf. *Tefila leMoshe*, ff. 235b–236a.

35 Cordovero is fond of this term, which is of paramount importance in the talismanic model. See, e. g., *Tefila leMoshe* (Cordovero 1892), ff.4a, 10a, 29b, 57b, 67b, 190b, 213a; *Or yakar* on the *Zohar* (Cordovero 1972), XII:1–2; and *Or yakar* on *Tikune Zohar* (Cordovero 2009), VI:384–386. See also above, n. 26. Interestingly, in *Tefila leMoshe*, f. 29b, in connection with the commandments, Cordovero distinguishes between deed and speech as paralleling spiritual and material, which amounts to a different axiology from the translated passage. The manner in which the verbal activity operates is intimated by the syntagm *ruḥaniyut ha'otiyot*, the spirituality within the letters, or better: sounds. See also his *Eilima rabati* (Cordovero 1881), f. 132d. In *Tefila leMoshe*, f. 189b, Cordovero speaks of "the spirituality of the star," *ruḥaniyut hakokhav*, and the worshipers of

ing, a vocal activity, the effluence is brought down from the highest level within the theosophical structure to the lowest of the *sefirot*, the tenth power, called *Malkhut* or the Kingdom of God. This feminine divine power is described as the receptacle of the divine effluence drawn down by the act of blessing. Cordovero insists that the obligation of the worshipper is to draw the effluence down into this last divine power, a process that I referred to above as theurgy. The worshipper's approach is informed by some form of *devotio* to the divine Female, and his disinterested acts should be understood as dedicated to Her, without any expectation of a personal recompense.

The kabbalist also mentions the descent of the divine power to the lower entities, most probably the lower world. That would be an instance of the talismanic model. However, he does not recommend here that the person do this, for it is imagined to be the prerogative of the divine Female, as we learn from the verse quoted from Proverbs. Thus, this power has a passive role: She is the vessel or bucket that receives the divine influx because of the human action – and yet it is She that distributes it to the lower realm. We have here a combination of theurgy – the drawing down for the sake of the Female – with some implied form of magical act, evinced by the descent of the power onto the lower worlds. More important, from the present point of view, is the fact that the blessing that brings down the divine influx needs a vessel, a human action that differs from the blessing, a concrete act that serves as receptacle of the divine power. The Female is compared to this concrete act, which is described as strictly necessary in order to prevent the influx from descending into the domain of the demonic powers, the externals.

The kabbalist then associates the rabbinic statement about "a blessing [pronounced] in vain" (cf. BT *Temura* 4a) – that is, a verbal activity not associated with the performance of a commandment – with a talmudic statement, widely cited among kabbalists, about spilling "semen in vain," an act that is emphatically forbidden (BT *Nida* 13a).[36] To make sense of these two interdictions, Cordovero resorts to theosophy. The term "vessel" stands here both for the vessel used to collect the divine emanation and for the Female's womb, which receives the *semen virilis*.[37] Indeed, the distinction between the divine powers as vessels and the divine presence within them – also described as *sefirot*, but *sefirot* of

---

the stars (i.e., pagans) – a clear example of the impact of astral magic. In some cases *ruḥaniyut* stands for the spiritual aspect of the *sefirot* that can be drawn down. In *Or yakar* on *Tikune Zohar* (VI:386), Cordovero refers to a certain *Book of Talismans*, *Sefer hatalisma'ot*.

36 See Pachter 2006.

37 See Idel, forthcoming, Appendix 5.

the essence of God – is a major element in Cordovero's theosophy.[38] This dual vision of the sefirotic realm is projected here onto the polarity between deed and vocal activity, on the one hand, and a halakhic type of sexual activity that necessitates the presence of a male and a female, on the other. This polarity differs from that of deed versus intention (*kavana*), which is more widespread in Kabbalah.[39]

Note the role played by linguistic associations in this kabbalistic discourse. The term *levatala*, in vain, is found in both rabbinic statements, but in very different contexts. However, Cordovero believes in the relevance of the shared term, and he associates the two statements by identifying what he views as a common structure: A meaningful religious experience is compounded of a polarity that is meaningful also in theosophical terms, symbolized by a couple that is sexually differentiated. This is a widespread exegetical strategy in the type of Kabbalah under discussion, and particularly in Cordovero's vast opus. It assumes that a certain type of supernal order constellates both this world and the religious texts, and discerning this order enables one to make sense of statements that are, prima facie, unrelated and hardly understandable.[40]

Rationalizations in Context

The last passage, in my opinion, reflects a major concern within the theosophical-theurgical Kabbalah. Kabbalists who belonged to these schools were concerned with strengthening the status of the performative aspect of religion by means of a theosophical system that responded to human actions. Rationalization, in this context, thus deals not so much with beliefs as with actions. It is the latter that need to be explained by means of theosophical speculation, which is meaningless unless it serves as the framework of a *modus operandi*. The "ratio" is therefore conjoined and largely subordinated to the performative. This is why, in the history of Kabbalah, theosophies changed dramatically while the performative aspects of Judaism changed far less. As a nineteenth-century Hasidic master put it, "there is an infinite number of rationales" for the commandments, but not one commandment should be added because of any of these rationales.[41] The

38 See, e. g., Ben-Shlomo 1965.
39 See, e. g., Scholem 1989:195–196, 209, 243–248, 416–419; Tishby 1991:941–974; Gottlieb 1976:38–55; Idel 1993c, 1994b.
40 See also Idel 2002:449–460.
41 See Shapira 1921:fols.17b, 86d.

theosophical-theurgical Kabbalists were concerned more with the efficacy of the ritual than with the absoluteness of the theosophy. One can infer their special interest in worship as against than speculation from their frequent self-descriptions as *ba'ale ha'avoda*, "masters of worship."[42] The various theosophical systems constellate halakhic activity by offering meanings that are absent in the first two layers of classical Judaism. This type of subordination has been overlooked in scholarship of Kabbalah, which tends to emphasize the importance of theosophical structures in the expositions of Kabbalah, generating what can be called a "Reuchlinization" of Kabbalah.[43]

However, there are also other forms of rationalization, which are basically concerned with the meanings attributed to Judaism's tenets and beliefs. Unlike the effectively disjunctive philosophical interpretations of the performative religion as containing spiritual elements that supersede the performing body, Cordovero's passage represents a wider, conjunctive phenomenological structure. From this point of view, many of the philosophical interpretations developed in the Middle Ages are closer to a Paulinian religious structure, and that is one reason why the most important controversy in the Jewish Middle Ages revolved around Maimonides' *Guide for the Perplexed.*

In modern times, that is, since the late eighteenth century, the importance of these forms of rationalization has declined, and in their place have emerged other types of rationale for the religious life in Judaism, such as the centrality of the emotional life in east European Hasidism, and, in Central Europe, what were conceived as ethical or rational interpretations of Judaism. Modern Jews, including many scholars, accustomed as they are to the dramatic medieval shift in Jewish religion, view these developments as authentic expressions also of the two earlier layers of Judaism. This is evident in the writings of a series of philosophers who were well acquainted with various forms of Judaism, such as Moses Mendelssohn, Hermann Cohen and Yeshayahu Leibowitz, to name only a few outstanding examples, an approach all the more fascinating for the perceived consonance of medieval philosophical trends with those in vogue in Germany, where these philosophers lived or studied. With the decline in some Jewish circles of the understanding of earlier forms of Judaism as performative, the rationalization of performance also declined, to be replaced by the rationalization of more abstract matters, like ethics and theology, so that a concept like ethical monotheism emerged as a rationalization of the alleged mission of the Jews. There is no

42 See, e.g., the title of one of the best summaries of Kabbalah, written in the early sixteenth century, R. Meir ibn Gabbai's *Sefer 'Avodat hakodesh*.
43 See Idel 2004b; 2007:634–635; 2008b; Liebes 1992.

better illustration of this shift than the interesting story told by Gershom Scholem about his father, who transgressed by smoking on the eve of the Sabbath, but contended that the Jews had already fulfilled their mission of spreading ethical monotheism among the gentiles.[44] These shifts in rationalization have their own wider rationales.

Judaism as a whole was not transformed or rationalized by these sorts of rationalizations. They formed part of an elite type of speculation that only rarely touched the Jewish masses, even in the centers where they were formulated. Bound up as they were with the efforts of minority elites to be accepted by the majority culture, they hardly affected Jews living in environments in which there was less concern with rationalizing religion. Indeed, the majority of Jews have lived throughout the centuries without significant forms of rationalization, as can be seen not only from the lives of ordinary religious Jews even today, but also from the content of the most voluminous and influential type of Jewish religious literature written by elite figures, the halakhic literature, which deals with the various aspects of the performance of the commandments.

References

Abulafia, Abraham. *Sheva' netivot haTora*, ed. A. Gross. 2000. Jerusalem: Yerid haSefarim.

—. *Sefer sitre Tora*, ed. by A. Gross. 2002. Jerusalem. Ms. Paris BN 774.

Atlan, Henri. 1986. "Une rationalité symbolique." *Les nouveaux Cahiers*, 86:43–51.

Austin, J.L. 1962. *How to Do Things with Words*. Oxford: Clarendon Press.

Ben-Sasson, Hillel, and Moshe Halbertal. 2012. "The Divine Name YHVH and the Measure of Mercy." In J. Garb, R. Meroz and M. Niehoff (eds.), *And This Is for Yehuda: Studies Presented to Our Colleague Professor Yehuda Liebes*. Jerusalem: Mandel Institute of Jewish Studies–Bialik Institute. 53–69. Hebrew.

Ben-Shlomo, Joseph. 1965. *The Mystical Theology of Moses Cordovero*. Jerusalem: Mossad Bialik. Hebrew.

Cordovero, Moshe. 1881. *Eilima rabati*. Lemberg (Lviv).

—. 1892. *Tefila leMoshe*, I. Przemyśl: Zupnik, Knoller and Hammerschmidt.

—. 1972, 1985. *Or yakar* on the *Zohar*, vols. XII, XIII. Jerusalem.

—. 2009. *Or yakar* on *Tikune Zohar*, vol. VI. Jerusalem.

Elkayam, Avraham. 1990. "Between Referentialism and Performativism: Two Approaches in Understanding the Kabbalistic Symbol." *Daat*, 24:5–40. Hebrew.

Farber, Assi. 1996. "The Shell Precedes the Fruit: On the Question of the Source of the Metaphysical Existence of Evil in Early Kabbalistic Thought." In H. Pedaya (ed.), *Myth in Judaism*. Beer Sheva: Ben Gurion University Press. 118–142. Hebrew.

44 Scholem 2012:11.

Fenton, Paul B. (Ynnon). 1992. "Shem Tov Ibn Falaquera and the Theology of Aristotle." *Daat*, 29:27–40. Hebrew.

Gottlieb, Ephraim. 1976. *Studies in Kabbalah Literature*. Edited by J. Hacker. Tel Aviv: Tel Aviv University. Hebrew.

Harvey, Steven. 1992. "Did Maimonides' Letter to Samuel ibn Tibbon Determine Which Philosophers Would Be Studied by Later Jewish Thinkers?" *Jewish Quarterly Review*, 83:51–70.

Heller-Wilensky, Sara. 1967. "R. Isaac ibn Latif: Kabbalist or Philosopher?" In A. Altmann (ed.), *Jewish Medieval and Renaissance Studies*. Cambridge (MA): Harvard University Press.

Idel, Moshe. 1983. "The Magical and Neoplatonic Interpretations of Kabbalah in the Renaissance." In B.D. Cooperman (ed.), *Jewish Thought in the Sixteenth Century*. Cambridge (MA): Harvard University Press. 186–242.

—. 1987. *The Mystical Experience in Abraham Abulafia*. English transl. by J. Chipman. Albany: SUNY Press.

—. 1988. *Kabbalah: New Perspectives*. New Haven: Yale University Press.

—. 1990. "Maimonides and Kabbalah." In I. Twersky (ed.), *Studies in Maimonides*. Cambridge: Cambridge University Press. 31–81.

—. 1993a. "Jewish Kabbalah and Platonism in the Middle Ages and Renaissance." In Lenn E. Goodman (ed.), *Neoplatonism and Jewish Thought*. Albany: SUNY Press. 319–331.

—. 1993b. "Some Remarks on Ritual and Mysticism in Geronese Kabbalah." *Jewish Thought and Philosophy*, 3:111–130.

—. 1993c. "Kabbalistic Prayer in Provence." *Tarbiz*, 62:265–286. Hebrew.

—. 1994a. "Kabbalah and Elites in Thirteenth-Century Spain." *Mediterranean Historical Review*, 9:5–19.

—. 1994b. "The Mystical Intention of the Eighteen Benedictions by R. Isaac Sagi Nahor." In M. Oron and A. Goldreich (eds.), *Massu'ot: Studies in Kabbalistic Literature and Jewish Philosophy in Memory of Prof. Ephraim Gottlieb*. Jerusalem: Mossad Bialik. 25–52. Hebrew.

—. 1995a. *Hasidism: Between Ecstasy and Magic*. Albany: SUNY Press.

—. 1995b. "On Talismatic Language in Jewish Mysticism." *Diogenes*, 43/2:23–41.

—. 1998. "Nahmanides: Kabbalah, Halakhah and Spiritual Leadership." In M. Idel and M. Ostow (eds.), *Jewish Mystical Leaders and Leadership*. Northvale: Jason Aronson. 15–96.

—. 2002. *Absorbing Perfections: Kabbalah and Interpretation*. New Haven: Yale University Press.

—. 2003. "On Some Forms of Order in Kabbalah." *Daat*, 50–52:xxxi–lviii.

—. 2004a. "Hermeticism and Kabbalah." In P. Lucentini, I. Parri and V.P. Compagni (eds.), *Hermeticism from Late Antiquity to Humanism*. Turnhout: Brepols. 389–408.

—. 2004b. "On the Theologization of Kabbalah in Modern Scholarship." In Y. Schwartz and V. Krech (eds.), *Religious Apologetics: Philosophical Argumentation*. Tübingen: Mohr. 123–174.

—. 2005. *Kabbalah & Eros*. New Haven: Yale University Press.

—. 2007. *Ben: Sonship in Jewish Mysticism*. London–New York: Continuum.

—. 2008a. *The Angelic World: Apotheosis and Theophany*. Tel Aviv: Miskal–Yedioth Ahronoth. Hebrew.

—. 2008b. "Johannes Reuchlin: Kabbalah, Pythagorean Philosophy and Modern Scholarship." *Studia Judaica*, 41:30–55.

—. 2009. “On the Performing Body in Theosophical-Theurgical Kabbalah: Some Preliminary Remarks.” In M. Diemling and G. Veltri (eds.), *The Jewish Body: Corporeality, Society, and Identity in the Renaissance and Early Modern Period*. Leiden: Brill. 251–272.
—. 2011a. “The Triple Family: Sources for the Feminine Perception of Deity in Early Kabbalah.” In E. Baumgarten, A. Raz-Krakotzkin and R. Weinstein (eds.), *Tov Elem – Memory, Community and Gender in Medieval and Early Modern Jewish Societies: Essays in Honor of Robert Bonfil*. Jerusalem: Mossad Bialik. 91–110. Hebrew.
—. 2011b. *Saturn’s Jews: On the Witches’ Sabbat and Sabbateanism*. London: Continuum.
—. 2012. “On the Secrets of the Torah in Abraham Abulafia.” In B. Brown, M. Lorberbaum, A. Rosenak and Y.Z. Stern (eds.), *Religion and Politics in Jewish Thought: Essays in Honor of Aviezer Ravitzky*. Jerusalem: Israel Democracy Institute. 418–430. Hebrew.
—. 2013. “The Pearl, the Son and the Servants in Abraham Abulafia’s Parable.” *Quaterni di Studi Indo-Mediterranei*, 6:103–134.
—. 2017. “The Womb and the Infinite in R. Moshe Cordovero’s Kabbalistic Thought.” *Pe‘amim*, 104:41–64. Hebrew.
—. Forthcoming. *“Male and Female”: Equality, Female’s Theurgy, and Eros – R. Moshe Cordovero’s Dual Ontology*.
Isaac of Acre, *Otsar ḥayim*. Ms. Moscow-Guenzburg 775. n. d.
Liebes, Yehuda. 1992. “New Directions in the Study of Kabbalah.” *Pe‘amim*, 50:150–170. Hebrew.
—. 1993. *Studies in Jewish Myth and Jewish Messianism*. Albany: SUNY Press.
—. 2008. *Collected Essays on the Jewish Myth*. Jerusalem: Carmel. Hebrew. Marx, Alexander. 1935. “Texts by and about Maimonides.” *Jewish Quarterly Review*, 25:371–428.
Naeh, Shlomo. 1997. “*Poterion en cheiri kyriou*: Philo and the Rabbis on the Powers of God and the Mixture in the Cup.” *Scripta Classica Israelica*, XVI (= H.M. Cotton, J.J, Price and D.J. Wasserstein [eds.], *Studies in Memory of Abraham Wasserstein*, II): 91–101.
Netton, I.R. 1982. *Muslim Neoplatonists: An Introduction to the Thought of the Brethren of Purity (Ikhwan al-Safa)*. London: Allen & Unwin.
Pachter, Shiloh. 2006. “Shemirat haberit: The History of the Prohibition of Wasting Seed.” Ph. D. Dissertation, Hebrew University of Jerusalem. Hebrew.
Pines, Shlomo. 1955. “La longue récension de la théologie d’Aristote dans ses rapports avec la doctrine isma’elienne.” *Revue des etudes islamiques*, 32:7–20. (Reprinted in S. Stroumsa [ed.], *The Collected works of Shlomo Pines*, III. Jerusalem: Magnes. 390–403.)
—. 1980. “Le *Sefer ha-Tamar* et les Maggidim des Kabbalistes.” In G. Nahon and Ch. Touati (eds.), *Hommage à Georges Vajda*. Louvain: Peeters. 333–363.
—. 1988. “On the Term *Ruḥaniyyut* and Its Sources and on Judah Halevi’s Doctrine.” *Tarbiz*, 57:511–540. Hebrew.
Scholem, Gershom. 1989. *Origins of the Kabbalah*, English transl. by A. Arkush, ed. R.J. Zwi Werblowsky. Princeton–Philadelphia: Princeton University Press–JPS.
—. 2012. *From Berlin to Jerusalem*. Philadelphia: Paul Dry Books,
Searle, John R. 1969. *Speech Acts: An Essay in the Philosophy of Language*. Cambridge: Cambridge University Press.
Shapira, Tsvi Elimelech, of Dinov. 1921. *Derekh pikudekha*. Lemberg (Lviv).
Sonne, Isaiah. 1939. “Mamonides’s Letter to Samuel b. Tibbon according to an Unknown Text in the Archives of the Jewish Community of Verona.” *Tarbiz*, 10:135–154, 309–332. Hebrew.
Stern, Samuel M. 1971. “Ibn Masarra, Follower of Pseudo-Empedocles – An Illusion.” *Actas IV congresso de estudios ‘arabes e islamicos, Coimbra–Lisboa, 1 a 8 de Setembro de 1968*. Leiden: Brill. 325–337.

Stroumsa, Sarah, and Sara Sviri. 2009. "The Beginnings of Mystical Philosophy in Al-Andalus: Ibn Masarra and His *Epistle on Contemplation*." *Jerusalem Studies in Arabic and Islam*, 36:201–253.

Tishby, Isaiah. 1991. *The Wisdom of the Zohar: An Anthology of Texts*. English transl. by D. Goldstein. London–Washington: Littman Library.

Urbach, Ephraim E. 1979. *The Sages: Their Concepts and Beliefs*, vol. I. English transl. by I. Abrahams. Jerusalem : Magnes Press.

Werblowsky, R.J. Zwi. 1977. *Joseph Karo: Lawyer and Mystic*. Philadelphia: Jewish Publication Society.

Wolfson, Elliot. 1988. "Mystical Rationalization of the Commandments in *Sefer ha-Rimmon*." *Hebrew Union College Annual*, 59:217–251.

Wolfson, Harry A. 1982. *Philo: Foundation of Religious Philosophy*. Cambridge (MA): Harvard University Press.

Zimmermann, F.W. 1986. "The Origins of the so-called *Theology of Aristotle*." In J. Kraye, W.F. Ryan and C.B. Schmitt (eds.), *Pseudo-Aristotle in the Middle Ages: The Theology and Other Texts*. London: Warburg Institute. 110–240.

Christoph Markschies

Origen of Alexandria: The Bible and Philosophical Rationality, or: Problems of Traditional Dualisms

The thesis to be presented in this paper is relatively simple: I wish to demonstrate that a central element of rationalization, and not only in Antiquity, lies in resolving *dualisms*, or more precisely, dual models of reality. If we subscribe to Carl Friedrich Gethmann's process-oriented definition of "rationality" as "developing processes for the discursive upholding of claims to validity,"[1] then "rationalization" would be defined as the optimization of the discursive upholding of validity claims. The Christian religion asserted such validity claims in Antiquity: It intended that the consensus within a specific religious group as to the truth of certain doctrines and behavioral prescriptions should be shared by the entire society.

One notable rationalistic impulse was provided by the so-called Christian Alexandrians, and not by coincidence, as the already Hellenized Judaism of Alexandria had laid the foundations for it, and the city's character as a center of learning was fertile ground for such a rationalizing impulse.[2] The Christian Alexandrians, principally Clement of Alexandria (c. 140/150–220 CE) and Origen (c. 185–254 CE), argued for the validity of Christian precepts regarding the world and of behavioral prescriptions according to contemporary criteria of rationality; in contrast to the preceding generations of Christian theologians, they were familiar with those criteria from the source texts of Platonic and Stoic philosophy and not just from compendia or general educational tracts.[3] These Alexandrians optimized the hitherto prevalent ways of reflecting upon Christianity as it had existed from the earliest days of Christendom, from Paul in the first century and through apologists such as Justin and bishops like Irenaeus of Lyons in the second century. We can join Gethmann in regarding such a purposeful optimization of rationality as "rationalization."[4]

1 Gethmann 1995: col. 468. See also Koch 2016 and Sperber 1985:89. I published parts of this argument more extensively in my German article "Origenes und Paulus" (Markschies 2015).
2 For the relationship between religion and rationalization in general cf. especially Max Weber and his concept of the "disenchantment of the world": Drehsen 2009; Schluchter 1976.
3 See Markschies 2012.
4 Gethmann 1995: col. 463.

https://doi.org/10.1515/9783110446395-006

What I am concerned with herein is a single such optimization process, namely, the resolving of insufficiently complex dualisms. Here rationalization does not mean the simplification of, say, a mythological conception of the world through reduction to certain suitable principles, but rather the addition of complexity to an insufficiently complex theory. The principal aim of this paper, then, is to demonstrate that modern scholarship has failed to perceive this increased complexity through the dissolution of dualisms in its reconstruction of the teachings of the Alexandrians as an ensemble of dualisms, and in particular in its treatment of the dualism of the Bible versus Philosophy, thus leveling the *differentia specifica* between the pre-Alexandrian and Alexandrian eras of Christian theology.

For obvious reasons, I will focus on a single Christian Alexandrian, Origen, who is justifiably to be regarded as the first Christian polymath of antiquity.[5] He lived in Alexandria until the thirties of the third century, first as a teacher of grammar and student of the Platonic philosopher Ammonius Saccas, and later as a teacher at a sort of Christian private university. From the 230s until his death in the mid-250s, at the behest of the bishops of Caesarea and Jerusalem, he worked as a preacher in a small church near the port of Caesarea and as a gifted teacher at a Christian educational institution, which taught the entire educational canon of antiquity and, as its pinnacle, Christian theology.

Origen overcame the dualism of "Bible versus Philosophy," which shaped the Christian theology of the second century and in particular the so-called Gnostic systems and their contestation within the majority church, but his transcendence of it has been given too little attention in the sweep of scholarship, especially in the twentieth century. One can – with a nod to a currently popular paradigm – describe his thinking, more appropriately than in such dualisms, as a *non-hierarchical network of knowledge systems continuously reconfigured according to current requirements*. By "knowledge" – to formulate a bare-bones working definition – I mean some part of the entirety of all reality-interpreting descriptions of elements of that reality, where "reality" is understood not as something which is perceived simply as a possibility but as something asserted to be "real."[6] In using the term "system of knowledge" I am describing a systematic ordering of knowledge associated with a particular validity claim.

If "knowledge" only ever exists in multidimensional relations in which, for instance, mental and epistemic structures overlap ("Origen *knows* something" and "Origen knows *something*"), it becomes clear that systematization or ordering

5 Cf., e. g., Nautin 1977 and Vogt 2002.

6 Detel 2009:184–186; Sarasin 2011:159; for more in general: Mittelstrass 1996; Anacker 2004.

consists in a particular arrangement of knowledge according to certain of its individual relations. Such a systematization or ordering of knowledge into a knowledge system can occur in two fundamental ways: either in the form of a stable hierarchy, as in a hierarchy tree; or in the form of a network of essentially decentralized, plural nodes or foci. In an important article entitled "Was ist Wissensgeschichte,"[7] Philipp Sarasin, a historian who now teaches in Zurich, described how, in a modern conception of the history of knowledge, "knowledge systems" are viewed not as hierarchical structures of more and less useful, more and less important, or permitted and forbidden, as in previous centuries, but rather as networks of knowledge stores in which the focus is placed here or there based on circumstances. Thus, knowledge systems are comparable to neural networks in the brain, in which, rather than some central control center determining the hierarchy of all processes, neural circuitry emerges in decentralized processes – in processes that develop and pathways that perpetuate themselves.[8]

Heretofore, Origen's thinking has often been described as a singular, strictly hierarchical and therein completely stable system of knowledge; scholars were long concerned only with the question of whether the top level of this knowledge system was a theology based on biblical texts or a philosophy drawn from Platonic writings. What is surprising about this question is its construal of biblical theology and Platonic philosophy as two stable entities completely autonomous from one another, as distinct to the observer as two blocks of marble in a landscape. One need not, as Ulrich Berner did in his 1981 volume on Origen in the "Erträge der Forschung"[9] series, comb through the entirety of the secondary literature on the Alexandrian theologian, collected in three massive volumes,[10] to recognize the bitter dispute being waged among scholars as to how the two knowledge systems – biblical theology on the one hand and Platonic philosophy on the other – are hierarchized in the case of Origen. On the one hand there are very simple models: My Roman Catholic Patristic teacher in Tübingen, Hermann Josef Vogt, propounded the basic dogma of Catholic French Origen scholarship, which acknowledged the Christian Alexandrian as having been well versed in philosophy but supposed him to have remained loyal to biblical norms in all cases of conflict between biblical texts and Platonic philosophy.[11] For Vogt, as, for example, for Henri Crouzel, Origen is at core a biblical theologian, with a knowledge system

7 Sarasin 2011.
8 On the structure of neural networks see Singer 2001 and 2002.
9 Berner 1981.
10 Crouzel 1971, 1982, 1996.
11 Vogt 1999, esp. 191–195; 2002.

in which the biblical-theological and Platonic-philosophical systems are clearly hierarchized.[12] The counter-model to this interpretation, not coincidentally, was asserted by Protestant theologians such as the reformed French theologian Eugène de Faye (1860–1929), in a major, three-volume work published between 1923 and 1928.[13] According to de Faye, Origen was the first Christian thinker to introduce basic concepts of Middle Platonic philosophy into the interpretation of the Christian Bible and thus into theology; he was much more committed to philosophical concepts like the two-world doctrine, the priority of spiritual being over material reality and so on than to biblical concepts.[14]

Of course there were always moderating concepts floating around, and even Crouzel and de Faye were not so radically one-sided as I have portrayed them here for reasons of economy and illustration. The most appealing example of such a middle way comes to us via Adolf von Harnack's very late article on Origen in the fourth volume of the second edition of the Protestant encyclopaedia *Die Religion in Geschichte und Gegenwart*, which appeared in 1930, the year of Harnack's death.[15] On the one hand, Harnack emphasizes that Origen, with his philosophical theology, had presented "merely a variation of the post-Platonic Stoic system" and speculated in a rather elevated fashion on biblical texts from within the orbit of these philosophical orientations. On the other hand, Harnack wisely observes that this speculation is "bound in its understanding of the Bible to the rule of faith ... which the church, following in the apostolic tradition, developed from the Bible according to O(rigen) in contrast to the false understanding of the heretics."[16] The rule of faith, *regula fidei* or κανὼν τῆς πίστεως,[17] is the formulation – still free in terms of language – of basic truths of the Christian faith such as the affirmation of the one God, the one Christ and the one church. And then Harnack gives us this image: "The church gnostic is like an airship pilot; though he may lift off and rise up to the sun, his balloon is a captive one that can never lose contact with the firm ground of the rule of faith."[18]

---

12 Crouzel 1962:215–216; 1989:156–163.

13 De Faye 1923–1928.

14 De Faye 1928:286: "Y avait-il donc chez Origène deux homes, un philosophe et un croyant? Une cloison étanche les séparait-elle? ... Nous estimons qu'Origène m'avait aucune peine à passer de l'un à l'autre, parce que le philosophe et le croyant, le didascale et le prêtre, n'étaient que les deux côtés d'une seule et même personnalité. ... Sa philosophie était saturée d'esprit chrétien, comme sa foi était imbue de sa pensée religieuse."

15 Harnack 1930.

16 *Ibid.*:783.

17 Ohme 1998:1–17, esp. 2–3.

18 Harnack 1930:783.

No matter how the relationship between biblical theology and Platonic philosophy in Origen was defined, it was popular to describe his system of knowledge as a hierarchy of knowledge stores that could be separated into two static blocks. Harnack's differentiation between a down-to-earth interpretation of the Bible oriented towards the rule of faith, the *regula fidei*, and an aloof, airy or elevated realm of philosophical speculation is perhaps the clearest metaphor for how knowledge stores are modeled as separate entities and how systems of knowledge are seen to a great extent as hierarchically organized systems.

If we stay with the more recent history of knowledge, a notable representative of which is the aforementioned science historian Philipp Sarasin, and describe systems of knowledge much more strongly as a network of fluid hierarchizations reconfigured according to current requirements, this of course also changes how we describe the relationship between biblical theology and Platonic philosophy in Origen compared to the classic concepts of the twentieth century, represented on the one hand by Crouzel and Vogt, and on the other by de Faye and, to an extent, by Harnack.

To the question of whether Origen was loyal to the Bible or to the philosophy of Plato, one might now, somewhat flippantly, respond: "It depends."[19] It depends, for example, on whether this exegete and thinker of Antiquity was even aware of a conflict that we nowadays believe to exist. It depends on the context he was writing in at any given time, or rather, as Sarasin puts it, on "forms of representation and the mediality of knowledge." More simply, he tended to platonize less in sermons than he did in the famous "fundamental writings," Περὶ ἀρχῶν/ *De principiis*.[20] To be sure, Origen's sermons were directed to his very ordinary congregants in a Mediterranean harbor town and provincial capital, while the fundamental writings are presumably the closing lecture at his private university, aimed at presenting students with a comprehensive view of all known knowledge stores against the background of the concept of God, Creation and the Revelation, together with an appropriate understanding of these. In other words, the aim of the sermons was to invite non-academics – if I may again put it in anachronistic terms – to readings of the Bible and afterwards, in the sermon, to examine more closely what they had heard.[21] In the lecture hall, by contrast, Origen's students were given to understand that the pagan canon of teachings not only fit in well with Christian theology (or "Christian philosophy," as Origen called it[22]) but

19 For this question cf. now Edwards 2002.
20 Lies 1992:6–23.
21 Markschies 1997; Monaci Castagno 1987:50–64.
22 Markschies 2007a:70–75.

should, as it were, be framed by it and integrated into a truly comprehensive, convincing and appropriate system. In other words, these teachings can be presented and learned within a hierarchical system of knowledge, which, in theory, is naturally so in accordance with God's will. But this we can label "theology as prescribed"; "theology as practiced" might well be quite different. However, though I cannot show this in detail in the present framework, the fluid structure of the network differentiates Origen's thinking in the third century from Christian concepts of the second century – for example, among the apologists of Irenaeus.

I would like, in conclusion, to illustrate my thesis once again by taking a brief look at an example – that of anthropology. For many obvious reasons, I will concentrate on one commentary; I will therefore not be looking at the homilies on the First Epistle to the Corinthians, which I have been trying to edit for years from fragments of catenae, but will look instead at the Commentary on the Epistle to the Romans, edited by Caroline Hammond Bammel,[23] which, however, is available to us only in the abridged and dogmatically corrected and/or updated Latin translation by Rufinus of Aquileia and some Greek fragments, mainly from the Byzantine Chain Commentaries, the above-mentioned catenae.[24] In this translation, completed in 406 CE, fifteen books were abridged to ten (there really is something in the old preconception that Greek was more abundant and Latin briefer, to recall once again, albeit partly with tongue in cheek, the highly problematic folk psychologies that were so popular in Antiquity[25]).

Origen wrote this commentary around 150 years before Rufinus translated it, in 243–244, after he had already lived, preached and taught in Caesarea for ten years.[26] It was the mature late work of a man who had once been a sixteen-year-old grammar teacher, but who had long since become a teacher of theology renowned throughout the Empire and a highly respected scholar, as shown by the enthusiastic graduation speech of Gregor Thaumaturgus.[27] Having dealt elsewhere with Origen's Commentary on Romans in terms of its antique literary context and its interpretative methodology,[28] I shall now concentrate on his anthropology as demonstrated in this work.

---

23 Hammond Bammel 1990, 1997, 1998; on the biblical text see Hammond Bammel 1985.
24 Mühlenberg 2012; 1989.
25 Cicero, *Tusculanae disputationes* II 6: "eadem enim dicuntur a multis, ex quo libris omnia referserunt"; Gigon 1973.
26 Cf. the introduction by Theresia Heither to her edition and translation: Heither 1990:7–41, esp. 7–15.
27 Crouzel and Brakmann 1983; Markschies 2007a:73–74, 102–104.
28 Markschies 1999.

In Origen's eyes, anthropology undoubtedly belongs to the particularly weighty theological problems highlighted, discussed and examined by Paul in the Epistle to the Romans, the treatment and resolution of which only the similarly consummate interpreter could adequately reflect and comment upon. The Commentary's presentation of the basal constitution of man as comprising mind and body, with the soul as an intermediary between the two,[29] poses less of a problem than the freedom with which the thus-constituted man can behave – or not, as the case may be – in the face of divine law. It is this problem that I would like to look at in the following paragraphs, because it is here that the Pauline and Platonic (and also the Stoic) elements in Origen's thinking – or simply his system of knowledge – can be followed so well.

It can be shown that Origen reads his Pauline text with a solid belief that man is free in his decision-making and in his decisions for or against God.[30] Thus, for our modern tastes, Origen comes into considerable conflict with the deterministic motifs in the Epistle to the Romans, particularly in the seventh and ninth chapters. However, the matter is not as simple as might be presumed on the basis of the above-described conception of a hierarchizing conflict between the two "blocks" of a biblical – or, more precisely, Pauline – anthropology, on the one hand, and a philosophical – or, more precisely, Platonic – anthropology with Stoic elements, on the other. In the first and second book of his Commentary on Romans, Origen speaks in very Pauline terms of the power of sin[31] – for example, in the nice image of man as a house with two doors to the soul, allowing desire to enter on one side and virtue on the other. If virtue is spurned, it departs from that place, leaving the man who has thus fallen to succumb to his desires, in the way described by Paul at the beginning of the Epistle to the Romans.[32]

---

29 Origenes/Rufinus, *Commentarii in epistulam ad Romanos* I 21, *ad Romanos* 1:24–25 (Hammond Bammel 1990:88, ll. 40–47 = Heither 1990:148, 10–24): "Frequenter in scripturis inuenimus et a nobis saepe dissertum est quod homo spiritus et corpus et anima esse dicatur. Uerum cum dicitur quia caro concupiscit aduersus spiritum spiritus autem aduersus carnem, media procul dubio ponitur anima quae uel desideriis spiritus adquiescat uel ad carnis concupiscentias inclinetur; et si quidem se iunxerit carni unum cum ea corpus in libidine et concupiscentiis eius efficitur, si uero se sociauerit spiritui, unus cum ea spiritus erit." Cf. also Theiler 1970.

30 For an overview see Perrone 2000; for context see Dihle 1985:124–126 and in general Benjamins 1994.

31 Heither 1990:111–126.

32 Origenes/Rufinus, *Commentarii in epistulam ad Romanos* I 21, *ad Romanos* 1:24–25 (Hammond Bammel 1990:90, ll. 85–94 = Heither 1990:152, 10–20): "Ponamus esse aliquod domicilium, in quo cum corpore et spiritu uelut cum duobus consiliariis habitet anima; pro foribus uero huius domicilii astare pietatem omnesque cum ea uirtutes; ex alia uero parte impietatem omnesque luxuriarum ac libidinum formas et expectare animae nutum, quem ex duobus pro foris obser-

At the beginning of the Commentary, then, there is not much evidence of the light image of a human being who is free to decide, which Origen depicts mainly in his Commentary on the seventh chapter, where he simply assumes it axiomatically with certain philosophical prerequisites. One can say, perhaps, that within the network of knowledge that marks Origen, the Pauline texts he admires sometimes have a strong influence, and their anthropological concepts come into the foreground, overlaying others that originate more from Platonic or Stoic philosophy.

However, in other places – or, to use Sarasin's term, within other contexts – the network of knowledge may be organized very differently. I have already pointed out how Origen, in the sixth book of the Commentary, assumes axiomatically that man has the freedom to choose for or against divine law. The human being is made in God's image and would for that reason alone be free. He is responsible to God and free for that reason as well. Only Gnostic heresies can put determination or even predestination in the place of freedom of decision.[33] However, how does Origen explain passages such as Romans 7:19 – "For I do not do the good I want to do, but the evil I do not want to do"[34] – in which Paul speaks of the good not being able to manifest itself, although the will is there? Commenting on this verse, Origen invokes the prosopopoeia (προσωποποΐία), a typical method of literary hermeneutics drawn from the pagan art of interpretation:[35] "Paul, as a teacher of the church, himself takes on the role of the weak."[36] That is, Paul makes use of the literary device of speaking in the form of several different persons. Origen, we may

uantibus chorum introduci ad se desideret, quem repelli. Nonne, si spiritui obtemperans et meliori usa consiliario pietatis et pudicitiae ad se euocauerit chorum, ille alius spretus repudiatusque discedet?"

33 Origenes/Rufinus, *Commentarii in epistulam ad Romanos* VI 1, *ad Romanos* 6:12–14 (Hammond Bammel 1997:456, l. 28 – 457, l. 38 = Heither 1990:192, 10–21): "Illud tamen aduerte, quod ostendens in nostra potestate situm, ut non regnet in corpore nostro peccatum, praeceptum dat apostolus dicens: 'Non ergo regnet peccatum in uestro mortali corpore ad oboediendum de deriis eius.' Nisi enim esset in nostra potestate, ut non regnaret in nobis peccatum, praeceptum utique non dedisset. Quomodo ergo possibile est, ut peccatum in carne nostra non regnet? Si faciamus illud, quod idem apostolus dicit: 'Mortificate membra uestra, quae sunt super terram,' et si semper mortem Christi in corpore nostro circumferamus. Certum namque est, quia ubi mors Christi circumfertur, non potest regnare peccatum."

34 Οὐ γὰρ ὃ θέλω ποιῶ ἀγαθόν, ἀλλὰ ὃ οὐ θέλω κακὸν τοῦτο πράσσω. For one of a great many secondary works see Vollenweider 1989:339–374.

35 Villani 2008.

36 Origenes/Rufinus, *Commentarii in epistulam ad Romanos* VI 9, *ad Romanos* 7:14–25a (Hammond Bammel 1997:509, ll. 45–47 = Heither 1990:270, 22–23): "... hic iam tamquam doctor ecclesiae personam in semet ipsum suscipit infirmorum."

infer, did not perceive his interpretation of the seventh chapter of the Epistle to the Romans as a philosophical remodeling of Pauline theology, espousing, against the literal sense of the Epistle, a certain position concerning man's freedom of decision; he saw it, rather, as the product of a literary analysis, the identification of the prosopopoeia. He thus, as we would put it today, linked different knowledge stores – literary, philosophical and theological – in a context-related, decentralized, non-hierarchical network, enabling him to offer a different interpretation here than in the commentary on the first chapter of the Epistle.

While the present framework does not allow me to examine the picture I have drawn here in more detail, I believe I have shown that one cannot use the dual model of a conflict between biblical texts and philosophical theories to describe the fluidity of the systems of knowledge that Origen deploys, which are reconfigured according to his current requirements. The dual, hierarchical, conflictual approach thus misses the point of his thinking. And it should be clear, without saying too much, that this flexibilization of knowledge stores in Origen may be described as a rationalization or optimization of the Christian strategy of argumentation for its claims to the validity of its own theory.

References

Anacker, Michael. 2004. "Wissen VI. 19. u. 20. Jahrhundert." In: *Historisches Wörterbuch der Philosophie*, XII. Darmstadt: Wissenschaftliche Buchgesellschaft. Cols. 891–900.

Benjamins, Hendrik S. 1994. *Eingeordnete Freiheit: Freiheit und Vorsehung bei Origenes* (Supplements to Vigiliae Christianae, 28). Leiden–New York–Köln: Brill.

Berner, Ulrich. 1981. *Origenes* (Erträge der Forschung, 147). Darmstadt: Wissenschaftliche Buchgesellschaft.

Crouzel, Henri. 1962. *Origène et la Philosophie* (Théologie, 52). Paris: Aubier.

—. 1971. *Bibliographie critique d'Origène* (Instrumenta Patristica, 8). Steenbrugis, in Abbatia Sancti Petri – The Hague: Nijhoff.

—. 1982. *Supplément I* (Instrumenta Patristica, 8A). Steenbrugis, in Abbatia Sancti Petri – The Hague: Nijhoff.

—. 1989. *Origen* (English transl. by A. Stanley Worrall). Edinburgh: T & T Clark.

—. 1996. *Supplément II* (Instrumenta Patristica, 8B). Steenbrugis, in Abbatia Sancti Petri – Turnhout: Brepols.

Crouzel, Henri, and Heinzgerd Brakmann. 1983. "Gregor I der Wundertäter." *Reallexikon für Antike und Christentum*, XII. Stuttgart: Hiersemann. Cols. 779–793.

De Faye, Eugène. 1923–1928. *Origène: Sa vie, son œuvre, sa pensée*, I–III. Paris: Leroux.

Detel, Wolfgang. 2009. "Wissenskulturen und universale Rationalität." In: Johannes Fried und Michael Stolleis (eds.), *Wissenskulturen: Über die Erzeugung und Weitergabe von Wissen*. Frankfurt–New York: Campus. 181–214.

Dihle, Albrecht. 1985. *Die Vorstellung vom Willen in der Antike*. Göttingen: Vandenhoeck & Ruprecht.

Drehsen, Volker. 2009. "Religion und die Rationalisierung der modernen Welt: Max Weber (1864–1920)." In: idem, *Der Sozialwert der Religion: Aufsätze zur Religionssoziologie*, eds. Christian Albrecht, Hans Martin Dober and Birgit Weyel. Berlin–New York: De Gruyter. 41–95.

Edwards, Mark. 2002. *Origen against Plato*. Aldershot: Ashgate.

Gethmann, Carl Friedrich. 1995. "Rationalität." *Enzyklopädie Philosophie und Wissenschafts-theorie*, III. Stuttgart: Metzler. Cols. 468–481.

Gigon, Olof. 1973. "Cicero und die griechische Philosophie." In: Hildegard Temporini (ed.), *Von den Anfängen Roms bis zum Ausgang der Republik: 4: Philosophie und Wissenschaften* (Aufstieg und Niedergang der römischen Welt, I.4). Berlin–New York: De Gruyter. 226–261.

Hammond Bammel, Caroline Penrose. 1985. *Der Römerbrieftext des Rufin und seine Origenes-Übersetzung* (Vetus Latina: Arbeiten zur Geschichte der lateinischen Bibel, 10), Freiburg: Herder.

— (ed.). 1990. *Der Römerbriefkommentar des Origenes: Kritische Ausgabe der Übersetzung Rufins, Buch 1–3* (Vetus Latina. Arbeiten zur Geschichte der lateinischen Bibel, 16). Freiburg: Herder.

— (ed.). 1997. *Der Römerbriefkommentar des Origenes: Kritische Ausgabe der Übersetzung Rufins, Buch 4–6*, eds. Hermann Josef Frede and Herbert Stanjek (Vetus Latina: Arbeiten zur Geschichte der lateinischen Bibel, 33). Freiburg: Herder.

— (ed.). 1998. *Der Römerbriefkommentar des Origenes: Kritische Ausgabe der Übersetzung Rufins, Buch 7–10*, eds. Hermann Josef Frede and Herbert Stanjek (Vetus Latina: Arbeiten zur Geschichte der lateinischen Bibel, 34). Freiburg: Herder.

Harnack, Adolf von. 1930. "Origenes." *Religion in Geschichte und Gegenwart*, IV. 2nd edition, Tübingen: Mohr-Siebeck. 781–787.

Heither, Theresia. 1990. *Translatio Religionis: Die Paulusdeutung des Origenes in seinem Kommentar zum Römerbrief* (Bonner Beiträge zur Kirchengeschichte, 16). Vienna: Böhlau.

Koch, Anton Friedrich. 2016. "Rationalität im Gespräch: Grundlegendes aus philosophischer Perspektive." In: Markus Mühling, Christina Drobe, Dirk-Martin Grube, Alexander Kupsch, Paul Silas Peterson and Martin Wendte (eds.), *Rationalität im Gespräch – Rationality in Conversation: Philosophische und theologische Perspektiven – Philosophical and Theological Perspectives* (Marburger Theologische Studien, 126). Leipzig: Evangelische Verlagsanstalt. 11–22.

Lies, Lothar. 1992. *Origenes' 'Peri Archon': Eine undogmatische Dogmatik* (Werkinterpre-tationen). Darmstadt: Wissenschaftliche Buchgesellschaft.

Markschies, Christoph. 1997: "... für die Gemeinde im Grossen und Ganzen nicht geeignet? Erwägungen zu Absicht und Wirkung der Predigten des Origenes." *Zeitschrift für Theologie und Kirche*, 94:39–68. (Reprinted in Markschies 2007b:35–62).

—. 1999. "Origenes und die Kommentierung des paulinischen Römerbriefs: Einige Bemerkungen zur Rezeption von antiken Kommentartechniken im Christentum des dritten Jahrhunderts und ihrer Vorgeschichte." In: Glenn W. Most (ed.), *Commentaries – Kommentare* (Aporemata, 4). Göttingen: Vandenhoeck & Ruprecht. 66–94.

—. 2007a. *Kaiserzeitliche christliche Theologie und ihre Institutionen: Prolegomena zu einer Geschichte der antiken christlichen Theologie*. Tübingen: Mohr-Siebeck.

—. 2007b. *Origenes und sein Erbe: Gesammelte Studien* (Texte und Untersuchungen, 160). Berlin–New York: De Gruyter.

—. 2012. *Hellenisierung des Christentums: Sinn und Unsinn einer historischen Deutungskategorie* (Theologische Literaturzeitung. Forum, 25). Leipzig: Evangelische Verlagsanstalt.
—. 2015. "Origenes und Paulus: Das Beispiel der Anthropologie." In: Jörg Frey and Benjamin Schließer, with Veronika Niederhofer (eds.), *Der Philipperbrief des Paulus in der hellenistisch-römischen Welt* (Wissenschaftliche Untersuchungen zum Neuen Testament, 353). Tübingen: Mohr-Siebeck. 349–372.
Mittelstrass, Jürgen. 1996. "Wissen." *Enzyklopädie Philosophie und Wissenschaftstheorie*, IV. Stuttgart: Metzler. Cols. 717–719.
Monaci Castagno, Adele. 1987. *Origene predicatore e il suo pubblico*. Mailand: Angeli.
Mühlenberg, Ekkehard. 1989. "Katenen." *Theologische Realenzyklopädie*, XVIII. Berlin–New York: De Gruyter. 14–21.
—. 2012. "Catena, II: Christianity." *Encyclopedia of the Bible and Its Reception*, IV. Berlin–New York: De Gruyter. Cols. 1061–1064.
Nautin, Pierre. 1977. *Origène: Sa vie et son œuvre* (Christianisme antique, 1). Paris: Beauchesne.
Ohme, Heinz. 1998. *Kanon ekklesiastikos: Die Bedeutung des altkirchlichen Kanonbegriffes* (Arbeiten zur Kirchengeschichte, 67). Berlin–New York: De Gruyter.
Perrone, Lorenzo. 2000. "Libero Arbitrio." In: Adele Monaci Castagno (ed.), *Origene: Dizionario – La cultura, il pensiero, le opere*. Rome: Città Nuova. 237–243.
Sarasin, Philipp. 2011. "Was ist Wissensgeschichte?" *Internationales Archiv für Sozialgeschichte der Deutschen Literatur*, 36:159–172.
Schluchter, Wolfgang. 1976. "Die Paradoxie der Rationalisierung: Zum Verhältnis von 'Ethik' und 'Welt' bei Max Weber." *Zeitschrift für Soziologie*, 5:256–284.
Singer, Wolf. 2001. "Zur Struktur der neuronalen Netzwerke vgl. Wolf Singer, Ignorabimus? – Ignoramus: Wie Bewußtsein in die Welt kam." *Berlin-Brandenburgische Akademie der Wissenschaften: Jahrbuch 2000*. Berlin: Akademie Verlag. 115–124.
—. 2002. "Wahrnehmen, Erinnern, Vergessen: Über Nutzen und Vorteil der Hirnforschung für die Geschichtswissenschaft – Eröffnungsvortrag des 43. Deutschen Historikertags am 26. 09. 2000 in Aachen." In: idem, *Der Beobachter im Gehirn: Essays zur Hirnforschung* (Suhrkamp Taschenbuch Wissenschaft, 1571). Frankfurt a. M.: Suhrkamp. 76–89.
Sperber, Dan. 1985. "Anthropology and Psychology: Towards an Epidemiology of Representations." *Man*, 20:73–89.
Theiler, Willy. 1970. "Die Seele als Mitte bei Augustin und Origenes." In: idem, *Untersuchungen zur antiken Literatur*. Berlin: De Gruyter. 554–563.
Villani, Andrea. 2008. "Origenes als Schriftsteller: Ein Beitrag zu seiner Verwendung von Prosopopoiie, mit einigen Beobachtungen über die prosopologische Exegese." *Adamantius*, 14:130–150.
Vogt, Hermann Josef. 1999. "Beobachtungen zum Johannes-Kommentar des Origenes." In: idem, *Origenes als Exeget*. Paderborn: Schöningh. 187–206.
—. 2002. "Origenes." *Lexikon der antiken christlichen Literatur*. Freiburg im Breisgau: Herder. Cols. 528–536.
Vollenweider, Samuel. 1989. *Freiheit als neue Schöpfung: Eine Untersuchung zur Eleutheria bei Paulus und in seiner Umwelt (Forschungen zur Religion und Literatur des Alten und Neuen Testaments, 147)*. Göttingen: Vandenhoeck & Ruprecht.

Aryeh Kofsky and Serge Ruzer

Theodore of Mopsuestia: Rationalizing Hermeneutics and Theology

One of the salient features of the so-called Antiochene School or tradition is its penchant for a type of historical-grammatical and literal-critical exegesis of the Old Testament that may be branded rationalistic hermeneutics. In this study we focus on Theodore of Mopsuestia (ca. 350–428), the illustrious representative of the Antiochene tradition, later extolled in the East Syrian church as "The Interpreter" (ܡܦܫܩܢܐ) – highlighting the implications of his underlying rationalism for both Old and New Testament hermeneutics. Theodore's rationalism goes hand in hand with a low Christology, which, responding to the contemporaneous challenges of the late fourth and early fifth centuries, especially Arianism and Apollinarianism, emphasized Christ's humanity. This will be another focus of our study.

Theodore's master, Diodore of Tarsus, the Antiochene school's first prominent figure and perhaps its true founder, was a disciple of Eusebius of Emesa, a native of Edessa (c. 300),[1] who was distinguished by the literalist tendency of his exegesis.[2] In Diodore, in turn, we find some precedents for Theodore's principal stance of loose-union Christology. For Diodore, the incarnation is reduced to an indwelling of the Logos: The Logos assumed flesh but did not *become* flesh. Christ is thus perceived as two persons, whose loose union is described in typically Antiochene terms as "assumption," "clothing" or "indwelling."

Notwithstanding Diodore's use of Greek terminology and theological polemics, the basic underlying incarnational concept of the "assumed man" and the indwelling Logos, with its emphasis on Christ's humanity and the devaluation and relativization of his divinity, do not seem all that different from the earlier crude Christology of Aphrahat.[3]

Traits of Theodore's Old Testament Exegesis

In his exegesis, Diodore followed the rationalistic interpretative tradition of Eusebius of Emesa, insisting on a literal and historical method, strenuously opposing "the old wives' tales of the allegorists" and not seeking a hidden meaning in the

1 See Hill 2005a. On Eusebius of Emesa, see Buytaert 1949; Winn 2011.
2 See Ter Haar Romeny 1997.
3 See Ruzer and Kofsky 2010:7–40.

https://doi.org/10.1515/9783110446395-007

text.[4] In his partially recovered *Commentary on Psalms*, he allows messianic relevance to only four Psalms (2, 8, 44 and 109).[5] This calls to mind, *mutatis mutandis*, Ephrem the Syrian's general inclination toward literal interpretation and "low anthropology."[6] Unfortunately, we are dependent mostly on insufficient fragments for the reconstruction of Diodore's theology and exegesis.[7]

Thanks to Theodore of Mopsuestia, who would further refine and expand the ideas of his master, our picture of the Antiochene tradition becomes more detailed.[8] Theodore was less a speculative theologian than an exegete. In his exegesis he demonstrates acquaintance with Jewish traditions and usages and applies them in his critical views of Scripture, a practice astutely noted by Leontius of Byzantium with regard to Theodore's commentary on the book of Psalms: "Following usage of the Jews, he [Theodore] referred all the psalms to Zerubbabel and Hezekiah. He applied to the Lord only three psalms."[9] Moreover, Theodore was inclined to accept only those Old Testament books recognized by the Jews, apparently according to the Palestinian Jewish canon; thus, he does not quote the Old Testament apocrypha, which apparently did not belong in his canon. There is insufficient evidence for us to be sure that Theodore knew Hebrew, though he often uses the terms "Hebrew voice" and "Hebrew idiom" and refers to the original Hebrew text as the authentic source for correct understanding and the vehicle of revelation.[10] Indeed, a conspicuous trait of the Antiochenes is their close relationship to literalist trends in Jewish exegesis.[11] This may also account for Theodore's mitigated

---

4 Diodore, *Comm. on Psalms* 6.1, ed. Olivier 1980:77. See also Petit et al. 2011:i–xxxix.

5 On Diodore's commentary on Psalms, see Rondeau 1969–1970 and 1982, I:93–102; Diodore, *Commentary on Psalms 1–51*, ed. Hill 2005; Wayman 2014.

6 The similarity between the Antiochene school and Ephrem's literalism and anti-allegorism, especially in his *Commentary on Genesis*, has already been noted by Ter Haar Romeny (1997:93). See also Kofsky 2013 and Ruzer and Kofsky 2010:41–60.

7 On Diodore's theology, see Sullivan 1956:181–196 and Grillmeier 1975:352–360. On Diodore's exegesis, see Schweizer 1941; Thome 2004.

8 On Theodore's theology, see also Grillmeier 1975:421–439 and Norris 1963. On Antiochene Old Testament hermeneutics, see Hill 2005b:85–182; Schäublin 1974, 1988; and Zaharopoulos 1989. On Theodore's hermeneutics, see also Simonetti 2006.

9 Leontius of Byzantium, *Deprehensio ... super Nestorianos*, ed. Migne 1865:1365D. Theodore in fact considered the same four psalms recognized by Diodore as messianic prophecies. See Hill 2004; O'Keefe 2000.

10 Theodore, *Comm. on Psalms* 127, 133, 195, 249, ed. Devreese 1939; Zaharopoulos 1989:56–57. Theodore's disciple Theodoret of Cyrrhus – another great representative of the school – also shows familiarity with the works of Jewish authors and Jewish traditions, and even uses Jewish material as background illustrations for his argument.

11 Nevertheless, for elements of the moderate "spiritual" exegesis in the Antiochene tradition, see Nassif 1993, 1996.

supersessionism and relatively moderate attitude toward Jews in general.[12] On occasion, Theodore also introduces variant Syriac readings from the Peshitta, sometimes preferring the Syriac to the Greek text, but he appears to have lacked a solid knowledge of Syriac and to have depended in this regard on oral information and Syriac exegetical traditions.[13]

We have noted Theodore's strong opposition to Christological interpretations of the psalms and other messianic *testimonia* entrenched in patristic literature; he likewise denies pre-incarnation revelations of the Logos and the Holy Spirit to patriarchs and prophets.[14] According to Theodore, Old Testament prophecy as a whole does not present Christ directly but only lends itself to such interpretation because of its "hyperbolic" imagery, rich metaphorical meaning and symbolism. This is part of Theodore's biblical theology of progressive revelation, which would eventually pertain even to Jesus' human development, in his rejection of Jesus' apocryphal childhood miracles.[15]

Theodore of Mopsuestia as a New Testament Exegete

In his *Commentary on John*, which has survived in its entirety in Syriac translation, Theodore points to some of the parameters underlying his New Testament exegetical strategies, especially with regard to the Fourth Gospel.[16] Throughout the *Commentary*, the author stresses its polemical setting and declared objective of refuting heresy – primarily that of the Arians and the Apollinarians – paying special attention to verses exploited by the heretics (ܗܪܣܝܘ̈ܛܐ).[17] In addition, he indicates his intention to focus on questions that present a difficulty to the reader of the Gospel rather than to supply a full running commentary (*Comm.* 4.15–17;

12 Kofsky and Ruzer 2014.

13 E.g., Theodore, *Comm. on Habakkuk*, ed. Migne 1864:437C; *Commentary on Zephaniah* 1:6, ed. Migne 1874:452D. Cf. van Rompay 1997.

14 See Theodore, *CH*, ed. Mingana 1932:27.

15 See Hill 2005b:85–182; Kofsky and Ruzer 2013b:570–595; Simonetti 2006; Zaharopoulos 1989.

16 We generally concur with Thome's (2008:37) conclusion that the Syriac translation of the *Commentary* provides a closer reflection of the original Greek text than the surviving Greek catena fragments.

17 E.g., *Comm.* 3.7–10, 5.6–7; Eng. 1–2. For anti-Arian arguments, see, e.g., *Comm.* 8–14, 18, 25; Eng. 5–12. For a discussion of the anti-Arian polemics in the *Commentary*, see Thome 2008:315–334.

Eng. 1). While generally restricting himself to concise explanations, he nevertheless comments on most of the verses.[18]

As in Theodore's other exegetical works, here, too, one notes a distinctly anti-allegorical stance informing his mode of interpretation, as well as a penchant for etymology (*Comm.* 18.10–15; Eng. 8–9).[19] He shows a distinct preference for rational-contextual down-to-earth interpretation, with attention constantly paid to the "customary way of saying things" and, consequently, the *ordinary meaning* of those things as attested in Scripture. A telling example is found in his interpretation of the story of the blind man at the beginning of John 9, culminating in Jesus' teaching that the man had been born blind not because he had sinned, but "so that God's works might be revealed in him" (9:3). According to Theodore, this is again "Scripture's idiomatic way of saying things" (ܐܝܟ ܥܝܕܗ ܕܟܬܒܐ ܐܡܪ, κατὰ τὸ τῆς γραφῆς ἰδίωμα λέγει), and it does not imply that the man was made blind in order to manifest God's powers; rather, this was a birth defect (ܕܗܘ ܡܘܡܐ ܟܝܢܐܝܬ ܠܕܢܚܗ) that would become instrumental for Jesus' miracle (*Comm.* 184.25–29; Eng. 84).

Theodore similarly elaborates on the meaning of the title "son of God" in the Gospel according to the putative usage of Jesus' Jewish milieu: "Nathanael said that he was the *son of God* not because he knew of his divine birth [ܡܘܠܕܐ ܐܠܗܝܐ], but because it was *a familiar way of saying things*, since those who by their own *moral virtue drew near to God were called sons of God* [ܡܛܠ ܕܒܢ̈ܝܐ ܕܐܠܗܐ ܡܬܩܪܝܢ ܗܘܘ ܗܢ̈ܝ ܐܢܫܐ ܐܝܠܝܢ ܕܒܡܝܬܪܘܬܗܘܢ ܩܪܝܒܝܢ ܗܘܘ ܠܐܠܗܐ]" (*Comm.* 53.18–22; Eng. 25).[20] Theodore also characteristically interprets Thomas's exclamation upon witnessing Jesus' post-Easter appearance – "My Lord and my God!" (John 20:28) – not as addressed to Jesus but as praising God for the miracle of Jesus' bodily resurrection, since, according to Theodore, Thomas, who had just touched the body of Jesus, would not be expected to call him "God" (*Comm.* 358.5–11; Eng. 166).

A different aspect of Theodore's rational and critical approach to the sacred text may be seen in his bold assertion that not everything in the Gospel was actually penned by the Evangelist. He thus claims that its concluding words (John 21:24–25) were "not by John, but by someone else" (ܕܠܘ ܕܝܘܚܢܢ ܐܝܬܝܗܘܢ ܐܠܐ

18 See Theodore's own description of his approach in *Comm.* 232.21–25; Eng. 106–107.

19 See Thome 2004.

20 Cf. the habitual Jewish exegesis of the "sons of God" in Gen 6:4 (e. g., in the Aramaic Targum) as "sons of the chosen elite"; and see Flusser 2001:113–123. Theodore also explains the rhetorical question of Nathanael, "Can anything good come from Nazareth?" (John 1:46), by suggesting – apparently on the basis of "the Galilee of the Gentiles" in Isa 9:1–2 and Matt 4:15 – that the village of Nazareth at that time was much despised by the Jews because its inhabitants were mostly gentiles (ܕܡܢ ܚܢܦ̈ܐ, ὑπ' ἐθνικῶν; *Comm.* 52.1–5, Eng. 24).

ܠܐܚܪܝܢܐ ܐܢܫ ܐܚܪܢܐ ܗܘܝ, ταῦτα τὰ ῥήματα οὐκ εἰσὶ τοῦ εὐαγγελιστοῦ, ἀλλ' ὑπό τινος φιλοπόνου ἐνετέθη; *Comm.* 364.4–6; Eng. 169).[21]

Further salient features of Theodore's exegesis include a fondness for psychological interpretation of protagonists' motives;[22] his observation that in Scripture, especially in the Old Testament, "different times are simply placed together without distinction," enabling him to reconstruct a more reasonable temporal framework for the text;[23] and his keen awareness of the logical implications of the text's literal meaning.[24] In some cases he does not hesitate to go against the current, as in his elaboration on the story of the paralytic cured by Jesus at Bethzatha on the Sabbath (John 5:2–9):

> Some have actually composed words of praise for the paralytic's actions ... How could the paralytic be worthy of praise when he revealed our Lord to the Jews who had even openly threatened him ... as a transgressor of the law? ... Rather, in order to comply with the rules of the Jews, he [the paralytic] betrayed his own benefactor ... following his own evil will. (*Comm.* 101–102; Eng. 47)

Theodore regards the Fourth Gospel as later than the Synoptics. He assumes John's familiarity with his predecessors and views him – like Luke, who so presents himself at the beginning of his Gospel – as aiming to supply necessary clarifications and in general to complete what is lacking in the Synoptic account. He explicitly criticizes the Synoptics for having "had no care for the order of the

---

21 One may note that the Greek version here seems to include an editorial embellishment (φιλοπόνου) – an example of the paraphrastic nature of the catenae Greek fragments of the *Commentary*.

22 See, e.g., his interpretation regarding some of the apostles' initial hesitancy to follow Jesus, *Comm.* 50.26–51.1; Eng 24; and cf. his observation about Mary's conduct in Cana: "His mother, *according to the habit of mothers*, incited him to perform a miracle, wanting the greatness [ܪܒܘܬܗ] of her son to be revealed" (*Comm.* 56.7–11; Eng. 26). For the patristic exegesis of the Cana episode, see Smitmans 1966.

23 See note 1 above. For the application of this hermeneutical principle to the New Testament, see, e.g., *Comm.* 29.16–19; Eng. 14, where John 1:5 ("The light shines in the darkness and the darkness did not grasp it") is interpreted as referring to the future, namely, Jesus' advent, and not to the beginning of creation.

24 Thus, for example, he concludes from John the Baptist's words in John 1:32 ("I saw the Spirit descending from heaven like a dove") that the descending Spirit "*was not seen by all* those present but only by John in a sort of spiritual vision" – otherwise "it would *have been superfluous* to say that 'John testified, saying 'I saw the spirit'" (*Comm.* 45.18–30; Eng. 22). Another example is found in *Comm.* 90.1–6; Eng. 42, where Theodore deduces from John 4:18 that the Samaritan woman concealed the details of her problematic marital history from her countrymen. See also *Comm.* 50.18–21, 98.19–23, 338.14–18; Eng. 24, 46, 156.

events" (ܘܠܐ ܗܟܢܐ ܐܬܥܒܕ ܠܗܘܢ ܥܠ ܛܟܣܗܘܢ ܕܣܘܥܪ̈ܢܐ; *Comm.* 76.12–13; Eng. 35).[25] Thus, regarding John the Baptist's encounters with Jesus on the bank of the Jordan River (John 1:29–36), Theodore claims:

> No other Evangelist was diligent in saying that these things happened on the first day, those on the second and those others on the third. Rather, each of them simply recorded the events [themselves]. The blessed John [the Evangelist], intending to report also the omitted things, which in his opinion had to be related completely, developed his story also according to chronological order [ܘܫܘܚ ܕܝܢ ܠܛܟܣܐ ... ܐܬܚܫܒܬ ܠܗ ܕܫܘܥܝܬܗ ܐܦ ܠܛܟܣܐ ܕܙܒܢܐ ܠܐܝܠܝܢ ܕܫܒܝܩܬܐ]. (*Comm.* 48.7–15; Eng. 23)[26]

Theodore also attributes various disagreements among the Synoptics to the fact that they did not "coordinate their opinions [ܬܪܥܝܬܗܘܢ]" (*Comm.* 325.20–30; Eng. 150–151).[27] This seems to presuppose that some of them might have erred in details of their accounts, for instance regarding the "times and hours" of Jesus' crucifixion (*Comm.* 334.2–3; Eng. 154). Theodore nevertheless insists apologetically that in the essential details the Evangelists demonstrate overwhelming harmony (ܫܘܝܘܬܐ ܣܓܝܐܬܐ; *Comm.* 340.4–10, 341.7–12; Eng. 157–158). He is ready to admit that even John does not always adhere to a consistent chronological order, but he presents this as deriving from an inherent scriptural trait: "Words, in fact, are not placed and coordinated precisely in divine books" (ܠܐ ܓܝܪ ܚܬܝܬܐܝܬ ܡܬܛܟܣܢ ܘܣܝܡܢ ܡܣܝܡܢ ܕܡ̈ܠܐ ܒܟܬܒ̈ܐ ܐܠܗ̈ܝܐ; *Comm.* 256.2–4; Eng. 117).

Theodore sees John as consciously avoiding the repetition of details already supplied by earlier accounts; only when the narrative requires it does he recount them briefly.[28] Thus, for example, the Evangelist relates only those events linked to John the Baptist and told by others that are necessary for the narrative, complementing them with stories omitted by his predecessors (*Comm.* 8.10–16, 28.14–16, 232.12–14; Eng. 3, 13, 106). Theodore also notes: "In some passages where he [the Evangelist] mentions a sign already related by the others, he undoubtedly does it for a specific purpose" (*Comm.* 8.21–23, 64.1–8; Eng. 4, 30). Sometimes, however, the Interpreter complements John's narrative with details that he deems important which are found only in the Synoptics, presenting them, quasi-Diatessarically, as if they were included in the Fourth Gospel. Thus, elaborating on John 1:15,

---

25 See also *Comm.* 85; Eng. 39–40.

26 See also the discussion regarding the events in Cana (*Comm.* 55.18–56.2; Eng. 26), where Matthew is criticized for lacking care for the proper order of events.

27 On the apologetic treatment of Gospel contradictions in early Christian literature, see Merkel 1971.

28 See, e. g., *Comm.* 43.18–24; Eng. 21, and *Comm.* 325–326; Eng.150–152. Cf. *Comm.* 335.17–20; Eng. 155.

Theodore rephrases the speech of John the Baptist, adding the Synoptic motif of Jesus' baptism, whose inclusion the Evangelist, according to him, had considered superfluous, as it was already recorded by the Synoptics: "This is the one about whom I [the Baptist] said, 'After me comes a man who will certainly *be considered inferior to me* because testimony about him came from me, *and he will be baptized by me*'" (*Comm.* 37.7–15; Eng. 18).[29] Theodore also believed that John intentionally suppresses "those things that personally concern him," and when he does relate to events in which he himself was involved, "he avoids subscribing his name" (*Comm.* 49.15–17; Eng. 23).

John's most prominent contribution, however, is his introduction of crucial theological elements lacking in the earlier accounts:

> He certainly praised the writers [of the earlier Gospels] for their consistency and truth [ܠܫܪܪܗܘܢ ܕܫܠܡܘܬܐ]. He said, however, that some details [ܢܘܕ̈ܪܐ] had been neglected by them – especially certain miracles that needed to be related – and that doctrine [ܡܠܦܢܘܬܐ, τὰ διδασκαλικά] was almost entirely absent from their books. He also added that, since they had mostly discussed in detail the advent of the Lord in the flesh [ܡܬܝܬܝܘܬܗ ܕܒܣܪ ܡܫܝܚܐ, περὶ τῆς ἐν σαρκὶ τοῦ χριστοῦ παρουσίας], the question of his divinity [ܐܠܗܘܬܗ, περὶ θεότητος] could not be omitted; otherwise, with the passing of time, people having grown accustomed to their testimony might think of the Lord only as he appeared from their account. (*Comm.* 7.9–18; Eng. 3)

In a sense, for Theodore, the Gospel of John represents the completion of all the important elements missing from the other Gospels (*Comm.* 9.1–3; Eng. 4). This manifestly presupposes a critical approach to the Synoptic tradition. In fact, according to Theodore, John's reworking of the inherited tradition benefited from the superior authority and faith that he gained from his closeness to Jesus and his having been "endowed with a greater grace [ܛܝܒܘܬܐ, χάρις] for his love" (*Comm.* 7.5; Eng. 3). Thus, comprehension of John's theological thought is regarded as more useful than that of the other Evangelists (ܝܬܝܪ ܡܢ ܟܠ ܡܟܪܙܐ; *Comm.* 4.3; Eng. 1).[30] For Theodore, notably, Paul also expressed the same Logos-theology as was spelled out in John, balancing between the Scylla of Arian distinction and the Charybdis of monarchian Sabellianism (*Comm.* 24.25 ff; Eng. 11).[31]

---

29 See also Theodore's harmonizing approach regarding the different versions of Jesus' anointment in Bethany (*Comm.* 236.22–30; Eng. 108).

30 One may note that, unlike the early sixth-century Philoxenus of Mabbug, who likewise compared the Christological stances of John and the Synoptics, Theodore does not attempt to claim that the Synoptics indicated the same Christological truths. See Ruzer and Kofsky 2010:131–134.

31 Theodore appeals here to Heb 1:3.

The Balancing Logic of Theodore's Christological Hermeneutics

The theological and especially the Christological views of Theodore of Mopsuestia have been addressed repeatedly in the research of the last half-century. Since his major theological treatise, *On the Incarnation*, has been lost,[32] even greater importance for reconstructing Theodore's Christology must be assigned to his under-studied *Commentary on John*, along with his *Catechetical Homilies*. In fact, the extant Greek and Latin fragments of the *De Incarnatione* correspond closely to Theodore's Christology in the *Commentary*.[33]

Of the numerous commentaries on almost the whole of the New Testament penned by Theodore, only his short commentaries on the minor Pauline epistles, surviving in Latin,[34] and the *Commentary on John*, in Syriac, have been fully preserved.[35] As noted, Diodore of Tarsus had already laid down the main contours of what would become the characteristic "Antiochene stance" on Christology, especially the cardinal distinction between the Logos (son of God) and the *homo assumptus*. For Diodore, Mary is the mother of a man who is conjoined to the Logos and deified because of this conjunction (*synapheia*). Diodore's refusal to admit the predication of human attributes to the Logos reduced the incarnation to an indwelling of the Logos, which therefore cannot be called "the son of David." The Logos assumed flesh but did not *become* flesh. To safeguard the divinity of the Logos, another ultimate subject had to be found for these human predicates. Thus, Christ was essentially perceived as two entities loosely united via "assumption," "clothing" or "indwelling" – the typical Antiochene terminology. The difference between indwelling in Christ and in the prophets was only a matter of duration and degree. Diodore's stance, his insistence on the complete humanity of Christ, should be understood in the general context of Julianist, Arian and Apollinarian polemics.[36] Regrettably, the surviving fragments are insufficient for us to compose an adequate picture of Diodore's theology and hermeneutics.[37]

---

32 On Theodore's Christology, see, e. g., Abramowsky 1961; Galtier 1957; Grillmeier 1975:421–442; McLeod 2009:34–63; Norris 1963; Sullivan 1956. For the extant fragments of *De Incarnatione*, see Jansen 2009:234–291.

33 For a synthesis of the Christology reflected in the fragments of *De Incarnatione*, see Jansen 2009:152–206. See also Kofsky and Ruzer 2013a, 2014.

34 On Theodore's commentaries on the Pauline epistles, see Wickert 1962. See also more recently Greer 2010.

35 See Theodore, *Comm. on Colossians*, ed. Greer 2010:394–395. For a detailed study of the *Commentary on John*, emphasizing the work's textual aspects, see Thome 2008.

36 See Beeley 2011.

37 See Greer 1966; and see the works cited in note 7, above.

Further elaborating on these ideas, Theodore of Mopsuestia would endeavor to combine the Logos and "the man" in the more balanced and intricate concept of a loose unity and, most prominently, to expand the scope of applied hermeneutics.[38] Although the extent of Theodore's dependence on Diodore is sometimes difficult to assess, it is clear that for him, too, the polemical context, which he stressed in his *Commentary on John*, constituted a major axis and impetus for his theological elaborations.[39] We will address here some quasi-rational aspects of Theodore's responses to these challenges and the ways in which they shaped his theology and especially his Christological thinking, as reflected mainly in the hermeneutics of the *Commentary on John*.

Theodore's Trinitarian ideas do not differ essentially from the Nicene outlook as developed in response to the Arian challenge throughout the fourth century. They have been amply studied, and so we will examine them only briefly, especially with regard to their polemical concerns, hermeneutical context and Christological implications.

In his commentary on the Johannine Prologue, Theodore addresses major Arian theological arguments: that the Logos was created; that it is not a truly divine hypostasis; and that it was created as a medium for the creation of the world and perhaps even exclusively of life. Against these doctrines, Theodore reestablishes that the Logos is a divine hypostasis, coeternal and consubstantial with the Father, proceeding from him but not made by him, and that its existence is not a function of its role in the creation (*Comm.* 14.5–15, 18.5–8, 112.9–14; Eng. 6–7, 8–9, 52).[40] The Evangelist wanted to show that "the Son was always with the Father and that he is of the *same nature* [ܒܟܝܢܐ ܕܫܘܐ ܠܗ, ὅμοιος τὴν φύσιν] and *a partner* [ܡܫܘܬܦ, κοινωνός] *with him in creation*," whose role is in no way limited

38 See the works cited in note 8, above.

39 E. g., *Comm.* 3.7–10, 5.6–7; Eng. 1–2. See also Theodore, *Comm. on Philippians*, ed. Greer 2010:322–323. For discussions of Arianism, see Barnes and Williams 1993; Böhm 1991, 2006; Gregg and Groh 1981; Hanson 1988; Kannengiesser 1983; Williams 1983. For anti-Arian arguments, see, e. g., *Comm.* 8–14, 18, 25; Eng. 5–12. For a discussion of the anti-Arian polemics in the *Commentary*, see Thome 2008:315–334. Theodore refers explicitly to the Arian Asterius, who wrote a commentary on John, which is lost. It appears that at least some of his allusions to the Arian interpretation of verses from John refer to that work – see *Comm.* 4.14–5.14, 210.16–25; Eng. 1, 96. He also refers to Eunomius (*Comm.* 3.7–13; Eng. 1). For Apollinarius and Apollinarianism, see Lietzmann 1904; Spoerl 1994.

40 See also Theodore, *CH* 1–3, ed. Mingana 1932:23/123–124, 30/132–133, 40/144–146. Theodore is aware that John's Prologue is an elaboration of the opening verses of Genesis and pits the terminology of Genesis – "one day" and not "first day" – against the Arian interpretation of John 1:1. Cf. *Genesis rabba* 3:8–9 (ed. Theodor–Albeck 1965), where the meaning of "one day" in Gen 1:5 likewise does not mean "the first day." Cf. Theodore, *Comm. on Philippians*, ed. Greer 2010:314–315.

to the creation of life (*Comm.* 25.11–16, 26.5–19; Eng. 12, 2).[41] According to the Interpreter, the Evangelist further emphasizes that the Son "has no communion [of nature (ܫܘܬܦܘܬܐ, κοινωνία)]" with the created things (ܒܪ̈ܝܬܐ) (*Comm.* 24.29 – 25.1; Eng. 12).

Theodore presents his arguments as a discourse on the meaning of "in the beginning" (John 1:1) and the unity of divine substance in philosophy and Scripture (*Comm.* 12.20–25; Eng. 6).[42] He thus rejects an Arian interpretation of John 1:1 as referring to the "beginning" of the Logos, claiming that in the Scripture "the beginning" indicates something that is not preceded by anything else (*Comm.* 16.17 – 17.2, 25.1–6; Eng. 8, 12).[43] This is another example of Theodore's predilection for studying the meaning and usage of scriptural words and idioms to substantiate his hermeneutics. In a similar vein, he argues that, although elsewhere in Scripture *meltha* (Logos) does not necessarily mean hypostasis, here it clearly does (*Comm.* 21.3–8; Eng. 10). Moreover, according to Theodore, the Evangelist here intentionally avoids applying to the Logos the appellation "Son" in order not to mislead the reader with regard to his/its eternity (*Comm.* 18.4–10; Eng. 8).[44] For Theodore, not only John but also Paul, and in fact Jesus himself, expressed the same Logos-theology, which is nothing but Theodore's own version of post-Nicene theology (*Comm.* 24.25 ff; Eng. 11).[45] Theodore moreover discusses polemically, albeit in passing, the divine status of the Spirit, contested in his time by the so-called *pneumatomachoi*, those who "diminished the person of the Spirit [ܡܒܨܪܝ ܗܘܘ ܠܩܢܘܡܗ ܕܪܘܚܐ]" (*Comm.* 296:19–21, Eng. 136, commenting on John 16:12–14).[46] The Interpreter thus asserts that the Spirit, being uncreated and unique, was not included among "all things" – both visible and invisible (ܡܬܚܙܝ̈ܢ ܘܠܐ ܡܬܚܙܝ̈ܢ) – made through the Logos (John 1:3); it is united exclusively

41 Cf. Aphrahat, according to whom the world was not created via Christ (see Ruzer and Kofsky 2010:12–16).

42 Theodore's opening of his commentary with a discussion of the various meanings of "beginning" is structurally similar, *mutatis mutandis*, to Origen's opening of his commentary on John. See Origen, *Comm. on John* 1.90, ed. Preuschen 1903.

43 See also Theodore, *CH* 3, ed. Mignana 1932:41/146–147.

44 In a similar vein, Theodore asserts that Scripture uses a variety of appropriate appellations to indicate the divine nature, e.g., "our God is a consuming fire" (Heb 12:29). Cf. Jansen 2009:249, 251, 253 (Frags. 23, 25, 31).

45 Theodore appeals here to Heb 1:3. Cf. Theodore, *CH* 2–3, ed. Mingana 1932:28–29/129–130, 36/140–141.

46 See also Theodore, *CH* 1, 9, ed. Mingana 1932:23–24/127–128, 100/219–221.

with the Father and the Son (ܢܩܦ ܕܝܢ ܠܐܒܐ ܘܠܒܪܐ ܒܠܚܘܕ) (*Comm.* 26.19 – 27.30; Eng. 12–13).[47]

Arian Christology was viewed as posing three main difficulties: (1) Its Logos-sarx Christology (admittedly, not an exclusively Arian trait), in which the Logos, a created entity subject to change, replaces the human *nous* in Christ and thus denies full humanity to Christ, might impair the principle that "what is not assumed is not saved [*quod non est assumptum, non est redemptum*]"; (2) it conceives not of the true incarnation of a deity but only of the incarnation of a created, albeit heavenly, being; and (3) the concept of a tight union between the Logos and humanity in Christ raises the problem of their reciprocal influence and hence the possible transformation of both. These difficulties were compounded by the Apollinarian anti-Arian solution, according to which a divine, *non-created* Logos replaced the human *nous* in a full-union incarnation.

In response to these challenges, Diodore of Tarsus had already emphasized the essential distinction between the Logos and the *homo assumptus*.[48] This dichotomy was, in turn, perceived as problematic, and it is here that Theodore, though he generally followed Diodore's scheme, aspired to a more adequate concept of conjunction, expressed in his elaborate idea of the "dignity" of the assumed man as a divine power bestowed on him by the Logos. Theodore further develops his characteristic emphasis on the communication between the Logos and the assumed man of the Messiah through a loose conjunction due to the difference between their natures, illustrated by the union of husband and wife.[49] With him, however, this conjunction is mediated and expressed through the dignity of the Logos bestowed on and empowering the assumed man.[50] Through the conjunction with the Logos, the assumed man also participates in the other divine persons, the Father and the Spirit.[51] Through Christ, humanity will also share in this dignity.[52]

Theodore is clearly motivated by the need to repel the attempts of the Arians to violate the notion of divine transcendence. He is always motivated by a

---

47 Theodore further claims that the divine nature and essence of the Spirit were clearly acknowledged by the participants in the Nicene Council; see *CH* 9, ed. Mingana 1932:96–97/220–221.

48 See Sullivan 1956:352–360.

49 See Theodore, *CH* 8, ed. Mingana 1932:90/207; Jansen 2009:236, 244 (Frags. 3, 12).

50 See note 1 for these principles of Antiochene doctrine. See also Theodore, *CH* 3, 5, 8, ed. Mingana 1932:37, 51, 89–90; Jansen 2009:239, 245, 252 (Frags. 6, 13, 28); and Theodore, *Comm. on Colossians*, ed. Greer 2010:372–373.

51 See Jansen 2009:257 (Frag. 41).

52 Jansen 2009:240 (Frag. 7). On Theodore's anthropology in soteriological context, see Kofsky and Ruzer 2013c.

quasi-rational concern not to confuse the godhead with the creature. As a result, the closeness of the conjunction of God and man is loosened. Vis-à-vis the Arians and Apollinarians, the synthesis between the immanence and transcendence of God in Christ and in humanity is to be such that both the divinity of the Logos and the integrity of humanity in Christ are preserved.

The concept of *prosopon* plays a special part in Theodore's understanding of Christ. Theodore rejects the Logos-sarx model of incarnation and, following Didymus, advocates the Logos-anthropos scheme, with its emphasis on Christ's human soul:

> The disciples of Arius and Eunomius say that he [Christ] took a body but not a soul [ܕܦܓܪܐ ܫܩܠ ܐܡܪܝܢ ܢܦܫܐ ܕܝܢ ܠܐ ܠܡ]; the divine nature, they say, takes the place of the soul [ܐܠܐ ܚܠܦ ܢܦܫܐ ܟܝܢܐ ܠܡ ܕܐܠܗܘܬܐ]. And they lower the divine nature of the Unique [Son; ܝܚܝܕܝܐ] to the point [of saying] that he declines from his natural grandeur and performs the actions of the soul, by enclosing himself in the body and accomplishing everything to make it subsist [ܠܩܘܝܡܗ]. Consequently, if the divinity takes the place of the soul [ܕܗܘܬ ܢܦܫܐ ܡܡܠܠܐ], it [i. e., the body] had neither hunger, nor thirst, nor was it tired, nor did it have need of food; for all this happens to the body because of its weakness [ܡܚܝܠܘܬܗ] and because the soul is not equipped to satisfy the needs which it has, save according to the law of the nature [ܢܡܘܣܐ ܕܟܝܢܐ] which God has given it.[53]

Thus, according to the Arians, the Logos is combined with the body in a vital unity. According to Theodore, however, such a symbiosis contradicts Christ's true nature. If Christ was hungry and thirsty, and suffered, it could only be because the functions of life were performed by his human soul. Both body and soul, then, had to be assumed to enable the death of the body and the sins of the soul. Thus, Christ assumed a soul and by the grace of God brought it to immutability and to full dominion over the sufferings of the body.[54] The difference between this picture of Christ and that of the Logos-sarx Christology is clear. The human nature of Christ regains its real physical-human inner life and its capacity for action. The created soul provides the life for the body of Christ and is also the principle of the acts decisive for our redemption. Theodore demonstrates the activity of the assumed man against Apollinarius:

> Moreover [the divine Son] furnished his cooperation in the proposed works to the one who was assumed. Where does this [cooperation] entail that the deity had replaced the [human] *nous* [*sensus*] in him who was assumed? For it was not his wont to take the place of the

---

53 Theodore, *CH* 5, ed. Mingana 1932:55; see also ed. Tonneau (1949); translation according to Norris 1963:150. Cf. *CH* 3, ed. Mingana 1932:40–41.
54 Theodore, *CH*, ed. Mingana 1932:14 (introduction). See also Jansen 2009:241 (Frag. 7).

> *nous* ... But suppose, as you would have it, that the deity took the role of the *nous* in him who was assumed. How was he affected with fear in his suffering? Why, in the face of immediate need, did he stand in want of vehement prayers – prayers which, as the blessed Paul says, he brought before God with a loud and clamorous voice and with many tears? How was he seized with immense fear, such that he gave forth fountains of sweat by reason of his great terror?[55]

Apollinarius and Theodore both agree that redemption is achieved through the moral integrity inherent in the immutability of the spiritual principle in Christ. But while Apollinarius regards the Logos as this principle, Theodore emphasizes the enhanced human soul of Christ.[56] The human is the victor over sin and death, albeit only with God's grace. The redeeming sacrifice of Christ is now seen as an act of his "human decision."[57] When the complete humanity of Christ is thus emphasized, it is only logical that the distinction of his natures and the question of their unity have to be stressed.[58]

This loose-union Christology adheres to a single subject in Christ; but the two complete natures seem to be united only superficially, through "one *prosopon*" produced by the Logos, not as an essential *prosopon* but as one of "dignity," given to the assumed man.[59] This is apparently the channel for infusing humanity with "dignity." In other words, this conjunction is not a combination of the two natures to form a new one, but rather an equality of dignity now shared by Christ's human nature and the hypostasis of the Logos. Christ's *prosopon* is thus the ultimate expression of the close conjunction between his humanity and the hypostasis of the Logos.[60] It is also the channel through which grace operates in the spiritual development of the assumed man and his soteriological powers and acts. All this has a distinctively relativizing effect on the perception of the divine presence in the Messiah.

---

55 Theodore, *Comm. on Paul*, ed. Swete 1880, II:315; Norris 1963:204.

56 Norris 1963:186–189.

57 Theodore, *CH* 15, ed. Mignana 1933:71 ff.

58 Cf. Theodore, *CH* 11, ed. Mingana 1933:2. This distinction of natures is further exemplified in Theodore's statement that at the time of Jesus' death the Logos is separated from the assumed man yet "remains close to him"; *CH* 8, ed. Mingana 1932:87.

59 See Norris 1963:228–229.

60 On Theodore's concept of *prosopon*, see also Grillmeier 1995:433; Jansen 2009:239, 244 (Frags. 6, 12).

Revelation as Progressive Evolution

A close reading of Theodore's surviving commentaries on John and on the minor Pauline epistles reveals their salient feature, namely, the Interpreter's perception of a gradual – possibly didactically motivated – development in the unfolding of Christological truths to Jesus' followers. This concept of "progressive revelation" appears not to be limited to the issue of Christology but to function as a guiding principle in the elaboration of various key trajectories imparting divine knowledge throughout the history of salvation. The following discussion examines the rationalizing aspects of this hermeneutical strategy, applied successively to pre-incarnation sacred history, to the apostles' and disciples' cognitive development and, finally, to the gradual development of Jesus' divinely enhanced humanity.

From Biblical Past to Incarnation

According to a conception found in early Christian thought, including such prominent early Greek Christian writers as Justin, Irenaeus, Origen and Eusebius, the Logos had been revealed personally to the righteous (ܙܕܝ̈ܩܐ) – the patriarchs and prophets – in the biblical past in quasi-angelic form.[61] Theodore regards this idea as unacceptable and seems to associate it with contemporary heretical, primarily Arian, views. For him, it was only in the incarnation that the Logos was revealed hypostatically and seen, whereas God's words had earlier been conveyed through angelic intermediaries (*Comm.*18–19; Eng. 9). He invokes John 1:18 ("No one has ever seen God") as a proof that the Logos had never been directly "seen" before the incarnation (*Comm.* 42.29 – 43.6; Eng. 20). Theodore further interprets John 1:9–10 as distinguishing between the Logos's manifestation in the flesh (its "coming into the world") and its omnipresence in the world ("he was in the world") even before that, "according to his *hypostasis and his nature*" (ܒܩܢܘܡܘܬܗ ܓܝܪ ܒܪ ܘܒܟܝܢܘܬܗ, τῇ γὰρ ὑποστάσῃ ... κὰι τῇ φύσει; *Comm.* 32.3–13; Eng. 15).[62]

Theodore claims that the notion of serial pre-incarnation appearances of the Logos was widespread among John's Jewish contemporaries. What clearly under-

61 Justin Martyr, *Dialogue with Trypho*, ed. Goodspeed 1914:56; Irenaeus of Lyons, *Against Heresies* 3.11.8, 4.5.2–3, 4.7.2–4, 4.9.1, 4.10.1, ed. Rousseau et al. 1965–1982:100, 152 f, 210 f, 263 f, 293 f; Origen, *Commentary on John* 1.37, 6.17, ed. Preuschen 1903; Eusebius of Caesarea, *Eclogae Propheticae* 1.3, ed. Migne 1857; idem, *Historia Ecclestiastica* 1.2.7–8, ed. Schwartz 1903; idem, *Demonstratio Evangelica* 5.9.8, ed. Heikel 1913. See also Pines 1987. It may be worth noting that this motif is absent in Aphrahat's writings (see Ruzer and Kofsky 2010:16).

62 See also Fatica 1989.

lies his polemical strategy here is his apprehension that such a position jeopardizes the revelatory uniqueness of the incarnation event by relativizing the divine manifestation in the humanity of Christ. Theodore's staunch opposition to this view may have been influenced by an identification of this conception as rooted in Late Antique Judaism, where it prevented the Jews from accepting the revelation of the incarnation and recognizing its unique character.[63]

Nevertheless, while struggling to uphold the uniqueness of the incarnation, Theodore retains the aspect of continuity – the basic perception of the Logos as the voice proclaiming God's will (ܡܛܠ ܗܕܐ ܩܪܝܗܝ܆ ܡܠܬܐ ܐܝܟ ܡܢ ܕܡܫܘܕܥ ܠܢ ܨܒܝܢܗ ܕܐܒܐ) and as God's intermediary in his dealings with the world and humanity throughout sacred history (*Comm.* 18.20–21; Eng. 9). Theodore thus confirms that the Logos had conveyed its messages to ancient Israel, albeit indirectly, and this in turn informs his perception of the revelatory development from the biblical past to the Messiah. It seems that Theodore ascribes a similar indirectness even to the famous angelic vision of Isaiah 6, in which, he asserts, the prophet was able to perceive only the glory (ܫܘܒܚܐ, δόξα) of the triune deity, whereas the divine nature remained incomprehensible (ܟܝܢܐ ܐܠܗܝܐ ܗܘ ܕܠܐ ܡܬܕܪܟܢܐ; *Comm.* 248.10–17; Eng. 114). The revelation's oblique character in the past prevented Israel from "recognizing its Lord" (ܠܐ ܐܫܬܘܕܥܘ ܠܡܪܗܘܢ, τὸν οἰκεῖον δηοπότην; *Comm.* 32.14–15; Eng. 15). Though Theodore takes for granted the primordial hypostatic existence of the Logos, he may be retaining here an earlier restrictive concept of the pre-incarnation Logos as the voice and message of God, notably expressed by Aphrahat in the early fourth century.[64]

The Disciples' Cognitive Development

Though Theodore regards the incarnation as a direct personal revelation of the Logos in humanity and a watershed in the unfolding history of salvation, he recognizes that even Jesus' disciples were not ready fully to apprehend the divine truth of the incarnation, because of their deficient conceptual preparation. His model of the disciples' gradual enlightenment is informed by the Gospel narrative with its inherent dynamic and tension.

The *Commentary on John* provides many examples of the disciples' cognitive deficiency. During Jesus' lifetime, they thought of him in "a human way" (ܡܛܠ ܕܐܢܫܐܝܬ ܒܒܪܢܫܐ ܡܬܪܥܝܢ ܗܘܘ ܠܡܫܝ̈ܚܐ; *Comm.* 221.23–24; Eng. 102), addressing him as an

63 See the discussions in Boyarin 2003; 2004.
64 See Ruzer and Kofsky 2010:10–11.

admirable man (ܓܒܪܐ ܬܡܝܗܐ) who performed many wonders through his superior powers (ܒܡܝܬܪܘܬܗ). Theodore insists that before the crucifixion they did not have a proper understanding of Christ as "God the Logos" (ܐܠܗܐ ܡܠܬܐ; *Comm.* 224.16–21; Eng. 103).[65] For instance, faced with Jesus' cleansing of the Temple (John 2:13–19), they believed that by driving away the sellers of cattle and sheep he had merely abolished the market; had they recognized the incarnate Logos, they would have realized that what they were witnessing was in fact a new phase in salvation history and that Jesus' act "in truth ... meant that the sacrifices of dumb animals [ܚܝ̈ܘܬܐ ܚܪ̈ܫܬܐ] were to be abolished" (*Comm.* 61.29 – 62.1; Eng. 29). This is an illuminating example of how, despite his clearly stated hermeneutic preference, Theodore retains his basic propensity for literal, historically contextualized interpretation, which he ascribes here to the unaware disciples.

A rather blatant example of this propensity is found in the Interpreter's claim that the disciples, expressing their shock at Jesus' words in John 6:58, had completely misunderstood the symbolic nature of the Eucharist established by their master (*Comm.* 151; Eng. 70).[66] In light of the disciples' innate incapacity, Jesus reveals to them only partial knowledge of his powers – hinting at his "secret omniscience" (ܕܟܣܝܐ ܫܠܡܗ ܝܕܥ ܟܠ ܡܕܡ ܗܘ) – to gradually (ܒܙܒܢܐ ܗܘܐ) prepare them for eventual comprehension of his divine nature (*Comm.* 52.15–20, 273.30 – 274.1; Eng. 25, 126). According to Theodore, this didactic stratagem, addressing the widely acknowledged cognitive paradox of the incarnation, is part of a broader strategy on Jesus' part to avoid public exposure of his divinity: "Though it would have been appropriate [ܠܚܡܐ] for him to be acknowledged as God ... he nonetheless protected himself" from this impression (*Comm.* 100.29 – 101.5; Eng. 47).[67] Thus, according to the interpretation suggested in the *Commentary*, Jesus' words in John 16:28, "I *came from* the Father," are used in deference "to the human opinion about him" (ܡܣܬܒܪܢܘܬܐ ܕܗܘ ܒܢ̈ܝ ܐܢܫܐ ܣܝܡ ܗܘܘ ܠܗ) that he was only a human messenger of God, though actually the speaker here, who is the Logos dwelling in him, cannot be separated from his *communion* (ܫܘܬܦܘܬܐ) with the Father (*Comm.* 303.17–21; Eng. 140).

65 See also *Comm.* 226.15–18, 238.15–16; Eng. 104, 109.

66 Theodore's understanding of the Eucharist is further addressed in Kofsky and Ruzer 2013c. This may imply a polemical stance against a literal understanding of the Eucharist. On Theodore's views on the Eucharist in the *Comm. on John*, see Ducros 1949:366–367. For a similar polemic on the Eucharist, see Ruzer and Kofsky 2010:69–72.

67 Theodore's notion here may very well have been informed by the inherent logic of the Gospel narrative, the so-called Messianic secret, which modern scholarship discerns especially in Mark. See, e.g., Wrede 1971.

Jesus conceals the divine nature hidden within him because it is *necessary for the plan of salvation* (ܡܛܠ ܣܢܝܩܘܬܐ ܕܡܕܒܪܢܘܬܐ ܕܡܣܬܒܪܢܐ): "My time will come when I will clearly make known what I am before everyone" (ܢܗܘܐ ܠܝ ܙܒܢܐ ܐܡܬܝ، ܕܒܓܠܝܐܝܬ ܐܘܕܥ ܠܟܠܢܫ ܡܢ ܕܐܝܬܝ). This refers to Jesus' resurrection and the following events (*Comm.*155.9–14; Eng.72). Jesus is also portrayed as first demonstrating his powers in acts and only thereafter explicating certain elements of his teachings – another didactically motivated strategy based on a psychological truism (*Comm.* 194.25–28; Eng. 89).

Within this general didactic approach, according to Theodore, Jesus uses a complementary tactic, throughout his ministry and until its very end, of giving indications which, though unintelligible at the time, would be preserved by the tradition and eventually deciphered by the disciples in light of his resurrection (*Comm.* 114.1–5, 269.24 – 270.7; Eng. 53, 124). The things he said of himself (ܥܠܝܗܝܢ ܐܝܠܝܢ ܥܠ ܢܦܫܗ ܐܡܪ), especially those that would happen later, such as the resurrection, ascension and second coming, were related *allegorically* (ܒܦܠܐ̈ܬܐ) and would only then be properly understood (ܗܘ ܕܝܢ ܒܫܘܠܡܐ ܘܒܣܘܟܠܐ ... ܕܡܫܝܚܐ ܕܣܘܟܠܐ ܢܕܥܘܢ ܗܘܢ; *Comm.* 206.4–11; Eng. 94).[68] At certain key points, then, the events *experienced by the assumed man* (ܒܪܢܫܐ ܕܐܬܢܣܒ) hinted at the nature of God the *Logos, dwelling in him* (ܟܝܢܗ ܕܐܠܗܐ ܡܠܬܐ ܕܥܡܪ ܗܘܐ ܒܗ), but his dignity (ܪܒܘܬܗ) would not properly be understood before the end (*Comm.* 242–243; Eng. 111).[69] Similarly, such natural phenomena as the earthquake and the sun's eclipse (brought forth by the Logos) would be grasped as pointing to the true identity of the crucified one only after the resurrection (*Comm.* 261.21–29, 308.16–19; Eng. 120, 142). Theodore specifies further that Jesus' words in John 14:6–7 – "If you had known me, you would have known my Father also" – indicate that the disciples, at that point, like all of Jewry, did not have accurate knowledge of the Father (ܠܐܒܐ ܡܬܒܝ̈ܢ ܠܗܘܢ; *Comm.* 267.27–30; Eng. 123).

Thus, the final phase of enlightenment comes after Jesus' resurrection. Yet even then full enlightenment does not occur instantaneously; it, too, is distinguished by a gradual development. In a programmatic statement, commenting on John 20:29, Theodore highlights the key events signaling the advance of the disciples' apprehension on the way to Christological *gnosis*, which characteristically belong to the post-resurrection time: "Three times grace was given to the disciples who believed: in the mission to the gentiles, after the resurrection and

68 See also *Comm.* 266.21 – 267.9; Eng. 122.
69 Cf. *Comm.* 258.30 – 259.2; Eng. 119: "I foretell *the facts before the event* so that, *when they happen, you will know who I am.*"

at Pentecost" (ܒܬܪܥܝܬܐ ܕܠܘܬ ܡܢܝ̈ܢܐ ܘܒܬܪ ܡܫܬܥܐ ܘܡܩܘܒܠܢܘܬܐ; *Comm.* 358.12–14; Eng. 166).

Within this general outlook, Theodore emphasizes the novelty of the post-resurrection understanding granted to the disciples in contrast to their earlier cognitive deficiency: "The disciples understood nothing of what happened before his resurrection [ܕܠܐ ܡܕܡ ܡܢ ܐܝܠܝܢ ܕܡܬܥܒ̈ܕܢ ܗܘ̈ܝ ܡܕܡ ܡܣܬܟܠܐ ܡܣܬܟܠܝܢ ܗܘܘ ܬܠܡܝ̈ܕܐ] … but only received such *grace of true comprehension* [ܠܛܝܒܘܬܐ … ܕܒܐܝܕܗ ܡܕܡ ܢܕܥܘܢ ܫܪܝܪܐܝܬ, ἔτυχον χάριτος … ὡς πάντα τρανῶς εἰδέναι] after his resurrection" (*Comm.* 238.14–24; Eng. 109). This post-resurrection enlightenment would be mediated through the Holy Spirit, as intimated by Jesus' words on the future guidance of the Spirit (John 16:13) and by the traditional narrative of the descent of the Spirit in Acts 2 (*Comm.* 273.8–9; Eng. 125 – commenting on John 14:16–17). Given that the Spirit had been instrumental in the disciples' partial Christological comprehension during Jesus' lifetime, Theodore asserts its crucial role in their final doctrinal enlightenment, not "through speech but communicating to their souls the revelation of the doctrine through an ineffable mystery" (ܠܘ ܕܝܢ ܒܡܠܬܐ ܡܠܦ ܗܘܐ ܪܘܚܐ ܠܬܠܡܝ̈ܕܐ ܐܠܐ ܒܐܪܙܐ ܕܠܐ ܡܬܡܠܠ ܓܠܝܢܐ ܕܝܘܠܦܢܐ ܠܢܦܫܬܗܘܢ ܡܫܘܬܦ ܗܘܐ). This complemented the preparatory figurative sayings of the "only begotten" (ܝܚܝܕܝܐ), which they were unable to understand properly at the time, especially when he spoke about his nature (ܟܝܢܗ; *Comm.* 294.25 – 295.1; Eng. 136).[70]

Paradoxically, it is ultimately this quasi-mystical illumination that conveys elements of speculative theology to the disciples, who now receive a clear understanding of the Father – namely, that "the Father had begotten the Son from his substance [ܡܢ ܐܝܬܗ]" (*Comm.* 302.5–7; Eng. 139 – commenting on John 16:25). In other words, the disciples, John included, had learned the kernel of the Nicene outlook after Jesus' resurrection and ascension, and, similarly, they now acknowledged the post-Nicene addition that the Spirit is of the same substance (ܐܘܣܝܐ) as the Logos and the Father (*Comm.* 357.3–5; Eng. 165). Moreover, they also comprehend:

> the nature [ܟܝܢܐ] of the Father, the dignity [ܪܒܘܬܐ] of the Son, the communication of his essence [ܫܘܬܦܘܬܐ ܕܐܝܬܘܬܗ] and the perfect similarity of his nature in the divine plan [ܡܕܒܪܢܘܬܐ] worked out among humanity. [They] will also come to know the great dignity conferred upon him and the identity of the one who is in him, and what conjunction [ܢܩܝܦܘܬܐ] is between him and the one who – notwithstanding the difference of the natures [ܫܘܚܠܦܐ ܕܟܝܢ̈ܐ] – could exist in him through the power [ܚܝܠܐ] of the one who made it so. (*Comm.* 294.2–16; Eng. 135)

70 See also Ferraro 1986; Kofsky and Ruzer 2013b:181.

This passage clearly represents the essence of Theodore's or, more broadly, the Antiochene Christology, with its characteristic emphasis on the communication between the Logos and the assumed man of the Messiah through a loose conjunction due to the difference of their natures. This conjunction is mediated and expressed through the dignity of the Logos bestowed on and empowering the assumed man.[71] The disciples' enlightenment thus was not limited to the Nicene Trinitarian doctrine but further included chief aspects of Theodore's Antiochene stance.[72] It is this full theological enlightenment that transforms the humanity of the disciples, endowing them with supernatural power (ܚܝܠܐ ܕܠܥܠ ܡܢ ܟܝܢܐ) and eternal life (ܚܝܐ ܕܠܥܠܡ ζωὴν αἰώνιον; *Comm.* 308.7–12, 356.15–17; Eng. 142, 165).

Even the post-resurrection enlightenment is presented as gradual, its first stages still characterized by the disciples' incomplete knowledge. Thus, Theodore emphatically claims not only that the apostles did not know Christ perfectly before his resurrection, but that even afterwards they still had their doubts about it (ܕܐܦܠܐ ܫܠܝܚ̈ܐ ܫܠܝܡܐܝܬ ܩܕܡ ܩܝܡܬܗ ܝܕܥܝܢ ܗܘܘ ܠܡܫܝܚܐ ܐܠܐ ܕܐܦ ܡܢ ܒܬܪ ܩܝܡܬܗ ܟܠ ܡܬܦܠܓܝܢ ܗܘܘ ܒܪ̈ܥܝܢܝܗܘܢ ܥܠ ܗܕܐ ܕܗܘܐ; *Comm.* 226.15–18; Eng. 104). The almost obvious illustration of this post-resurrection cognitive deficiency is provided by the abovementioned Thomas episode in John 20:24–28, where Theodore once more exemplifies his penchant for a rational exegetical approach, highlighting logical implications of the literal understanding. Against the widespread understanding that Thomas's skepticism was a sign of weak faith, Theodore contextualizes his behavior as most realistic and adequate at this stage, since, objectively, Thomas was not yet *able* to discern the divine nature in Christ. Thus, rather than being blameworthy, Thomas becomes a legitimate representative of the whole group of Jesus' followers. Accordingly, as noted above, Thomas's exclamation in John 20:28 ("My Lord and my God") could not, in truth – contrary to prevailing exegesis – be addressed to Jesus in this early post-resurrection phase. Theodore states unequivocally that Thomas, who had just touched the body of Jesus and *had not yet been taught* that the risen one was divine, could not have been expected to call the latter "God." In exclaiming "My Lord and my God," the "doubting disciple" was merely praising God for the miracle of Jesus' bodily resurrection (*Comm.* 358.3–11; Eng. 166).[73]

---

71 For these principles of Antiochene doctrine, see above.

72 See McLeod 1999.

73 Interestingly enough, this exegetical solution still persists on the margins of modern scholarly exegesis.

Human Development in Christ

As noted, a consequence of the aspiration to safeguard the divinity of the Logos within the anti-Arian context was that another ultimate subject had to be found for the human predicates of Christ related in the Gospel account. Thus, the loose-union model employed to this end had to be complemented through its specific implementation in the idea of the human development of the *homo assumptus*, leaving the Logos unaffected and unchanged by the processes undergone by Christ's dignity-enhanced humanity. The framework of gradual progress characterizing Theodore's historical hermeneutics is finally epitomized in his concept of Jesus' own biographical development.

The quasi-scholastic question of the precise moment of the incarnation, namely, the moment of the union between the Logos and humanity, remained undetermined in Christological discourse for a long time after Theodore.[74] He seems to distinguish pre-union and post-union phases following Mary's impregnation. In the former, the Logos is present, but no union is as yet effected; in the latter – at an undefined moment of the pregnancy or at the very moment of birth – the union comes about through the mediation of the Spirit. This motif of the Spirit as the active agent in the incarnation is a traditional feature derived from its prominent place in the birth narratives of Matthew and Luke. Theodore's adaptation of this motif to the claim of a pre-union stage can be understood in the context of his overall developmental scheme and loose-union Christology, as the application of a residual sort of adoptionism to the early period of the pregnancy: "Christ-in-the-flesh, when he was not yet in his nature – namely, conjoined with God the Word – necessarily needed the mediation of the giving of the Spirit" (ܡܫܝܚܐ ܕܒܒܣܪ ܡܛܠ ܕܠܐ ܗܘܐ ܒܟܝܢܗ ܗܘܐ ܐܝܟ ܕܢܬܢܩܦ ܠܐܠܗܐ ܡܠܬܐ ܐܠܨ ܐܝܟ ܐܬܚܫܚ ܠܗ ܡܢ ܡܨܥܝܘܬܐ ܕܝܗܒܘܬܗ ܕܪܘܚܐ; *Comm*. 296.26–29; Eng. 137).

This developmental pattern continues also after the incarnation. Theodore discerns two consecutive functional modes of the Logos on the humanity in the Messiah – potential and operative. This is dictated by Theodore's insistence on full humanity as the subject of development in Christ, which had to be emphasized against Arian and Apollinarian views (*Comm*. 33–34; Eng. 16).[75] He relates the first mode, when empowerment by the Logos was not yet active, to the period between the incarnation and Jesus' anointment by the Spirit at baptism. This seems to be

74 See, e.g., Philoxenus, *Commentary on the Gospel of John* 4, pp. 9, 17, 42; Ruzer and Kofsky 2010:131.

75 See also Lorenz 1983.

the background to Theodore's fierce rejection of the apocryphal stories of Jesus' childhood miracles in the Infancy Gospels: "It is certainly foolish [ܕܫܛܝܘܬܐ] to believe that any of those events reported about our Lord during his childhood [ܒܛܠܝܘܬܗ] ever happened" (*Comm.* 59.3–12; Eng. 28).[76]

The second, operative mode is initiated by the Holy Spirit at Jesus' baptism, which is explicitly marked by Theodore as conferring the additional grace of empowerment: "The descent of the Spirit [ܡܚܬܬܗ ܕܪܘܚܐ] was not useless even for him [Christ] with regard to the conferring of grace [ܡܘܗܒܬܐ ܕܛܝܒܘܬܐ]" (*Comm.* 80.7–9; Eng. 37).[77] This grace sets in motion Jesus' public ministry, miraculous powers and moral perfection, newly acquired by virtue of his enhanced humanity: "After receiving every perfect grace [ܛܝܒܘܬܐ ܡܫܡܠܝܬܐ], which he received thanks to his anointing [ܡܫܝܚܘܬܐ], he lived a life of great integrity [ܫܦܝܘܬܐ ܡܝܬܪܬܐ ܕܕܘܒܪ̈ܐ] in a way that is not possible for human nature [ܐܝܟܢܐ ܕܟܝܢܐ ܐܢܫܝܐ ܠܐ ܡܫܟܚ ܐܬܕܒܪ]" (*Comm.* 296.29 – 297.2; Eng. 137).[78] Similarly to what Augustine would claim with regard to humanity in general, Theodore presupposes with regard to Christ a need for an additional influx of God's grace in order for him to achieve moral perfection.[79] Theodore thus appears to advocate a notion of development in Christ's human nature that reaches its perfection in the anointment by the Spirit, which becomes, in effect, the crowning stage of the incarnation. This enhanced human nature, however, is no longer an ordinary human nature: It now participates in the divine goodness (ܪܫܝܬܐ ܕܟܠܗܘܢ ܛܒܬܐ) on behalf of all humanity, which will "participate in all the things that happened to him" (*Comm.* 297.2–7; Eng. 137). This future stage of humanity is described as a "natural conjunction" (ܢܩܝܦܘܬܐ ܟܝܢܝܬܐ) with the enhanced assumed man, by way of "a small portion" (ܡܢܬܐ ܙܥܘܪܬܐ) of his grace, paralleling the full-fledged conjunction of

76 It seems, however, that in his earlier *De Incarnatione* (ed. Jansen 2009:240–243, Frags. 7–8, 11) Theodore subscribed to the slightly more conventional view that the human mental and moral development of Jesus between the incarnation and baptism was intensified under the influence of the Logos compared to other humans. Yet this development admittedly remains limited compared to the post-baptism phase.

77 See also Theodore, *CH* 7, ed. Mingana 1932:80.

78 In *De Incarnatione* (Jansen 2009:252–253, Frag. 30), Theodore, referring to the Annunciation story in Luke, remarks that the name Jesus is the appellation for the son born, whereas the title "Son of High" is the sign for the dignity empowering the *homo assumptus* in baptism to perform his messianic works. See also Theodore, *Comm. on 1 Timothy*, ed. Greer 2010:610–611.

79 See, e.g., Augustine, *De spiritu et littera* 5, ed. Bright 1914:27–29; *Ep.* 217 (to Vitalis), ed. Migne 1865b:978–989; *De correptione et gratia* 34–38, ed. Migne 1865a:936–940.

the assumed man with the Logos achieved at baptism through the Spirit (*Comm.* 298.16–18; Eng. 137).[80]

Following the internal logic of the Gospel narrative, Theodore also seeks to conceptualize in Christological terms the events of the post-resurrection stage. He thus incorporates it into his overall scheme of the progressive development of Jesus' humanity. He takes care to emphasize that the sayings in John regarding the resurrected Christ and his ascension refer to the assumed man and not to the Logos, which remains immutable – one more indication of Theodore's loose-union Christology:

> The Son of Man will ascend [ܢܣܬܠܩ] into heaven, and this is something that has never happened to anyone until now. Therefore, when he ascends, he will clearly demonstrate the *nature dwelling in him* [ܟܝܢܐ ܕܥܡܪ ܒܗ] that naturally descended without moving [ܕܢܚܬ ܠܐ ܒܫܘܢܝܐ] from any place ... He [the Logos] therefore assumed him [Jesus] into heaven [ܠܗ ܠܫܡܝܐ] as the one who must be exalted over everything. (*Comm.* 72.5–16; Eng. 34)[81]

This new glorious state of Christ's humanity is described in terms of fulfilling the potential of the dignity bestowed on it, which in turn finally allows the suspended recognition by the disciples and others of the indwelling Logos: "The dignity of the assumed man was so great that it was perceived that God dwelled in him" (ܗܟܢܐ ܗܘܬ ܪܒ ܝܩܪܗ ܕܒܪܢܫܐ ܕܐܬܢܣܒ، ܕܢܬܝܕܥ ܕܐܠܗܐ ܥܡܪ ܒܗ; *Comm.* 310.15–16; Eng. 143, with a slight change).[82] Jesus is presented as being aware of the gap between his human state and dignity and his future post-resurrection glory and dignity (*Comm.* 255.14–18; Eng. 117).

This post-resurrection enhanced human state is, moreover, perceived as derived from a *new mode of conjunction* or an even higher degree of realization of the potential of the union in incarnation. This new phase enables a stronger union with the Logos: "He [the assumed man] separated his person from other human

---

80 On the soteriological functions of Christ's humanity in Theodore, see McLeod 2005; Koch 1965. Since Theodore's elaboration of his concept of human development in Christ is conditioned by exegetical constraints, it remains fragmentary and occasionally somewhat ambiguous. However, it can safely be inferred that the fullest conjunction of incarnation in Jesus' lifetime is achieved only through the grace of the Spirit in baptism. For Theodore's notions of grace, see Dewart 1971. In *De Incarnatione* (Jansen 2009:250; Frag. 24), Theodore further asserts that the Logos brought the *homo assumptus* to perfection through suffering.
81 Cf. *Comm.* 152.9–19, Eng. 70. See also Bruns 1995; El-Khoury 1990.
82 See also the Greek fragment of the commentary to John 17:4–5: "Reveal me to them making known to them my divine nature [τὴν θείαν μου φύσιν] ... the invisible one, through which my glory is also made manifest [τὴν ἀόρατον, δι' ἧς καὶ ἡ δόξα μου γίνεται καταφανής]." Cf. Theodore, *Comm. on Philippians*, ed. Greer 2010:322–323.

beings ... by indicating that he had received a *more excellent* grace [ܦܪܝܫ ܕܝܢ ܗܢܝ ܡܘܗܒܬܗ، ܕܢܒܗܘܢ ܥܠ ܠܡܫܘܬܦܘܬܐ ܡܫܬܪܪܬܐ ܕܥܡ] through which he is joined together with God the Logos like a *real* son [ܢܩܝܦܘܬܐ ܕܥܡ ܐܠܗܐ ܡܠܬܐ ܒܕܡܘܬܗ ܕܒܪܐ ܫܪܝܪܐ]" (*Comm.* 350.19–22; Eng. 162). The upgraded conjunction finds its principal manifestation in Jesus' ascension and his newly acquired universal dominion (ܡܪܘܬܐ ܕܥܠ ܟܠ, τὴν κατὰ πάντων ἐξουσίαν; *Comm.* 306.26–30; Eng. 141).

This finally leads to the perfect conjunction (ܢܩܝܦܘܬܐ ܡܫܡܠܝܬܐ, ܓܡܝܪܐܝܬ) of Jesus with the Father, mediated through the Logos, as was proclaimed separately in advance, according to Theodore, by both Jesus and the Logos (*Comm.* 273.5–9, 271.3–4; Eng. 125, 124). This new phase of conjunction with the Father is manifested in the greater glory of the assumed man in his post-resurrection heavenly existence: "As a result of ascending to heaven, I achieve greater glory in my conjunction with the Father" (ܐܦ ܕܝܢ ܠܫܘܒܚܐ ܡܫܬܡܠܐ ܐܢܐ ܘܡܬܥܠܝܢܘܬܐ ܡܫܬܘܕܥܐ ܚܠܦ ܐܢܐ ܕܐܝܬܘܗܝ ܒܢܩܝܦܘܬܐ ܕܥܡ ܐܒܐ, δοκῶ ἐν μείζοσιν ἀναβιβάζεσθαι εἰς οὐρανοὺς ...; *Comm.* 278.19–21; Eng. 128). Theodore also indicates here the polemical implication of his position: In contradistinction to the heretics (the Arians) who exploit John 14:28 ("I go to the Father; for the Father is greater than I") to prove that the nature of the Father is greater than that of the Son-Logos, Theodore claims that Jesus referred here to the enhanced mode of conjunction of the assumed man and not to the "Logos, whose divine nature did not suffer the torment of the cross" (ܠܐ ܗܘܐ ܟܝܢܗ ܕܐܠܗܐ ܡܠܬܐ ܡܩܒܠ ܗܘܐ ܚܫܐ ܕܙܩܝܦܐ; *Comm.* 278.29 – 279.1; Eng. 128).[83]

Theodore's reiterating this perception again and again suggests that it is not only a reaction to a localized exegetical constraint but also a reflection of a core element of his outlook, one that he succinctly summarizes in the context of his comments on John 17:11:

> When our Lord wanted to put an end to that death and make humanity imperishable [ܠܐ ܡܬܚܒܠܢܘܬܐ] ... he assumed one man as the principle of all, in which God the Logos dwelled. He caused *him* to perform and endure all the things that happen to human beings while living a life of the utmost integrity ... But after he rose from the dead, he was born into another life ... as *a new imperishable man* [ܒܪ ܐܢܫܐ ܚܕܬܐ ܠܐ ܡܬܚܒܠܢܐ ܐܬܝܠܕ ܠܚܝܐ ܐܚܪܢܝܐ ܢܝܚܐ ܘܡܫܝܢܐ], and after receiving *the entire gift of the Spirit* [ܘܡܟܠ ܕܟܠܗ ܡܘܗܒܬܐ ܕܪܘܚܐ ܢܣܒ], he easily [ܕܠܐ ܠܐܝܘܬ] did all the things that were required in this world for our salvation. Since he received immortality *after his resurrection*, he [the *man*] was made Lord of all in his *conjunction* with God the Logos [ܒܢܩܝܦܘܬܗ ܕܥܡ ܐܠܗܐ ܡܠܬܐ ܡܪܐ ܕܟܠ ܗܘܐ]. (*Comm.* 313.19–30; Eng. 145)

It is apparent here and elsewhere in the *Commentary on John* that the body of the assumed man in his post-resurrection existence acquires a new physical

83 See Simonetti 1970.

mode: "he [the resurrected Jesus] had assumed forever the sublime and admirable garment of incorruptibility" (ܠܒܘܫܐ ܪܒܐ ܘܬܡܝܗܐ ܢܣܒ ܗܘܐ ܠܥܠܡ ܕܠܐ ܡܬܚܒܠܢܘܬܐ, τῷ εἰς ἀφθαρσίαν μεταχωρήσαντι σώματι; *Comm.* 347.9–11; Eng. 160).[84] This dramatic change pertains not only to his human body but also to his human soul, which now finally becomes immutable, similarly to the Logos: "[The resurrected Jesus] had received a better life in an imperishable body and an immutable soul" (ܒܦܓܪܐ ܠܐ ܡܬܚܒܠܢܐ ܘܢܦܫܐ ܠܐ ܡܫܬܚܠܦܢܝܬܐ; *Comm.* 347.4–6; Eng. 160).[85] Although the concept of imperishability is not peculiar to Theodore, it is integrated idiosyncratically into his overall scheme of a progressive upgrade of the humanity of the assumed man, resulting from the enhanced conjunction with the Logos and, correspondingly, the realization of the full potential of grace through the Holy Spirit after resurrection.[86] This further emphasizes that Jesus' humanity – body and soul – even in its dignity-enhanced state after his baptism, was not yet fully perfected.

Conclusion

Theodore of Mopsuestia stands out as a prominent representative of the Antiochene tradition's general predilection for literal, historical-grammatical interpretation of Scripture. This contextualizing approach, which in Theodore's case is pointedly applied not only to the Old but also to the New Testament, may be branded as rationalistic hermeneutics. The present study has identified some important implications of Theodore's underlying critical logic for his exegetical strategies, attested especially in his New Testament commentaries. Furthermore, it has shown that for Theodore these strategies are characteristically integrated into his overall scheme of low loose-union Christology, which emphasizes the

---

84 See also *Comm.* 350.5–8; Eng. 162; *CH* 15, ed. Mingana 1933:75. The new mode of bodily existence in immortal nature renders material nutrition superfluous; hence, Theodore explicates Jesus' post-resurrection meal with the disciples as a mere didactic stratagem tailored to strengthen the disciples' belief in his bodily resurrection (*ibid.*:78). In his *Comm. on 1 Timothy*, Theodore spells out that in the ascension Christ was made "clearly visible" (*perspicuus*) to the angels (ed. Greer 2010:612–613).

85 See also Theodore, *CH* 5, 8, ed. Mingana 1932:60, 85; *Comm. on Ephesians*, ed. Greer 2010:190–191. In *CH* 14, Theodore specifies that although the assumed man did not sin during his lifetime, he only became immune to sin with the acquisition of incorruptibility in the resurrection (ed. Mingana 1933:67).

86 On the earlier history of the concept of incorruptibility, see de Andia 1986; Athanasius, *De Incarnatione* 7.5, 20.2, ed. Migne 1857:cols. 109A, 132A.

humanity of Christ and is elaborately adapted to the needs of constructing a coherent Christological logic in the face of the challenges of the time, posed particularly by Arianism and Apollinarianism.

As part of his Christological hermeneutics and in accordance with his penchant for historical contextualization, Theodore advances a model of progressive evolutionary revelation or, in other words, his own version of *praeparatio evangelica*. We have indicated the centrality of the concept of progressive development as a core hermeneutical principle grounded in the Interpreter's theological outlook. We have further argued that Theodore applied his development-centered interpretation to a variety of central issues in the Gospel narrative – both to Israel's sacred history and, idiosyncratically, to the post-incarnation period. The latter is likewise distinguished by gradual disclosure of Christological truths, as the disciples' initial cognitive deficiency is progressively mended.

Moreover, the general framework of gradual development is not limited to progressive revelation but is finally epitomized in Theodore's conception of Jesus' own biographical development – more precisely, in his conception of the mode of union in the incarnation. Following the logic of the Gospel narrative, Theodore seeks to conceptualize in Christological terms not only the core events of Jesus' life but also those of the post-resurrection stage, incorporating them into his overall scheme of the progressive development of Jesus' humanity, apparently confronting the Logos-sarx Christology of his opponents.

Theodore's bold and consistent portrait of Christ's development and gradual realization of the dignity potential, or, in other words, the postponement of his full divinization to beyond the limits of his lifetime, seems unprecedented, and it is indicative of Theodore's original genius, recruited to the polemics of his time. This underlying development leitmotif appears to be a radical expression of Theodore's rationalistic hermeneutics employed within the constraints of contemporary theological discourse.

References

Works by Theodore of Mopsuestia

CH, ed. Mingana = *Commentary of Theodore of Mopsuestia on the Nicene Creed* (= *Catechetical Homilies* 1–10), ed. A. Mingana. 1932 (Woodbrooke Studies, 5); *Commentary of Theodore of Mopsuestia on the Lord's Prayer and on the Sacraments of Baptism and the Eucharist* (= *Catechetical Homilies* 11–16), ed. Mignana. 1933 (Woodbrooke Studies, 6). Cambridge: Cambridge University Press.

CH, ed. Tonneau = *Catechetical Homilies*, ed. and French transl. by R. Tonneau. 1949. Vatican City: Bibliotecca Apostolica Vaticana.

Comm. = *Commentary on John*, ed. and Latin transl. by J.M. Vosté. 1940 (CSCO Scriptores Syri 4.3). Louvain: Ex Officina Orientali. Greek fragments: see Devreese 1948:305–419. English transl. of the Greek fragments: see Kalantzis 2004.
Comm., Eng. = *Commentary on the Gospel of John*, ed. Joel Elowsky and English transl. by M. Conti. 2010. Downers Grove, IL: InterVarsity Press.
Comm. on Colossians, Ephesians, Philippians, Timothy = *Theodore of Mopsuestia: Commentary on the Minor Pauline Epistles*, ed. Rowan A. Greer. 2010. Atlanta: SBL.
Comm. on Habakkuk = *Commentary on Habakkuk*, ed. J.P. Migne. 1864 (PG 66). Paris: Imprimerie Catholique.
Comm. on Paul = *Theodori Episcopi Mopsuesteni in Epistolas B. Pauli Commentarii*, ed. h. B. Swete. 1880. Cambridge: University Press.
Comm. on Psalms = *Commentary on Psalms*, ed. R. Devreese. 1939. Vatican City: Bibliotecca Apostolica Vaticana.
Comm. on Zephaniah = *Commentary on Zephaniah*, ed. J.P. Migne. 1864 (PG 66). Paris: Imprimerie Catholique.
De incarnatione – see Jansen 2009.

Other Works

Abramowsky, Luise. 1961. "Zur Theologie Theodors von Mopsuestia." *Zeitschrift für Kirchengeschicte*, 72:263–293.
de Andia, Ysabel. 1986. *Homo vivens: Incorruptibilité et divinisation de l'homme selon Irénée de Lyon*. Paris: Etudes Augustiniennes.
Athanasius. *De Incarnatione*, ed. J.P. Migne. 1857 (PG 25). Paris: Imprimerie Catholique.
Augustine. *St. Augustine: De spiritu et littera*, ed. W. Bright. 2014. London: Clarendon Press.
—. *De correptione et gratia*, ed. J.P. Migne. 1865a (PL 44). Paris: Garnier fratres.
—. *Epistolae*, ed. J.P. Migne. 1865b (PL 33). Paris: Garnier fratres.
Barnes, Michel R., *and* Daniel H. *Williams (eds.). 1993. Arianism after Arius*. Edinburgh: T. & T. Clark.
Beeley, Christopher A. 2011. "The Early Christological Controversy: Apollinarius, Diodore, and Gregory Nazianzen." *Vigiliae Christianae*, 65:376–407.
Böhm, Thomas. 1991. *Die Christologie des Arius: Dogmengeschichtliche Überlegungen unter besonderer Berücksichtigung der Hellenisierungsfrage*. St. Ottilien: EOS.
—. 2006. "The Exegesis of Arius: Biblical Attitude and Systematic Formation." In Charles Kannengiesser (ed.), *Handbook of Patristic Exegesis: The Bible in Ancient Christianity*. Leiden: Brill. 687–705.
Boyarin, Daniel. 2003. *Sparks of the Logos: Essays in Rabbinic Hermeneutics*. Leiden: Brill.
—. 2004. *Border Lines: The Partition of Judaeo-Christianity*. Philadelphia: University of Pennsylvania Press.
Bruns, Peter. 1995. *Den Menschen mit dem Himmel verbinden: Eine Studie zu den Katechetischen Homilien des Theodor von Mopsuestia*. Leuven: Peeters.
Buytaert, Éloi Marie. 1949. *L'héritage littéraire d'Eusèbe d'Émèse: Étude critique et historique*. Louvain: Bureaux du Muséon.
Devreese, Robert. 1948. *Essai sur Théodore de Mopsueste*. Vatican: Biblioteca Apostolica Vaticana.

Dewart, Joanne McWilliam. 1971. *The Theology of Grace of Theodore of Mopsuestia*. Washington, DC: Catholic University of America Press.
Diodore of Tarsus, *Commentarii in Psalmos*, ed. J.M Olivier (CCG 6). 1980. Turnhout: Brepols.
—. *Commentary on Psalms 1–51*, English transl. by R.C. Hill. 2005. Atlanta: Society of Biblical Studies.
Ducros, Xavier. 1949. "L'eucharistie chez Théodore de Mopsueste d'après son commentaire sur l'évangile selon saint Jean." *Actes du XXIe congrès international des orientalistes, Paris, 23–31 juillet 1948*. Paris: Imprimerie Nationale. 366–375.
El-Khoury, Nabil. 1990. "Der Mensch als Gleichnis Gottes: Eine Untersuchung zur Anthropologie des Theodor von Mopsuestia." *Oriens Christianus*, 74:62–71.
Eusebius of Caesarea. *Eclogae Propheticae*, ed. J.P. Migne. 1857 (PG 22). Paris: Imprimerie Catholique.
—. *Historia Ecclesiastica*, Book I, ed. E. Schwartz. 1903. In *Eusebius Werke*, II (GCS). Leipzig: Hinrichs.
—. *Demonstratio Evangelica*, ed. i. A. Heikel. 1913. In *Eusebius Werke*, VI (GCS). Leipzig: Hinrichs.
Fatica, Luigi. 1989. "Il commento di Teodoro di Mopsuestia a Giovanni, 1, 1–18." *Koinonia*, 13:65–78.
Ferraro, Giuseppe. 1986. "L'esposizione dei testi pneumatologici nel commento di Teodoro di Mopsuestia al Quarto Vangelo." *Gregorianum*, 67:265–295.
Flusser, David. 2001. *Jesus*. Jerusalem: Magnes.
Galtier, Paul. 1957. "Theodore de Mopsueste: Sa vraie pensé sur l'incarnation." *Recherches de science religieuse*, 45:161–186, 338–360.
Genesis rabba, ed. J. Theodor and C. Albeck. 1965. Jerusalem: Wahrmann.
Greer, Rowan A. 1966. "The Antiochene Christology of Diodore of Tarsus." *Journal of Theological Studies*, 17:327–341.
— (ed.). 2010. *Theodore of Mopsuestia: Commentary on the Minor Pauline Epistles*. Atlanta: SBL.
Gregg, Robert C., and Dennis E. *Groh*. 1981. *Early Arianism: A View of Salvation*. Philadelphia: Fortress.
Grillmeier, Aloys. 1975. *Christ in Christian Tradition*, I. London: A.R. Mowbray.
—. 1995. *Christ in Christian Tradition*, II, part 2. London: A.R. Mowbray.
Hanson, Richard Patrick Crosland. 1988. *The Search for the Christian Doctrine of God: The Arian Controversy 318–381*. Edinburgh: T. & T. Clark.
Hill, Robert Charles. 2004. "His Master's Voice: Theodore of Mopsuestia on the Psalms." *Heythrop Journal*, 45:40–53.
—. 2005a. "Diodore of Tarsus as Spiritual Director." *Orientalia Christiana Periodica*, 71:413–430.
—. 2005b. *Reading the Old Testament in Antioch*. Leiden: Brill.
Irenaeus of Lyons. *Against Heresies*, ed. A. Rousseau, L. Doutreleau, B. Hemmerdinger and C. Mercier. 1965–1982. Paris: Éditions du Cerf.
Jansen, Till. 2009. *Theodor von Mopsuestia: De incarnatione – Überlieferung und Christologie der griechischen und lateinischen Fragmente einschließlich Textausgabe*. Berlin: De Gruyter.
Justin Martyr. *Dialogue with Trypho*, ed. E.J. Goodspeed. 1914. Göttingen: Vandenhoeck and Ruprecht.
Kannengiesser, Charles. 1983. "Arius and the Arians." *Theological Studies*, 44:456–475.
Koch, Günter. 1965. *Die Heilsverwirklichung bei Theodor von Mopsuestia*. Munich: Hueber.

Kofsky, Aryeh. 2013. "Theology and Hermeneutics among Syriac Christianity, Greek Christianity and Contemporaneous Judaism (4th–5th Centuries): Paradigms of Interactions." *Orientalia Christiana Analecta*, 293:75–90.

Kofsky, Aryeh, and Serge Ruzer. 2013a. "Shaping Christology in a Hermeneutical Context: Theodore of Mopsuestia's Endeavor in Face of Contemporaneous Challenges." *Adamantius*, 19:256–275.

—. 2013b. "Theodore of Mopsuestia on Progressive Revelation and Human Development in Christ." *Revue biblique*, 120:570–595.

—. 2013c. "Anthropology and Soteriology in Theodore of Mopsuestia's *Commentary on John*." *Annali di storia dell' esegesi*, 30:63–78.

—. 2014. "Theodore of Mopsuestia's Hermeneutics: Transformed Theology in Response to Fourth-Century Crises." *Vox Patrum*, 34:221–238.

Leontius of Byzantium. *Deprehensio et triumphus super Nestorianos*, ed. J.P. Migne. 1865 (PG 86a). Paris: Imprimerie Catholique.

Lietzmann, Hans. 1904. *Apollinaris von Laodicea und seine Schule: Texte und Untersuchungen*. Tübingen: Mohr.

Lorenz, Rudolf. 1983. "Die Christusseele im Arianischen Streit: Nebst einigen Bemerkungen zur Quellenkritik des Arius und zur Glaubwürdigkeit des Athanasius." *Zeitschrift für Kirchengeschichte*, 94:1–51.

McLeod, Frederick G. 1999. *The Image of God in the Antiochene Tradition*. Washington, DC: Catholic University of America Press.

—. 2005. *The Roles of Christ's Humanity in Salvation: Insights from Theodore of Mopsuestia*. Washington, DC: Catholic University of America Press.

—. 2009. *Theodore of Mopsuestia*. London–New York: Routledge.

Merkel, Helmut. 1971. *Die Widersprüche zwischen den Evangelien: Ihre polemische und apologetische Behandlung in der Alten Kirche bis zu Augustin*. Tübingen: Mohr Siebeck.

Nassif, Bradley. 1993. "The 'Spiritual Exegesis' of Scripture: The School of Antioch Revisited." *Anglican Theological Review*, 70:437–470.

—. 1996. "'Spiritual Exegesis' in the School of Antioch." In idem (ed.), *New Perspectives on Historical Theology: Essays in Memory of John Meyendorff*. Grand Rapids: Eerdmans. 343–377.

Norris, Richard Alfred. 1963. *Manhood and Christ: A Study in the Christology of Theodore of Mopsuestia*. Oxford: Clarendon Press.

O'Keefe, John. J. 2000. "'A Letter that Killeth': Toward a Reassessment of Antiochene Exegesis; or Diodore, Theodore, and Theodoret on the Psalms." *Journal of Early Christian Studies*, 8:88–104.

Origen. *Commentary on John*, ed. E. Preuschen. 1903. Berlin: De Gruyter.

Petit, F., L. van Rompay and J.J.S. Weitenberg (eds.). 2011. *Eusèbe d'Émèse: Commentaire de la Genèse*. Leuven: Peeters.

Pines, Shlomo. 1987. "God, Glory and Angels According to a Second-Century Theology." *Jerusalem Studies in Jewish Thought*, 6:1–14. Hebrew.

Rondeau, Marie-Josèphe. 1969–1970. "Le 'Commentaire des Psaumes' de Diodore de Tarse et l'exégèse antique du Psaume 109/10." *Revue d'histoire des religions*, 176:5–33, 153–188; 177:5–33.

—. 1982. *Les commentaires patristiques du Psautier*. Rome: Pont. Institutum Studiorum Orientalium.

Ruzer, Serge, and Aryeh Kofsky. 2010. *Syriac Idiosyncrasies: Theology and Hermeneutics in Early Syriac Literature*. Leiden: Brill.

Schäublin, Christoph. 1974. *Untersuchungen zu Methode und Herkunft der antiochenischen Exegese*. Cologne–Bonn: Hanstein.

—. 1988. "Die antiochenische Exegese des Alten Testaments." In Damaskinos Papandreou (ed.), *L'Ancien Testament dans l'église*. Chambésy: Éditions du Centre orthodoxe du Patriarcat oecuménique. 115–128.

Schweizer, Eduard. 1949. "Diodor als Exeget." *Zeitschrift für die neutestamentliche Wissenschaft*, 40:33–75.

Simonetti, Manlio. 1970. "Giovanni 14:28 nella controversia ariana." In Patrick Granfield and Josef A. Jungmann (eds.), *Kyriakon: Festschrift Johannes Quasten*, I. Münster: Aschendorff. 151–161.

—. 2006. "Theodore of Mopsuestia." In Charles Kannengiesser (ed.), *Handbook of Patristic Exegesis: The Bible in Ancient Christianity*. Leiden: Brill. 799–828.

Smitmans, Adolf. 1966. *Das Weinwunder von Kana: Die Auslegung von Jo 1,2–11 bei den Vätern und heute*. Tübingen: Mohr.

Spoerl, Kelley McCarthy. 1994. "Apollinarian Christology and the Anti-Marcellan Tradition." *Journal of Theological Studies*, 43:545–568.

Sullivan, Francis Aloysius. 1956. *The Christology of Theodore of Mopsuestia*. Rome: Pontificia Università Gregoriana.

Ter Haar Romeny, R. Bas. 1997. *A Syrian in Greek Dress: The Use of Greek, Hebrew and Syriac Biblical Texts in Eusebius of Emesa's Commentary on Genesis*. Leuven: Peeters.

Thome, Felix. 2004. *Historia contra Mythos: Die Schriftauslegung Diodors von Tarsus und Theodors von Mopsuestia im Widerstreit zu Kaiser Julians und Salustius' allegorischem Mythenverständnis*. Bonn: Borengässer.

—. 2008. *Studien zum Johanneskommentar des Theodor von Mopsuestia* (Bonn: Borengässer.

van Rompay, Lucas. 1997. "Antiochene Biblical Interpretation: Greek and Syriac." In Judith Frishman and Lucas van Rompay (eds.), *The Book of Genesis in Jewish and Oriental Christian Interpretation*. Louvain: Peeters. 103–123.

Wayman, Benjamin D. 2014. *Diodore the Theologian: Πρόνοια in his Commentary on Psalms 1–50*. Turnhout: Brepols.

Wickert, Ulrich. 1962. *Studien zu den Pauluscommentaren Theodors von Mopsuestia als Beitrag zum Verständnis der antiochenischen Theologie*. Berlin: Alfred Töpelmann.

Williams, Rowan. 1983. "The Logic of Arianism." *Journal of Theological Studies*, 34:56–81.

Winn, Robert E. 2011. *Eusebius of Emesa: Church and Theology in the Mid-Fourth Century*. Washington, D.C.: Catholic University of America.

W. Wrede, William. 1971. *The Messianic Secret* (English transl. by J.C.G. Greig). Cambridge: Clarke.

Zaharopoulos, Dimitri. Z. 1989. *Theodore of Mopsuestia on the Bible: A Study of his Old Testament Exegesis*. New York: Paulist Press.

Yonatan Moss

"I Trapped You with Guile": Rationalizing Theology in Late Antiquity

"[W]e only rationalize things that are disturbing and important.
Our rationalizations are our personal mythologies."
Phillips 2012:ix

Introduction: Cognitive Dissonance after Chalcedon

Some time in the late 630s, a precocious young monk by the name of Anastasius travelled from St. Catherine's Monastery in Sinai to Alexandria in order to participate in a series of public debates about the nature of Jesus.[1] The question at stake, over which devout Christians had been arguing passionately for more than two hundred years, was whether Christ had one or two natures. When he walked on this earth, did Jesus comprise two natures – one human, one divine – or was his nature singular? The issue had been determined in 451, at a large, imperially sponsored ecclesiastical council in Chalcedon, in favor of the two-nature (Diphysite) position. But many Christians, particularly in the eastern provinces of the empire, refused to accept the Chalcedonian definition of the faith and zealously upheld a one-nature (Miaphysite) Christology. The question long remained a burning issue for masses of believers.

In Alexandria, Anastasius, himself a dedicated Chalcedonian, debated John of Zyga and Gregory of Nystazon, two leaders of the city's Miaphysite community, whom Anastasius dubs "Theodosians," after the city's influential sixth-century Miaphysite patriarch.[2] Looking back as an old man in the Egyptian desert, probably some fifty years after the debates took place, Anastasius described the events in his *Hodegos* (Guide along the right path), a theological handbook for the Diphysite polemicist.[3] The elderly monk offered the following account of his actions leading up to one of the debates:

1 For the dating of the debates and an assessment of Anastasius, see Richard 1958:34.
2 On Theodosius see Van Roey and Allen 1994; Grillmeier and Hainthaler 1995:53–59; and see below.
3 Anastasius is thought to have composed the work in its present form in the late 680s on the basis of a series of accounts that he had written earlier in his career. See Richard 1958:32, Uthemann 1981:ccxi–ccxii, ccxviii.

https://doi.org/10.1515/9783110446395-008

> [H]aving heard a few days before the debate that the Theodosians had sent for John and Gregory, their top leaders, to face us, I sat down and composed a dogmatic tome as if in the name of Flavian, the bishop of Constantinople who was murdered by Dioscorus for confessing in Christ two indivisibly united natures in one composite hypostasis.[4] In this tome I preserved, as it were, the aim and meaning of the holy fathers with all precision; I did, however, slightly change their expressions into certain other, synonymous phrases. Thus, for example, in place of "form" I put "essence," and in place of "earthy" I put "earthborn," and in place of "suffering" I put "cross." I did this in order to demonstrate to all that it is on hateful and quarrelsome grounds, rather than out of the love of truth, that they oppose the Council of Chalcedon, the blessed Flavian, and St. Leo's *Tome*.[5]

Convinced that the Miaphysite objections to Chalcedon were at root more political than theological, Anastasius devised a clever ruse to expose his opponents' true colors.[6] He assembled a string of quotations from theologians of the fourth and fifth centuries, such as Basil of Caesarea, Gregory of Nazianzen and Cyril of Alexandria, who were all considered authoritative by Diphysites and Miaphysites alike. He concealed the sources of these passages and, in the manner of most plagiarists, slightly altered certain phrases so as to make them not immediately recognizable to his audience.[7] He then presented the passages as all stemming from the pen of the mid-fifth-century patriarch of Constantinople, Flavian, in a letter allegedly written to Leo of Rome. Since it was Leo's letter to Flavian, his so-called *Tome*, which lay at the foundation of the Chalcedonian definition, Ana-

4 Dioscorus of Alexandria was condemned at the Council of Chalcedon for having convened a council at Ephesus in 449 that pushed a Miaphysite agenda and deposed and exiled the Diphysite Flavian of Constantinople, ultimately causing the latter's death. Anastasius goes on to explain that he pretended that Flavian had sent this epistle to Leo of Rome, another stalwart Diphysite. It was upon the latter's *Tome*, addressed to Flavian, that the Council of Chaledon based its definition of faith.

5 Anastasius, ed. Uthemann 1981:181–182 (10.2.7.51–66): [Π]ρὸ μικρῶν ἡμερῶν τῆς διαλέξεως ἀκούσας, ὅτι τοὺς ἀκρέμονας καὶ ἐξάρχους αὐτῶν μετεστείλαντο – λέγω δὴ τὸν Ἰωάννην καὶ Γρηγόριον – οἱ Θεοδοσιανοὶ πρὸς τὸ ἡμῖν παρατάξασθαι, καθεσθεὶς συντέταχα τόμον δογματικὸν ὡς ἐξ ὀνόματος Φλαβιανοῦ τοῦ ἐπισκόπου Κωνσταντινουπόλεως τοῦ φονευθέντος ὑπὸ Διοσκόρου διὰ τὸ ὁμολογεῖν ἐν Χριστῷ δύο ἡνωμένας ἀδιαιρέτως φύσεις ἐν μιᾷ συνθέτῳ ὑποστάσει. Ἐν ᾧ τόμῳ τὸν μὲν σκοπὸν καὶ τὸ φρόνημα τῶν ἁγίων πατέρων μετὰ πολλῆς τινος τῆς ἀκριβείας ἐφύλαξα, μικρὸν δὲ τὰς αὐτῶν ῥήσεις δι' ἑτέρων τινῶν ἰσοδυνάμων λέξεων ὑπαλλάξας τέθηκα, οἷον ἀντὶ «μορφῆς» «οὐσίαν» καὶ ἀντὶ «χοϊκοῦ» «γηγενὲς» καὶ ἀντὶ «πάθους» «σταυρόν», πρὸς τὸ δεῖξαι πᾶσιν, ὅτι ἐχθρωδῶς καὶ ἀντιπαθῶς, ἀλλ' οὐ φιλαλήθως ἐναντιοῦνται τῇ συνόδῳ Χαλκηδόνος καὶ τῷ μακαρίῳ Φλαβιανῷ καὶ τῷ Τόμῳ τοῦ ἁγίου Λέοντος. Translations here and throughout are my own unless indicated otherwise.

6 In addition to the above-quoted passage, see further the preceding and following passages: Anastasius, ed. Uthemann 1981:180–181, 182 (10.2.7.26–45, 66–70).

7 *Ibid.*:183–187 (10.2.7.83–160).

stasius knew that his opponents would heap curses upon any text associated with the names of these two bishops.[8]

The result of his ruse, according to Anastasius's own telling, was nothing short of spectacular. The anti-Chalcedonian leaders, John and Gregory, failed to recognize that the passages presented to them as the work of a man they considered an arch-heretic were in fact authored by many of their greatest heroes. Anastasius was able to induce his adversaries to anathematize the church fathers revered by them and him alike, and, more importantly, he thereby was able to prove that their hatred of two-nature Christology was more about the people associated with the idea than the idea itself. As a result, the audience gathered to witness the event nearly stoned Anastasius's adversaries.[9]

Nevertheless, while Anastasius – if he is to be taken at his word – scored a victory in the battle against his opponents, anyone reading other parts of his *Hodegos* is left deeply puzzled by the whole affair. Even the most cursory reading of the work reveals that one of the author's most oft-repeated lines of attack is the claim that the anti-Chalcedonians falsify patristic texts.[10] More specifically, Anastasius accuses his opponents of engaging in the same two forms of forgery that he proudly proclaims to have practiced himself. In the first instance, he claims that certain works that the anti-Chalcedonians cite as foundational to their one-nature theology were in fact written by radical Miaphysite theologians who deceitfully fathered them onto earlier patristic authorities.[11] This is hardly different from Anastasius's own act of fabricating the letter he claimed to have been written by Flavian. In addition to the accusations of full-fledged forgeries, Anastasius frequently censures his opponents for doctoring known patristic texts to suit their theological claims.[12] Is this not what Anastasius himself does

8 To anti-Chalcedonians, Leo's *Tome* was a metonymy for Chalcedon. See, e.g., the trial by fire involving the *Tome* described in John Rufus's anti-Chalcedonian tract *Plerophoria* (early sixth century), ed. Nau 1912:98; and see the discussion of this episode in Moss 2016b:119–120.
9 Anastasius, ed. Uthemann 1981:188 (10.2.7.160–173).
10 See, e.g., *ibid.*:188–189 (10.2.7.176–206), where Anastasius accuses the followers of Severus in Alexandria of consciously falsifying (φαλσεύοντες) the writings of the fathers, especially those of Cyril of Alexandria, by rewriting various statements that could be read as supportive of the doctrine of two natures. See also *ibid.*:8 (1.1.27–34), where Anastasius casts doubt on the whole procedure of demonstration by proof-text, because "passages can be corrupted" and "whenever you cite a proof-text to your opponent, he will immediately cite another proof-text, whether he be a heretic or a Jew."
11 *Ibid.*:143 (10.1.1.1–9), regarding proof-texts the Miaphysites wrote in the name of Cyril of Alexandria.
12 *Ibid.*:202 (12.1.9–20), 297–299 (22.3.18–70), 95–98 (6.1.31–106). In the last case, Anastasius compares Severus of Antioch's philological treatment of the fathers to Aquila's "Judaizing" Greek translation of Hebrew Scripture.

to the works of Basil, Cyril, John Chrysostom and others to make his point? It is no wonder that the Australian scholar of post-Chalcedonian theology, Pauline Allen, has labeled Anastasius's action here "freakish," describing it as "fighting fire with fire."[13]

Yet Anastasius himself sensed the self-contradictory nature of his actions. In an explanatory comment added to the text toward the end of his life, he implicitly admits the problematic nature of his forgery and attempts to defend it.[14]

> Scholion: We have narrated this affair so that the [Chalcedonian] scholars could employ the same method against their adversaries; after all, even the blessed Paul knew how to employ this kind of method; that is why he said to some: "I trapped you with guile" [2 Cor. 12:16].

Realizing the dishonest and inconsistent nature of his ruse, Anastasius appeals to the authority of the apostle known for his variability.[15] In the quoted sentence from the Second Letter to the Corinthians, Paul might indeed seem, at first blush, to encourage deceit in certain circumstances. Nevertheless, a closer examination of the sentence in its context reveals that Anastasius attributes to Paul an idea that is diametrically opposed to what Paul meant, or at least to what the exegetical tradition prior to Anastasius had taken him to mean.[16] In the letter, Paul fends off accusations leveled at him by some of the Corinthians that he had monetarily taken advantage of them. After addressing the accusation of direct misappropriation of their funds, he moves on in the verse in question to counter a further accusation of indirect appropriation. His accusers say that he has trapped them with guile: they claim that although he takes nothing himself, he sends his disciples to

---

13 Allen 1982:300–301, on the basis of the observations in Anastasius, ed. Uthemann 1981:8, at 1.1.29–30 ("Etsi ualde uituperat haereticos, ipse tomum Flauiani ad Leonem Magnum finxit"). See also Speyer 1971:96–97.

14 Anastasius, ed. Uthemann 1981:182 (10.2.7.76–79): Σχόλιον. Ταῦτα ἐκτιθέμεθα, ἵνα τῷ αὐτῷ τρόπῳ κέχρηνται οἱ φιλόπονοι κατὰ τῶν ἐναντίων. Ἐπεὶ καὶ ὁ μακάριος Παῦλος οἶδε τῷ τοιούτῳ τρόπῳ χρήσασθαι· διὸ καὶ ἔλεγε πρός τινας, ὅτι *Δόλῳ ὑμᾶς ἔλαβον.*

15 For the theme of Pauline variability and adaptability, see 1 Cor. 9:19–23 and Glad 2003. See further Anastasius, ed. Uthemann 1981:143 (10.1.1.26), for a similar defense, on the basis of Ps. 18:26 (17:27): "with the crooked, act crookedly"; and *ibid.*:193 (10.4.17): "We say this cunningly and not according to the truth" (πανούργως καὶ οὐ κατὰ ἀλήθειαν λέγομεν ταῦτα).

16 For the exegetical tradition of this verse, see, e.g., John Chrisostom, ed. Migne 1862 (PG 61):589 (*Homily* 27 on 2 Cor., 4); Theodoret of Cyrus, ed. Migne 1864:452 (*Commentary* on 2 Cor., *ad loc.*); and Cramer 1841:436. Speyer 1971:96 hints that Anastasius misinterpreted this verse: "beruft er sich missbräuchlich auf das Wort des Paulus."

collect money from them, which he then cunningly appropriates.[17] In the passage that follows Paul fends off this accusation as well.

Although this is the interpretation that best suits the letter's overall context, and it was universally proffered in the early church, as also in modern commentaries, Anastasius's reading of the verse is indeed possible on a literal level. But was this reading worth it, if the price was casting Paul as a swindler?

What induced Anastasius to forge a text, plagiarize from venerated authorities, twist the meaning of a biblical verse in the face of tradition and besmirch the apostle's morals? I submit that precisely the same post-Chalcedonian theological intellectual-cultural climate that encouraged the Sinaite monk to accuse others of forging patristic texts led him to engage in similar actions himself.[18] The Christological questions that occupied the minds of theologians leading up to and following the Council of Chalcedon were matters of technical philosophical debate that had not been entertained as such in Scripture or even in the works of Christian writers in earlier centuries. Nevertheless, the culture of theological debate from the fifth century onward was such that all arguments had to be founded on these earlier writings.[19] These texts were granted absolute, divinely inspired authority, and they were not allowed to contradict one another or say anything that would go against the arguments of a contemporary theologian.

Yet, composed at different times over a long period and in different parts of the Christian world, the writings of the Church Fathers, no less than the disparate documents that came to constitute Christian scripture, were riddled with inconsistencies and contradictions. All Christian theologians in the post-Chalcedonian period, on both sides of the Chalcedonian divide, thus operated in a constant state of cognitive dissonance, between what they wished the authoritative texts said and what, as they must on some level have realized, these texts said in reality.[20]

---

17 The modern interpretation of this verse follows the ancient one. See, e. g., Plummer 1915:363: "He is, of course, quoting his critics' estimate of him." The Revised Standard Version inserts the words "you say."

18 Besides Flavian's *Letter* to Leo, which Anastasius admits to having forged for polemical purposes, he seems to have forged at least one other text. See Uthemann 1981:ccxvi, note 61; and *ibid.*:300, note on 9.69, where it is convincingly argued (against Abramowski 1957:55–60) that Anastasius fabricated a text in the name of Andreas of Samosata.

19 See Gray 1982, 1989, 1996, 1997, 2006:25–28; and Graumann 2002.

20 See Gray 1982:66–70. Elsewhere, Gray (1997:196) writes of "the age's repressed, subconscious or semi-conscious tension about its reconstruction of the religious past in its struggle to achieve conformity."

Cognitive dissonance, a psychological term, might initially appear irrelevant to the study of theology in late antiquity.[21] However, bearing in mind the intensely personal nature of late ancient theological engagement, it makes sense to view it from a psychological angle. What we know about theology in this period we know thanks to texts that more often than not were written from a very subjective perspective. These texts do not come in the form of abstract creeds, but rather of letters addressed to particular people or tracts drafted in response to specific occasions, in which personal motives and tempers figure prominently alongside intellectual ideas and logical arguments. Even when it comes to the church councils, those for which we have surviving acts demonstrate that the discussions, far from being detached and objective, were strongly colored by passion, ambition and manipulation.[22]

When students of religion employ the term "rationalization" as an analytical category, it is usually in the sociological sense developed by Max Weber.[23] However, in the same years that Weber was developing his notion of the social rationalization that he thought characterized the modern age, Freud and his followers were using the same word to identify the psychological defense mechanisms used in everyday life.[24] Following the lead of Leon Festinger, general and social psychologists have fruitfully employed the term "rationalization" to understand the processes at play in the resolution of cognitive dissonances on both the individual and the group level.[25] Given both the personal nature of late ancient theological writing generally, and the specific cognitive dissonances involved in the absolutist post-Chalcedonian reliance on the authority of the fathers, I believe that the psychological application of "rationalization" can profitably be applied to the study of this material.

When viewed as a rationalization meant to resolve a situation of cognitive dissonance, the example of Anastasius of Sinai with which we opened can begin to make sense. Aware at some level of the dissonance between his practice of attack-

21 This technical psychological term, now in general parlance, was first coined and examined in Festinger 1957.

22 See MacMullen 2006. See also Leontius of Jerusalem's striking admission and his attempt to defend the practice of bribery at the Council of Chalcedon: Leontius, ed. Gray 2006:148–151.

23 See, e.g., Müller 1998; Rüpke 2012.

24 For Weber, see Sica 2000. For Freud's followers, see Jones 1908; Anna Freud 1937. For a comparison between Weber's and Freud's uses of rationalization for understanding culture, see Kaye 1992.

25 Festinger 1957; Anand et al. 2004; Fleming and Zyglidopoulos 2009. Müller (1998:367–368) mentions very briefly, in one paragraph, the psychological sense of rationalization but offers no discussion of its applications to the study of religion.

ing anti-Chalcedonian patristic forgeries and his own engagement in a similar act of forgery and misattribution, Anastasius attempts to resolve the contradiction by appealing to apostolic precedent and current polemical exigencies. Viewed from the outside, his attempts, as we saw above, come off as unsatisfactory. The contradiction has not really been resolved. But such exactly is the nature of rationalization. To the outside viewer, the dissonance does not go away once rationalizing excuses are provided.[26]

One may identify three major types of dissonance that post-Chalcedonian theologians had to cope with. The first concerns contradictions on the level of ideas or phraseology that existed either within the acknowledged corpus of church fathers (between two fathers or within the writings of one father) or, alternatively, between the writings of an earlier father and one's own notions.[27] Theologians on both sides of the Chalcedonian divide came up with a range of techniques for resolving such contradictions. Three of the main ones were *interpretive distinction*, which resolves the contradiction between two statements by assigning different meanings to each;[28] *historical and rhetorical contextualization*, which seeks to limit the absolute validity of one statement or the other by attributing its utterance to specific circumstances;[29] and *textual adjustment*, which deactivates the contradiction by changing the wording of one of the statements.[30] Since I have elsewhere treated this first type of dissonance and the three techniques that were used to resolve it,[31] I will dedicate the remainder of the present article to a discussion of the two other types of dissonance that we find post-Chalcedonian theologians attempting to minimize through rationalization.

The second type of dissonance relates to the question of forgery with which we began. In his elegant treatments of the transformation of post-Chalcedonian theological culture, Canadian patristics scholar Patrick Gray has shown how the demand for absolute unanimity among the fathers led to a proliferation of forger-

26 As recognized early on by Jones 1908:166. See further Adorno 1998:108.

27 See, e. g., Severus, ed. Hespel 1964:10; 13/8; 11 (Julian of Halicarnassus and Severus of Antioch, *Exchange of Letters*); here and throughout, the first page number or series of numbers refers to the text, the second to the French or English translation. And see Leontius, ed. Gray 2006:104–105 (*Testimonies of the Saints*), and further Gray 1989.

28 See, e. g., Severus, ed. Hespel 1968:28/23 (*Contra Additiones Juliani* 5–12); and Leontius, ed. Gray 2006:65–68 (*Testimonies of the Saints*). See further Moss 2013b; 2016a:123–126.

29 See, e. g., Severus, ed. Lebon 1949:1–2/1 (*Ad Nephalium*); and Anastasius, ed. Uthemann 1981:111, 289–290. See further Moss 2013b; 2016a:123–126.

30 See, e. g., Severus, ed. Hespel 1971:82–83/69 (discussed further below). See further Moss 2013b; 2016a:117–123.

31 See Moss 2013a, Chap. 4; 2013b; 2016a:106–139.

ies and falsifications on both sides of the Chalcedonian divide.[32] Anti-Chalcedonians in the fifth and sixth centuries famously relied on texts forged in the fourth century in the name of venerable third-century figures.[33] Chalcedonians freely manipulated many of the passages from the fourth- and fifth-century fathers that they quoted in their florilegia.[34] Gray correctly points out that the same sixth-century authors who accuse their opponents of relying on adulterated texts in order to prove their case can be shown to do the same when it comes to their own positions.[35] Rarely, however, do these theologians reflect on or attempt to defend the inconsistency of such behavior. We encountered at the outset one such case, where Anastasius of Sinai offers a rationalization for his own apparently inconsistent engagement in an act of literary falsification and misattribution, despite his zealous complaints against the forgeries to which his opponents have succumbed. In the following section, I will discuss another case of rationalization, this time offered by Severus of Antioch, on the other side of the Chalcedonian divide, for his reliance on a text under grave suspicion of being a forgery.

The third type of post-Chalcedonian rationalization of an apparent dissonance relates to what may be called the essential meta-challenge surrounding the transformation of theology after Chalcedon. If, as noted earlier, the church fathers had, in this period, become the sole and absolute sources of truth, the challenge was how to prove this very idea, itself pertaining to that theological truth, on the basis of the writings of the fathers themselves. In the final section of this paper I will analyze a rare passage from a late sixth-century treatise by Peter of Callinicum that attempts to meet this overarching challenge.

Rationalizing Forgery: Severus of Antioch

The towering early sixth-century leader of the mainstream opposition to Chalcedon, Severus of Antioch (d. 538), left an indelible mark on late Roman society and culture. He was instrumental in engineering the only significant – if ultimately temporary – reversal of imperial policy vis-à-vis Chalcedon in 512–518, during which time he himself served as patriarch of Antioch; and through his theolog-

32 Gray 1988.

33 These were the so-called Apollinarian forgeries produced by Apollinarius of Laodicea and his school in the late fourth century and "fathered" onto such third-century figures as Julius and Felix of Rome and Gregory the Wonderworker.

34 See Richard 1951:740–741; and see further the unpublished study by Richard referenced in Gray 1988:285, note 13.

35 Gray 1988:284–286; 2006:27.

ical engagements with Chalcedonian opponents he proved to be an unmatched polemicist. It is safe to say that no single sixth-century theologian, on either side of the Chalcedonian divide, exercised as much influence.[36]

In engagements with his opponents, Severus often accuses them of falsifying texts.[37] He distinguishes himself from them as one who carefully cites passages in their original contexts, from whole works, giving the exact sources of his citations, rather than relying on compilations prepared by others.[38] Due to the fact that some of his own writings had been tampered with, Severus was especially wary of the dangers of textual falsification.[39] He vehemently cites the withering verdict of the fathers and the harsh regulations of Roman law against forgers.[40]

Given all this, it is not surprising that Severus's Chalcedonian adversaries made sport of Severus's gullibility when it came to the Apollinarian forgeries that, so conveniently for the anti-Chalcedonians, proclaimed Christ's one, incarnate nature.[41] How did Severus himself respond to this apparent inconsistency? Although Chalcedonian-minded authors, beginning already in the mid-fifth century, had demonstrated with increasing sophistication the Apollinarian provenance of these texts variously attributed to Julius of Rome, Gregory the Wonderworker and Athanasius, the anti-Chalcedonian authors, including Severus himself, were usually silent on the matter.[42] This overall trend is evident in the reports of the conversations between representatives of the two sides hosted by the emperor Justinian in an attempt at reconciliation in 532. In the account surviving from the Chalcedonian side, the anti-Chalcedonian bishops are presented as having made no effort to counter the forgery allegations proffered by their

---

36 See Grillmeier and Hainthaler 1995:148, calling Severus "the leading theologian of his time."
37 See the evidence collected in Gray 1988:284–285.
38 See the evidence collected in Moss 2016a:112–113.
39 Severus, ed. Brooks 1902–1904:19–21, 504–505/18–19, 448.
40 *Ibid.*:76–77/69–70.
41 See Schwartz 1973:54.
42 The most thoroughgoing and famous surviving specimen of the Chalcedonian attack on the Apollinarian forgeries is the *Adversus fraudes Apollinaristarum*, attributed to Leontius of Byzantium of the mid-sixth-century. Daley (1978:lv–lviii) has argued that it was composed by Leontius of Byzantium in preparation for the conversations of 532. Rees (1968:241–242), however, identifies John of Scythopolis as the author. Leontius of Jerusalem, writing between 536 and 538, ascribes similar efforts to John of Scythopolis. See Gray 2006:122–123 (for John of Scythopolis) and *ibid.*:40 (for Gray's dating of Leontius's work). In either case, the *Adversus fraudes Apollinaristarum* would have been written in Severus's lifetime. For further examples of Chalcedonian attacks on the authenticity of the Apollinarian forgeries, both before and after the 530s, see Speyer 1971:95–98; Grillmeier and Hainthaler 1995:238–239.

opponent, Hypatius, bishop of Ephesus.[43] The report that has come down from the anti-Chalcedonian camp sidesteps the issue altogether by leaving out any mention of the forgery issue.[44]

Nevertheless, although anti-Chalcedonians generally preferred not to engage the question head-on, we do have a rare case where Severus rationalizes his acceptance of a text he knows was gravely suspected of being an Apollinarian fabrication.[45] The matter comes up in the course of a prolonged debate within the anti-Chalcedonian camp between Severus and his one-time ally, Julian of Halicarnassus. The debate, which produced an exchange of letters and tracts between the two bishops in the 520s, concerned the question of whether Jesus' body between the incarnation and the resurrection was corruptible (Severus's position) or not (Julian's position).[46] In a passage previously unnoticed in earlier scholarship on the history of the Apollinarian forgeries, Severus lambastes Julian for changing the wording of a text that they both held to have been written by Gregory the Wonderworker, in order to fend off Chalcedonian claims that it was an Apollinarian forgery.[47] Severus writes:

> Due to the fact that the most famous Gregory, in his *Exposition of the Faith, Point by Point*, has decreed an anathema on those who make of the trinity a tetrad by the division into two natures, those who profess the Jewish and abominable doctrines of Nestorius[48] wish to alienate and remove this treatise from the teacher and classify it among the texts belonging to the impious Apollinarius. Given that Gregory had written: "the mind [νοῦς] is unvan-

43 *ACO* IV.2, ed. Schwartz 1914:172–173. See Lietzmann 1904:124: "Die Severianer geben sich denn auch … keine weitere Mühe, das Gewicht der Zeugnisse zu verteidigen." See further, along the same lines, and Grillmeier and Hainthaler 1995:239.

44 Brock 1981:98, note 33; 119. See, however, the interesting comment in Grillmeier and Hainthaler 1995:238.

45 Several years earlier, in his *Against the Impious Grammarian*, written around 520, Severus had defended the authenticity of the wording of a passage from the same work to be discussed below. But no mention is made there of a Chalcedonian claim that the entire work was an Apollinarian forgery. See Severus, ed. Lebon 1938:99–102/78–80 (*Contra impium Grammaticum* 2.9). See also Grillmeier and Hainthaler 1995:53, who, after discussing the above-mentioned passage, write: "One would now have expected that the much more pressing problem of the Apollinarian forgeries in general would also have come up for discussion, something that would have suggested itself with the name of Gregory the Wonderworker and its misuse perpetrated by the Apollinarians."

46 See Draguet 1924; Grillmeier and Hainthaler 1995:79–111; Moss 2013a; 2016a.

47 For the history of this claim, with particular reference to this text (without mention of Severus's and Julian's treatments of the matter), see Caspari 1879:65–146, esp. 80–90; Spoerl 1991:66–94.

48 I. e., the Chalcedonians.

> quished by the passions of the soul and the flesh" – these besotted and ignorant phantasiasts [i. e., Julian and his party] had become convinced that these words were stained by falsification, rather than being an aid inspired by the truth, and as a result they erased the words "the mind [νοῦς] is unvanquished ..." Yet, truth requires no folly disguised as aid ... In fact, naming the Word of God "mind" [νοῦς] does not in itself fall under the charge of the blasphemies of Apollinarius, because the teachers of the orthodox faith call it by this name.[49]

Severus proceeds to cite two passages from the writings of the influential late fourth-century author Gregory Nazianzen that indeed seem to speak of the Word of God as "mind" (νοῦς).[50] He then goes on to accuse his opponents not only of tampering with the text by Gregory the Wonderworker, but also of misinterpreting it. For, he continues:

> In essence, it is by means of the totality and not by means of one [sole] passage or one part [alone] that one secures perfect knowledge of the doctrine of piety.[51]

By condemning a party within his own anti-Chalcedonian camp, Severus is able to fortify himself against Chalcedonian attacks on his uncritical acceptance of Apollinarian forgeries. Resolving the dissonance between his usual text-critical approach and his uncritical acceptance of these texts by compensation,[52] he shifts the spotlight from his own acceptance of Gregory the Wonderworker's text to the Julianists' tampering with it. It is the Julianists who are the forgers, since they admit to changing the wording of the text. This, Severus declares, is not how one goes about defending venerated texts suspected of being inauthentic. Instead, one must interpret them in light of one's knowledge of the full corpus. At the end of the day, only superior textual knowledge of the corpus as a whole can determine questions about the authenticity of individual texts and passages. Unlike Anastasius, who, as we saw at the outset, tried to fend off forgery by "fighting fire with fire," Severus does not himself engage in forgery. But he does condone the usage of texts that he must have realized had good reason to be suspected of

---

49 Severus, ed. Hespel 1971:82–83/69. According to Apollinarian Christology, the Logos occupied the place of Jesus' mind. Thus, language ascribing to Jesus' mind the divine quality of "being unvanquished by the passions" came off as Apollinarian.

50 Our ability to verify the meaning of these passages is limited, in that: (1) The text of the Syriac manuscript is partially effaced here; and (2) the sources of these passages have not been identified. See Hespel 1971:70, notes 1–3. Is it possible that these passages were not in fact originally written by Gregory Nazianzen?

51 Severus, ed. Hespel 1971:83/70.

52 On compensation as a mechanism for the resolution of cognitive dissonance, see Wicklund and Gollwitzer 2009:218–220.

being forgeries. He defends this position by shifting the conversation – in this case – from text-criticism to textual interpretation.[53]

As with Anastasius, Severus does not really resolve the dissonance between his stances toward his opponents and toward himself, but he does offer a certain justification for it. Our final example also involves justification, but the rationalization at play is less explicit than in the cases of Anastasius and Severus.

Fathering the Fathers: Peter of Callinicum

In the cases examined so far we have seen that rationalization occurs when there is an admission, even if implicit, of a certain dissonance or tension between a given assumption about a patristic text and an aspect of that text, or a claim made by others, that appears to contradict that assumption. I have so far focused on the dissonances that arose between individual texts, or between accusing others of accepting or producing forgeries and accepting or producing them oneself. Such dissonances were challenges that all post-Chalcedonian theologians had to reckon with. Patrick Gray is right in pointing out that these challenges were the direct result of an overall cultural paradigm shift, which Gray dubs "patrification," from a mode of theology that was essentially about ideas to a new mode that concentrated on authoritative sources.[54] The belief underlying this shift is well articulated by Peter of Callinicum, the sixth-century theologian we are about to discuss: "We have learned to follow the fathers' intention in everything, and to reckon their word and their understanding more authoritative and more secure than our own word and understanding."[55]

But this very transition involved a paradox. The writers whom post-Chalcedonian theologians turned to as authoritative, divinely inspired fathers did not themselves claim this kind of authority. Thus, the idea of granting such authority to the fathers was itself an innovation of the post-Chalcedonian age. Yet if they now had to "reckon [the fathers'] word and their understanding more authoritative" than their own, the challenge that faced post-Chalcedonian theologians was how to anchor this level of authority in the fathers themselves.

This paradoxical situation is comparable to the cognitive dissonances in other realms of theological activity. As with them, it is rare to find explicit engagements with the problem in the writings of the fifth- and sixth-century authors, and, as a

53 See Moss 2013a; 2016a:126–139.

54 Gray 1988, 1989.

55 Peter of Callinicum, ed. Ebied et al. 2003:384–385, their translation.

result, it is rare to find treatments of it in modern scholarship.[56] In the few cases where post-Chalcedonian authors do try to provide a justification from the fathers for their new concept of patristic authority, these efforts come off less as resolutions of the dissonance than as a form of rationalization.

Peter of Callinicum's sprawling work *Contra Damianum*, written in the late 580s, provides one such attempt. Peter served as anti-Chalcedonian patriarch of Antioch (in absentia) from 581 until his death in 591. *Contra Damianum* is an attack upon the contemporary patriarch of Alexandria, whose Christology, Peter believed, did not sufficiently separate the three persons of the Trinity. The treatise was originally written in Greek but survives, in incomplete form, only in Syriac.[57]

Peter dedicates the first half of Chapter 48 of Book 3, toward the very end of his lengthy treatise, to proving the proposition described above, according to which the "word and authority" of the fathers is absolutely superior to one's own authority. To overcome the challenge of proving an idea from sources that do not really support it, Peter recruits a literary genre that he employs regularly throughout his treatise, one that typifies post-Chalcedonian theology in general: the florilegium.[58] Characterized by strings of passages cited selectively from traditional sources to prove a point, the florilegium was ideally suited to the paradoxical task of transforming the tradition from within itself. It provided a systematic and rationalized means for sixth-century theologians to overcome the dissonance between what they wished their predecessors had said and what the latter actually said.[59]

Peter of Callinicum's florilegium on patristic authority comprises five citations from the fathers. The authorities cited are: (1) Theodosius, patriarch of Alexandria; (2) Gregory of Nazianzen; (3) Gregory of Nyssa; (4) Cyril of Alexandria; and (5) Severus of Antioch.[60] A citation from Basil of Caesarea is embedded in the passage from Theodosius.

---

56 Gray's interest was in identifying the post-Chalcedonian "patrification" of theology and its effects; he was less interested in explaining the processes by which this transformation was accomplished.

57 For background on Damian and Peter, see Grillmeier and Hainthaler 1995:75–81.

58 See Ebied and Wickham 1985:117: "Patristic theology may be said to aspire to the condition of the florilegium." See further Gray 1989:29–30; 1996:190; 2006:26.

59 It is precisely these aspects of the florilegium and of post-Chalcedonian theology in general that have frustrated some modern historians of theology. See, e. g., Moeller 1951:639, who recommends subjecting oneself to reading Leontius of Jerusalem daily as a penitential Lenten practice due to his tortuous "stammering scholasticism" ("scholastique balbutiante").

60 Peter, ed. Ebied et al. 2003:384–395. The text of this chapter has also come down independently in an unpublished Syriac manuscript containing a Syrian Orthodox florilegium on a

Before delving into the content of these passages, it is instructive to observe Peter's use of the formal possibilities of the florilegium to support his point. Rather than citing his five sources in chronological order, he first cites Theodosius, the latest; he then moves on to Gregory Nazianzen, the earliest, followed by the remaining authors in chronological order, ending with Severus of Antioch, who was Theodosius's master. Thus, the two sixth-century authors, Theodosius and Severus, frame the three fourth- and fifth-century authors – the two Gregories and Cyril.

I believe this arrangement is not accidental. By it, Peter of Callinicum accomplishes two things. First, he signals that his corpus is ahistorical. The fathers all think and express themselves as one; they are not bound by the normal processes of historical progression and development. Second, by situating Theodosius and Severus – two post-Chalcedonian authors already steeped in the patrification process – in the first and last positions, Peter creates an interpretive frame of reference for the passages from the three pre-Chalcedonian authors. One is more likely to read the middle of a text in light of its beginning and end than the reverse.

The florilegium not only provided Peter with the opportunity to arrange his sources in a targeted manner; it also enabled him to cite from them selectively. This can only be fully demonstrated by a thorough analysis of Peter's sources and his specific usage of them, which would go beyond the scope of this article. I will limit myself here to an analysis of the passages from Theodosius and Severus, with some brief comments on the other sources.

After introducing the overall theme of the florilegium, namely, the authority of the fathers' words, Peter continues:

> For, accurate Theodosius proved this by the divinely inspired words of Basil the Great, when he wrote in his *Discourse on Theology* in the following manner:
> Hence, bidding farewell to those who readily weave cobwebs of objections and speedily perfect thoughtless thoughts, and to the easy impious absurdities into which they slip especially from ignorance of the divine words, deceiving themselves rather than those they address, we ourselves will, so far as we can, collect and set down what we have received from our store-house (meaning from the divinely-inspired learning of the God-clad fathers), thinking that what comes from them will suffice right-thinking people for secure knowledge of the issue. For as to the man who does not follow the intention of the holy fathers at all points and does not reckon their word more powerful and more exact than his own notions, Saint Basil ruled that he deserves censure for his presumption, in the *Letter* he sent *to the*

range of subjects. The manuscript, BL Add. 12, 155, has been dated to 747. See Wright 1871:921, 955, 967; and Draguet 1924:83–85. That florilegium clearly borrowed this chapter from Peter of Callinicum rather than the reverse, as an earlier section, at BL Add. 12, 155, f. 56r, explicitly cites another passage from Peter of Callinicum.

> *Canoness*[61] *on the Trinity*, where he wrote as follows: "For not following the fathers and not considering their word more accurate than our own understanding deserves censure, because it is full of presumption." Therefore, we too will be right to import no addition and make no subtraction in the fathers' teaching.[62]

This passage offers a great demonstration of the authority of the fathers because of its recursivity. In order to prove the absolute authority of the words and ideas of the fathers, Theodosius, the father, is *cited, citing* his predecessor, Basil, the father, who seems to be making the same point. Peter attributes absolute authority to Theodosius, who attributes absolute authority to Basil, who, in turn, attributes absolute authority to *his* predecessors. Such recursive self-referentiality, comparable to depictions of the work of art or the artist within the work of art or of the novelist or her novel within the novel, serves to blur the boundaries between the author – of the novel, the work of art, or the theological florilegium – and his or her audience, and thus lends authority, or at least an aura of reality, to the author's claims.[63]

A closer look at the citations from Theodosius and Basil in their respective contexts, however, reveals that they were in fact making very different points. Theodosius's citation is taken from his *Theological Discourse*, written against proponents of the so-called "Tritheist" theology. Without getting too much into the intricacies of that dispute, which rocked the Miaphysite church in the second half of the sixth century,[64] we may simply observe that Theodosius's entire *Theological Discourse* is centered on patristic argumentation. The discussion is about very specific texts, patristic excerpts from a range of authors, which Theodosius's opponents had cited to prove their position, and which he reinterprets in light of other patristic excerpts in order to refute his opponents. Much of the debate had revolved around a short line from John Chrysostom's *Commentary on John*: οὗτος ὁ Λόγος οὐσία τις ἐστιν, "this Logos is a substance."[65] Theodosius's opponents claimed that saying that that the Word is *a* substance proves that it is in some sense a *different* substance from both the Father and the Spirit, and that therefore the three different persons of the Trinity are to be considered, at least in one sense, three separate substances or "natures." Theodosius countered by saying

---

61 Thus in the Syriac. The original Greek of Basil's letter reveals that it was addressed to a group of canonesses.

62 Peter, ed. Ebied et al 2003:384–387, their translation.

63 Dällenbach 1989:31–32. Compare this also to the striking self-referentiality of the Qurʾān, studied in Wild 2006. See further Moss 2016a:244.

64 For a brief overview, see Moss 2016b:130–131.

65 John Chrysostom, ed. Migne 1862 (PG 59):47 (*Homily* 4 on John, 1).

that although οὐσία normally means "substance," in this case Chrysostom meant it in the sense of hypostasis, and that the added τις does not involve division or a change in the divine substance.[66]

In keeping with the exegetical strategies commonly employed by post-Chalcedonian authors, Theodosius appeals to subtle interpretive distinctions in order to smooth over an apparent wrinkle in the perfect, harmonious system he attributes to the fathers. But this strategy contrasts sharply with the stance of Basil of Caesarea, as it emerges in the latter's very different fourth-century historical context as well as in the literary context of the letter from which his passage was excerpted. In that letter, Basil expresses his frustration with certain contemporaries who have rejected the *homoousios* formula, the heart of the Nicaean definition of faith.[67] In the full context of the letter, Basil's critique of those who do not accept the definition of the Nicene fathers is actually just one side of a contrastive μέν–δὲ sentence of the type commonly employed in literary Greek.[68] The following table demonstrates the changes and omissions Theodosius (and Peter in his footsteps) made to Basil's text:

Basil, *Epistle 52, apud se ipsum*	**Basil, *Ep.* 52, *apud* Theodosius *apud* Peter**
For **while** (μέν) not adhering to the fathers, and not considering their word more authoritative than **their** own opinion, is a thing liable for censure inasmuch as it is filled with impudence, yet, **on the other hand** (δέ), regarding with suspicion a doctrine with which others have found fault does somehow seem to free them from a portion of the blame.	For not adhering to the fathers and not considering their word more accurate than **our** opinions is a thing liable for censure inasmuch as it is filled with impudence.
Τὸ μὲν γὰρ Πατράσι μὴ ἀκολουθεῖν καὶ τὴν ἐκείνων φωνὴν κυριωτέραν τίθεσθαι τῆς **ἑαυτῶν** γνώμης ἐγκλήματος ἄξιον, ὡς αὐθαδείας γέμον· τὸ δὲ πάλιν ὑφ' ἑτέρων διαβληθεῖσαν αὐτὴν ὕποπτον ἔχειν, τοῦτο δή πως δοκεῖ τοῦ ἐγκλήματος αὐτοὺς μετρίως ἐλευθεροῦν.	ܗܝ ܓܝܪ ܕܠܐܒܗ̈ܬܐ ܠܐ ܢܩܦ: ܘܠܒܪܬ ܩܠܐ ܕܝܠܗܘܢ ܠܐ ܢܣܡ ܕܝܬܝܪ ܚܬܝܬܐ ܡܢ ܬܪ̈ܥܝܬܢ. ܠܐܪܫܢܐ ܫܘܝܐ ܒܗ̇ ܕܡܪܚܘܬܐ ܡܠܝܐ.

66 Theodosius, *Theological Discourse*, in Van Roey and Allen 1994:161–163, 196–198/232–235; see also 127, 134.
67 Basil of Caesarea, ed. Courtonne 1957:133 (*Letter* 52.1 – to the Canonicae).
68 For the gradual post-classical decline of this structure in documentary settings and its conscious retention in literary contexts, see Lee 1985:1–8.

In the letter, Basil offers a certain defense of those who dissent from an expression or a doctrine propounded by the fathers in cases where others have found fault with it. He goes on to cite, as an additional defense of this position – with which he disagrees – the third-century councils dealing with the case of Paul of Samosata, which had actually censured the term *homoousios* that he so eagerly seeks to defend.[69] Thus, this very passage from Basil, cited selectively by Theodosius in the sixth century to demonstrate the absolute authority of one's patristic predecessors, turns out, when read in its original context, to reflect characteristically fourth-century attitudes about the *contingent*, non-absolute nature of patristic authority.[70] Basil explicitly recognizes the polyphony of his predecessors and recruits it to offer a defense of his opponents! This is a far cry from the univocal conception of the patristic past advocated by Theodosius.

Moving on to the fourth- and fifth-century citations from Gregory of Nazianzen, Gregory of Nyssa and Cyril, an examination of their original contexts similarly reveals meanings very different from those that Peter assigns to them. I will not enter into a detailed discussion of these texts; the excerpts in the florilegium are long, and their full contexts are even longer! Suffice it to say that a similar process is at play in Peter's transformation of all three of them. In their original contexts, these texts can be shown to be speaking *not* of patristic authority but of scriptural authority. In fact, patristic argumentation plays no role whatsoever in any of the three works from which these passages are cited, Gregory of Nazianzen's *Invective against Julian*, Gregory of Nyssa's *Contra Eunomium* and Cyril's *Dialogues on the Trinity*.[71]

Peter presents Cyril's citations of Matt 10:20, "it is not you who speak, but the spirit of the father that speaks through you," and Matt 5:14, "you are the light of the world," as referring to the post-scriptural fathers, but an examination of the passage in its original context reveals that Cyril is clearly referring to the divinely-inspired apostles, the authors of the New Testament documents, since it is to citations from the Gospel of John, Acts and First John that he then applies these Matthean statements.[72] But Peter selectively leaves out these parts of the text, as he signals to the reader by separating his two citations with the words "and a little later" (ܘܒܬܪ ܙܥܘܪ̈ܝܬܐ).[73]

69 Basil, ed. Courtonne 1957:133.
70 On Basil's attitude toward his theological past see further Gray 1989:27.
71 See Ebied et al. 2003:386–390 for bibliographical details.
72 De Durand 1977:141, 147.
73 Peter, ed. Ebied et al. 2003:390–391.

As we saw with Theodosius's selective usage of Basil, so it is with Peter's selective usage of the two Gregories and Cyril. Cited out of the contexts of their original treatises, in a chapter introduced by a title indicating that they should be understood as referring to patristic authority, and surrounded by the passages from Theodosius and Severus, which also refer to patristic authority, these excerpts offer the reader almost no choice but to read them as demonstrations of the absolute authority of the church fathers.

It is the final passage from Severus – even more so than the Theodosian excerpt – that carries the patrification process to its furthest extreme. Cited from Severus's first full-length treatise against Julian of Halicarnassus, his *Critique of Julian's Tome*, the passage explicitly equates patristic authority with scriptural authority and presents that authority as all-encompassing. It extends to the very words used by the fathers, and it is exclusive: there is no truth outside what is expressed by the fathers. Paraphrasing the same verse from Matthew 10 that Cyril cited with reference to the biblical authors, "it is not you who speak, but your father who speaks through you," Severus enthusiastically applies it to the fathers. The Spirit guides the fathers not only in what they should say but also in what they should *not* say. This much can be found in Severus's text, both in its own context and as cited by Peter of Callinicum.

That the patrification process had reached this pitch by Severus's time should not surprise us. With Peter, however, another element is added. Peter subtly rewrites Severus to make the claim that the fathers not only are divinely inspired as to what they should say in their own historical contexts, but they are also given the gift of pronouncing answers to all questions that may arise in the future.

As with Theodosius's excerpt from Basil, here, too, a comparison of Peter's excerpt from Severus with witnesses of the full text reveals how Peter seems to have altered the text to maximize the effect of its message about the extent of patristic authority. Consider the following synoptic table:[74]

74 Peter, ed. Ebied et al. 2003:392–395; Severus, ed. Hespel 1964:23/17. It is interesting to note that BL Add. 12, 155 (above, note 60), which generally follows Peter's text very closely, in this case cites the reference for Severus's text, while Peter's text does not.

Severus, *Critique of Julian's Tome, apud se ipsum*	**Severus, *Critique of Julian's Tome, apud Peter***
For it was not they who spoke, according to the unlying word of our Savior, but it was "the Spirit of" their "Father speaking in" them, indicating what it is appropriate to say, and what they should not say, concerning the traps **that would arise among them** by the craftiness of the wicked heresies …	For it was not they who spoke, according to the unlying word of the Savior, but it was "the Spirit of" their "Father speaking in" them, indicating what they should say, and, again, what they should not say, concerning the cunning traps of evil heresies **that subsequently arose** …
ܠܘ ܓܝܪ ܗܢܘܢ ܡܡܠܠܝܢ ܗܘܘ ܐܝܟ ܒܪܬ ܩܠܗ ܠܐ ܡܟܕܒܬܐ ܕܦܪܘܩܢ. ܐܠܐ ܪܘܚܐ ܕܐܒܘܗܘܢ ܗܘ ܕܡܡܠܠ ܒܗܘܢ ܘܡܫܘܕܥ ܕܐܝܠܝܢ ܘܠܐ ܠܡܡܠܠܘ. ܘܬܘܒ ܐܝܠܝܢ ܠܐ. ܙܕܩ ܠܡܡܠܠܘ. ܠܦܘܬ ܡܟܡ̈ܢܐ ܕܗܘܝܢ ܗܘܘ ܒܝܢܬܗܘܢ ܡܢ ܢܟܝܠܘܬ ܒܝܫܘܬܗܝܢ ܕܗܪ̈ܣܝܣ.	ܠܘ ܓܝܪ ܗܢܘܢ ܐܢܬܘܢ ܗܘܘ ܗܠܝܢ ܕܡܡܠܠܝܢ: ܐܝܟ ܒܪܬ ܩܠܐ ܠܐ ܡܟܕܒܬܐ ܕܦܪܘܩܐ: ܐܠܐ ܪܘܚܐ ܕܐܒܘܗܘܢ ܕܡܡܠܠ ܒܗܘܢ.. ܘܡܫܘܕܥ ܗܠܝܢ ܕܙܕܩ ܕܢܐܡܪܘܢ: ܘܬܘܒ ܗܠܝܢ ܕܠܐ ܙܕܩ ܕܢܐܡܪܘܢ.. ܠܦܘܬ ܡܟܡ̈ܢܐ ܢܟ̈ܝܠܐ ܕܒܬܪܟܢ ܗܘܘ ܕܗܪ̈ܣܝܣ ܒܝܫܬܐ.

Speaking of the heretical traps, the Syriac translation, in the independent manuscript tradition of the treatise, uses the participial form of the verb "to be" combined with the perfect (ܕܗܘܝܢ ܗܘܘ, *dahweyn hwau*). This construction typically serves to render the Greek imperfect. Taken in conjunction with the suffixed preposition "among them" (ܒܝܢܬܗܘܢ, *baynothhon*), it must be understood in the frequentative sense: "the traps that would habitually arise among them." According to this version of the text, the fathers were indeed guided by the Spirit, but the guidance they received was intended to enable them to combat the heresies that arose *in their own times*.

However, when we turn to Peter's citation of Severus, we find the periphrastic Syriac participial + perfect construction replaced with the verb "to be" in the perfect (ܗܘܘ, *hwau*), accompanied by the adverb "afterwards" (ܒܬܪܟܢ, *botharkhen*). This requires a completely different translation. According to this version, Severus is referring not to the heretical traps that would habitually arise within the environment of the fathers in any given generation, but to the traps that would "subsequently arise," in future generations, coming *after* the fathers.[75]

75 To be sure, in contrast to the other cases discussed above, it is possible that in this case the difference between the two versions predated Peter's citation. There could have been two different Greek versions of the passage from Severus, in which case it would be impossible to discern which came first, although it should be noted that one of the manuscripts of the Syriac version of Severus's *Critique of Julian's Tome* is dated to April 528, very shortly after the date of composition in the early–mid 520s. See Draguet 1924:25; and Moss 2013a, Appendix 1. If so, it is possible that the "Severus" version came first. Another possibility is that the "Severus" version is indeed original but that the change found in Peter's text was introduced not by him but by his Syriac translator. Regarding these methodological possibilities, see Allen 1981:262–264. However,

Thus, while Severus himself was very much invested in the process of "patrifying" theology, it seems that Peter carried his work one step further. In Peter's hands, Severus is found to say that the patristic texts contain discussions of issues not only in their own times, but in all subsequent times as well.[76] Thus, Peter creates a beautiful recursive loop; through his subtle rewriting of Severus, he is able to meet the rare challenge of making the fathers father themselves. The past is made relevant to the present by being made to declare that it is an artifact of the future.

In sum, Peter of Callinicum, like virtually everyone participating in theological culture after the Council of Chalcedon, faced a degree of cognitive dissonance. How could the practice of anchoring all ideas in the past be anchored in the past, if this idea itself was an innovation? Although many must have experienced this dissonance, few attempted to overcome it. Using the florilegium, the poster-child method of post-Chalcedonian theology, Peter provided one such attempt. He made sophisticated use of the florilegium's possibilities of selection, juxtaposition and recension to build his case. Like Anastasius of Sinai's justifications for falsifying patristic texts, and Severus's defense of his reliance on writings that he must have known were not authentic, Peter's attempt turns out, upon close examination, to be more of a rationalization than a real solution to a problem that was, at root, insoluble. But, as British essayist Adam Phillips has elegantly observed, we rationalize precisely those things that are simultaneously disturbing and important to us. Our attempts to do so constitute our stories – our personal mythologies.[77] By focusing attention on three relatively rare instances of theological rationalization in the era after Chalcedon, I hope to have provided a unique glimpse of the mythologies of late ancient theological culture.

---

in light of the other cases discussed above of manipulations of patristic sources in support of notions of "patrification," the simplest explanation seems to be that it was indeed Peter himself who introduced this change.

76 See, however, Severus, ed. Hespel 1968:133/111, where he speaks of a treatise by Gregory the Wonderworker of the third century as preempting the heresies of the fourth-century Arius and Apollinarius. Ironically, precisely the same elements that led Severus to identify a link between this text of Gregory the Wonderworker and Apollinarius are those that led Severus's opponents to attribute the text *not* to Gregory but to an Apollinarian context.

77 Phillips 2012:ix.

References

Abramowski, Luise. 1957. "Zum Brief des Andreas von Samosata an Rabbula von Edessa." *Oriens Christianus*, 41:51–67.

Acta Conciliorum Oecumenicorum (*ACO*), IV.2: *Concilium Universale Constantinopolitanum sub Iustiniano habitum*, ed. Eduard Schwartz. 1914. Berlin–Leipzig: De Gruyter.

Adorno, Theodor W. 1998. *Critical Models: Interventions and Catchwords*. English transl. by Henry W. Pickford. New York: Columbia University Press.

Allen, Pauline. 1981. "Greek Citations from Severus of Antioch in Eustathius Monachus." *Orientalia Lovaniensia Periodica*, 12:261–264.

—. 1982. Review of Anastasius of Sinai, ed. Uthemann 1981. *Vigiliae Christianae*, 36:294–312.

Anand, V., B.E. Ashforth and M. Joshi. 2004. "Business as Usual: The Acceptance and Perpetuation of Corruption in Organizations." *Academy of Management Executive*, 18:39–53.

Anastasius of Sinai. *Anastasii Sinaitae Viae Dux*, ed. K.H. Uthemann. 1981 (Corpus Christianorum Series Graeca, 8). Turnhout–Leuven: Brepols–Leuven University Press.

Basil of Caesarea. *Saint Basile: Lettres*, I, ed. Yves Courtonne. 1957. Paris: Les Belles Lettres.

Brock, Sebastian. 1981. "The Conversations with the Syrian Orthodox under Justinian (532)." *Orientalia Christiana Periodica*, 47:87–121. Caspari, Carl Paul. 1879. *Alte und neue Quellen zur Geschichte des Taufsymbols und der Glaubensregel*. Oslo: P.T. Malling.

Cramer, J.A. (ed.). 1841. *Catenae Graecorum patrum in Novum Testamentum*, V. Oxford: Oxford University Press.

Daley, Brian E. 1978. "Leontius of Byzantium: A Critical Edition of his Works, with Prolegomena." Ph. D. Dissertation, University of Oxford.

Dällenbach, Lucien. 1989. *The Mirror in the Text*. English transl. by Jeremy Whiteley. Chicago: University of Chicago Press.

Draguet, René. 1924. Juli*en d'Halicarnasse et sa controverse avec Sévère d'Antioche sur l'incorruptibilité du corps du Christ. Louvain: Smeesters.*

De Durand, G.M. 1977. *Cyrille d'Alexandrie: Dialogues sur la Trinité*, II (Sources chrétiennes, 237). Paris: Édition du Cerf.

Ebied, Rifaat, and Lionel R. Wickham. 1985. "Timothy Aelurus: Against the Definition of the Council of Chalcedon." In Carl Laga, Joseph A. Munitiz and Lucas van Rompay (eds.), *After Chalcedon: Studies in Theology and Church History Offered to Professor Albert Van Roey for his Seventieth Birthday*. Leuven: Peeters. 115–166.

Ebied et al. 2003 – see Peter of Callinicum, ed. Ebied et al.

Festinger, Leon. 1957. *A Theory of Cognitive Dissonance*. Stanford: Stanford University Press.

Fleming, Peter, and Stelios C. Zyglidopoulos. 2009. *Charting Corporate Corruption: Agency, Structure and Escalation*. Northampton: Edward Elgar.

Freud, Anna. 1937. *The Ego and the Mechanisms of Defence*. English transl. by Cecil Baines. London: Hogarth Press.

Glad, Clarence E. 2003. "Paul and Adaptability." In J. Paul Sampley (ed.), *Paul in the Greco-Roman World*. Harrisburg: Continuum. 17–41.

Graumann, Thomas. 2002. *Die Kirche der Väter: Vätertheologie und Väterbeweis in den Kirchen des Ostens bis zum Konzil von Ephesus (431)*. Tübingen: Mohr Siebeck.

Gray, Patrick T.R. 1982. "Neo-Chalcedonianism and the Tradition: From Patristic to Byzantine Theology." *Byzantinische Forschungen*, 8:61–70.

—. 1988. "Forgery as an Instrument of Progress: Reconstructing the Theological Tradition in the Sixth Century." *Byzantinische Zeitschrift*, 81:284–289.
—. 1989. "'The Select Fathers': Canonizing the Patristic Past." *Studia Patristica*, 23:21–36.
—. 1996. "Through the Tunnel with Leontius of Jerusalem: The Sixth-Century Transformation of Theology." In Pauline Allen and Elizabeth Jeffreys (eds.), *The Sixth Century: End or Beginning?* Brisbane: Australian Association for Byzantine Studies. 187–196.
—. 1997. "Covering the Nakedness of Noah: Reconstruction and Denial in the Age of Justinian." *Byzantinische Forschungen*, 24:193–206.
—. 2006 – see Leontius of Jerusalem, ed. Gray.
Grillmeier, Aloys, and Theresia Hainthaler. 1995. *Christ in Christian Tradition*, II.2: *The Church of Constantinople in the Sixth Century*. English transl. by John Cawte and Pauline Allen. London–Louisville: Mowbray–Westminster John Knox.
—. 1996. *Christ in Christian Tradition*, II.4: *The Church of Alexandria with Nubia and Ethiopia after 451*. English transl. by O.C. Dean. London–Louisville: Mowbray–Westminster John Knox.
Hespel, Robert. 1971 – see Severus of Antioch, ed. Hespel 1971.
Jean Rufus. *Plérophories: Témoignages et revelations contre le concile de Chalcédoine*, ed. F. Nau. 1912 (Patrologia Orientalis, 8). Paris: Firmin-Didot.
John Chrysostom. *S. Joannes Chrysostomus*, ed. J.P. Migne. 1862 (PG 59, 61). Paris: Imprimerie Catholique.
Jones, Ernest. 1908. "Rationalization in Everyday Life." *Journal of Abnormal Psychology*, 3:161–169.
Kaye, Howard L. 1992. "Rationalization as Sublimation: On the Cultural Analyses of Weber and Freud." *Theory, Culture and Society*, 9:45–74.
Lee, J.A.L. 1985. "Some Features of the Speech of Jesus in Mark's Gospel." *Novum Testamentum*, 27:1–26.
Leontius of Jerusalem. *Against the Monophysites: Testimonies of the Saints and Aporiae*, ed. Patrick T.R. Gray. 2006. Oxford: Oxford University Press.
Lietzmann, Hans. 1904. *Apollinaris von Laodicea und seine Schule*. Tübingen: J.C.B. Mohr.
MacMullen, Ramsay. 2006. *Voting about God in Early Church Councils*. New Haven: Yale University Press.
Moeller, Charles. 1951. "Le chalcédonisme et le néo-chalcédonisme en Orient de 451 à la fin du VIe siècle." In Aloys Grillmeier and Heinrich Bacht (eds.), *Das Konzil von Chalkedon: Geschichte und Gegenwart*, I. Würzburg: Echter-Verlag. 637–720.
Moss, Yonatan. 2013a. "In Corruption: Severus of Antioch on the Body of Christ." Ph. D. Dissertation, Yale University.
—. 2013b. "'Packed with Patristic Testimonies': Severus of Antioch and the Reinvention of the Church Fathers." In Brouria Bitton-Ashkelony and Lorenzo Perrone (eds.), *Personal and Institutional Religion: Thought and Praxis in Eastern Christianity*. Turnhout: Brepols. 227–250.
—. 2016a. *Incorruptible Bodies: Christology, Society, and Authority in Late Antiquity* (Christianity in Late Antiquity, 1). Oakland: University of California Press.
—. 2016b. "Les controverses christologiques au sein de la tradition miaphysite: Sur l'incorruptibilité du corpus du Christ et autres questions." In Flavia Ruani (ed.), *Les controverses religieuses en syriaque* (Études syriaques, 13). Paris: Geuthner. 119–136.

Müller, Rudolph Wolfgang. 1998. "Rationalisierung." In Hubert Cancik et al. (eds.), *Handbuch religionswissenschaftlicher Grundbegriffe*, IV. Stuttgart: Kohlhammer. 363–376.
Peter of Callinicum. *Petri Callinicensis Patriarchae Antiocheni Tractatus Contra Damianum*, IV, ed. R.Y. Ebied, Albert van Roey, Lionel R. Wickham and Jacques Noret. 2003. Turnhout–Leuven: Brepols–Leuven University Press.
Phillips, Adam. 2012. "Introduction." In Hilda Doolittle, *A Tribute to Freud*. New York: New Directions.
Plummer, Alfred. 1915. *A Critical and Exegetical Commentary on the Second Epistle of St Paul to the Corinthians*. Edinburgh: T&T Clark.
Rees, Silas. 1968. "The Literary Activity of Leontius of Byzantium." *Journal of Theological Studies*, 19:229–242.
Richard, Marcel. 1951. "Les florilèges diphysites du Ve et du VIe siècle." In Aloys Grillmeier and Heinrich Bacht (eds.), *Das Konzil von Chalkedon: Geschichte und Gegenwart*, I. Würzburg: Echter-Verlag. 721–748.
—. 1958. "Anastase le Sinaïte, l'Hodegos et le monothélisme." *Revues des études byzantines*, 16:29–42.
Rüpke, Jörg. 2012. *Religion in Republican Rome: Rationalization and Ritual Change*. Philadelphia: University of Pennsylvania Press.
Schwartz, Eduard. 1973. *Drei dogmatische Schriften Justinians*, ed. Mario Amelotti et al. Milan: Giuffrè.
Severus of Antioch. *The Sixth Book of the Select Letters of Severus Patriarch of Antioch in the Syriac Version of Athanasius of Nisibis*, I–II, ed. and English transl by E.W. Brooks. 1902–1904. London: Williams and Norgate.
—. *Severi Antiocheni Liber contra impium Grammaticum*, ed. Joseph Lebon. 1938 (CSCO 111–112). Louvain: Secrétariat du CSCO.
—. *Severi Antiocheni Orationes ad Nephalium, eiusdem ac Sergii Grammatici epistulae mutuae*, ed. Joseph Lebon. 1949 (CSCO 119–120). Louvain: Secrétariat du CSCO.
—. *Sévère d'Antioche: La polémique antijulianiste*, I: *Trois Échanges de lettres et Critique du* Tome *de Julien*, ed. Robert Hespel. 1964 (CSCO 244–245). Louvain: Secrétariat du CSCO.
—. *Sévère d'Antioche: La polémique antijulianiste*, IIA: *Le Contra Additiones Juliani*, ed. Robert Hespel. 1968 (CSCO 295–296). Louvain: Secrétariat du CSCO.
—. *Sévère d'Antioche: La polémique antijulianiste*, III: *L'Apologie du Philalèthe*, ed. Robert Hespel. 1971 (CSCO 318–319). Louvain: Secrétariat du CSCO.
Sica, Alan. 2000. "Rationalization and Culture." In Stephen Turner (ed.), *The Cambridge Companion to Weber*. New York: Cambridge University Press. 42–58.
Speyer, Wolfgang. 1971. *Die literarische Fälschung im heidnischen und christlichen Altertum*. Munich: C.H. Beck'sche Verlagsbuchhandlung.
Spoerl, Kelly McCarthy. 1991. "A Study of the *Kata Meros Pistis* by Apollinarius of Laodicea." Ph. D. Dissertation, University of Toronto.
Theodoret of Cyrus. *Theodoretus Cyrensis*, ed. J.P. Migne. 1864 (PG 82). Paris: Imprimerie Catholique.
Uthemann, K.H. 1981 – see Anastasius of Sinai, ed. Uthemann.
Van Roey, Albert, and Pauline Allen. 1994. *Monophysite Texts of the Sixth Century*. Leuven: Peeters.
Wicklund, Robert A., and Peter M. Gollwitzer. 2009. *Symbolic Self-Completion*. New York: Routledge.

Wild, Stefan (ed.). 2006. *Self-Referentiality in the Qurʾān*. Wiesbaden: Harrassowitz.
Wright, William. 1871. *Catalogue of Syriac Manuscripts in the British Museum Acquired since the Year 1838*, II. London: British Museum.

Acknowledgement

Parts of this paper were presented at Yale University in the spring of 2012 at the invitation of Stephen J. Davis and Hindy Najman. I thank them both.

Moshe Sluhovsky

Rationalizing Visions in Early Modern Catholicism

When confronted with apparitions, spectral visions and miracles that allegedly took place in late medieval and early modern Europe, historians (and other scholars) tend to explain them away. They were not *really* supernatural transformations, strange occurrences, visual encounters with angelic, demonic or deceased entities, but natural events that pre-modern people failed to comprehend.[1] The events they described as supernatural or preternatural must have been meteorological anomalies, hallucinations resulting from this or that mental, medical or dietary condition, or dramatic psychological or psychopathological enactments of desires, fears and anxieties. Above all, we moderns agree – even though we no longer say so explicitly – that visions and other miraculous events were part of a pre-modern belief-system that was unscientific and irrational, and that, with the rise of modern science and naturalist reasoning since the second half of the seventeenth century, we have superseded this stage in human development. We may be culturally sensitive and not use the term "superstition" anymore, but it is always there, lurking offstage, smiling mischievously at our futile attempt to distance ourselves from earlier generations of positivist historians for whom "progress" described a clear path leading from darkness to light and from ignorance to modern rationalism.

Our very definition of modernity is founded upon maintaining this distance between the modern and the pre-modern age, a distance that is measured, among other criteria, by the replacement of Catholic beliefs with scientific, rational modes of thinking, and of a religious system that centers on rites and sensual experiences with theology of a Protestant type, an abstract belief system that does not need visual proofs and miracles to claim its truth (and in that sense we are all Protestants now).[2] We are modern insofar as we adhere to what intellectual

1 In this article I overlook the distinction between apparitions and visions. In general, visions are sensory experiences that bypass normal perception through the physical body and happen, so to speak, in the soul, while apparitions appear through the physical act of seeing. But since what interests me are late medieval and early modern attempts to rationalize both visions and apparitions within the contexts of the period's perception theory and its theological crisis, the distinction is not really important for my argument. See, however, Wiebe 1997, Newman 2005, Taves 2009 and Bilu 2013.

2 Weber (1946), Merton (1970), Cascardi (1992) and Dupré (1993) are among the most familiar proponents of this foundational narrative.

https://doi.org/10.1515/9783110446395-009

historian Martin Jay has called the "'rationalized' visual order" of the seventeenth century, which, among other things, denies a traditional Catholic belief in the existence of spectral visions.[3]

Obviously, no one doubts that medieval and early modern Europeans were "rational" in the sense that they employed theories of reasoning and causality and systems of classification, and that they attempted to consolidate their worldview on the basis of conformity to rules of logic. In pursuing this enterprise, late medieval and early modern thinkers generated scientific and rationalizing epistemologies to validate knowledge and to create a coherent explanatory system that approximated the "truth" about the laws and rules that govern the way the world operates.[4] My argument goes beyond this Thomistic self-evident assertion to suggest that, together with fellow philosophers and natural philosophers, and just like modern scholars, late medieval and early modern theologians participated in a continuous effort to develop strategies of rationalization that systematically, and by means of reasoned inquiry, not merely explained but also explained away most supernatural occurrences.

As such, my essay is an addition to the earlier efforts of Richard Kieckhefer and Stuart Clark (and others) to define the specific rationality of medieval and early modern beliefs in magic, miracles, visions and other supernatural and preternatural events, as well as to the argument of William M. Ivins, Jr., that the Renaissance perspective secured a new correspondence between objective reality and cognitive experience.[5] Late medieval and early modern explanations of visions and apparitions strove, just like our own, to be naturalistic and to disenchant the world as much as possible; but, unlike modern science, they left space for the exceptional, for God in his omnipotence to intervene and act as he wishes, in ways that do not necessarily accord with the laws of nature. Rationalization of religion, I therefore suggest, was an inherent element of late medieval and post-Tridentine Catholicism.

In the first part of the essay, I offer an overview of the current literature on late medieval theories of the connections between seeing and knowing and their epistemological, cognitive, physiological and psychological dimensions. I then address the impact of these late medieval theories on shifting understandings of spectral visions. In the final part, I argue that multiple historical processes in early modern Europe – among them the Reformation, the anxiety concerning witchcraft and the campaign against superstitious beliefs and practices, as well as

3 Jay 1993:45.
4 Clark 1997; Cameron 2010.
5 Kieckhefer 1994; Clark 2007; Ivins 1973; Dawes 2013.

the rise of philosophical skepticism, new developments in the fields of optics and perception and new materialistic approaches to the observable world – dramatically accelerated the systematic contraction of the realm of the supernatural that had begun in the late Middle Ages. This process culminated in a new rationalization of the theological discourse on matters relating to apparitions and spectral visions, and was echoed in Descartes' own thinking about visuality.

For late medieval theologians and philosophers, the key to making sense of the world was systematic observation. In this sense, theirs was already a "rationalized visual order." The word "evidence" is derived from the Latin verb *videre*, to see. Seeing offers empirically-observed evidence, and is therefore a guarantee of truth. Swedish linguist Åke Viberg informs us that this association between seeing and knowing obtains in practically *all* languages.[6] Seeing is knowing: The English words "wisdom," "witness" and "wise" are cognates of Latin *videre*. From their very inception, Christian theology, philosophy and anthropology have promoted the eye as the noblest of the senses. The Aristotelian doctrine of "species" was used by vision theorists to anchor visual veridicality. The correspondence between what is out there and what we see was guaranteed by this theory, according to which objects in the world replicate true resemblances and true impressions of themselves, known as species, which travel to the eyes and then through the optic nerves into the various ventricles of the brain, which is the computer where species are deciphered and stored.[7] In the species, the real is united with the human intellect and the outside with the inside, because the species is neither a copy nor a representation of an object but the intelligible object itself.

Intuitively, then, to deny the reality of things seen with the eyes is more difficult than to accept them, and this includes spectral visions and apparitions. Indeed, a special category, "occult" (literally "hidden"), was designated to describe powers and things whose existence in the world was beyond doubt and which operated according to precise rules while, nevertheless, being invisible to the human eye. The late medieval and Renaissance rise of natural magic and interest in the occult could be viewed, from this perspective, as part of the attempt to provide naturalistic and rational explanations for the ways nature works and to restrict as much as possible the realm of the supernatural.[8] But, importantly, the agents who were likely to appear in spectral visions – invisible beings such as Christ, the Virgin, angels, demons, saints and deceased ancestors – were never

6 Viberg 2001.
7 From Greek *spec* – what a thing looks like. See Pasnau 1997; Camille 2000; and Clark 2007:9–38.
8 Eamon 1994.

viewed as occultic. Their existence was beyond doubt, on account not only of their prominence in the belief system but also, partially, of their recurrent visual appearances. Often seen, they ought to be real. Apparitions appear not merely to one of the senses; they appear to the sense that has always been viewed as reliable and trustworthy above all others.[9]

Medieval philosophy and Christian theology, however, also maintained a profound distrust of the eye and acknowledged a disjuncture between appearance and reality. The senses often deceive, and there is no certitude that what appears to exist actually exists. To see is to believe, yet to trust the eye is to risk fraud and deception. Species transmit resemblances, but the devil and other distractions can skew the transmission. The eye arouses lascivious temptations and promotes idolatry, but the same eye enables veneration of icons and admiration of nature, God's creation. Comprehension of Christ's divinity depends upon the ocular testimony of witnesses to his Crucifixion and Resurrection, but also upon belief in what cannot and could not be seen, namely, the Incarnation. To get to "objective reality" we cannot use our eyes. Essential reality is invisible, and what we see, we see only seemingly, "through a glass, darkly," to use St. Paul's beautiful metaphor (I Corinth. 13:12).

Belief in Christ's Incarnation and the veracity of transubstantiation thus rested upon a complex relationship between exterior visible forms and interior *in*visible essences, while God's *potentia absoluta* and his liberty to perform miracles were not to be bound by laws of optics. No less important was the practical concern for maintaining a sense of the real and of visual certitude in daily life.[10] Theologians, natural philosophers and philosophers participated throughout the Middle Ages and the early modern period in the elaboration of sophisticated theories of optics, perception, psychology and cognition that would not contradict the theological truth of Revelation while also being commonsensical, reasoned and rational. A rational explanation of the reality of apparitions and visions had to supply an ocular theory that accounted for both visible and invisible realities at one and the same time, and that reaffirmed the compatibility of reason and faith.

Traditional medieval vision theory was, in fact, a "mis-vision" theory. It successfully maintained two contradictory positions, both affirming and denying the reliability of the senses. Too much insistence on physicality ran the risk of idola-

---

9 This is not to deny, of course, that visions of supernatural beings can also be heard, and (admittedly, less often) touched or smelled (but note the reduction of all sensory experience to the visual when we use the term "vision," an impoverishment that at the same time anchors the experience in the realm of evidence and certitude).

10 Denery 2005; Minnis 2009.

try, while emphasizing the immaterial facet of the invisible ran the risk of denying the truth of the Word made Flesh. Vision provided the most reliable access to the truth of the physical world, but it was impossible to distinguish between truth and falsity based on the sense of vision alone. This juggling act, with its wider implications for physiological and cognitive theories of vision, unavoidably generated a wealth of insights into thinking, not only about spiritual and physiological visions, but also about the shifting boundaries between the natural and the supernatural and about different categories of certitude and their social and cultural formations.

But while the nobility of sight was repeatedly asserted and celebrated, what seeing actually means was far from self-evident. What is the connection between the sensorial occurrence of seeing on the screen of what we today call the retina and the mental or cognitive consciousness of seeing? Was seeing a learned skill or a physiological given? Was it a result of rays projected from the eye (extromission) or of rays received from objects and caught by the eye (intromission)? Where does seeing take place: in the physical eye or in the brain? Or in both? Does human vision give reliable access to the real world? Is vision veridical? Do we see with the eye of the body or with the gaze of the mind (*acies animi* versus *acies mentis*)? In what experiential and sensory sense are apparitions or visions different from other ocular experiences? How are they different from seeing "real" objects? What makes seeing "real" physical objects real, but seeing spectral visions problematic?[11]

In asking these questions about visions, I am obviously focusing on one specific type of event that is commonly regarded as supernatural and preternatural. The scope of late medieval and early modern epistemological and theological concerns, though, was wider, and it also encompassed miracles: They, too, were witnessed and recorded; seen, and therefore necessarily true and real. And what was true of miracles and visions was also true of demonic possession and bewitchment, resuscitation of the dead and bilocation, magic and the sighting of prodigies and portents. While I will restrict my discussion to the rationalization of spectral visions and apparitions, it is important to keep in mind the relevance of the late medieval and early modern discussion I present to much larger epistemological and theological concerns.[12]

11 Lindberg 1976; Levin 1997.

12 On the wider contexts, see especially Daston 1991 and Daston and Park 1998. On apparitions of angels, see Marshall and Walsham 2006 and Walsham 2010. On the rationality of belief in demons, see Clark 1997, and on apparitions of the dead, see Gordon and Marshall 2000.

This discussion should help us rethink the transition from an alleged naïve and representational Aristotelian theory of visual realism by means of species to rational modernity and its alleged new perspectivist theory. This transition, it is often claimed, took place between the Renaissance and the seventeenth century, and reached its climax in the century of René Descartes, Francis Bacon, Johannes Kepler and the lens-grinder Baruch Spinoza.[13] The seventeenth century, according to this chronology, witnessed the "rationalization of sight," the victory of a new, naturalistic and rational ocular-centric culture, one that grounded truth in observable experiments capable of demonstrating mechanical and physical laws. This was the century of the birth of the modern scientific worldview, which privileged the visual over the textual and developed the sciences of the eye, establishing what Martin Jay has called the "secular autonomization of the visual as a realm unto itself."[14] But let us not forget that it was also the century of the baroque, with its manipulation of natural visual representations, its anamorphic paintings that presented distorted yet perspectival forms, and its dazzling and disorienting surplus of images.[15] Put differently, the early modern period witnessed more, much more, than a transition from one visual culture to another; it cannot be reduced to the era in which the supposed naiveté of medieval visual theory was rationalized by early modern science. It was, rather, a period of disorientation and confusion in all matters relating to truth claims and rationalization theories, to both presentation and representation.

Aristotle, Augustine and late medieval and early modern philosophers, natural philosophers and theologians, as previously mentioned, both promoted and rejected the intuitive connection between vision and truth. While they all agreed that visual perception was more reliable than other senses or faculties, they repeatedly warned that the connection between what the eyes see and what exists out there is, in reality, shaky. The history of these debates is beyond the focus of this essay, but the three most important philosophers of the fourteenth century participated in them. John Duns Scotus (d. 1308), William of Ockham (d. ca. 1348) and, especially, Nicole Oresme (ca. 1323–1382) challenged the reliability of our senses to assert anything about the world around us with any certitude. Given this inability, Ockham suggested relying on intuitive cognition rather than on optical perception. God, being benevolent, is a better guarantor of the reliability of seeing

13 Ivins 1973.

14 Jay 1993:44.

15 Merleau-Ponty 1968; Buci-Glucksmann 1986. But on the "scientific" facet of baroque visual culture, see now Gal and Chen-Morris 2013a, 2013b.

things. We see better when we see with the eyes of the mind than when we see with the eyes of the body, as Cicero and Virgil had been the first to suggest, and as generations of Christian theologians never tired of repeating (see, for example, Matt. 6:22).[16]

But could God himself deceive us? Could he have given us a deceptive and illusionary mechanism that makes us believe that we see things we do not actually see? This possibility was too radical even for Descartes to entertain, a point to which we will return. And yet, the basic assumptions made about the possibility of human knowledge and evidentiality and about the ways God chooses to act in the world always allowed for the possibility that God can deliberately confuse appearance with truth.[17] Many Christian theologians refused to consider this possibility, but some scholastics, among them Ockham, the fourteenth-century Italian Gregory of Rimini and the fifteenth-century German Gabriel Biel, considered this hyperbolic speculation a form of preemptive skepticism – of pushing an argument *ad absurdum* in order to assure its immunity to skeptical criticism.[18] St. Paul, in fact, had already assigned divine visual deceit a crucial role in the apocalyptic time, when "God will send them strong delusions and they will all believe a lie" (2 Thes. 2:11). But Paul immediately retracts his own bewildering possibility and attributes these displays of signs and wonders to Satan rather than to God.

Theologians' ambivalence about a deceptive God granted the Christian devil virtual independence. Satan is *simius Dei*, God's ape, the entity whose very essence is imitation and falsification. Satan is a master of mimesis, and often transforms himself into an angel of light (Corinth. 11:14) in order to deceive people. Such is his power over the natural world, including the natural processes of human perception and cognition, that he can create simulacra of perfect reality. He does so by manipulating and controlling species, by destroying the unity between an object and its intelligibility, between nature and its image, and between the known and the knower. Thus, the same species that guarantee and stabilize the veracity of sight are also the easiest targets of Satan's manipulations of it.

---

16 Hansen 1985; Tachau 1988; Minnis 2009; Denery 2005, 2009; Schreiner 2011:15–23; Fogleman 2009.

17 The Book of Deuteronomy tells us: "if there arise among you a prophet ... and he gives you a sign or wonder, and that sign or wonder comes to pass, of which he spoke to you, saying 'Let us go after other gods, which you have not known, and let us serve them,' you shall not hearken to the words of that prophet ... For the lord your God puts you to the proof, to know whether you love the Lord your God with all your heart and with all your soul" (Deut. 13:1–3). Not only do miracles and prophecies not provide solid ground for interpretation, but it appears that in order to know whether or not his followers are hypocrites, God himself tests them with false visions.

18 Groarke 1984; Grellard 2007; Perler 2010.

Note that these authors dealt not with spectral visions of the divine, the demonic or the angelic, but with perception of "real" or natural objects. They cared about the reliability of all things seen and the veracity of the sensory-cognitive-psychological experiences of perception itself. Apparent supernatural occurrences are always very likely to have natural causes, explained Oresme in his *De causis mirabilium* (c. 1370), and they are more likely to happen to people who have an abnormally active imagination, or are melancholic or sick. Brain injury, imbalance of bodily humors, fasting and over-exertion of the mind and body cause perceptual errors, and even theologians, he emphasized, have been known to mistake natural causes for miracles. The fearful are likely to identify natural occurrences with apparitions of demonic entities, while spiritually-inclined people are likely to see angels.[19]

The discussion of preternatural (or marvelous) and supernatural (or miraculous) visions was just one element in this larger discussion of cognition and perception. When examining visions or miracles, learned late medieval and early modern Europeans always maintained a hermeneutics of suspicion and developed an elaborate apparatus of investigatory and probative practices for their authentication. Their basic approach was to discredit all but a very few visions and miracles, and to find natural, materialistic and medical causes for as many marvelous occurrences as possible.[20] Apparitions were the consequence of vapors and exhalations rapidly inflaming and cooling in the upper regions of the air, or reflections from droplets of rain, or configurations of clouds. Intense concentration or mental fixation was also known to cause perceptual errors. Devout people see things not truly present. Focusing intensely on some venerated image (species) in their mind, they "see" it as if it were real. In other words, one sees not because the object is there to be seen but because one wishes to see it.

Above all, it was extremely difficult to distinguish between visions and dreams (and dreams themselves could result from all of the above causes, and then some).[21] Apparitions and spiritual visions were part of a conceptual continuum, the whole of which constituted an epistemological quandary. From an epistemological perspective, questions concerning spectral apparitions stood side by side with questions concerning the "visual transparency" of all sensory

19 Hansen 1985:160–163, 265.

20 Park 2006; eadem 2010.

21 Siraisi 1997:174–191; Clark 2007:301–327; Fogleman 2009; Amelang 2012; Plane and Tuttle 2013, and the bibliographies therein. Descartes, as is well known, argued that "there are never any sure signs by means of which being awake can be distinguished from being asleep." Descartes, ed. Cottingham et al. 1984, II:15. See also Nadler 1997.

experience. The difficulty in explaining "supernatural" visions was not in any way different from the difficulty in explaining perception itself. Seeing was not just believing, but also unbelieving; vision was always only mis-vision.

And yet, extraordinary sightings of angels, demons, revenants and other agents could not be ruled out altogether. The Bible reported them, numerous saints experienced them and many reliable people witnessed them. Late medieval and early modern mystics were well aware of the dangers of spectral deception. "Free me from deception," Saint Teresa of Avila pleaded to God (*Life* 29:5), and in her *Interior Castle* (1577), she repeatedly warned her followers against visions.[22] But the Deceiver was always waiting for his opportunity to lead spiritual people astray. Even if Satan could not operate against the rules of nature, as Aquinas had argued and the Flemish Jesuit Martin Delrio elaborated in his encyclopedic *Disquisitiones magicae* of 1599–1600, he could create simulacra of reality.[23] Protestant attacks on the entire edifice of the representation of the presence of God and the divine in the world, from miracles to the Mass, further called into question the reliability of all things seen. Most Catholic worship, Protestants challenged, is based on visual delusion.[24] Visions of Christ and the Virgin, or of saints and angels, apparitions of ghosts and of the dead and most miracles are either tricks of the devil or fraudulent fabrications of Catholic priests, they argued.[25]

The growing interest in magic and the manipulation of nature further exacerbated the instability of perception theory. In the mid-sixteenth century, the first Latin edition of Euclid was published in Paris (1557), and in his introduction the mathematician Jean Pena suggested that all apparitions should be attributed to natural effects. Heinrich Cornelius Agrippa and Giambattista Della Porta both wrote about the manipulation of visions by optical means, thus contributing to a growing skepticism concerning all things seen.[26] Catholics, confronted with the Protestant attack, created both an elaborate typology of visions and stringent rules of verification.[27] The revival of Thomism in the sixteenth century, culminating in Thomas Aquinas's elevation to Doctor of the Church in 1567, was part of this project of rationalizing the natural realm, as was the systematic effort to cleanse Catholicism of superstitious practices and beliefs that were, allegedly, contaminating its truth.[28] The probative technique of verifying visions, part and

22 Teresa of Avila, ed. Kavanaugh and Rodriguez 1976–1985, I, *Life*: 222; II, *Interior Castle*.
23 Clark 2007:123–134.
24 Eire 1986, 1990; Wandel 1995; Clark 2007:161–203.
25 See especially Lavater 1572.
26 See Clark 2007.
27 Newman 2005 offers a very good history of the medieval theology of spectral visions.
28 Campagne 2002.

parcel of this vast enterprise of redrawing the boundaries between the natural and the supernatural and between purified Catholicism and popular yet unauthorized versions of traditional Christianity, crystallized into a body of knowledge known as the discernment of spirits. This was the culmination of a 500-year theological effort to develop a coherent method of distinguishing between true and false visions and their good and evil instigators.

The most prominent among the hundreds of authors who wrote on this topic was the early fifteenth-century rector of the Sorbonne, Jean Gerson, whose treatises on it were imitated, copied, plagiarized and used throughout the early modern period. In accordance with cognitive and perceptual theories of the period, Gerson agreed that alleged encounters with spirits and alleged apparitions were more likely to have resulted either from natural causes or from disorderly thoughts, which were themselves shaped by excitation of the passions. The soul, always imaginative, fashions images, and often they are so vivid that it is impossible to distinguish simulacra of bodies from real bodies. A religious vision, a dream, a mad person's hallucination and a demonic illusion could all yield identical visual experiences. It is also impossible to identify whether they are external or internal and whether the instigator of a vision is God or Satan. So while discernment of spirits is crucial to preventing us from falling into error, Gerson failed miserably in his attempt to offer a cognitive method of discernment. Instead, he created a social hierarchy of reliabilities: The educated are more reliable than the unlearned; the wealthy are to be trusted more than the poor; and women's visions should always be viewed with the utmost suspicion.[29]

There is no point in reviewing this body of literature. The discernment of spirits was a field of incessant citation, reiteration and plagiarization.[30] Writing 300 years after Jean Gerson, Prospero Lambertini, the future Pope Benedict XIV, was still unable to move beyond Gerson's frustrated effort. In his *On the Beatification of the Servants of God and on the Canonization of the Blessed* (*De servorum Dei beatificatione et beatorum canonzatione*) (1734–1738), an encyclopedic treatment of all things supernatural, he settled for a discernment based on the moral outcome of the vision. If the vision asks the visionary to act against the commands of the church, or if it denies scriptural truths, or if it brings feelings of confusion and grief, it is obviously demonic. If it brings gladness, sweetness and love, it is clearly divine. But what if Satan acts as an angel of light, Lambertini then asked

29 Roth 2001; Caciola 2003; Elliott 2004; Anderson 2011.
30 Sluhovsky 2007; Copeland and Machielsen 2013.

himself? In the 1730s, just as 500 years earlier, Satan could still control and traverse the entire process of human cognition.[31]

Importantly, Lambertini's analysis was also the culmination of another process, namely, the rationalization (in the other, Weberian sense of the term) of the supernatural and the miraculous. The realm of the supernatural, which, over the previous centuries, had already been narrowed down, was now to be patrolled and guarded by a professional bureaucracy of parish priests, bishops and, on top of them, a special committee in Rome, the Congregation for Rites, which alone had the authority to authenticate miracles, visions, visionaries and other supernatural events, seers and beings. All of these agencies of control functioned according to judicial procedures that involved the collection of testimonies, the interrogation of witnesses and the assessment of both their reliability and their adherence to narrowly restricted preexisting notions of the supernatural.[32] "Evidentiary theology," to use Lorraine Daston's term, came to dominate all discussion of the supernatural. Early modern theologians, both Protestant and Catholic, referred to this body of knowledge as physico-theology, and between the fifteenth and the eighteenth centuries it generated an immense number of treatises, subfields, methods and internal debates.[33] It had one goal: To restrict the realm of the supernatural as much as possible and, with it, the constant danger of sensorial deception.[34] The few events "that did pass through the fine sieve of official scrutiny were backed by so much legal and medical evidence" that they are among the best-documented facts of early modern Europe.[35]

Nevertheless, the discernment of visions failed to solve the epistemological quandary it was created to solve, because there was no solution to the epistemological question of the veracity of all things seen. Along the way, the realm of the supernatural and preternatural was restricted, and a new consensus emerged that reports of visions and apparitions were never to be trusted. Probative inquests should refute rather than confirm testimonies of supernatural events, or so this new theology of suspicion instructed. Nature, theologians agreed with natural philosophers, works according to mechanistic and physical rules. But unlike the natural philosophers, who spoke of *laws* of nature and of probabilities, theologians insisted that nature's regularities were merely habitual patterns. The tran-

31 Lambertini 1734–1738; M. Rosa 1991; Vidal 2007, 2013.

32 Schroeder 1941:217; S. Rosa 1996; Klaniczay 2000; Brambilia 2003; Ditchfield 2007.

33 Vidal 2003.

34 For details, see Keitt 2004, 2005; Clark 2007; and Sluhovsky 2007.

35 Daston 1991:116, 121, following and quoting de Viguerie 1983.

scendental, while not bound by the laws of nature, operates according to them, but only so long as it does not choose to operate otherwise.

Protestant attacks on visions of Mary and angels and sightings of ghosts of the dead were not a rejection of apparitions *tout court*. Just like the Catholic discussion of these matters, Protestant thinking on visions was characterized by ambivalence.[36] The Bible explicitly supplied proof that God used the natural world as a medium of communication, and therefore a total rejection of optical encounters with supernatural beings contradicted both Scripture and God's free will. Visions of prodigies and signs in the sky were, in fact, extremely popular among early Protestants, who witnessed in such signs the End of Time. And while descriptions of visible angels were rejected as Catholic superstitions, Protestant theologians, including the Swiss Zwinglian pastor Ludwig Lavater (1527–1586), the most radical and most popular Protestant author on the topic, admitted that *invisible* angels intervened regularly on behalf of the faithful. The days of angelic *apparitions* had ended, he explained, yet angels themselves were alive and well, and therefore God *might* still reveal them at critical moments.[37] This was a loophole large enough for a host of angels to pass through.

By the seventeenth century, then, and in both belief systems, physical appearances of demons, angels, ghosts, fairies, saints, deceased relatives and the Virgin were considered extraordinary and very rare suspensions of the rules of nature. The confessional divide was not as significant as the shared understanding that no objective and reliable criteria for deciding the veracity of apparitions on visual grounds could possibly be sustained.[38] Both Protestants and Catholics opposed skeptical materialists who refused to admit that there are things supernatural, and both belief systems insisted that there are things that lie beyond natural causality and scientific explanation, and that no materialistic, rationalistic or medical theory could account for their veracity. Furthermore, in their attempts to rationalize and suspend the supernatural, authors on occasion developed alternative theories that were no less extravagant than miracles. Thus, for example, Protestants discussed supposedly natural qualities of minerals and liquids that would account for what Catholics regarded as the healing miracles that occurred in shrines and water sources.[39]

36 Walsham 1999; Cameron 2010:174–191; Soergel 2012.
37 Lavater 1572.
38 See Cameron 2010; Copeland and Machielsen 2013.
39 Walsham 2008; Jillings 2013.

The seventeenth century did indeed witness a short period of fetishization of the visualization of truth through public demonstrations of scientific experiments. The air pump, the vacuumed room and the use of condoms on copulating male frogs were all celebrated experiments that proved scientific truths by way of visual demonstration. But already by the second half of the seventeenth century, natural philosophers were arguing that mathematical probabilities and physical laws are infallible even when they cannot be demonstrated or even when they contradict what the physical eye sees. Thus, the rationalized science of the early modern period was as much a rejection as an affirmation of visuality: Accurate scientific observations relied on abstract mathematical laws that predetermined the reliability of the observed experience. The old suspicion of the eye, along with the assertion that the eye of the mind sees better than the eye of the body, came back to dominate scientific thought. None other than Descartes – the author of treatises on optics, who dissected a cow's eye and built his own *camera obscura*, and the man often credited with the breakthrough in vision theory – stated that "it is the soul that sees, and not the eye; and it does not see directly, but only by means of the brain."[40]

In his "demon hypothesis" in the first of his *Meditations on First Philosophy* of 1641, immediately following his adamant refusal to entertain the possibility that God is a deceiver and the entire visual world is a simulacrum, Descartes suggests the possibility that a malicious demon of the utmost power and cunning has turned every human experience into a delusion. Can we really be sure that our waking experience is not mere illusion, since these experiences are similar to what we see in dreams?[41] Richard Popkin, the great historian of the Western skeptical tradition, suggests that this thought experiment was both unprecedented and the most dramatic skeptical speculation in the entire tradition.[42] Following Stuart Clark, I want to argue that we have in fact already encountered this malicious demon; he is unmistakably the late medieval and early modern Satan who transforms himself into an angel of light, the trickster who destabilizes any attempt to trust both natural and supernatural experience.

My intention is not to participate in the obsessive search for origins that, itself, is a characteristic of modernity. I suggest, rather, that while late medieval and early modern theories and theologies of knowledge, cognition and perception failed in their attempts to create a method for discerning and authenticating spectral apparitions and visual experiences of the supernatural, they legitimized

40 Descartes, ed. Cottingham et al. 1984, I:172.
41 *Ibid.*, II:13. See also Scarre 1990; Wachbrit 1996; and Nadler 1997.
42 Popkin 1978:178; but see Groarke 1984 for precedents.

an intellectual climate receptive to ever more radical philosophical rationalization and skepticism. Recall how, in trying to determine the reliability of visions, Gerson ended up considering variables such as bodily condition, emotional state, age and above all the social standing and gender of the visionary. Put differently, the discernment of encounters with the supernatural led to the conclusion that human vision was interpretable, that it relied not on visual cognition itself but on social agreements. When Descartes explained that visions consist of "*judgments* about things seen," he was arguing for a social construction of reality.[43]

Descartes was also expressing an epistemological skepticism whose goal was to overcome radical skepticism, and which had been in the making for the previous three centuries. Descartes conceded what late medieval philosophers and theologians had already implicitly argued, namely, that seeing is not a natural process but a cultural and social habituation and negotiation, in which variables such as physical health, social and economic standing, intelligence and gender are of crucial importance. After all, the only way he managed to affirm the reliability of the senses was by entertaining and then dismissing the possibility that he himself might be insane:

> Perhaps I were to liken myself to madmen, whose brains are so damaged by the persistent vapors of melancholia that they firmly maintain they are kings when they are paupers, or say they are dressed in purple when they are naked, or that their heads are made of earthenware, or that they are pumpkins, or made of glass. But such people are insane, and I would be thought equally mad if I took anything from them as a model for myself.[44]

At the end of the day, and with a skeptical detour, the only guarantee Descartes had that the world was not one huge deception was his own unwillingness to consider himself insane; as Michel Foucault put it, the exclusion of folly was "the foundational act of the organization of a new order of truth."[45] The rationalization of vision derived not from new scientific insights as much as from an agreement to reject what society deemed irrational

Two parallel developments, then, led to the replacement of one way of accounting for apparitions and spectral visions with another. Perception theories could not in and of themselves solve the problem of visions, since the latter

43 Descartes, ed. Cottingham et al. 1984, II:295; cf. Judovitz 1993:72; Clark 2007:334–344. Stuart Clark's as yet unpublished "Visions and Knowledge in a Religious Context: Discernment of Spirits in the Age of Descartes" [2011] has significantly shaped my thinking on this point. I thank Professor Clark for sharing his paper with me prior to its forthcoming publication.
44 Descartes, ed. Cottingham et al. 1984, II:13.
45 Foucault 2012:96; and see Foucault 2006.

were not more unreliable than other types of ocular events and, like them, were a matter of social agreement. So it was not the epistemological or philosophical difficulties relating to the veridicality of the senses that led to the rejection of most claims of encounters with supernatural beings or with the souls or bodies of the dead. Rather, the new dismissal of visions that were allegedly experienced or witnessed by the poor, the uneducated, the marginal and by women was the product of a combination of factors: inter-religious disagreements regarding the veracity of things seen and unseen; the efforts of both Catholics and Protestants to resist skeptical materialists; and a growing need to control the spiritual experiences of unqualified (and "superstitious") people – be they women, physically ill, spiritually-enthusiastic or mad. What mattered most to the early modern Catholic Church (as also to most Protestant denominations) was the Church's control of the social affirmation of the reliability of visions and its monopoly on determining what they signified. Things seen with the eyes no longer corresponded to images in the brain. Instead, what was seen was more like words and signs – conveying social meanings that had to be deciphered.[46]

References

Amelang, James S. 2012. "Sleeping with the Enemy: The Devil in Dreams in Early Modern Spain." *American Imago*, 69:319–352.

Anderson, Wendy L. 2011. *Discernment of Spirits: Assessing Visions and Visionaries in the Late Middle Ages*. Tübingen: Mohr Siebeck.

Bilu, Yoram. 2013. "'We Want to See our King': Apparitions in Messianic Habad." *Ethos*, 41:98–126.

Brambilia, Elena. 2003. "La fine dell'esorcismo: Possessione, santità, isteria dall'età barocca all'illuminismo." *Quaderni storici*, 112:117–163.

Buci-Glucksmann, Christine. 1986. *La folie du voir: De l'esthétique baroque*. Paris: Galilée.

Caciola, Nancy. 2003. *Discerning Spirits: Divine and Demonic Possession in the Middle Ages*. Ithaca: Cornell University Press.

Cameron, Euan. 2010. *Enchanted Europe: Superstition, Reason, and Religion, 1250–1750*. Oxford: Oxford University Press.

Camille, Michael. 2000. "Before the Gaze: The Internal Senses and Late Medieval Practices of Seeing." In Robert S. Nelson (ed.), *Visuality Before and Beyond the Renaissance: Seeing as Others Saw*. Cambridge: Cambridge University Press. 197–223.

Campagne, Fabián Alejandro. 2002. *Homo Catholicus, Homo Superstitiosus: El discurso antisupersticioso en la España de los siglos XV a XVIII*. Buenos Aires: Miño y Dávila.

Cascardi, Anthony J. 1992. *The Subject of Modernity*. Cambridge: Cambridge University Press.

46 Cf. Foucault 1970: Chaps. 2–3. Foucault calls the process a transition from resemblance to representation.

Clark, Stuart. 1997. *Thinking with Demons: The Idea of Witchcraft in Early Modern Europe*. Oxford: Oxford University Press.
—. 2007. *Vanities of the Eye: Vision in Early Modern European Culture*. Oxford: Oxford University Press.
—. [2011]. "Visions and Knowledge in a Religious Context: Discernment of Spirits in the Age of Descartes." Paper presented in the Clark Library, UCLA, October 2011.
Copeland, Clare, and Jan Machielsen (eds.). 2013. *Angels of Light? Sanctity and the Discernment of Spirits in the Early Modern Period*. Leiden: Brill.
Daston, Lorraine. 1991. "Marvelous Facts and Miraculous Evidence in Early Modern Europe." *Critical Inquiry*, 18:93–124.
Daston, Lorraine, and Katharine Park. 1998. *Wonders and the Order of Nature, 1150–1750*. New York: Zone Books.
Dawes, Gregory W. 2013. "The Rationality of Renaissance Magic." *Parergon*, 30:33–58.
Denery, Dallas G. II. 2005. *Seeing and Being Seen in the Later Medieval World: Optics, Theology and Religious Life*. Cambridge: Cambridge University Press.
—. 2009. "Protagoras and the Fourteenth-Century Invention of Epistemological Relativism." *Visual Resources*, 25:29–51.
Descartes, René. *The Philosophical Writings of Descartes*, ed. John Cottingham, Robert Stoothoff and Dugald Murdoch. 1984. 3 vols. Cambridge: Cambridge University Press.
Ditchfield, Simon. 2007. "Tridentine Worship and the Cults of the Saints." In Ronnie Po-chia Hsia (ed.), *The Cambridge History of Christianity: Reform and Expansion, 1500–1660*. Cambridge: Cambridge University Press. 201–224.
Dupré, Louis. 1993. *Passage to Modernity: An Essay in the Hermeneutics of Nature and Culture*. New Haven: Yale University Press.
Eamon, William. 1994. *Science and the Secrets of Nature: Books of Secrets in Early Modern Culture*. Princeton: Princeton University Press.
Eire, Carlos M.N. 1986. *War Against the Idols: The Reformation of Worship from Erasmus to Calvin*. Cambridge: Cambridge University Press.
—. 1990. "The Reformation Critique of the Image." In Robert W. Scribner (ed.), *Bilder und Bildersturm in Spätmittelalter und in der frühen Neuzeit*. Wiesbaden: Harrassowitz. 51–68.
Elliott, Dyan. 2004. *Proving Women: Female Spirituality and Inquisitional Culture in the Later Middle Ages*. Princeton: Princeton University Press.
Fogleman, Andrew. 2009. "Finding a Middle Way: Late Medieval Naturalism and Visionary Experience." *Visual Resources*, 25:7–28.
Foucault, Michel. 1970. *The Order of Things: An Archaeology of the Human Sciences*. New York: Random House.
—. 2006. "My Body, This Paper, This Fire" (1972). In idem, *History of Madness*. New York: Routledge. 550–574.
—. 2012. *Du gouvernement des vivants: Course au Collège de France (1979–1980)*. Paris: Gallimard and Seuil.
Gal, Ofer, and Raz Chen-Morris. 2013a. *Baroque Science*. Chicago: University of Chicago Press.
—. (eds.). 2013b. *Science in the Age of Baroque*. Dordrecht: Springer.
Gordon, Bruce, and Peter Marshall (eds.). 2000. *The Place of the Dead: Death and Remembrance in Late Medieval and Early Modern Europe*. Cambridge: Cambridge University Press.
Grellard, Christophe. 2007. "Scepticism, Demonstration and the Infinite Regress Argument (Nicholas of Autrecourt and John Buridan)." *Vivarium*, 45:328–342.

Groarke, Leo. 1984. "Descartes' First Meditation: Something Old, Something New, Something Borrowed." *Journal of the History of Philosophy*, 22:281–301.

Hansen, Bert. 1985. *Nicole Oresme and the Marvels of Nature: A Study of His* De causis mirabilium. Toronto: Pontifical Institute of Medieval Studies.

Ivins, William M. Jr. 1973. *On the Rationalization of Sight: With an Examination of Three Renaissance Tests on Perspective* [1938]. New York: De Capo.

Jay, Martin. 1993. *Downcast Eyes: The Denigration of Vision in Twentieth-Century French Thought*. Berkeley: University of California Press.

Jillings, Karen. 2013. "Scotland's 'Naturall Elixirs' and 'Sacred Liquors': Explaining the Medicinal Power of Mineral Waters." *Parergon*, 30:59–79.

Judovitz, Dalia. 1993. "Vision, Representation, and Technology in Descartes." In David M. Levin (ed.), *Modernity and the Hegemony of Visions*. Berkeley: University of California Press. 63–86.

Keitt, Andrew. 2004. "Religious Enthusiasm, the Spanish Inquisition, and the Disenchantment of the World." *Journal of the History of Ideas*, 65:231–250.

—. 2005. *Inventing the Sacred: Imposture, Inquisition, and the Boundaries of the Supernatural in Golden Age Spain*. Leiden: Brill.

Kieckhefer, Richard. 1994. "The Specific Rationality of Medieval Magic." *American Historical Review*, 99:813–836.

Klaniczay, Gábor. 2000. "I miracoli e i loro tetomoni: La prova dei soprannaturale." In Paolo Golinelli (ed.), *Il Pubblico dei santi: Forme e livelli di ricezione dei messaggi agiografici*. Rome: Viella. 259–287.

Lambertini, Prospero. 1734–1738. *De servorum Dei beatificatione, et beatorum canonizatione*. Bologna: Longhi.

Lavater, Ludwig. 1572. *Of Ghostes and Spirites Walking by Nyght* [1569]. London: n. p.

Levin, David M. 1997. *Sites of Visions: The Discursive Construction of Sight in the History of Philosophy*. Cambridge, Mass.: MIT Press.

Lindberg, David C. 1976. *Theories of Vision from Al-Kindi to Kepler*. Chicago: University of Chicago Press.

Marshall, Peter, and Alexandra Walsham (eds.). 2006. *Angels in the Early Modern World*. Cambridge: Cambridge University Press.

Merleau-Ponty, Maurice. 1968. *The Visible and the Invisible*. Evanson, Ill: Northwestern University Press.

Merton, Robert K. 1970 [1938]. *Science, Technology and Society in Seventeenth-Century England*. New York: Harper Torchbooks.

Minnis, Alastair. 2009. "Medieval Imagination and Memory." In idem and Ian Johnson (eds.), *Cambridge History of Literary Criticism*, II: *The Middle Ages*. Cambridge: Cambridge University Press. 239–274.

Nadler, Steven. 1997. "Descartes' Demon and the Madness of Don Quixote." *Journal of the History of Ideas*, 58:41–56.

Newman, Barbara. 2005. "What Did It Mean to Say 'I Saw'? The Clash between Theory and Practice in Medieval Visionary Culture." *Speculum*, 80:1–43.

Park, Katharine. 2006. *Secrets of Women: Gender, Generation, and the Origins of Human Dissection*. New York: Zone Books.

—. 2010. "Holy Autopsies: Saintly Bodies and Medical Expertise, 1300–1600." In Julia Hairston and Walter Stephens (eds.), *The Body in Early Modern Italy*. Baltimore: Johns Hopkins University Press. 61–73.

Pasnau, Robert. 1997. *Theories of Cognition in the Later Middle Ages*. Cambridge: Cambridge University Press.
Perler, Dominik. 2010. "Could God Deceive Us? Skeptical Hypotheses in Late Medieval Epistemology." In Henrik Lagerlund (ed.), *Rethinking the History of Skepticism: The Missing Medieval Background*. Leiden: Brill. 171–192.
Plane, Ann Marie, and Leslie Tuttle (eds.). 2013. *Dreams, Dreamers, and Visions: The Early Modern Atlantic World*. Philadelphia: University of Pennsylvania Press.
Popkin, Richard H. 1978. *The History of Scepticism from Erasmus to Spinoza*. Berkeley: University of California Press.
Rosa, Mario. 1991. "Prospero Lambertini tra 'regolata devozione' e mistica visionaria." In Gabriella Zarri (ed.), *Finzione e santità tra medioevo ed età moderna*. Turin: Rosenberg and Selleir. 521–550.
Rosa, Susan. 1996. "Seventeenth-Century Catholic Polemics and the Rise of Cultural Rationalism: An Example from the Empire." *Journal of the History of Ideas*, 57:87–107.
Roth, Cornelius. 2001. *Discretio Spirituum: Kriterien geistlicher Unterscheidung bei Johannes Gerson*. Würzburg: Echter.
Scarre, Geoffrey. 1990. "Demons, Demonologists and Descartes." *Heythrop Journal*, 31:3–22.
Schreiner, Susan E. 2011. *Are You Alone Wise? The Search for Certainty in the Early Modern Era*. New York: Oxford University Press.
Schroeder H.J. (ed.). 1941. *Canons and Decrees of the Council of Trent: Original Text with English Translation*. St. Louis: Herder.
Siraisi, Nancy G. 1997. *The Clock and the Mirror: Girolamo Cardano and Renaissance Medicine*. Princeton: Princeton University Press.
Sluhovsky, Moshe. 2007. *Believe Not Every Spirit: Possession, Mysticism, and Discernment in Early Modern Catholicism*. Chicago: University of Chicago Press.
Soergel, Philip. 2012. *Miracles and the Protestant Imagination: The Evangelical Wonder Book in Reformation Germany*. Oxford: Oxford University Press.
Tachau, Katherine H. 1988. *Vision and Certitude in the Age of Ockham: Optics, Epistemology, and the Foundations of Semantics, 1256–1345*. Leiden: Brill.
Taves, Ann. 2009. *Religious Explanation Reconsidered*. Princeton: Princeton University Press.
Teresa of Avila, *The Collected Works of Teresa of Avila*, ed. Kieran Kavanaugh and Otilio Rodriguez. 1976–1985. 3 vols. Washington, DC: ICS.
Viberg, Åke. 2001. "The Verbs of Perception." In Martin Haspelmath, Ekkehard König, Wulf Oesterreicher and Wolfgang Raible (eds.), *Language Typology and Language Universals: An International Handbook*. Berlin: De Gruyter. 165–185.
Vidal, Fernando. 2003. "Extraordinary Bodies and the Physicotheological Imagination." In Lorraine Daston and Gianna Pomata (eds.), *The Faces of Nature in Enlightenment Europe*. Berlin: Berliner Wissenschafts Verlag. 61–96.
—. 2007. "Miracles, Science, and Testimony in Post-Tridentine Saint-Making." *Science in Context*, 20:481–508.
—. 2013. "Prospero Lambertini's 'On the Imagination and Its Powers.'" In Maria Teresa Fattori (ed.), *Medicina e diritto nei trattati di Prospero Lambertini – Benedetto XIV*. Rome: Storia e Letteratura. 297–318.
de Viguerie, Jean. 1983. "Le miracle dans la France du XVIIe siècle." *XVIIe siècle*, 35: 313–331.
Wachbrit, Robert. 1996. "Cartesian Skepticism from Bare Possibility." *Journal of the History of Ideas*, 57:1009–1029.

Walsham, Alexandra. 1999. *Providence in Early Modern England*. Oxford: Oxford University Press.
—. 2008. "Sacred Spas? Healing Springs and Religions in Post-Reformation Britain." In Bridget Heal and Ole Peter Grell (eds.), *The Impact of the European Reformation: Princes, Clergy, and People*. Aldershot: Ashgate. 209–230.
—. 2010. "Invisible Helpers: Angelic Intervention in Post-Reformation England." *Past and Present*, 208:77–130.
Wandel, Lee Palmer. 1995. *Voracious Idols and Violent Hands: Iconoclasm in Reformation Zurich, Strasbourg, and Basel*. Cambridge: Cambridge University Press.
Weber, Max. 1946. "Science as Vocation." In *Max Weber: Essays in Sociology*. Edited by Hans Heinrich Gerth and C. Wright Mills. New York: Routledge. 129–155.
Wiebe, Philip H. 1997. *Visions of Jesus: Encounters from the New Testament to Today*. Oxford: Oxford University Press.

Simon Gerber

“They Shall Be All Taught of God”: Schleiermacher on Christianity and Protestantism

Religion as Intuition and Feeling

> Therefore it is time to take up the subject from the other end and to start with the sharp opposition in which religion is found over against morals and metaphysics. That was what I wanted. ... Religion's essence is neither thinking nor acting, but intuition and feeling. ... Praxis is an art, speculation is a science, religion is sensibility and taste for the infinite.[1]

Thus wrote the young Reformed chaplain Friedrich Schleiermacher in 1799. His friends from the Berlin romantic circle had urged him to write a philosophical book, and so Schleiermacher had taken advantage of a stay of several months at Potsdam as a vicarious court preacher, far from his ordinary affairs as hospital chaplain at the Charité in Berlin. The result was five apologetic speeches on religion, addressed to its cultural despisers. When Enlightenment theologians had defended religion, they had tried to show its utility for the common life: Religion makes a man moral; it helps one to achieve virtue and blissfulness. You do not like those “poorly stitched together fragments of metaphysics and morals that are called rational Christianity,”[2] Schleiermacher tells the despisers of religion; nor do I. But, he says, I can show you what is genuine religion; it belongs properly to human nature, but nowadays it is “held in a despicable slavery.”[3]

Now, what kind of feeling and intuition would be genuine religion, freed from that slavery? It is an intuition of the universe that seeks to “accept everything individual as a part of the whole and everything limited as a representation of the infinite.”[4] If you view the world around you not only as an aggregation and accumulation of separate particulars to be explored and worked upon, but, rather, you feel everything, including yourself, as belonging to the one universe and representing the universe, you are religious.

1 Schleiermacher 1799:50, 52 f (1984:211 f; 1996:22 f).

2 *Ibid.*:25 (1984:199; 1996:12).

3 *Ibid.*:26 (1984:199 f; 1996:13).

4 *Ibid.*:56 (1984:214; 1996:25).

https://doi.org/10.1515/9783110446395-010

A crucial point for the interpreters is the question of whether religion as intuition, according to Schleiermacher, is an attitude only of passiveness and affection, or whether elements of activity – that is, of interpretation and construction of the particulars, perceived as the one coherent universe, also pertain to it.[5] Later on, in his scientific system of philosophy and theology, Schleiermacher modified intuition into his theory of feeling as immediate self-consciousness, which is the point of indifference preceding intellect and will. This immediate self-consciousness continues unchanged while acts of reflection and of will alternate and relieve one another. Religion is feeling and has its anthropological place at the very base, in the immediate self-consciousness, beyond intellect and will (or, as the Speeches have it, beyond metaphysics and morals).[6] It is the feeling of absolute dependency, the feeling of one's relation to God.[7]

Back to the Speeches on Religion! Religion as intuition of the universe has two peculiar attributes: it is individual, and it seeks community and communication. A particular religion or individual instance of religion arises "through free choice by making a particular intuition of the universe the center [or central intuition or fundamental intuition] of the whole of religion and relating everything therein to it."[8]

Such arbitrarily centralized intuitions are the positive religions, despised and rejected by the friends of enlightenment, who prefer a natural or rational religion that can be common to all.[9] Schleiermacher replies:

> So-called natural religion is usually so refined and has such philosophical and moral manners that it allows little of the unique character of religion to shine through.[10] ...
> You will find that precisely the positive religions are these determinate forms in which infinite religion manifests itself in the finite, and that natural religion cannot claim to be something similar inasmuch as it is merely an indefinite, insufficient and paltry idea that can never really exist by itself.[11]

On the other hand, individuality and positiveness of religion do not mean that each individual has his own hermetically secluded religion. On the contrary:

---

5 Cf. Albrecht 1994; Grove 2004; Lauster 2011.
6 Schleiermacher 1806:44–78 (1995:43–64); 2002, I:141–143 (Dialectics, lectures 1814/15, lesson 35, § 214 f); 1830–1831, I:§ 3.2–5 (2003, I:22–32).
7 Schleiermacher 1830–1831, I:§ 4 (2003, I:32–40).
8 Schleiermacher 1799:259 f, cf. 265 (1984:303, cf. 305 f; 1996:104, cf. 106).
9 Cf., e.g., Kant 1794:167–183 (1914:115–124); 1798:70–115 (1917:48–69).
10 Schleiermacher 1799:243 (1984:296; 1996:98).
11 *Ibid.*:248, cf. 274 f (1984:298 f, cf. 309 f; 1996:100, cf. 109).

> Once there is religion, it must necessarily also be social. That not only lies in human nature but also is preeminently in the nature of religion. You must admit that it is highly unnatural for a person to want to lock up himself what he has created and worked out. ... But the most proper object of this desire for communication is unquestionably that where man originally feels himself to be passive, his intuitions and feelings.[12]

Christianity

What is Christianity? It is one positive religion among others, one of the forms in which infinite religion realises itself. And what is its *differentia specifica* among religions? According to the Speeches on Religion, the original intuition of Christianity is:

> the intuition of the universal straining of everything finite against the unity of the whole and of the way in which the deity handles this striving, how it reconciles the enmity directed against it ... Corruption and redemption, enmity and mediation are two sides of this intuition that are inseparably bound to each other.[13]

Thus, the problem of human history and of religion itself is the material for the original intuition of Christianity; among religions, Christianity is raised to a higher power.[14]

The introductory paragraphs of Schleiermacher's Dogmatics, his "Glaubenslehre," undertake a definition of Christianity from the perspective of philosophy of religion and apologetics. Christianity is a monotheistic religion, above Judaism and Islam, the purest realisation of the monotheistic idea that has up to now appeared in history.[15] Its piety is teleological; that is, Christianity refers to the ethical idea of a coming kingdom of God.[16] And its peculiarity is that everything relates to the redemption accomplished by Jesus of Nazareth. Jesus is the principal object of Christian piety. He has more dignity than Moses has for the Jews or Mohammed for the Muslims, because Jesus is not only a teacher or prophet of a

---

12 *Ibid.*:177 (1984:267; 1996:73).
13 *Ibid.*:291 (1984:316; 1996:115).
14 *Ibid.*:293 f (1984:317 f; 1996:116).
15 Schleiermacher 1830–1831, I:§ 8.4, 9.2 (2003, I:70 f, 78–80). Judaism, because of Jehova's predilection for Abraham's offspring, is akin to fetishism; from the notions of Jehova's commanding will and of his reward and retribution for all human deeds it ensues that Jewish consciousness of God relates more to the active than to the passive states of human consciousness. Islam, by virtue of its passionate and sensual character and its aesthetic fatalism, has analogies with polytheism.
16 *Ibid.*, I:§ 9 (2003, I:74–80).

doctrine, who has to follow the doctrine himself. For Christians, Jesus is the one who is without sin and doesn't need redemption for himself; his position as the Redeemer is not amidst his congregation but over against it.[17]

Since all positive religions emerge from an individual and original religious intuition, Christianity is not the continuation or perfection of the Old Testament religion. Rooted in Old Testament and Jewish monotheism, Christianity is nevertheless a new religious idea.[18] In his fifth Speech on Religion, Schleiermacher had already declared:

> [E]very intuition of the infinite exists wholly for itself, is dependent on no other, and has no other as a necessary consequence.[19] ...
> I hate that type of historical reference in religion. Its necessity is a far higher and eternal one, and every beginning in it is original.[20]

Insofar as the apostles' preaching was addressed to Jews as well as to Gentiles, Christianity stands in an equal relation to both.[21]

What Schleiermacher writes at the beginning of the "Glaubenslehre" in order to define Christianity from an external point of view, he expresses at the beginning of his lectures on church history as his confession of faith: First of all, Christianity begins with Christ. Christ is neither a reformer of Judaism nor merely a wise man like the antique philosophers; he is the beginner of something new, and the history of Christianity is the evolution and realization of that new thing in the world. Second, that which is new in Christ is a religious idea, and so it can also be called a divine revelation. It is destined to be conveyed to the whole human race.[22] So Schleiermacher's confession of faith refers both to the religious originality of Christ and Christianity and to the universal tendency.

Consequently, the introduction to the "Glaubenslehre" numbers among the natural heresies of Christianity two views that deny the universal salvation accomplished by Christ: Pelagianism and Manichaeism. Pelagianism (historically, an early fifth-century view that contradicted the doctrine of original sin and taught the participation of the human free will in salvation) refers here to the notion that humanity, or a part of it, has no real need for redemption by Christ. Manichaeism (historically, a late-antique syncretistic religion combining a doc-

17 *Ibid.*, I:§ 11.4 (2003, I:98–101).
18 *Ibid.*, I:§ 12.1 (2003, I:103).
19 Schleiermacher 1799:249 (1984:299; 1996:100).
20 *Ibid.*:287 (1984:314; 1996:114).
21 Schleiermacher 1830–1831, I:§ 12.2 (2003, I:103–105).
22 Schleiermacher 2006:22, 473 f (Church History, lectures 1821/22, lesson 2).

trine of salvation with a dualistic philosophy of nature alloying elements of Zoroastrism, Hellenism, Gnosticism, Judaism and Christianity), conversely, refers to the idea that parts of humanity cannot be redeemed by Christ, because they are too wicked to receive redemption.[23] Both views are heretical, for the notion that all of humanity needs salvation and is redeemed by Christ's work of salvation is essential to Christian faith.

According to Schleiermacher, Christianity represents what is, for the present, the highest degree of evolution among religions.[24] Nevertheless, there is no reasonable evidence of the truth of Christian religion. A religion whose truth is proved would no longer be religion, but philosophical metaphysics.[25]

Is Schleiermacher's theory of religion a kind of rationalization of religion? Yes and no. No, because it strictly separates religion from philosophical doctrines of God, metaphysics and philosophical ethics; Schleiermacher denies that utility and rationality are criteria of religion's value. Yes, because this separation hangs together with a transcendental philosophy and theory of human self-consciousness[26] and with a certain ethical theory of culture that gives religion a distinct place within human culture and history.[27] All of these fit together, and none can be assigned logical priority. For example, Schleiermacher rejects the idea of God's wrath. Is that because he thinks it is not compatible with the God preached by Jesus,[28] or because God, as the absolute subject implicitly presupposed by every act of human thinking,[29] cannot be angry? We do not know, nor did Schleiermacher.

---

23 Schleiermacher 1830–1831, I:§ 22.2 (2003, I:156–158). Cf. Schleiermacher 1843:369 f (Christian Ethics, lectures 1822/23).

24 In Schleiermacher's historical thought there is an ambiguity between the individuality of the historical phenomena stressed by him and the universal goal of all human development; cf. Pauck 1970:49–51.

25 Cf. Schleiermacher 1829:492–496 (1990:348–352); 1830–1831, I:§ 3.4 (2003, I:27–29).

26 The young Schleiermacher borrows from Immanuel Kant the criticism of conventional metaphysics and of the ontology of substance, but he doesn't follow Kant's proof of God's existence by practical reason. With Baruch Spinoza, Schleiermacher agrees that the object of religion is not a personal God standing outside and over against the world, but the whole and infinite, which (contra Spinoza, but according to Friedrich Heinrich Jacobi's interpretation of Spinoza) is not an intellectual intuition, but an intuition by feeling – the intuition of the universe. Spinoza's infinite is changed into a Kantian form of intuition. Cf. Arndt 2011.

27 Cf., e. g., Schleiermacher 2006:13 f (Introduction to Church History, lectures 1806, lesson 4); 1913:310–318 (Ethics, lectures 1812/13, doctrine of goods, detailed explication, § 204–251).

28 Cf., e. g., Schleiermacher 1831:189; 2015:400 (Sermon 159 on 2 Corinthians 5:17 f, October 24, 1830).

29 Cf. Schleiermacher 2002, I:108, 119–122, 136 f, 141–150 (Dialectics, lectures 1814/15, lessons 19,

To the philosopher Friedrich Heinrich Jacobi, who had declared himself a heathen by reason but a Christian by feeling, Schleiermacher wrote, "My philosophy and my Dogmatics are strictly resolved not to contradict each other." They are like the two foci of an ellipse.[30]

Catholicism and Protestantism

"They shall be all taught of God, and they shall not teach every man his brother." With this combination of biblical citations (John 6:45, Jeremiah 31:34, Hebrews 8:11), Schleiermacher describes the end and the aim of the development of Christianity.[31] All of humanity is redeemed by Christianity. The spread of Christianity throughout the human race has two functions, extension and intension: propagating the Christian faith to those that do not yet have it, and increasing the piety of those who have it already.[32]

The early Christian church was stamped by Jewish culture and tradition. As it is disseminated to the nations, Christianity interacts with many cultures and languages and takes in some peculiarities, ideas and practices from which it must later be purified. The intension of Christianity has to correct what came into it by way of extension. Thus, the state and condition of the Christian church in the world are always developing and changing, and various forms of Christianity emerge that often are in competition with each other.[33]

Of these several forms of the Christian church, there are two in which Schleiermacher has a special interest: Roman Catholicism und Protestantism. Protestantism is Schleiermacher's own form of the Christian church, on whose behalf he practices theology, while Roman Catholicism is the form from which he most dissociates himself and with which he is chiefly in contest. In the "Glaubenslehre," he declares:

25, 31 and 35–39, §§ 163–166, 183 f, 200–202, 214–223).

30 Cf. Schleiermacher 1994:395 f (letter to Friedrich Heinrich Jacobi, March 30, 1818).

31 Schleiermacher 2006:24, 480 (Church History, lectures 1821/22, lesson 5); 2006:684 (Church History, lectures 1825/26); 1829:494 (1990:350).

32 Schleiermacher 2006:22, 474 (Church History, lectures 1821/22, lessons 2 and 3); 1843:373–377 (Christian Ethics, lectures 1822/23).

33 Schleiermacher 2006:22–24, 474–480 (Church History, lectures 1821/22, lessons 3–5); 1843:209 (Christian Ethics, lectures 1826/27); 2005:468 f (Ecclesiastical Statistics, lectures 1833/34, lesson 2).

> An explanation of the Dogmatics of the occidental church in the present cannot be indifferent to the opposition between Roman Catholicism and Protestantism; it has to belong to one of these two parts.[34]

In his lectures on ecclesiastical statistics, Schleiermacher tells the students some features of Roman Catholicism: The proceedings at the election of a pope are "a regular form of irregularities, indecencies, intrigues and God knows what else."[35] Around St. Agnes' Church at Rome, the lambs are fed up: Their wool is used as the material of the archiepiscopal capes. A house at Loretto is said to be the very house where it was announced to St. Mary that she was the elected mother of the Saviour; when the Saracens occupied Palestine, angels lifted the house from Nazareth and brought it to Italy. The monks and clergymen in Spain and Portugal are weaker in their education than any monk far away in the Syrian desert. A nunnery near Lisbon was long a harem for the king and princes. Processions, bullfights and fireworks are indispensable to the celebration of a holiday.[36]

So Roman Catholicism might seem to be the unreasonable and Protestantism the reasonable form of occidental Christianity. But Schleiermacher himself wouldn't maintain that. The peculiarities of South European Catholicism stem from its isolation; the more isolated Catholicism is, the more superstitious it becomes. In France and Germany, Catholics have to compete with Protestantism, and here we find Catholic erudition, the art of preaching, biblical studies and but little superstition.[37] The actual difference between the two occidental churches is a sociological one; it refers to their respective relations between the clerics and the laics.

Education and Autonomy of the Laity

Any religion strives for communication, sociability and organization. The two essential functions of a religious community are those of the clerics and the laics; the former act more spontaneously and as instructors, while the latter are more passive and receptive.[38] In Catholicism, the distinction between clerics and laics is very strict. Catholic clerics are priests who mediate between God and the con-

34 Schleiermacher 1830–1831, I:§ 23, Leitsatz (2003, I:160).
35 Schleiermacher 2005:251 (Ecclesiastical Statistics, lectures 1827, lesson 16).
36 Schleiermacher 2005:273 f (Ecclesiastical Statistics, lectures 1827, lesson 24).
37 Schleiermacher 2005:297 f, 358–360, 371 (Ecclesiastical Statistics, lectures 1827, lessons 30, 47 and 50).
38 Schleiermacher 1913:359–361 (Ethics, lectures 1812/13, Perfect ethical forms, § 196–209); 1830–1831, I:§ 6.4, II:§ 133 (2003, I: 57 f, II:342–346).

gregation, and the laics must obey the priests, especially their father confessors. Without a priest there is no access to God for the faithful; the priest rules the conscience of the layperson. Protestants, by contrast, believe that every faithful person is a priest who has access to God. Clergymen are the teachers and instructors of the congregation; their function is to help the laics attain religious independence and autonomy, first of all by instructing them in how to read and understand the New Testament by themselves.[39]

The basic difference between the two churches is this different comprehension of the function of the clerics toward the laics, but it calls forth further differences. Protestantism has a natural interest in national education, while in Catholic states education is a work of opposition to the church.[40] According to Catholic doctrine, the priest is above the secular government, since the government officials are laic, and so the church requires clerical immunity to criminal procedures by the secular justice system.[41] Since Protestant churches, by contrast, do not constitute an interstate organisation, many Protestants believe the church to be an institution of the state; they might learn from Catholics that it is otherwise and that an interstate association of Protestant national churches might be desirable.[42] Finally, in the Protestant church individuals and laics have the competence to criticize the organized bodies of the church and to discuss whether the church has deviated from the doctrine of the New Testament. It was in this way, as a purification and alteration of the church starting from below and from individuals, that the reformation began and the Protestant church arose. According to Catholic doctrine, individuals must be obedient to the clerical representatives of the church;[43] any disobedience is destructive, and the state of Protestantism is the best illustration of what results therefrom.[44]

Measured by the aim and end of Christianity, Protestantism is a more developed form of Christianity than Catholicism. For Protestantism to have emerged, the intension of Christianity must have proceeded far enough for the laics, step for by step, to have come of age and need less teaching by their brothers, the

39 Schleiermacher 1843: Beilage 148; 175 f, 519–521 (Christian Ethics, lectures 1822/23); 1843:208, 366 f, 432, 434, 522–524 (Christian Ethics, lectures 1826/27); 2005:298–300, 394, 396 f (Ecclesiastical Statistics, lectures 1827, lessons 31, 56–57).

40 Schleiermacher 2005:322 f (Ecclesiastical Statistics, lectures 1827, lesson 37).

41 Schleiermacher 2005:249 f, 374, 392 (Ecclesiastical Statistics 1827, lessons 17, 50 and 55).

42 Schleiermacher 1821:458 (1995:319); 2005:378, 394–396 (Ecclesiastical Statistics, lectures 1827, lessons 51 and 56).

43 Schleiermacher 1843:182–205 (Christian Ethics, lectures 1822/23).

44 Schleiermacher 2005:383, 388 (Ecclesiastical Statistics, lectures 1827, lessons 53 and 54); 1830–1831, I:§ 24.3 (2003, I:166 f.).

clerics, than they needed in the times of the apostles, the church fathers and the medieval bishops.[45] Since then, they have advanced on the path to equality with their teachers. At the end of this development there will be no more extension and teaching of Christianity, except for the education of children.[46] But that is still far in the future.

References

Albrecht, Christian. 1994. *Schleiermachers Theorie der Frömmigkeit* (Schleiermacher-Archiv, 15). Berlin–New York: De Gruyter.

Arndt, Andreas. 2011. "On the Amphiboly of Religious Speech." In Dietrich Korsch and Amber L. Griffioen (eds.), *Interpreting Religion* (Religion in Philosophy and Theology, 57). Tubingen: Mohr. 99–111.

Grove, Peter. 2004. *Deutungen des Subjekts* (Theologische Bibliothek Töpelmann, 129). Berlin–New York: De Gruyter.

Kant, Immanuel. 1794. *Die Religion innerhalb der Grenzen der bloßen Vernunft²*. Königsberg: Nicolovius.

—. 1798. *Der Streit der Facultäten*. Königsberg: Nicolovius.

—. 1914 [1797]. *Die Religion innerhalb der Grenzen der bloßen Vernunft: Die Metaphysik der Sitten* (Akademie-Ausgabe, 6). Berlin: Reimer.

—. 1917 [1798]. *Der Streit der Facultäten: Anthropologie in pragmatischer Hinsicht* (Akademie-Ausgabe, 7). Berlin: Reimer.

Lauster, Jörg. 2011. "Religion as Feeling." In Dietrich Korsch and Amber L. Griffioen (eds.), *Interpreting Religion* (Religion in Philosophy and Theology, 57). Tubingen: Mohr. 73–84.

Pauck, Wilhelm. 1970. Schleiermacher's Conception of History and Church History. *Journal for Theology and the Church*, 7:41–67.

Schleiermacher, Friedrich. 1799, 1806, 1821. *Über die Religion*. Berlin: Unger; 2nd (1806) and 3rd (1821) editions, Berlin: Reimer.

—. 1829. "Dr. Schleiermacher über seine Glaubenslehre, an Dr. Lücke." *Theologische Studien und Kritiken*, 2:255–284, 481–532.

—. 1830–1831. *Der christliche Glaube nach den Grundsäzen der evangelischen Kirche im Zusammenhange dargestellt²*. I–II. Berlin: Reimer.

—. 1831. *Predigten in Bezug auf die Feier der Uebergabe der Augsburgischen Confession* (Predigten, Sechste Sammlung). Berlin: Reimer.

45 Schleiermacher 2006:24, 480 f, 629 (Church History, lectures 1821/22, lessons 5 and 91–93); 2006:680 f, 684–686 (Church History, lectures 1825/26); 1843:324–326, 432 (Christian Ethics, lectures 1826/27); 2005:322 f, 396 f (Ecclesiastical Statistics, lectures 1827, lessons 37 and 57); 1830–1831, II:§ 88.3 (2003, II:25).

46 Schleiermacher 2006:24, 480 (Church History, lectures 1821/22, lesson 5); 1843:373 (Christian Ethics, lectures 1822/23); 2006:684 f (Church History, lectures 1825/26); 1830–1831, II:§ 119.3, 120 Zusatz, 125.1, 157.1, 164.1 (2003, II: 264 f, 276 f, 300 f, 456 f, 494 f).

—. 1843. *Die christliche Sitte nach den Grundsäzen der evangelischen Kirche im Zusammenhange dargestellt*, ed. Ludwig Jonas (Sämmtliche Werke, I/12). Berlin: Reimer.
—. 1913. *Entwürfe zu einem System der Sittenlehre*, ed. Otto Braun (Werke, 2; Philosophische Bibliothek, 137). Leipzig: Meiner.
—. 1984. *Schriften aus der Berliner Zeit 1796–1799*, ed. Günter Meckenstock (Kritische Gesamtausgabe, I/2). Berlin–New York: De Gruyter.
—. 1990. *Theologisch-dogmatische Abhandlungen und Gelegenheitsschriften*, ed. Hans-Friedrich Traulsen in cooperation with Martin Ohst (Kritische Gesamtausgabe, I/10). Berlin–New York: De Gruyter.
—. 1994. "Schleiermacher an Jacobi, 30. März 1818," ed. Andreas Arndt and Wolfgang Virmond. In Walter Jaeschke (ed.), *Religionsphilosophie und spekulative Theologie: Quellenband* (Philosophisch-literarische Streitsachen, 3.1). Hamburg: Meiner. 394–398.
—. 1995. *Über die Religion, (2.–)4. Auflage; Monologen, (2.–)4. Auflage* (Kritische Gesamtausgabe, I/12), ed. Günter Meckenstock. Berlin–New York: De Gruyter.
—. 1996. *On Religion*^{2}, English transl. and ed. by Richard Crouter. Cambridge: Cambridge University Press.
—. 2002. *Vorlesungen über die Dialektik*, ed. Andreas Arndt, I–II (Kritische Gesamtausgabe, II/10). Berlin–New York: De Gruyter.
—. 2003. *Der christliche Glaube, 2. Auflage (1830/31)*, ed. Rolf Schäfer, I–II (Kritische Gesamtausgabe, I/13). Berlin–New York: De Gruyter.
—. 2005. *Vorlesungen über die kirchliche Geographie und Statistik*, ed. Simon Gerber (Kritische Gesamtausgabe, II/16). Berlin–New York: De Gruyter.
—. 2006. *Vorlesungen über die Kirchengeschichte*, ed. Simon Gerber (Kritische Gesamtausgabe, II/6). Berlin–New York: de Gruyter.
—. 2015. *Predigten: Fünfte bis Siebente Sammlung*, ed. Günter Meckenstock (Kritische Gesamtausgabe, III/2). Berlin–Boston: De Gruyter.

Johannes Zachhuber

Christian Theology as a Rationalization of Religion: The Case of the Nineteenth-Century Research University

Theology as Rationalization

Rationalization is not a univocal concept. Notwithstanding the powerful and suggestive way in which Max Weber summarized his understanding of Western culture and its development with the help of this term, it is far from obvious that the various features of the modern world that he enlisted as proof for the historical uniformity of its meaning are all species of a genus called rationalization. Care and a healthy dose of skepticism are therefore needed in any approach to this topic if one is to avoid falling victim to the spell of the Weberian narrative.[1]

Urging care is not, however, the same as denying any value to Weber's observations. My attempt to think about theology, and more specifically about theology within the modern university, in terms of rationalization inevitably follows the Weberian trajectory to a certain extent. The existence of systematic theology was, after all, one notable feature which, according to the great sociologist, was indicative of the West's unique intellectual tradition.[2] While I shall remain noncommittal, for the purposes of this paper, about any claims to Western exceptionalism, I shall argue that Christian theology *can* be understood as a rationalization of this religion. By this I imply more than the conventional notion of theology as "faith seeking understanding" or as the *ratio fidei*;[3] theology "rationalizes" in very practical ways. By making the faiths of individuals compatible, it allows for, or at least facilitates, the creation of a faith community; and through its critical function, it adjudicates between competitive truth claims made by different believers or groups of believers. In a word, its "rational" character "rationalizes" and thus tames, restrains and controls religion. It is therefore unsurprising that

1 For a summary of Weber's position see his "Vorbemerkung" in Weber 1988:1–16.

2 *Ibid.*:1.

3 For these formulations see Anselm of Canterbury, ed. Davies and Evans 1998:87 (*Proslogion: Premium*).

https://doi.org/10.1515/9783110446395-011

Christian theology has been described as a "function of the Church":[4] Historically and sociologically, this is undoubtedly accurate insofar as theology has facilitated the integration of religious diversity into a single, hierarchical institution.

The Church, however, was not the only institution concerned to control religious activities. In many ways, the modern European state has been predicated from its inception in the seventeenth century on the idea that religion is dangerous and must be contained. Religious policies in Europe, whether conservative or liberal, have long been determined by a fear of religion, originating in the religious wars of the early modern period.[5] Religious establishment was as much an instrument of controlling religion as a means of supporting it. In this regard, too, theology had its role to play; the state's willingness to fund theological faculties was at least partly an expression of its hope and expectation that theology would endorse and underwrite the "rationalized" form of religion attractive from the point of view of the state. As we shall see, theologians were perfectly aware of this rationale and willing to appeal to it when defending the legitimacy of their discipline within the modern university.

If Christian theology thus "rationalizes" religion, it would be wrong to ignore that it was also an object of rationalization. Church and state, in different ways, have sought (and seek) to "rationalize" theology so that its results will strengthen rather than undermine their attempts to control religion. This, too, has undeniably positive aspects, insofar as funding and institutional support have been provided in the interest of the pursuit of high-quality theological scholarship and training. Yet the Janus-headed nature of rationalization is never far away; theology is empowered but also constrained by all these attempts. Theologians who resist this pressure risk being branded as heretics or academic failures, but that is often only because they are marked out as incompatible with the specific rationality demanded by the ecclesial institution or by the terms of the country's religious arrangement.

One major route this rationalization has taken since the high Middle Ages is the integration of theology into the university, to which both Church and state have contributed throughout the centuries, albeit in different ways and with varying degrees of enthusiasm. The university offers a fascinating illustration of the dual and ambiguous nature of rationalization. Intended as the institution *par excellence* of rationality, knowledge and learning, it is the place that ought to be dominated by reason alone. And yet its rationality also tames, constrains and excludes. Some premises are acceptable, others are not; some questions are

---

4 Barth 1955:1.

5 Cf. Zachhuber 2010:150–153.

admissible, others excluded. A certain type of thinker works well in this institution, while others who are equally or more creative do not. In a word, an institution founded on the principle of rationality *in and of itself* produces a social discipline.

This is not a particularly new or original insight,[6] but the fact and the extent to which theology offers itself as a test case for this observation has been less noted.[7] Theology is always and has always been a marginal member of the university. To be sure, it was given the title of queen of the sciences in the medieval university. However, its status and position within the overall system of human knowledge represented by the *universitas litterarum* was controversial and contested right from the beginning, as borne out by the immense energies invested in discussions of the question of whether it was a "science."[8]

My subsequent argument rests on the assumption that to consider theology a science is the supreme expression of the specific rationalization of theology within the university. Here, again, this rationalization has two aspects. On the one hand, integration into the framework of the university triggers a new level of rational reflection within theology, going beyond what has been practiced in and recognized by the Christian Church throughout its history: the formation and development of doctrine, the interpretation of Scripture (exegesis), and reflections about the forms of Church organization and governance (canon law), about events in its history (Church history) and about its relationship to rival accounts of reality (apologetics). Viewing theology as a science adds another layer of questions concerning the internal coherence of the various branches of theology (do all these diverse undertakings form a single discipline?), its methodology (how should investigation and debate about them be conducted?) and its epistemological principles (where do their insights originate? what are the sources and the

6 The classical exposition of this view is Weber's famous essay *Wissenschaft als Beruf*: Weber 1994:1–23.

7 Weber himself, interestingly, offers a brief discussion of theology in *Wissenschaft als Beruf*, *ibid.*:21–22. He states: "all theology is rationalization of the possession of sacred values."

8 A brief note on terminology: In this paper, I shall use "science" to translate Latin *scientia* and German *Wissenschaft*, both of which are abstract nouns derived from the verb "to know" and thus denoting a system of knowledge in the broadest possible sense. While English "science" used to have a similarly broad meaning, this changed in the mid-nineteenth century. Increasingly, "science" came to refer more specifically and exclusively to the natural sciences. When John Henry Newman, in *The Idea of a University*, discussed the question of whether theology was "a science," this already sounded archaic (Newman 1996:26). Today, the older meaning of the term has become obsolete. It is therefore not ideal to use it, but since there is no appropriate English equivalent available, it seems to be the least problematic solution to a veritable terminological conundrum.

criteria for distinguishing right from wrong, the appropriate from the less appropriate, in this process of reflection?). In this sense, theology in the university can be seen as theology in a higher order of rationality, extending the range of the questions to the principles and coherence of the discipline.

On the other hand, it is far from obvious that a stringent application of these criteria is even possible in the case of theology. It may well be argued that subjection to the agenda implied in this form of "rationalization" cripples theological reflection in such a way as effectively to rob it of its most productive and creative power.[9] The argument *against* the acceptance of theology as a science has therefore always been pressed from two seemingly contradictory angles: On the one hand, it has been the battle-cry of those who would prefer to oust theology as "irrational" from the realm of respectable academic learning and study; on the other, it has been the project of those who fear that "scientific theology" risks giving up too much of what is essential for the faith-guided reflection of which the Church and its believers are in need; that it stifles spirituality; that it invites skepticism if not atheism.

The conflict as such is well known; yet I would argue that it, too, can be inscribed into the logic of double rationalization: If theology exercises rationalization with regard to the faith community and is itself the object of rationalization within the university, it finds itself, unsurprisingly, pulled in these two directions: It can always be accused either of being lacking in rationality or of displaying too much of it (a charge frequently expressed by invoking the word "rationalistic"). This dynamic is arguably not new to Western modernity,[10] but it plays out in a particularly illuminating way in nineteenth-century German universities. It helps explain some very characteristic theological transformations and developments that occurred during this time, or so, at least, I shall argue.[11]

These nineteenth-century debates were inevitably informed and shaped by issues arising from the specifically modern transformation of Christian thought: the rise of biblical criticism, Kantian and post-Kantian philosophy, and history of dogma, to name but a few. Notably, however, the seventeenth and eighteenth-century authors who spearheaded the early forms of modern theology showed little or no interest in the question of whether or in what sense theology was a science. The latter question came to the fore precisely with thinkers whose activity

---

9 Webster 2005:11–31.

10 Interesting cases from the pre-modern age would include Origen, John Philoponus and Abaelard.

11 In what follows I take up and develop further material that I presented in my article on "Wissenschaft," Zachhuber 2013d:479–498.

was directly related to the organization of theology within the academy. This is true of Friedrich Schleiermacher, whose reflections on the topic resulted directly from his involvement in the foundation of the University of Berlin in 1810, but also of John Henry Newman, who lectured on *The Idea of a University* as rector of the newly established Catholic University in Dublin in the 1850s, and even of Wolfhart Pannenberg's extended reflections on *Theology and the Philosophy of Science* (a rather misleading rendering of *Wissenschaftstheorie und Theologie*), which were written at the height of the institutional controversies about the West German university in the early 1970s.[12]

At the same time, it is instructive to note that the question of whether theology is *scientia* was by no means rhetorical when it was first raised in the thirteenth century; in fact, the caveats and reservations expressed by those who discussed it back then in many ways anticipate later controversies and may thus indicate problems transcending the specific parameters of *Wissenschaft* as conducted within the modern academy. Without going into the details of the medieval debate, it may be useful to summarize some key problems as a heuristic starting point to the more detailed analysis of the modern discussion. It will turn out that all the fundamental problems recur; the modern theories that will be discussed in the remainder of my paper can be understood as seeking to address one or more of them within their own specific historical and intellectual environment.

First, how can a field of study be a science if it relies for its premises or principles on revelation? According to Aristotle, demonstration is only possible from principles that can either be demonstrated or are self-evidently known.[13] While we can make deductions from information obtained from others, we will never know those principles with certainty. Aquinas argued that such knowledge was possible as long as the principles were known to God and to the saints and accepted as revelation by everyone else,[14] but William of Ockham, for one, strongly disagreed:

> It is absurd to claim that *I* have scientific knowledge with respect to this or that conclusion by reason of the fact that *you* know principles which I accept on faith because you tell them to me. And, in the same way, it is silly to claim that *I* have scientific knowledge of the conclusions of theology by reason of the fact that *God* knows principles which I accept on faith because he reveals them.[15]

12 Schleiermacher 1956:219–308; Newman 1996; Pannenberg 1973.
13 Aristotle, *Analytica Posteriora* I 2 (71^b 19–25).
14 Thomas Aquinas, *Summa Theologiae* I, q. 1, art. 2, resp.
15 William of Ockham, ed. St. Bonaventure, NY, 1967:199; English text: Freddoso 2000:334.

This problem lingers in the modern debate primarily in a historicist transformation, famously formulated by Lessing, who held that "accidental truths of history can never become the proof of necessary truths of reason."[16]

Second, how do the various parts of theology form a unit? This problem is illustrated by the ambiguous use of theology, which is sometimes employed more narrowly to denote speculative reflection about Christian doctrine, but in the academic context usually denotes the ensemble of exegetical, historical, doctrinal and practical disciplines. What unites them, and how are they, in this form, distinct from and yet analogous to subjects like philosophy, history, physics or linguistics? In the German tradition, this problem is usually referred to as that of the "theological encyclopedia," and its treatment is closely related to the discussion of theology as *Wissenschaft*.[17]

Third, what methodologies ought to be used in the pursuit of theology, and what criteria are acceptable in adjudicating conflicting judgments? From the mid-nineteenth century, conceptions of science increasingly emphasized its procedural aspect, thus bringing this particular problem to prominence. Frequently, the question of theology's character as *Wissenschaft* is all but identified with its willingness to succumb to rational enquiry and its readiness to accept whichever conclusion is best supported by argument and evidence.

Fourth, how precisely is theology as a rational enterprise related to Christian faith and practice? Is faith merely a motivating factor for intellectual interest in theological enquiry, or does it, in its own specific structure, influence the actual operation and practice of theology? If the former, theology can easily appear indifferent or even implicitly hostile to faith; in fact, the academic and public prestige of certain theologians has – not only in modernity – often evoked sustained criticism from within the faith community. Yet if theology is in any more specific way beholden to its basis in Christian faith, this might appear to be in tension with, or even in contradiction to, the detached and impartial attitude required of the "scientist" with regard to their object of study.

These four questions offer a helpful structure and framework for the specific rationalization of theology as science that happened as part of its institutionalization in the university. They all triggered *both* intellectual reflection and disciplinary restriction. In the remainder of my paper, I shall investigate in more detail three paradigmatic responses to this challenge in the nineteenth century. As we shall see, these theories differed rather obviously in their conception of theology, but also in their conception of rationality. In fact, it may be most helpful to dif-

16 Lessing 1897:5; idem, ed. Chadwick 1956:53.
17 On the history of significance of "encyclopedia" see now: Purvis 2014.

ferentiate them as seeking to integrate theology into a framework of a practical rationality (Friedrich Schleiermacher), a scientific rationality (David Strauss) or a historical rationality (Ferdinand Christian Baur; Albrecht Ritschl).

Friedrich Schleiermacher's Concept of Theology as "Positive Science"

The problem of theology's place in a system of knowledge was not new to modernity. Developments from the late eighteenth century, however, created conditions that elicited new answers to most aspects of this problem. The first response I shall discuss goes back to Friedrich Schleiermacher (1768–1834). Characteristically, it was developed in the immediate context of the debates about university reform that took place in Prussia at the very beginning of the nineteenth century and ultimately led to the foundation of the University of Berlin. I cannot here discuss in any detail this fascinating public controversy, in which many leading German intellectuals of the time participated.[18] Suffice it to say that in spite of all the differences between individual discussants, they shared certain premises, the first of which was that *Wissenschaft* in the true sense was philosophy. This, of course, had been Aristotle's position, and indeed we may roughly sketch the consensus among these early nineteenth-century German thinkers by saying that their notion of science combined the Aristotelian tradition of philosophy as the systematic organization of knowledge with more romantic ideas of an organic unity-in-multiplicity. This is significant: These debates are often hailed as the intellectual origin of the modern research university, but in many ways they espoused remarkably conservative positions; the truly revolutionary views, as we shall see, were to emerge much less spectacularly.

Schleiermacher agreed with these assumptions; for him, too, *Wissenschaft* in the proper sense was philosophy,[19] but the latter, for him, always had to operate embedded in its cultural context. This stance permitted him to defend the traditional structure of the university: Theology, law and medicine all depend on regular exchange with and insights from philosophy, but philosophy itself would be incomplete without those extensions, because rational reflection cannot ever be conducted in abstraction from the concrete realities of nature and culture.[20] Schleiermacher was deeply skeptical about the ability of the human mind

18 For a full account of those debates see Howard 2006.
19 Schleiermacher 1956:258–260.
20 At the heart of Schleiermacher's philosophy stands ethics understood as a system of goods.

to construct a system of thought capable of explaining reality in its fullness – hence his opposition to Fichte and Hegel and his advocacy of a dialogical epistemology as first philosophy.[21] Rationality and hence knowledge and *Wissenschaft* are fundamentally dependent on communication and exchange; they are always perfectible and never complete.

It is this open system of science that facilitated theology's inclusion in the university. Schleiermacher did not claim that theology was an indispensable part of a system of knowledge, nor did he accept for theology any narrow definition of science as normative. In fact, his argument for the retention of the traditional "higher faculties" is remarkably conservative: This particular structure had emerged "naturally"[22] and for this reason had continued for so long. The Faculty of Theology, in particular, was founded by the Church

> in order to preserve the wisdom of the Fathers; not to lose for the future what in the past had been achieved in discerning truth from error; to give a historical basis, a sure and certain direction and a common spirit to the further development of doctrine and Church.[23]

In other words, theology exists because the Church was in need of rational reflection about its doctrines and practices, and this was best achieved by permitting these issues to be openly debated in permanent exchange with all other areas of human knowledge. Theology is to be taught in the university because the public has an interest that this be done well: The public, too, we might say, benefits from a rationally reflected form of religion. In this sense, theology is what Schleiermacher called "positive science" (*positive Wissenschaft*), a discipline that is constituted not by systematic deduction from the idea of knowledge, but by a practical need.[24] Yet it is not merely a trade, as theology, for its proper exercise, requires a solid and permanent exchange with *Wissenschaft* proper, that is, philosophy.[25]

Along the same lines, Schleiermacher argued in his *Brief Outline of the Study of Theology* that theology derives its internal unity not from its place within a system of *Wissenschaft*, but, again, from the practical need of the Church to have appropriately trained leaders.[26] It is this purpose that serves as the organizing

---

For a brilliant and brief summary of these ideas see his academy lectures *On the Highest Good*: Schleiermacher 2011:535–553, 657–677; English text: idem, ed. Froese 1992.

21 Schleiermacher 2002:378.

22 Schleiermacher 1956:257.

23 *Ibid.*:258.

24 Schleiermacher 1993:1.

25 Schleiermacher 1956:258–259.

26 Schleiermacher1993:2–3.

center of theology as *Wissenschaft* for Schleiermacher, and the philosophical and historical parts of the discipline are instrumental to this ultimate goal. Schleiermacher's argument can easily appear pragmatic, almost opportunistic. It is therefore important to see how it is embedded in his broader conception of rationality. A rational reflection on religion, we might paraphrase, cannot and must not abstract itself from its practical and cultural setting (and thus from religious communities), as rationality itself only comes to fulfillment through recognition of those realities.

What exactly does this mean for theology as a rationalization of religion? Let me return at this point to the four questions I formulated at the end of the first section.

First, like Thomas Aquinas, Schleiermacher accepts that theology is based on principles that are not themselves part of science. For Aquinas, these principles had been revealed and passed down to us through the authority of the teaching magisterium of the Church; the theologian thus relies on somebody else's knowledge for his work. Schleiermacher does not appeal to supernatural facts, but in his theory, too, the theologian is dependent for his work on something external to scientific rationality: the existence of the church as a historical and social reality. One might say that in practice the difference between the two is small; after all, revelation *in practice* is always (or almost always) accessible only as historical information, whether contained in biblical texts or in authoritative writings of the ecclesiastical tradition. Yet it seems clear that, nevertheless, something fundamental is at stake here, which may be called the historicization of religion. In *The Christian Faith* Schleiermacher argued that the utter novelty of a historical movement, which cannot be deduced from previous events, is the only reasonable meaning that the word "revelation" could possibly have.[27] It is precisely this inscrutable reality of Christianity as a historical and social formation (which Schleiermacher calls the church) that provides an extra-philosophical focal point of reference for theology in Schleiermacher's theory.

It is thus evident, second, that this same historical and social reality of Christianity is also the principle that unites the various philosophical, historical and practical fields pertaining to it.

As for methodology, thirdly, this is where Schleiermacher's concept is perhaps most evidently *wissenschaftlich*. Not only must all theological work be conducted in ways that can stand up to the highest standards of academic enquiry, but theologians must also constantly be aware of possible cross-references and interferences between their theological and related non-theological work.

27 Schleiermacher 1999:71–74.

Finally, what about the relationship between theology and faith? Schleiermacher draws a clear distinction between religion and theology. The former is a fundamental dimension of human nature, the latter a second-order discourse about it. Thus, theology would seem primarily to be a historical and philosophical interpretation of the faith that exists within the Christian community at a given time and of its historical emergence. Yet, for Schleiermacher, theology is not merely descriptive. Its reflection can and indeed has to be critical, and in this sense it offers a "rationalization" of religion. Still, it is needed by the few who have responsibility for shepherding the flock, not by the individual believer. While Schleiermacher chose Anselm's motto *credo ut intelligam* to adorn the title page of *The Christian Faith*, his view clearly was that individual faith, or religion, does not need theological reflection, but only its own social and historical manifestation in an increasingly extended group.[28]

The last point, in particular, helps us understand how, according to Schleiermacher, theology "rationalizes" religion. He is utterly explicit about the relationship between theological reflection and the need to govern and administer a large group of religious individuals. Theology is not, for him, a project for individual enlightenment; it is an elite project, a tool for those to whom religious leadership has been entrusted. This is not to say that Schleiermacher does not see theology as the rationality of faith in the more traditional sense. He clearly does; in fact, it is obvious that he considers religion to have its own specific form of rationality, which it is the task of theology to establish. As far as the individual is concerned, however, faith is enough! Religion can exist without theology, but for its organization and government, rationality is needed.

This theological rationality, then, is evidently at least partly instrumental. But Schleiermacher does not only affirm for theology the task of "rationalizing" religion; he also affirms the need for theology to be rationalized by virtue of its inclusion in the modern university. The methods it uses must be the same as those employed in other disciplines. In fact, Schleiermacher argues that a professor of theology who does not make an effort to contribute actively to philosophy – in the wide sense, including not only metaphysics and ethics but also philology and history – deserves to be ridiculed or even excluded from the university.[29] At one level, this is a demand for what we would now call interdisciplinary competence: Students of theology may expect of their teachers the ability and the willingness to traverse the distance between their theological area of expertise and related philosophical fields. The moral theologian must be conversant in ethics, the New

28 Schleiermacher 1993:2.
29 Schleiermacher 1956:261.

Testament scholar in classics, the systematic theologian in logic and metaphysics and so forth.

At the same time, however, the methodological homogeneity that Schleiermacher prescribes for every participant in the academy constrains and disciplines individual fields, and in particular theology. In fact, Schleiermacher's advocacy of a universal standard of research methodology without any acknowledgement of the potential complications arising from this principle for theology appears almost naïve. Did he not realize that the application of those methods was most likely to yield results different from, if not in outright contradiction to, traditional Christian views? It appears that he thought (much like his idealist contemporaries) that historicism could be contained by proper philosophical reflection, and while he himself, more than Hegel, engaged in exegetical and historical work, the results of that work soon became the butt of ridicule because of their lack of critical edge.[30] Be this however as it may, there is no doubt that theology is "rationalized" by virtue of Schleiermacher's principle of its methodological convertibility with philosophy; once again, this combines the advancement of intellectual insight with the imposition of order and discipline.

Schleiermacher's view of theology, then, advocates rationalization in a specific and nuanced sense. On the one hand, theology rationalizes religion by establishing its inherent rationality. Since Schleiermacher recognizes religion as a *sui generis* phenomenon in human culture, its rational reflection has to take this character into account and therefore draws on a broad and inclusive conception of rationality. At the same time, theology also rationalizes by imposing order and discipline on religious communities. This is acknowledged insofar as theology is defined as a tool for church leadership. Schleiermacher's support for theology's inclusion in the university is equally ambiguous, insofar as his advocacy of an open concept of rationality must be balanced against his demand for total convertibility of research methodologies across subjects, opening up the potential for a considerable amount of "rationalization" of which he himself, interestingly, seems to have been unaware.

Theology as the Science of Religion

While Schleiermacher insisted on the need for rational reflection upon religion (and thus for "rationalization" of religion), for him this included the need for rationality to respect, we might say, the independence and autonomy of religion

30 See the account in Schweitzer's authoritative *Quest of the Historical Jesus*: Schweitzer 1910:62.

as a field of human life. We encounter a very different view only a few decades later among the younger members of the so-called Tübingen School, a group of mostly historical theologians initiated by the Tübingen scholar Ferdinand Christian Baur (1792–1860). Here, the ideal of scientific theology is employed with a polemical edge against more traditional (and thus less "rational") forms of theology. In an editorial in the newly established *Theologische Jahrbücher*, Baur's son-in-law, Eduard Zeller (1814–1908), declared in 1841 that this journal "starts from the idea of free *Wissenschaft.*" The primary imperative of the yearbook, he continued, was "to accept freedom and consistency of thought as necessary and justified even within theology."[31]

The change in tone cannot be explained merely by the more animated temper of public debate in the lead-up to the storms of 1848. Zeller and his colleagues argued on the basis of a new understanding of *Wissenschaft* that was about to take over as the dominant model, heavily informing all public perceptions and expectations of academic work. This development happened largely outside theology; it also seems to have taken hold, at least initially, without great fanfare, simply by being accepted by an increasing number of researchers.[32] Due to the intellectual clamor surrounding the foundation of the University of Berlin, that date is often associated with the shift to modern notions of science, but, as I noted above, the conceptions proffered by the protagonists of that debate were not revolutionary. The revolution happened more silently: By 1840, it was clear that *Wissenschaft* was in practice now defined with reference not to a universality of knowledge, but to the formal rules of a particular procedure.[33] It thus became dynamic and open, geared towards the progressive discovery of new knowledge, which, however, could never be more than provisional. Any firm adherence to philosophical or religious principles was therefore ruled out; in fact, any predisposition of the individual academic came to be considered at best indifferent and, more often than not, problematic with regard to the scientific goal.

It is easy to see that Zeller's emphatic affirmation of theology as *Wissenschaft*, committed to research that is free and unconstrained by political and religious preconceptions, corresponds to this new idea. Yet he was not the first to espouse this as an ideal. If the broader transformation of the notion of *Wissenschaft* during this

31 Zeller 1842.
32 Cf. the famous opening line of A. Trendelenburg's *Logische Untersuchungen*: "The sciences happily try their own peculiar paths, but often without reflection about their method, as they are interested in their object, not in their procedure." Trendelenburg 1840:iv–v. On Trendelenburg see now Beiser 2013.
33 Schnädelbach 1984:91.

time happened silently and gradually, the situation in theology was very different indeed: The normative claim of the new ideal was enunciated with the loudest and shrillest possible fanfare in the one book that captured and divided public attention as few others had done before or after, David Friedrich Strauss's *Life of Jesus*.[34] Strauss (1808–1874), with his notorious gift for polarization, presented himself in this book as the representative of a modern, scientific mindset, in conscious contrast to the old-fashioned, albeit erudite, theologians around him. For this novel approach, he coined a new phrase which soon became the watchword for guardians of *Wissenschaftlichkeit* across disciplines: *Voraussetzungslosigkeit*, absence of presuppositions. Strauss's intention to provoke controversy by indicating irreconcilable differences between the old and the new became even more marked in his subsequent *Glaubenslehre*, published in 1841/42, whose subtitle promised to describe the Christian doctrine of faith "in its historical development and in its struggle with modern science."[35]

Strauss soon came to the conclusion that the rational standards of "modern" science left no room for theology. Yet this does not mean that his ideas are insignificant to the problem of religion's "rationalization." Strauss's own very specific concept of how religion ought to be rationalized can be gleaned from his argument, advanced in an earlier publication, that the task of the exegete was critically to unravel the seeming historicity of the biblical narrative.[36] This was necessary, he held, in order to prepare the ground for the philosophical restoration of the Christian truth by the more speculative disciplines. Precisely the same logic underlies his advocacy of the "mythical interpretation" of the gospel in the *Life of Jesus*; as the long final chapter of that work makes clear, Strauss hoped to show that the truth of the Christological dogma would become apparent after all erroneous attempts to tie it to the historical Jesus had been rejected.[37]

Strauss thus did have his own answers to our initial questions, and they were very different from Schleiermacher's.

First, insofar as it aims at a virtual transformation of faith into knowledge, the principles of theology are ultimately derived from speculative philosophy.

Second, as this knowledge can only be attained once the illusion that historical knowledge could have religious significance has been dispelled, critical exegesis and historical theology in general have a necessary role to play within the discipline. However, this role is wholly negative; it does not yield historical

34 Strauss 1835.
35 Strauss 1841/42.
36 Strauss 1839.
37 Strauss 1835:736.

knowledge but rather destroys the deceptive certainty created by the narrative spell of the biblical stories, thus paving the way for the constructive task of philosophical theology.

Third, it might seem that the question of methodology is easily answered from Strauss's point of view, but I would like to sound a note of caution here. Notwithstanding his rhetorical appeal to modern science, Strauss's conception of theology was deeply indebted to German Idealism and especially to Hegel's philosophy. Strauss himself admits this freely[38] but is rather unclear about the particular relationship between these two sources of his model.

Fourth and finally, it is significant that theology, for Strauss, is in principle relevant to every believer, as its purpose is the elevation of historical faith to speculative knowledge.[39] Theology is "faith seeking understanding," or more precisely, faith being transformed into understanding or knowledge.

Theology, for Strauss, rationalizes religion in a somewhat violent, even revolutionary (in the Marxist sense) manner. That is because the rationality of faith, for him, is originally hidden in a pre-rational, mythical narrative. Theology is a midwife assisting in the delivery of rational truth from its earlier container, and this cannot be accomplished without pain. Theology thus imposes on religion not so much the order and structure of a university discipline but the insights of modern scientific rationality. Whereas for Schleiermacher theology was a tool of Church government and therefore needed the space of the state-funded university, Strauss's theology offers a program for general, popular education, because the transformation of faith into knowledge must be appropriated by each person individually.

It can therefore be argued that this form of rationalization, while it originated in the university, was not ideally suited to it, or in fact to any institutional environment. Strauss intends to "rationalize" religion not in the interest of the Church or the state, but for the needs of the emerging class of the reading public; and the latter certainly embraced his teachings with enthusiasm.[40] One may even speculate that Strauss's personal departure from the university, though it owed much to a deeply problematic political constellation, was not without an inner logic: The type of rationalization his theology proposed was ultimately incompatible with that required by the institution.

---

38 *Ibid.*:vi.
39 *Ibid.*:742–743.
40 Graf 1982:16–18.

Theology as History of Religion

For all these reasons, Strauss's influence on university theology was limited. Much more influential was a view that may appear closely related, because it also relied heavily on the results of the critical study of the Bible and Christian tradition. According to this theory, biblical and historical theology contributed positively to theology's rational enterprise by reconstructing the history behind the available textual sources. This conception of scientific theology can be called historicist in the strict sense of the term. In different ways, it underlies the work of the two foremost German Protestant theological schools of the nineteenth century, the Tübingen School and the Ritschl School, and it was therefore crucial to this period's flourishing of historical theology. While in some ways it may be legitimate to see in Strauss an extreme proponent of this approach – and it is certainly the case that he continued to haunt the theologians associated with these schools – I shall argue that the rationalization of religion that they sought was very different from his vision.

The origins of the historicist conception can be traced back to Friedrich Wilhelm Joseph Schelling's lectures *On University Studies*, written in 1803 and thus belonging to the debate that preceded the foundation of the University of Berlin, which had also produced Schleiermacher's programmatic treatise on university education. Schelling suggests an outlook for theology that is strongly informed by history and justified by Christianity's influence on historicization:

> This is the great historical thrust of Christianity; this is the reason for which a Christian science of religion must be inseparable from, indeed wholly one with history. But this synthesis with history, without which theology itself could not be thought, in turn requires as its condition a higher Christian view of history.[41]

Religion's rationality is here closely aligned with its historicity; this is because the philosophical understanding of history has such an important place in Schelling's own thought.[42] In this sense, the "higher Christian view of history" is here explicitly enlisted to justify an idealist philosophy of history. At the same time, his formulation contains a methodical demand for the thorough historicization of theology. In the context of Christianity, a "science of religion" must be not only "inseparable" from but "wholly one" with history. Christian theology, in

---

41 Schelling 1956:69.

42 See Schelling 1857:593–603. On Schelling's philosophy of history in this work see Danz 2001:69–82.

other words, does not merely have a historical component; it is, strictly speaking, its own history. Such an ideal form of historical theology is, however, only possible on the soil of Christianity – just like Schelling's philosophy, which reaches this insight.

Schelling's intuition is developed into a veritable theory by Ferdinand Christian Baur, founder of the Tübingen School and teacher of both Strauss and Zeller.[43] For him, theology is *Wissenschaft* insofar as it offers a full integration of philosophy and history, centered on the notion of the Incarnation. The idea, as well as the reality, of God's becoming, in Christ, part of human history transforms the latter from an arbitrary sequence of isolated events into an orderly whole which in its entirety conforms to and reveals the divine plan. Yet if history is thus endowed with meaning and significance, it also and by the same token becomes the primary source of religious insight and truth. Only Christianity enables such historicism, which is far from relativist, but the product of this new perception of humankind's development in its turn takes on a normative role for Christian theology as well. Theology in its entirety, then, becomes something like a philosophy of the history of religion that develops its truth claims through historical analysis and, concurrently, allows the result of its historical work to be interpreted in light of philosophical insights.

In practical terms, this meant that the argument for the absoluteness of Christianity became the linchpin for this understanding of theology. Absoluteness here does not signify the broader assumption that Christianity is set apart from other religions as the full and ultimate revelation of truth; it refers to the more specific idea that historical work is able to establish absolute value judgments. The study of the history of religions, properly considered, thus proves not merely that Christianity is the highest or the most advanced of them; it reveals the religion of the Incarnation as the "religion of religions," as religion in itself and thus qualitatively different from all others.

Ernst Troeltsch (1865–1932) recognized the centrality of this argument in making the case, in his landmark 1902 book *The Absoluteness of Christianity and the History of Religion*, that the impossibility of establishing such absoluteness within a historicist framework pulled the rug out from under all those attempts.[44] Yet in pointing out the failure of this project, Troeltsch was not triumphalist. He himself strongly sympathized with an approach to theology that started from the historicist turn, which he saw as irrevocable.

43 Cf. Zachhuber 2013b:25–72. For Baur's debt to Schelling see Zachhuber 2013a:151–170.
44 Troeltsch 1902.

How does this model reply to the questions standing in the background of the whole debate? In response to the first question about the principles that determine theological work, the possibility that these could be inaccessible to general knowledge is emphatically excluded. The alternative to accepting this premise, it is argued, would be to reduce theology to *private* opinion and thus take away precisely what this form of the rationalization of religion is meant to achieve, namely, public justification of the tenets of the Christian faith.[45]

Secondly, the unity of theology as one science within this model is tantamount to the unity of historical and systematic theology. As such, it is much more rigorously conceived than in Schleiermacher's theory, which had been willing to allow for a variety of disciplines within theology, bound together by their common purpose with regard to Church governance. Ultimately, the unity of the discipline is guaranteed by its common object or field of research, that is, religion. Historical and systematic interpretations go hand in hand in religion's elucidation, aimed at justifying the claims of Christianity to be the true religion that enables full knowledge of God.

It is evident, thirdly, that issues of procedure or method are central to this model. Theology is *Wissenschaft* insofar as it is willing to adopt the same standards of rational, intellectual investigation that are accepted in other disciplines, certainly in philosophy or history, but possibly also in the sciences. Here, the procedural emphasis of the "new" conception of science from the 1830s makes itself felt, even though its affirmation in the German context often had as a tacit premise an idealist philosophy of history. Indeed, the adoption of this idealist philosophical framework assuaged the worry that the acceptance of empirical and open-ended methods of research in theology could ultimately lead to results incompatible with the fundamental tenets of Christianity. In practice, of course, this presupposition was frequently shaken, and that is why this model regularly gave way to the variety encountered in Strauss, who viewed critical results obtained from historical and exegetical studies as a cathartic corrective to a naïve, literalist faith, as (seemingly) suggested by Paul's statement that "the letter kills but the Spirit gives life" (2 Cor. 3:6).

What, finally, is the consequence of the adoption of this model for the relationship between faith and its rational reflection in theology? It might appear to be largely negative or at least critical; after all, proponents of this model have been the most willing to employ the word *wissenschaftlich* with a normative emphasis in the direction of those seemingly less willing to adopt a critical stance towards traditional faith. Yet things are not quite so simple and straightforward. In fact,

---

45 Pannenberg 1973:333–334.

some individual proponents of this model were rather conservative theologically. What unites them is the view that faith in itself is cognitive and therefore can and ought to be rationally elucidated. This is in stark contrast to Schleiermacher, for whom individual faith does not need theological reflection. Baur and his successors all agree that this quasi-Kantian attempt to "annul reason to make room for faith"[46] was essentially a disingenuous, pseudo-intellectual trick.

Theology, then, is unequivocally affirmed by this group of academics as a rationalization of religion. The primary basis of this affirmation is their firm conviction that the Christian faith in and of itself is strictly rational and therefore capable and indeed in need of rationalization. Its rationality, they claim, is essentially historical in character and as such convergent with the kind of historical reason that underpinned much of German scholarship across the disciplines throughout the nineteenth century. Of the three models, this one was arguably the most attuned to the institutional environment of the modern research university, and that may well explain why its proponents achieved unrivalled prestige and accolades within the academy. In this model, theology is constructed as a single discipline with a clearly defined object of research, religion, using a generally recognized methodology (mostly historical and philological) in its open-ended exploration. The internal structure of theology is derived from this systematic and constructive approach; exegetical and systematic disciplines jointly contribute to the task of theology.

It may appear that this model rationalizes less in the way of imposing order and discipline than the two previous types did. In contrast to Schleiermacher, its proponents largely refrained from direct applications of their work to the governance of the church. Unlike Strauss, they did not seek to revolutionize the way people practice their faith. And yet one must not underestimate the extent to which this type of theology "rationalized" religion. Given its historicist cast, the list of starkly normative as well as controversial statements issued by these theologians is astoundingly long, from Baur's gnostic interpretation of Christianity to Ritschl's rejection of anything smacking of "mysticism" to Harnack's critique of the Apostle's Creed. While the adherents of this model varied in their precise visions, they shared the assumption that their theological system enabled them to make definitive pronouncements on matters of faith and practice. Their theologies were systematically conceived accounts of what could and could not be admitted as genuine expressions of the Christian faith.

46 Kant 1996:31.

Conclusion

In this paper, I have argued that the concept of theology as science or *Wissenschaft* is a specific form of making religion rational, which, I suggest, owes its existence to the institutionalization of theology within the university. In the nineteenth century, it essentially took three forms. In many ways, these were inspired by different understandings of rationality as well as of religion: Schleiermacher thought human rationality had to take cognizance of external reality, including religion in both its individual and its communal dimensions; Strauss found the truth of religion in speculative philosophy and therefore used historical criticism to dismantle its traditional historical narrative; Baur and his heirs believed that it was history that brought out the rationality of religion.

All three also, in different ways, exhibited the more instrumental side of rationalization: Schleiermacher explicitly connected theology with the need to organize and govern the church; Strauss assigned an almost revolutionary task to theology in the program of transforming faith into knowledge; while Baur, Ritschl and their students systematized historical and systematic insights in a way that would make certain elements of the Christian tradition acceptable while rejecting others.

All three, finally, show distinct traces of the rationalization imposed on theologians by the nineteenth-century research university. Theology is redefined along the lines of what is acceptable within this framework. Schleiermacher can be said to have pushed hardest against this trend in advocating a broad and inclusive notion of rationality for the future university. Yet in practice he, too, accepted the existence of a single standard of respectable academic methodology as the yardstick by which everyone, including the theologian, would be measured.

More could be said about the critical reception of these theories in both the academy and wider society, but I would like to conclude this paper on a different note. If it is true that theology's rationalization of religion has a Janus head, what about the object of this rationalization? Does the Christian faith thrive when it is rationalized in this sense? Or is it stifled? Any answer to this, I would suggest, walks a tightrope. Theological rationalization is good and indeed necessary for the religion insofar as it cultivates and improves its humane potential. It can provide a space for critical reflection, deepening doctrinal and ethical views and calling into question long-cherished ideas and practices incompatible with the principles of the faith.[47] Yet it is not a good in itself. Arguably, therefore, the resistance that any such attempt encounters is not just reactionary or fundamentalist,

47 Cf. Zachhuber 2013c:216.

but a reminder that the measure of rationalization is its ability to work on and with the living reality of religious faith; otherwise it will indeed be, as Max Weber famously put it, an "iron cage" from which the spirit has escaped.[48]

The same could also be said of the university: Its rationalization of all the fields of human knowledge is good insofar as it contributes to their improvement and flourishing, but it is not a good in itself. And perhaps it can be said that the existence of theology in the university, with its constant resistance to any attempt at full rationalization, is a useful reminder of this very fact.

References

Anselm of Canterbury. *The Major Works*, ed. Brian Davies and G.R. Evans. 1998. Oxford: Oxford University Press.

Barth, Karl. 1955. *Kirchliche Dogmatik*, I/1. Zürich: Evangelischer Verlag Zollikon.

Beiser, Frederick C. 2013. *Late German Idealism: Trendelenburg & Lotze*. Oxford: Oxford University Press.

Danz, Christian. 2001. "Geschichte als fortschreitende Offenbarung Gottes." In idem, C. Dierksmeier and C. Seysen (eds.), *System als Wirklichkeit: 200 Jahre Schellings "System des Transzendentalen Idealismus."* Würzburg: Königshausen & Neumann. 69–82.

Freddoso, Alfred J. 2000. "Ockham on Faith and Reason." In P.V. Spade (ed.), *The Cambridge Companion to Ockham*. Cambridge: Cambridge University Press. 326–349.

Graf, Friedrich Wilhelm. 1982. *Kritik und Pseudo-Spekulation: David Friedrich Strauß als Dogmatiker im Kontext der positionellen Theologie seiner Zeit*. Munich: Kaiser.

Howard, Thomas A. 2006. *Protestant Theology and the Making of the Modern German University*. Oxford: Oxford University Press.

Kant, Immanuel. 1996. *Critique of Pure Reason*. English transl. by W. Pluhar. Indianapolis: Hackett.

Lessing, Gotthold Ephraim. 1897 [1777]. *Über den Beweis des Geistes und der Kraft* (G.E. Lessing's Gesammelte Werke, 13). Edited by K. Lachmann and F. Muncker. Leipzig: Göschen. (Reprinted 1968. Berlin: de Gruyter).

—. 1956. *Lessing's Theological Writings*. English transl. by H. Chadwick. Stanford: Stanford University Press.

Newman, John Henry. 1996. *The Idea of a University*. Edited by F.M. Turner. New Haven–London: Yale University Press.

Pannenberg, Wolfhart. 1973. *Wissenschaftstheorie und Theologie*. Frankfurt a. M.: Suhrkamp.

Purvis, Zachary. 2014. "Theology and University: Friedrich Schleiermacher, Karl Hagenbach, and the Project of Theological Encyclopaedia in Nineteenth-Century Germany." DPhil. Dissertation, University of Oxford.

Schelling, Friedrich Wilhelm. 1857 [1800]. *System des transzendenten Idealismus* (Sämmtliche Werke, I/5). Edited by K.F.A. Schelling. Stuttgart–Augsburg: Cotta.

48 Weber 1988:203–204.

—. 1956 [1803]. "Vorlesungen über die Methode des akademischen Studiums." In E. Anrich (ed.), *Die Idee der deutschen Universität.* Darmstadt: Wissenschaftliche Buchgesellschaft. 1–123.

Schleiermacher, Friedrich. 1956 [1809]. "Gelegentliche Gedanken über Universitäten im deutschen Sinn, nebst einem Anhang über eine neu zu errichtende." In E. Anrich (ed.), *Die Idee der deutschen Universität.* Darmstadt: Wissenschaftliche Buchgesellschaft. 219–308.

—. 1992. *On the Highest Good.* Edited by H.V. Froese. Lewiston–New York: Edwin Mellen Press.

—. 1993 [1830]. *Kurze Darstellung des theologischen Studiums zum Behuf einleitender Vorlesungen*, § 1. Edited by H. Scholz. Darmstadt: Wissenschaftliche Buchgesellschaft.

—. 1999 [1830/31]. *Der christliche Glaube nach den Grundsätzen der Evangelischen Kirche im Zusammenhange dargestellt*, § 10, Zusatz. Edited by M. Redeker. Berlin–New York: De Gruyter.

—. 2002. *Vorlesungen über die Dialektik* (Kritische Gesamtausgabe, II/10). Edited by Andreas Arndt, 1–2. Berlin–New York: De Gruyter.

—. 2011 [1827, 1830]. *Über den Begriff des höchsten Gutes: Erste Abhandlung; Zweite Abhandlung* (Kritische Gesamtausgabe, I/11). Edited by M. Rößler. Berlin–New York: De Gruyter.

Schnädelbach, Herbert. 1984. *Philosophy in Germany, 1831–1933.* English transl. by E. Matthews. Cambridge: Cambridge University Press.

Schweitzer, Albert. 1910. *The Quest of the Historical Jesus: A Critical Study of Its Progress from Reimarus to Wrede.* English transl. by W. Montgomery and F.C. Burkitt. London: Adam and Charles Black.

Strauss, David Friedrich. 1835. *Das Leben Jesu*, I–II. Tübingen: Osianer.

—. 1839. Review of Carl Rosenkranz, *Encyclopädie der theologischen Wissenschaften* (1832). In idem, *Charakteristiken und Kritiken: Eine Sammlung zerstreuter Aufsätze aus den Gebieten der Theologie, Anthropologie und Ästhetik.* Leipzig: Wigand. 213–234.

—. 1841/42. *Die christliche Glaubenslehre*, I–II. Tübingen: Osiander.

Trendelenburg, Friedrich A. 1840. *Logische Untersuchungen.* Berlin: Bethge.

Troeltsch, Ernst. 1902. *Die Absolutheit des Christentums und die Religionsgeschichte.* Tübingen: Mohr.

Weber, Max. 1988. *Gesammelte Aufsätze zur Religionssoziologie*, I. Tübingen: Mohr.

—. 1994. *Wissenschaft als Beruf* (Studienausgabe der Max-Weber-Gesamtausgabe, I/17). Tübingen: Mohr Siebeck.

Webster, John. 2005. *Theological Theology.* In idem, *Confessing God: Essays in Christian Dogmatics*, II. London: T & T Clark International.

William of Ockham. 1967. *Ordinatio I, prologue, q. 7* (Opera Theologica, 1). St. Bonaventure, NY: Franciscan University Press.

Zachhuber, Johannes. 2010. "Religion und Politik in Europa und den USA: Überlegungen zur transatlantischen Hermeneutik." *Jahrbuch Ökonomie und Gesellschaft*, 22:139–166.

—. 2013a. "Ferdinand Christian Baurs Schellingrezeption: Einige Gedanken zu den geschichtsphilosophischen Grundlagen der Tübinger Schule." In C. Danz (ed.), *Schelling und die historische Theologie des 19. Jahrhunderts.* Tübingen: Mohr Siebeck.

—. 2013b. *Theology as Science in Nineteenth Century Germany: From F.C. Baur to Ernst Troeltsch.* Oxford: Oxford University Press.

—. 2013c. "The Rhetoric of Evil and the Definition of Christian Identity." In P. Fiddes and J. Schmidt (eds.), *Rhetorik des Bösen – Rhetoric of Evil.* Würzburg: Ergon. 193–217.

—. 2013d. “Wissenschaft.” In N. Adams, G. Pattison and G. Ward (eds.), *The Oxford Handbook of Theology and Modern European Thought.* Oxford: Oxford University Press. 479–498.
Zeller, Eduard. 1842. “Vorwort.” *Theologische Jahrbücher*, 1:iv–viii.

Volker Gerhardt

Die Rationalität des Glaubens: Über die wechselseitige Angewiesenheit von Glauben und Wissen

1. Ein Begriff unter Vorbehalt. Wenn Soziologen von der „Rationalisierung der Religion" sprechen, meinen sie die Anpassung von Formen und Inhalten des Glaubens an Verhaltensnormen der ihn umgebenden Gesellschaft. Die Rede setzt voraus, dass es überhaupt Rationalisierungsprozesse in menschlichen Gesellschaften gibt. Blickt man auf den zunehmenden Einsatz von Techniken, bedenkt man die Indienstnahme der Schrift, den Aufbau arbeitsteiliger Institutionen, die Rolle der Wissenschaften, die Abhängigkeit von einem zunehmend regulierten Verkehr zu Land, zu Wasser und in der Luft sowie die inzwischen nahezu alles durchdringende Geltung des Rechts, liegt es nahe, in alledem Rationalisierungsgewinne zu sehen, die den Prozess der Zivilisierung befördern.

Doch ein Anarchist, ein Pessimist oder ein Rousseauist könnte darin auch das Gegenteil von dem vermuten, was er für wünschenswert, gut begründet und damit für vernünftig hält. Und da die Schäden und Verluste durch Rationalisierung jederzeit hoch gewesen sind, könnte die Gegenrechnung weitere Opponenten auf den Plan rufen. Die sogenannte Netzdebatte führt das derzeit in unüberbietbarer Widersprüchlichkeit vor Augen.

Selbst ein aufgeklärter Anwalt der Vernunft könnte angesichts der breiten Spur der Gewalt, die alle Kultivierung und Zivilisierung der Menschheit bis in die Gegenwart nach sich ziehen, davor zurückschrecken, hier eine sich durch Gründe ausweisende *ratio* am Werk zu sehen; mag sein, dass er sich mit dem technischen Ausdruck der „Rationalisierung" eher anfreunden kann. Fraglich aber bleibt die Rede von der Rationalisierung gesamtgesellschaftlicher Einrichtungen und Vorgänge allemal. Man müsste sie vorab als Teile eines „Systems" ausweisen, um mit wirklich guten Gründen von Rationalisierung sprechen zu dürfen; dabei darf man den Verdacht, ein „Systemtheoretiker" zu sein, nicht scheuen. Da nicht nur Luhmann, Hegel, Kant und Leibniz, sondern auch Thomas und Aristoteles zu dieser Spezies gehören, muss der Verdacht nicht schrecken.

Die grundsätzlichen Bedenken gegen die soziologische Diagnose, ihre technische Terminologie und ihre metaphysischen Konsequenzen lassen sich zurückstellen, um im interdisziplinären Gespräch über die infrage stehenden Sachverhalte zu sprechen: Darin können wir zugestehen, dass die mit dem Prozess der Zivilisierung verknüpfte Rationalisierung gesellschaftlicher Prozesse auch die

https://doi.org/10.1515/9783110446395-012

Religionen nicht ungeschoren lässt. Selbst wenn eine Religion nur die überlieferte Botschaft ihres Glaubens zu verkünden suchte, wäre sie dem gesellschaftlichen Wandel unterworfen. Und solange sich in diesem Wandel ein wie auch immer beschaffener Rationalisierungsgewinn ausmachen lässt, kann man nicht ausschließen, dass die betroffenen Religionen daran ihren Anteil haben.

Die Frage ist nur, ob es in jedem Fall *dieselbe* Rationalität ist, die für die Ökonomie, die Politik und die Religion in Anschlag gebracht wird. Und selbst wenn dies der Fall sein sollte: Wird sie zu *allen* Zeiten als solche erkannt und angenommen? Mit Sicherheit nicht. Denn es ist ja schon in den weniger problematisch erscheinenden Handlungsfeldern nicht nur aktuell umstritten und im historischen Rückblick durchaus fraglich, was als „rational" und damit als *gut begründet, vorteilhaft, bleibend, weiterführend* oder auch nur als *zeit-* und *kostensparend* bewertet werden kann.

Von den Religionen ist bekannt, dass ihnen im Gang ihrer Geschichte viel zugemutet worden ist, gegen das sie sich selbst entschieden zur Wehr gesetzt haben. Gelegentlich konnten sie sich ihm durch Rückzug in die Askese, zumindest in die ostentative Weltverleugnung entziehen. Die Verfolgung durch Andersgläubige hat dennoch nur selten nachgelassen. Sie war besonders unerbittlich, wenn es zu Abspaltungen kam, die als jederzeit bereit stehendes Movens der Religionsgeschichte gelten können. Alles, was in deren mehrtausendjähriger Blutspur zu zeitweiligen Institutionalisierungen geführt hat, hat seine „Rationaliät", die aber stets unterschiedlich bewertet worden ist. So braucht man in der Annäherung an das Jahr 2017 nur die naheliegende Frage aufzuwerfen, ob Luthers Reformation „rational" gewesen ist, um sicher zu sein, dass es hier im breiten Spektrum zwischen römisch-katholischen, orthodoxen Christen und protestantischen Christen mehr als bloß eine Auffassung gibt.

Ziehen wir ein uns heute zwar weniger beschäftigendes, aber vermutlich über die Zukunft aller Religionen entscheidendes Beispiel heran: Die mit der politischen Öffnung der griechischen *poleis* im 7. und 6. Jhdt. v. Chr. durchgesetzte Verlegung der Grabstätten aus der Mitte der Städte an deren Peripherie kann als Rationalisierung politischer Kooperation gewertet werden. Denn so wurden Übersichtlichkeit entlang der Verkehrsachsen der jeweiligen Siedlung und Platz für zentrale Versammlungsplätze geschaffen. Beides kann man als günstige Voraussetzung einer auf allgemeine Einsicht und breite Mitwirkung aller Bürger ausgerichteten politischen Organisation ansehen. Die Toten wurden nunmehr am Stadtrand bestattet, wo alsbald auch Tempel zu besuchen waren, so dass die *agora* im Zentrum für Volksversammlungen und als Marktplatz zur Verfügung stand.[1]

1 Hölscher 1998.

Tatsächlich hat das den Reformschub begünstigt, dem die antiken Monarchien im griechischen und römischen Raum zum Opfer fielen. Er hat das Experiment mit der Demokratie und der Republik ermöglicht; beide begreifen wir, trotz der zahllosen missglückten Versuche und der unzähligen Kriege, die um sie führt worden sind, als „rational", weil sie als Voraussetzung der Hoffnung angesehen werden können, die wir mit Blick auf die Beteiligung aller, auf die Wahrung grundlegender Rechte und die arbeitsteilige Wahrnehmung politischer Leitungsaufgaben bis heute für vernünftig halten.

Die damit eröffnete Chance zur Konzentration der Religion auf spirituelle Aufgaben kann man ebenfalls als „rational" ansehen, obgleich die einst im Dienst an den griechischen und römischen Heiligtümern stehenden Tempelpriester das anders gesehen haben.[2] Sie hatten einen Verlust an Einfluss auf die Politik ihrer Städte zu erleiden und folglich auch eine Schwächung ihrer Rolle als Anwälte ihres Glaubens. Das kann von einem Vertreter dieses Glaubens schwerlich als „rational" verstanden worden sein. Gleichwohl haben jene Recht, denen es um die Geltung politischer Prinzipien sowie um die Kontrolle der politischen Administration zu tun ist. Sie haben auf der Dominanz politischer Herrschaft zu bestehen, weil anderes der Wille aller nicht gewahrt werden kann. Und dieser Überzeugung kann schwerlich widersprochen werden, solange die Politik den Glauben derer, auf deren Mitwirkung sie sich stützt, nicht erzwingt und nicht verbietet.

Wir haben somit mindestens zwei grundsätzlich verschiedene Gesichtspunkte, für die Bewertung einer Rationalisierung der Religion, und die Frage ist, ob es einen einheitlichen Maßstab geben kann.

2. Eine Hoffnung freisetzende Zumutung. Die mit der skizzierten Arbeitsteilung zwischen Politik und Religion verbundene Rationalisierung ist beachtlich, und man ist geneigt, das von den Gläubigen verlangte Opfer für eine Zumutung zu halten. Müssen die Religionen sich nicht als Anwälte ihres Gottes verstehen, in dessen Namen sie alles entscheiden, was er ihnen zu tun geboten hat? Kann man im Ernst verlangen, dass sich die Anhänger eines Gottes einer gar nicht durch Gott legitimierten Macht vorschreiben lassen, was zu tun ist und was nicht?

Für religiöse Menschen sind das existenzielle Fragen. Verstehen sie ihren Glauben als Auftrag, im Dienst ihres Gottes zu leben, dessen Ansehen sie zu mehren haben, müssen sie bereits die Trennung von geistlich-religiöser und weltlich-politischer Macht als demütigend empfinden. Wenn sie die Allmacht

2 Ein frühes Beispiel bietet die Klage des Tempelpriesters Euthyphron in Platon gleichnamigen Dialog.

ihres Gottes zu vertreten haben, kann nur er ihnen Einhalt gebieten, nicht aber eine ihm gar nicht anhängende Macht. Also kann ihnen die spirituelle Hoheit über die Gläubigen nicht genügen; sie beanspruchen vielmehr, auch den alltäglichen Lebensvollzug unter das göttliche Gebot zu stellen, und suchen Einfluss auf die gesellschaftliche Ordnung im Ganzen zu nehmen. Auf diese Weise sind so gut wie alle Glaubensgemeinschaften in die politischen Kämpfe der bisherigen Weltgeschichte verstrickt. Über Jahrtausende hinweg waren die Gläubigen (und insbesondere ihre Repräsentanten) davon überzeugt, dass es in der Logik des Gottesglaubens liegt, in seinem Geist über Gläubige und Ungläubige zu herrschen.

In den Ohren der Europäer, die haben lernen müssen, dass nicht der neutrale Staat der ärgste Feind der Religionen ist, sondern dass es die Religionen selber sind, die sich bis aufs Blut bekriegen, klingt bereits die totsichere Unterscheidung zwischen „Gläubigen“ und „Ungläubigen“ wie ein Rückfall in vergangen geglaubte Zeiten. Sie haben die zusätzliche Lektion erteilt bekommen, dass Religionen den allerschlimmsten Feind in jenen haben, die aus vermeintlich reiner Wissenschaft einen politischen Glauben an sich selber propagieren, der von jeder religiösen Überlieferung befreit.

Ob diese Lektion auf Dauer wirkt, muss bezweifelt werden. Aber zunächst, so hofft man zumindest mit Blick auf Deutschland und Westeuropa sagen zu können, hat die Schreckensherrschaft der totalitären Ideologien das Vertrauen in die neutralisierende Leistung des allein auf das Recht gegründeten Staates gestärkt. So könnte den in ihren Gegensätzen befangenen Religionen der Weg zu einer Rationalität eröffnet werden, mit deren Hilfe sie einem Glauben folgen könnten, der sich in seinem Anspruch auf die individuelle Lebensführung beschränkt und auf staatsförmige Machtansprüche verzichtet.

Um zu verstehen, wie schwer es einer Religion fällt, die Ausübung politischer Herrschaft anderen zu überlassen, braucht man nur die so gut wie alle Lebensbereiche umfassende Geltung einer göttlichen Botschaft zu bedenken. Natürlich kann es Ausnahmen und nicht im einzelnen geregelte Handlungsfelder geben; in Naturreligionen und unter der Obhut einer Vielzahl vielleicht sogar konkurrierender Götter bleibt vieles offen, das in der Frühzeit der Religionen Raum für kulturelle Erprobungen gelassen hat.[3]

---

3 Herodot berichtet, wie man in seiner Zeit, also um die Mitte des 4. Jhdts. v. Chr., aus der interkulturellen Erfahrung der Vielfalt der in Griechenland, Nordafrika, Kleinasien und Asien versammelten Religionen dasjenige auszuwählen und auszuprobieren sucht, was am vielversprechendsten erschient und das größte Heil zu bieten hatte. Das war auf kulturelle Praktiken bezogen, in deren Kern bereits die individuellen Überzeugungen derjenigen wirksam waren, die von den

Doch seit der Vorherrschaft der mit universellen Lehren auftretenden Großreligionen des Altertums, also seit etwa zweieinhalbtausend Jahren, kommt das immer seltener vor. Und da sich alles menschliche Leben in sozialen Zusammenhängen vollzieht, erscheint es abwegig, die Gebote Gottes nur auf den Einzelnen zu beziehen. Denn was immer er tut, hat Voraussetzungen bei und Folgen für seinesgleichen; das meiste dürfte überdies direkt auf andere und ihre mögliche Mitwirkung bezogen sein.

Eine fortgeschrittene Zivilisation, ohne die es keine der heute bekannten „Weltreligionen" gäbe, vorausgesetzt, hat jedes Handeln eine gesellschaftliche Dimension, der jederzeit eine politische Bedeutung zukommen kann. Somit könnte es aussichtslos erscheinen, religiöse Lehren von politischen Ansprüchen freizuhalten. Die aus Staatsräson verlangte politische Enthaltsamkeit der Religionen scheint daher etwas Unmögliches zu fordern. Eine „Rationalisierung", die das erzwingt, könnte auf das Verbot des praktizierten Glaubens hinauslaufen.

Dennoch ist das, was der in religiösen Fragen neutrale Staat verlangt, im Effekt keineswegs so neu, wie es scheint. Es gibt schon eine ältere Demütigung des religiösen Menschen, die nicht erst den modernen Staaten vorausliegt, sondern die schon in der Antike empfunden worden ist: Die Kränkung liegt darin, dass es *überhaupt andere Religionen* gibt, an die zu glauben – aus der Sicht der Rechtgläubigen – nur als Frevel angesehen werden kann. Wer in dieser Lage nicht seinen eigenen Glauben dadurch zu retten versucht, dass er die Einstellung aller Andersgläubigen zwar für falsch und abwegig hält, sie zugleich aber nach dem Modell von Völkern und Staaten denkt, die sich zwar eines schönen Tages erobern, einverleiben und damit auch bekehren lassen, vorerst aber als leidiges Übel hingenommen werden müssen – der kann nur zu leicht seinem eigenen Glauben untreu werden.

Immerhin hat die Duldung der nicht zu ändernden Realität religiöser Gegensätze zur Idee politischer Koexistenz geführt, die Toleranz ermöglicht – wenn zunächst auch nur nach Art einer aufgenötigten Schwäche. Im Vergleich mit dem bloßen Ertragen der Andersgläubigen war es jedoch ein Rationalitätsgewinn, fordern zu können, den Glauben der Anderen nicht nur als solchen hinzunehmen, sondern ihn anzuerkennen und zu achten. Diese Einsicht erhält mit der Proklamation des Menschenrechts im 18. Jahrhunderts universelle Gültigkeit[4] und

anderen Religionen Kenntnis hatten und sich von ihnen überzeugen ließen. – Für die Frühzeit vorstaatlicher Religionen sei auf das von Robert N. Bellah eindrucksvoll interpretierte Material verwiesen: Bellah 2012.

4 Zur Geschichte der Toleranz siehe: Forst 2003.

sie findet ihre Steigerung in der Profilierung des Prinzips der Individualität,[5] das im individuellen Unterschied als solchem einen unschätzbaren Vorteil für die Kultur, die Politik sowie für den Einzelnen selbst zu erkennen vermag.

Gemessen am theologischen Universalitätsanspruch des Glaubens an einen einzigen, alles umfassenden göttlichen Willen erscheint diese Reduktion der Verbindlichkeit des göttlichen Gebots auf die Lebensführung des Einzelnen beinahe selbst schon wie eine Preisgabe des religiösen Glaubens. Die machthabenden religiösen Institutionen warnen denn auch vor der „subjektivistischen" Aushöhlung der kirchlichen Lehre und sehen mit der Einheitlichkeit des Bekenntnisses den Glauben selbst in Gefahr.

In der Tat kann die Individualisierung des Glaubens als weitere Zumutung erscheinen, die alle empören könnte, die den Glauben für eine gemeinschaftliche Form des menschlichen Bewusstseins halten. Sie wollen den Glauben nur dort gelten lassen, wo es die ihm entsprechenden Lebensformen gibt, und sie neigen dazu, ihn nur dann anzuerkennen, wo er institutionalisierten Geboten folgt. Mit diesem Verständnis hat man „Ketzer" verfolgt und Mystiker als Verräter an der Gemeinschaft geächtet.[6] Damit dürften auch die von den Amtskirchen alleingelassenen und gleichwohl für ihren Glauben in den Tod gegangenen Opfer der totalitären Vernichtungsmaschinerie nicht als „Christen" bezeichnet werden.[7]

3. Drei Stufen der Rationalisierung des Glaubens. Mit der von niemandem ernsthaft erwogenen Konsequenz eines generellen Ausschlusses von Gläubigen, die als Märtyrer isoliert und in den Tod getrieben worden sind, soll nur die Absurdität benannt werden, die darin bestünde, die skizzierte Abfolge der Rationali-

---

5 Kant erhebt dieses Prinzip zum Kerngedanken seiner Ethik, wenn der dem kategorischen Imperativ die Fassung gibt, dass die Menschheit „in der Person eines jeden Menschen" gewahrt werden soll. Die damit sachlich erfolgte Zuspitzung auf das Individuum wird von Wilhelm von Humboldt sowie – in Berufung auf ihn und Sokrates – von John Stuart Mill ausdrücklich gemacht. Dazu vom Verf.: Gerhardt 2007:64–76.

6 Als Beispiel mag die durch Albertus Magnus gutgeheißene Ausrottung jener Dominikaner genügen, die sich unter Berufung auf das Paulus-Wort (Kor.3, 17: „Wo aber der Geist des Herrn ist, da ist Freiheit") als *spiriti libertati* um eine spirituelle Vertiefung ihres Glaubens bemühten. Die Anklage gegen Meister Eckhart war vermutlich auf seine Verbindung zu den Brüdern und Schwestern des „freien Geistes" gegründet. Näheres dazu im Kommentar zu: Porete 1987.

7 Ich verweise auf Dietrich Bonhoeffer, Alfred Delp und Helmuth James von Moltke, an deren Bedeutung ich im Beschluss meines Versuchs über das Göttliche: Gerhardt 2014a, erinnert habe. Dass damit keine Sonderstellung des christlichen Glaubens behauptet werden soll, wird in der abschließenden Erinnerung an das Schicksal des Hamburger Rabbiners Joseph Carlebach kenntlich gemacht.

sierung der Religionen zu verwerfen. Halten wir fest: Der *erste* Schritt besteht im *Verzicht auf den Totalitätsanspruch* einer Religion, indem sie sich mit ihrer regionalen oder nationalen Dominanz, als Religion unter anderen Religionen abfindet.

Der *zweite* Schritt erfolgt mit der *Tolerierung* nicht allein der Existenz, sondern des *Existenzrechts* der anderen Religionen, die man in ihrer Eigenart zu schätzen vermag.

Der *dritte* Schritt bietet sich mit der anerkannten *Individualisierung* des Glaubens an, die sowohl innerhalb wie auch außerhalb der bestehenden Religionsgemeinschaften stattfinden kann. Dieser vorerst letzte Schritt wird von manchen Religionen mit besonderem Argwohn betrachtet. Dazu besteht kein Anlass, sofern der Glauben von der Schuldfähigkeit des Einzelnen und damit von seiner Verantwortung vor Gott ausgeht. Das ist in der Tradition des Alten Testaments angelegt und wird im Neuen Testament mit der an jeden Einzelnen ergehenden Aufforderung einer unbedingten Nachfolge Jesu zum tragenden Prinzip des Glaubens.[8]

Es ist offenkundig, dass mit diesen drei Stufen der Rationalisierung des Glaubens kein historisches Gesetz beschrieben ist, das sich überall in verbindlicher Zeitfolge vollzieht. Es gibt, wie wir wissen, große Unterschiede zwischen den einzelnen Religionsgemeinschaften sowie zwischen den verschieden geographischen, kulturellen und nationalen Regionen. Die hier bestehenden Differenzen können zu größten Abweichungen führen, die wir derzeit sowohl innerhalb der christlichen Kirchen wie auch innerhalb der islamischen Welt oder der buddhistischen Schulen vorfinden. Die Spannungen zwischen den Gläubigen in Europa und Nordamerika einerseits und denen in Südamerika, Afrika und Asien andrerseits bedrohen die Einheit nicht nur der römischen Kurie.

Auch die Ungleichzeitigkeiten zwischen den Weltreligionen sind nicht zu übersehen. Aber es wäre voreilig, daraus den Schluss zu ziehen, nur eine oder nur zwei oder drei dieser Religionen seien zu der geschilderten Rationalisierung fähig. Die Charakterisierung der drei Entwicklungsschritte legt vielmehr nahe, dass alle Religionen zu einer solchen Entwicklung fähig sind, sobald sie über die ökonomischen, politischen und kulturellen Voraussetzungen verfügen, die jedem Individuum eine eigenständige, selbstbestimmte Lebensführung ermöglichen.

Doch dass auch hier nicht automatisch mit mehr Liberalität und Individualität zu rechnen ist, zeigt die Entwicklung der christlichen Kirchen in der westlichen Zivilisation: Je mehr sie genötigt sind, auf machtpolitische Ambitionen zu verzichten und die Verfügung über Leib und Leben ihrer Anhänger in die politi-

---

8 Dazu vom Verf.: Gerhardt 2002:1–16.

sche Obhut des Staates zu geben, umso entschiedener neigen sie zum Oktroi ethischer Wertungen. Noch ehe sie den Versuch unternehmen, ihre eigenen Anhänger auf den von ihnen gedeuteten Willen Gottes zu verpflichten, versuchen sie ihre moraltheologischen Ansichten zu staatlich sanktionierten Gesetzen zu erheben und für alle Bürger verbindlich zu machen. Obgleich sie zu schwach sind, ihre Auffassungen zur Empfängnisverhütung, zur *In-vitro-fertilisation*, zur Leihmutterschaft oder zur Sterbehilfe bei ihren Gläubigen durchzusetzen, versuchen sie ihre Auffassung für alle Bürger verbindlich zu machen.[9]

Diese seit Jahren in so gut wie allen westlichen Staaten betriebene Zwangsmissionierung in Fragen der Selbstbestimmung am Lebensanfang und am Lebensende widerspricht der längst zu einer Selbstverständlichkeit gewordenen Trennung von rechtsstaatlicher Organisation und kirchlicher Seelsorge. Sie belegt, wie schwer den Kirchen die Rationalisierung ihrer Religion selbst unter den Bedingungen einer rechtlich geordneten gesellschaftlichen Arbeitsteilung des politischen und des geistlichen Lebens fällt. Gleichwohl muss sie zur Grundlage des zivilisierten Daseins werden, wenn der Stellvertreterkrieg zwischen den Gewalten im Himmel und auf Erden auch nur im Grundsatz beigelegt werden soll.

Dass der Streit zwischen den staatlichen und den religiösen Institutionen in Einzelfragen jederzeit aufflammenden kann und dann auch von den Kirchen mit der jeder Organisation offenstehenden Mitteln der Meinungsbildung befördert werden kann, ist damit nicht bestritten. Nur muss klar sein, dass die Kirchen dann als Interessenvertreter auftreten, so wie es auch die Gewerkschaften, die Wirtschaftsverbände oder die wissenschaftlichen Vereinigungen zu tun pflegen. Die zivilisierende Rationalisierung erlaubt es den Religionen nicht, in der Berufung auf das Göttliche einen politischen Vorteil geltend zu machen.

Das Beispiel der Bioethik zeigt, wie schwer es den christlichen Kirchen selbst in etablierten Demokratien fällt, dem Rationalisierungsgebot zu folgen. Zwar haben sie auf hoheitliche Ansprüche verzichtet, doch dafür fordern sie, gleichsam kompensatorisch, die Oberhoheit in den Fragen der Moral und der Lebensführung. Während sie dem Staat die Gewalt über äußere Güter überlassen, nehmen sie die Herrschaft über das Gewissen aller Bürger in Anspruch. Trotz ihres Verzichts auf die Staatsgewalt, lassen sie nicht vom Alleinvertretungsanspruch über das moralische Bewusstsein aller ab und gebärden sich als Vollstrecker einer

9 Beispiele sind die Empfängnisverhütung, das Verbot der Abtreibung (insbesondere auch das der Spätabtreibung), die Präimplantationsdiagnostik (PID) oder die Selbstbestimmung im Sterben lassen. Siehe dazu vom Verf.: Gerhardt 2014b.

ethischen *volonté generale*, der die im Grundrecht der Würde garantierte Selbstbestimmung des Einzelnen zum Opfer fällt.

Das sei nur angemerkt, um kenntlich zu machen, dass die Rationalisierungserwartung auch auf der Stufe der Individualisierung von den Religionen Opfer verlangt, die Glaubensgemeinschaften in Fragen der Lebensführung nur zögernd erbringen. Doch die in vielen Fällen gefundenen parlamentarischen und juridischen Kompromisse lassen erkennen, dass hier ein Lernprozess im Gang ist, der auf die Kirchen zurückwirken wird.

Von grundsätzlicher Bedeutung ist hingegen die Frage, ob sich Religionen überhaupt rationalisieren lassen: Kann sich ein auf das Seelenheil gerichteter Glauben jemals damit abfinden, einem stets auch parteiliche Interessen verfolgenden Gebot der Politik unterworfen zu sein? Könnte der Glauben, der ein Absolutes zu seinem Inhalt hat, nicht *a priori* unfähig sein, überhaupt Kompromisse einzugehen, wie sie die Rationalisierung von ihm verlangt?

Das ist die Frage, auf die in den folgenden Punkten eine Antwort skizziert wird. In ihr wird das Feld der historischen Betrachtung nur gestreift, um einer philosophisch-theologischen Erwägung Raum zu geben, die sich ganz auf die Natur des Glaubens beschränkt, um zu zeigen, dass der Glauben selbst eine Rationalität zu Ausdruck bringt, die es sowohl den Religionen wie auch dem Gläubigen leicht machen müsste, die Notwendig einer vernünftig abgewogenen Einbindung der Religion sowohl in die erfahrene wie auch in die rationale erschlossene Welt einzusehen.

4. Glauben als rationaler Umgang mit dem Wissen. Es kann gar nicht sein, dass der Glauben an eine göttliche Macht schon von sich aus Kompromisse mit weltlichen Mächten ausschließt. Die Relativität der Autorität natürlicher Verhältnisse und gesellschaftlicher Instanzen mag noch so offenkundig sein: Sie können vielmehr sowohl den Einzelnen wie auch ganze Gemeinschaften von Gläubigen mit guten Gründen veranlassen, klug und behutsam mit ihrem Glauben umzugehen. Denn so umfassend und über alles erhaben Gott auch gedacht werden muss: Im menschlichen Glauben, in dem er einzig gegenwärtig ist, wird selbst Gott zu einer weltlichen Größe, die grundsätzlich weder einer Prüfung noch einem Vergleich noch einem Zweifel an seiner Wirksamkeit entgehen kann.

Tatsächlich kommt der geglaubte Gott im menschlichen Dasein selbst nur als eine relative Größe vor, die ihre unbedingte Geltung allein im Bewusstsein des ihm ergebenen Menschen annehmen kann. Nach der wörtlichen Bedeutung von „Rationalisierung", die stets eine „Logifizierung" durch Sprechen und Denken einschließt, ist der geglaubte Gott immer nur ein Gedanke, der selbst auf Rationalisierung beruht und ihr hinfort auch unterliegt. Der Gott, auf den wir uns vor anderen Mächten und Kräften einstellen, ist auf seine sich im Glauben entfaltende Kraft beschränkt. Er steht keineswegs als die eindeutig als Gott bekannte Größe vor aller Augen. Vielmehr ist er – als geglaubte Größe – gerade auch nach Ansicht derer, die ihm folgen, auf die Kraft des Glaubens angewiesen, um in dem vom Menschen erhofften Sinn als Gott erkennbar und tätig zu sein.

Was aber für den im Glauben gewahrten Gott gilt, muss auch für die den Glauben sichernde Religion Bestand haben. Es würde nicht weit führen, wollte man, nachdem schon Gott und der Glauben, auf ihm beruhen, die Religion dem Rationalisierungsanspruch entziehen. Es ist vielmehr so, das sowohl der Glauben wie auch die ihn tragende, stützende, zuweilen aber schwächende Religion selbst als Folge und Ausdruck eines rationalen Umgangs des Menschen mit sich und seinen Kräften ist: Mit Hilfe des Begriffs eines Gottes bringt der Mensch das unfassliche Ganze seines Daseins in die Stellung eines Gegenübers, dem er als Mensch entsprechen kann. Die Rationalität dieses Aktes liegt darin, dass die Welt, zu der das Individuum mit allen seinen Kräften gehört, in die Position eines bedeutungsvollen Ganzen gebracht wird, zu dem sich das Ganze der Person dieses Individuums wie zu seinesgleichen verhalten kann.

Diese Einstellung auf ein weltumspannendes Ganzes, zu dem man selbst gehört, das jedoch in seiner Größe, Vielfalt, Tiefe und Bedeutung alles übersteigt, was als einzelner Sachverhalt erkannt oder gedacht werden kann, erfolgt nicht im *Wissen* – sondern in einer das Wissen überbietenden und es zugleich weitertragenden, gleichwohl aber auf ihm beruhenden – Leistung, die wir *Glauben* nennen.

Also kann es bei der Rationalisierung der Religion immer nur um Fragen der Wahrnehmung des Glaubens gehen, also darum, wie er verstanden, gedeutet, zur Geltung gebracht und gelebt werden kann. Der Glauben ist Ausdruck der Annäherung an ein Absolutes, das von Menschen selbst nicht als Absolutes erfasst und schon gar nicht nach Art einer absoluten Größe zur Wirkung gebracht werden kann. In diesem Fall könnte es noch nicht einmal Widerstand gegen das Göttliche geben. Der Glauben ist ursprünglich durch das Wissen relativiert. Man tut ihm also keinen Zwang an, wenn man ihn durch Wissen reguliert – vorzugsweise durch das Wissen, über das der Gläubige selbst verfügt.

Glauben kann man als die Fähigkeit beschreiben, unter höchst unvollkommenen endlichen Bedingungen in der Überzeugung von etwas zu leben, das in seiner Bedeutung alles bloß endliche – und insofern unvollkommene – Wissen übersteigt. Für die Entfaltung dieser Fähigkeit kann es günstige und weniger günstige Bedingungen geben, diese Chance wahrzunehmen. Aus menschlicher Perspektive, in die wir uns gerade als Gläubige mehr oder weniger bewusst, mehr oder weniger verständig einlassen, folgen wir bereits einer Rationalität des stets begrenzten, lückenhaften und überdies auch noch wandelbaren Wissens, sobald wir ausdrücklich glauben. Denn irgendwie glauben wir immer irgendetwas; und wenn uns das Wissen, wie es in allen Fragen von lebensgeschichtlicher Bedeutung der Fall ist, im Stich lässt, bleibt uns ohnehin nur die mit dem Glauben gepaarte Hoffnung.

Darin liegt eine unschätzbare Rationalität der bewussten Beziehung zur Welt. Denn man stelle sich vor, auf dem weiten Meer des Nicht-Wissens, auf dem sich zu bewegen für den Menschen „Leben" heißt, gäbe es außer den verstreuten Inseln unseres Wissens nichts als Nacht und Vergessen: Dann bliebe dem Menschen neben dem Wissen außer einem blinden Trieb nichts, was ihm Mut machen, ihn auf- und ausrichten und dabei auch anleiten könnte. Er dürfte noch nicht einmal Ahnungen oder Hoffnungen haben, in denen allemal Reste eines Wissens wirksam sind. Tatsächlich aber wirkt seine in vertrauter Umgebung erworbene Weltkenntnis weiter, und leitet ihn selbst dort, wo sie ihn nicht mehr sicher zu tragen vermag, durch Mutmaßungen und Schlussfolgerungen, durch Ahnungen und Erwartungen an. Ohne sie – somit auch ohne das in ihnen angenommene Wissen – könnte es durch keine Hoffnungen geleitet werden, die wiederum im Glauben ihre habituelle Festigkeit erlangen.

Gleichwohl wäre es absurd anzunehmen, Hoffnung und Glauben könnten das Wissen ersetzen. Beide sind vielmehr in allen ihren Schattierungen auf das Wissen angewiesen. Besser gesicherte, mehr Einzelheiten einbeziehende und größere Zusammenhänge beachtende Kenntnisse können daher ein willkommenes Mittel sein, den Glauben zu belehren oder zu vertiefen. In Einzelfällen kann es immer sein, dass ein Glauben durch ein Wissen gänzlich unwahrscheinlich gemacht wird oder gar ersetzt werden kann. Wer aber, wie mancher ahnungslose Aufklärer meint, der Glauben ließe sich eines Tages vollständig durch das Wissen ersetzen, der weiß nicht, wie begrenzt das Wissen ist, an das er selbst in fataler Weise glauben muss, wenn er ihm zutraut, es könne eines Tages den Glauben überflüssig machen.

Der religiöse Glauben, von dem wir sprechen, kann schon deshalb durch kein Wissen ersetzt werden, weil er sich auf etwas bezieht, von dem gar kein Wissen möglich ist. Denn sein „Gegenstand" ist das Ganze des Weltzusammenhangs, der zwar durch die Vernunft erschlossen, aber nicht nach Art eines Sachverhalts gewusst werden kann. Zwar kann man behaupten, dass einen dieses Ganze bestenfalls als bloßes Gedankengebilde interessiere; man kann ihm methodologische Funktionen zugestehen, die uns die Rede vom „Weltall" oder von der „Ewigkeit" ermögliche, aber eben darin nur eine technische Leitung erbringe, die in der Wissenschaft, in der Raumfahrt oder in der Literatur die Rede von den Grenzen des Wissen erleichtere; insofern könne es sogar einen Sinn haben, von „Ganzheiten" oder „Einheiten" zu sprechen. Aber das mache es noch lange nicht sinnvoll, an ein derartiges Ganzes zu *glauben*.

Was aber ist, wenn Menschen es dennoch tun? Wenn es für sie Bedeutung hat, sich in ihrem Dasein auf die Welt als Ganze zu beziehen, weil sie den Eindruck haben, dass jenes Ganze, das sie selber sind, in Korrespondenz zum Ganzen des Daseins allererst den Rang erhält, dem sie ihm in ihrem – ebenfalls als Ganzes verstandenen Leben – zu wahren suchen? In dieser Korrespondenz von Welt und Person verliert der Begriff des Ganzen seinen rein methodologischen Charakter, und gewinnt eine existenzielle Bedeutung, die es erlaubt, seinem eigenen Leben ein Gewicht zu geben, das es in seinem bloß physischen Dasein niemals aufbieten kann.

Ist es angesichts dieser Verbindung von Wissen und Glauben zu viel gesagt, wenn ich behaupte, dass der Glauben selbst, das Wissen rationalisiert? Ist es nicht so, dass uns erst der Glauben erlaubt, auf eine verständige Weise mit dem Wissen umzugehen? Was erlaubt es uns, die verschiedenen „Inseln" unseres Wissens im Umgang mit unserem Körper, mit den sozialen Beziehungen im Haus und der im Spiel gewonnenen Erfahrungen, derart auf das Leben im Ganzen zu übertragen, dass wir nicht jederzeit fürchten müssen, in „andere Welten" zu gelangen, die uns überdies nötigen, die so unmittelbar erfahrene personale Ganzheit, in der wir uns selbst verstehen, preiszugeben? Hier wirkt ein Vertrauen sowohl in der theoretischen Übertragung wie auch in der praktischen Umsetzung unseres Wissens, das nach dem alltäglichen Verständnis des Wortes immer auch als „Glauben" bezeichnet werden kann.

Und wer wollte es uns verwehren, diese „verständige" Weise im alltäglichen Umgang mit dem Wissen spätestens dann „vernünftig" zu nennen, wenn es um die Beziehung nicht nur zwischen verschiedenen Situationen und Lebenslagen, sondern um die Einbindung des Wissens in das jeweils eigene Leben im Ganzen des zwar nur erschlossenen, aber gleichwohl als Totalität erfahrenen Weltzusammenhangs geht?

5. Die Korrelation von Wissen und Glauben. Wenn der Glauben in der Lage ist, dem Wissen eine einheitliche Wirkungsweise im menschlichen Dasein zu geben, kann er dem Wissen selbst nicht fremd sein. Es ist daher ein gravierendes Missverständnis, aus Glauben und Wissen einen Gegensatz zu machen. Zwar versteht man sofort, wie es zu gelegentlichen Oppositionen kommen kann: Wo sicheres Wissen ist, braucht man das, was Gegenstand des Wissens ist, nicht zu glauben; und wo das Wissen nicht ausreicht, aber dennoch Gewissheit verlangt wird, muss man eben glauben. Hinzu kommen zahllose Fälle, in denen etwas geglaubt wird, was gar nicht wahr ist, und vieles, das in den Augen vieler gar nicht wahr sein kann, dennoch Gegenstand gläubiger Verehrung ist. Schließlich gibt es ernst zu nehmende theologischen Äußerungen, die etwas für im höchsten Sinn glaubwürdig halten, weil es – schon aus rein logischen Gründen – kein Objekt des

Wissens sein kann.[10] Deshalb empfehlen gerade die radikalen Gottsucher in der Geschichte des Denkens sich in einer „Umkehr", einer inneren „Versenkung" oder in einem verzweifelten „Sprung" vom Wissen zu lösen, um so zu einem Glauben zu gelangen, in dem sie Gott nahe sind.[11]

Wer wollte bestreiten, dass es solche Erfahrungen der Annäherung an das Göttliche gibt? Wohl aber muss bezweifelt werden, ob der Zugang zum Glauben generell oder auch nur primär in der Abkehr vom Wissen gefunden werden kann? Denn die Ursprungsgeschichten aller großen afro-eurasischen Religionen enthalten eine andere Lehre: In Schöpfungs- oder Erweckungsmythen vergewissern sie sich des Wissens ihrer Zeit, das ihnen das Wirken eines göttlichen Urhebers anschaulich macht. Diese von tiefen Einsichten in den Gang der Dinge ausgehenden Erzählungen werden, kaum dass die Schrift erfunden ist, in eine urkundliche Form gebracht, um im Modus des Wissens von Generation zu Generation übermittelt zu werden. So verbürgen sie die sachhaltige Einheit einer Religion durch Schriftgelehrte und durch Lehren, die sich auf Tatsachen und Gründe berufen und mit Argumenten verteidigt werden.

Es ist ein kulturgeschichtliches Faktum ersten Ranges, dass alle heute weltweit operierenden Religionen parallel zu den sich gleichzeitig ausbreitenden Wissenschaften der Astronomie, der Medizin und des Rechts entstehen. Ganz abgesehen davon, dass ihnen die Techniken des Berg- und Brunnenbaus, des Verkehrswesens, des Befestigungs- und Kriegswesens sowie des Symbol- und Zeichengebrauchs vorhergehen, folgen die schriftlichen Notationen der Schöpfungsgeschichten den Errungenschaften, die mit der Archivierung der Handelserträge, der Steueraufkommen, der Grenzverläufe, der Geschlechterfolge, der diplomatischen Gesandtschaften und der Entdeckungsreisen gemacht werden.

Der Triumph des Wissens und der daraus bei großen Individuen entspringenden Weisheit, die in der Achsenzeit zwischen 700 und 400 v. Chr. verzeichnet werden, führen auch den Siegeszug der zumeist monotheistischen Religionen herauf, die bis heute die festen Begleiter der Kulturgeschichte der Menschheit geblieben sind. In ihr verbinden sich Wissen und Glauben, nicht zuletzt auch im Umgang mit den Techniken der Organisation und Kommunikation, zu *einem* Strang der Zivilisationsgeschichte der Menschheit. Historisch ist somit an der Parallelität des Aufkommens und der Verbreitung von Systemen des Wissens und des Glaubens nicht zu zweifeln.

---

10 Wie es das *credo quia absurdum* des Anselm von Canterbury nahelegt, ohne freilich auf eine Deutung festgelegt zu sein.

11 Ich belasse es bei einem summarischen Hinweis auf Augustinus, Hildegard von Bingen, Meister Eckhart, Pascal und Kierkegaard.

Nun muss selbst eine große Tradition zu gar nichts verpflichten. Deshalb ist es einen Hinweis wert, dass Wissen und Glauben bis heute auf das Engste miteinander verbunden sind: So hat bereits das Kind an das Wissen zu glauben, wenn es ihm mit dem geforderten Eifer nachkommen will. Das Gleiche gilt für den Zeitungsleser, den Weltreisenden oder den nach einer Lösung suchenden Forscher. Das derzeit gern beschworene Selbstbewusstsein der „Wissensgesellschaft" (die keineswegs erst mit den neuzeitlichen Wissenschaften oder dem Einsatz digitaler Medien beginnt) ist ein anschauliches Beispiel für einen exponierten Glauben an das Wissen. Trotz der Kritik an den neuzeitlichen Positivismen und ungeachtet der weit verbreiteten Fortschrittsskepsis, scheint der Glauben an das Wissen unvermeidlich. Er treibt alle an, die auf eine Bewältigung der ökonomischen und ökologischen Lebensrisiken setzen und leitet jeden, der sich Experten anvertraut, ob er nun zum Arzt oder zum Rechtsanwalt geht oder ins Flugzeug steigt.

Aber es ist nicht allein das Wissen der anderen, dem sich ein Patient, Klient oder Passagier anvertraut. Auch das eigene Wissen, auf das man bei Antritt der Reise, vor dem Examen oder bei einem Bewerbungsvortrag setzen muss, um überhaupt eine Aussicht auf Erfolg zu haben, hat einen aus Kenntnissen, Fertigkeiten und personaler Präsenz bestehenden Kern, an dem man, *sit venia verbo*, ebenfalls „glauben" muss. Es ist gewiss so, dass der Glaube an sich selbst und seine Fähigkeiten nicht die Reichweite des religiösen Glaubens erreicht. Aber ein Glaube an etwas, dessen wir uns nicht sicher sein können, ist es gleichwohl, und er betrifft etwas, auf das wir in der bevorstehenden Handlungslage notwendig angewiesen sind. Insofern liegt im Vertrauen in die eigenen Kräfte ein Paradigma des Vertrauens in den Weltzusammenhang, in dem wir uns mit der Erwartung auf Erfolg bewegen.

Schließlich ist da das uns jederzeit gewärtige Wissen von der Begrenztheit selbst des konsolidierten Wissens. Sogar ein erwiesenes mathematisches Urteil kann uns ratlos machen, wenn wir in einer Lage sind, in der es sich nicht anwenden lässt. Und alles empirische Wissen gilt nur, solange die Umstände Bestand haben, unter denen es gewonnen wurde und sich bislang bestätigt hat. Was also tun, wenn sich, wie es jederzeit der Fall sein kann, die Bedingungen geändert haben? Dann braucht man Urteilskraft, um vom Einzelfall auf ein uns nicht nach Art eines Objekts gegenüberstehendes Ganzes zu schließen oder um mit Blick auf ein Allgemeines ein uns nicht näher bekanntes Einzelnes zu exemplifizieren.

Die Erkenntnistheoretiker unterstellen in solchen Fällen „Einbildungskraft", erwähnen aber nicht das Selbst- und Weltvertrauen, dass dem Umgang mit einem Hiatus zwischen Wissen und Nicht-Wissen zugrunde liegt. Man kann auch auf das Verfahren von Versuch und Irrtum setzen. Wenn es ernsthaft geschieht, erfolgt das im Vertrauen darauf, dass sich nicht alles geändert hat und die Lösung im explorativen Einsatz des Wissens gefunden werden kann.

Man muss also nicht gleich niederknien und auf eine Erleuchtung warten. Aber sobald es um Lebensentscheidungen angesichts offener Zukunftsfragen geht, liegen die Grenzen des Wissens auf der Hand. Das Vertrauen in die eigenen Kräfte bedarf der Ergänzung durch das Vertrauen in das Kommende. Es ist damit auch im alltäglichen Verständnis dem religiösen Glauben nahe. Und sobald es dabei nicht nur um die persönliche, sondern auch um die der Kinder, der kommenden Generationen und der Menschheit geht, kann man sich mit dem nüchternen Pathos der Vernunftkritik „die Grenzen des Wissens" eingestehen, um zum „Glauben Platz zu bekommen".[12] Es ist dies ein Glauben, der seinen Sinn daraus bezieht, das zum Abschluss zu bringen, wozu die Mühen des Wissens nur Voraussetzungen schaffen, aber keine Gewissheit bieten können. Der Glauben bringt das Wissen zu einem Ende, mit dem der Mensch sich begnügen muss. Er bringt, um das technische Vokabular der Rationalisierung zu vermeiden, das menschliche Wissen zur Vernunft.

6. Glauben an der Lebensgrenze. Die vorgetragenen Bemerkungen werfen nur Schlaglichter auf eine erst seit Neuestem beharrlich verkannte Beziehung. Die klassische Philosophie des Altertums wusste von ihr und sie war in den Lehren der Metaphysik bis hin zu Kant, Fichte und Hegel bewusst. Sie wurde auch von großen Theologen, selbst wenn sie, wie Schleiermacher, das Gefühl zum Sensorium für das Göttliche erhoben, nicht vergessen. Denn der Glauben ist selbst – wie das Vertrauen, die Hoffnung und die Liebe – ein Gefühl, das in seiner Qualität verkannt wird, wenn man es zum Widersacher des Wissens erklärt.

So gleichgültig, ja, so borniert das Gefühl in manchen Lebenslagen einem bestimmten Wissen gegenüberstehen mag, so darf sein epistemischer Charakter nicht übersehen werden.[13] Denn das Gefühl des Glaubens sucht uns im Ganzen zu lenken und zu leiten; es erweist sich im evolutionären, kulturgeschichtlichen wie auch im biographischen Zusammenhang als durchaus gelehrig; und es ist nichts, von dem uns das Wissen jemals vollständig befreien könnte. Dies schon deshalb nicht, weil alles Wissen auf Gefühle angewiesen bleibt.

So gesehen, kommt die Vernunft dem Wissen erst in Verbindung mit dem Gefühl in vollem Umfang zu, und der Glauben ist das Gefühl, in dem die Vernunft zu ihrer Selbst und Welt umfassenden Gewissheit gelangt. In der unvollkommenen Endlichkeit des Daseins, von dem uns die Vernunft einen Begriff vermittelt, verdanken wir dem Glauben das Gefühl existenzieller Defizienz und möglicher

12 Kant 1911:19. Dazu: Rohs 2014.

13 Das war in den klassischen Affektlehren stets bewusst, wurde von Darwin in eindrucksvoller Weise bestätigt und ist in den letzten beiden Jahrzehnten zum bevorzugten Gegenstand der Debatte über Emotionen geworden. Dazu mit viel Material: Landwehr und Renz 2008.

Vollkommenheit. Er kann uns im Ganzen die Sicherheit geben, die in den kurzen Augenblicken des Lebens mit dem anerkannten Erfolg und der erwiderten Liebe verbunden sind. Es ist der Glauben, der einer Erwartung Dauer gewährt.

Je mehr wir wissen, umso größer wird die Einsicht in das, was mit dem Wissen nicht nur im Augenblick, sondern vermutlich auch auf lange Sicht verborgen bleibt. Da wir uns als handelnde und dabei notwendig viel erwartende und allemal auch manches hoffende Wesen mit dieser Einsicht nur schwerlich zufrieden geben können, greifen wir im Gefühl des Glaubens über die erkannten Grenzen aus, um mit größtmöglicher Konsequenz Weiterungen vorzunehmen, die dem begrenzten Wissen neue Räume des Hoffens eröffnen. Das Wissen von den Grenzen des Wissens soll unserer auf Handlungserfolge vorgreifenden Erwartung nicht entgegenstehen; nach Möglichkeit soll es die Aussicht auf Zufriedenheit mit dem erwarteten (und allemal bescheidenen) Ertrag unseres Tuns und Lassens eröffnen.

Schließlich gibt es die ebenfalls mit dem menschlichen Wissen verknüpfte Enttäuschung über das Leben insgesamt, die wir durch das Verlangen nach einem von den irdischen Lasten befreites Dasein nach dem Tod erträglich zu machen suchen. Wer hier nur auf die intellektuellen Kapazitäten des bewussten Erlebens, der Erinnerung und der kalkulierten Voraussicht setzt und dabei vergisst, dass alles dies einen affektiven Untergrund hat, dem dann (vielleicht erst im Bewusstsein der Gefährdung und bei nahendem Alter) in der Hoffnung auf ein „ewiges Leben" Rechnung getragen wird, macht es sich mit der angeblich rein affektiven Dimension des Glaubens zu einfach. Denn das Instrument rationaler Einsicht entgleitet dem Mensch nur im panischen Entsetzen und in bewusstloser Raserei, nicht aber solange er sein eigenes Ende irgendwie noch im Blick behalten kann. Es ist dies ein vom Gefühl durchsetztes, gegen Ende des Lebens vielleicht sogar vom Gefühl besetztes, aber immer noch so zu nennendes – *Denken.*

Noch im äußersten Punkt des Lebens: im Angesicht des Todes, in dem Bangen, Hoffen und Glauben in eine Sphäre überspringen, in der kein Wissen möglich ist, sind rationale Momente der Vorsicht und Rücksicht, der Berechnung, der Beherrschung und des Vergleichs am Werk. Selbst wer sich vor Höllenqualen fürchtet, muss in seinen letzten bewussten Regungen nicht von der Angst beherrscht zu sein. Sofern er noch bei Bewusstsein ist, dessen originäre soziale Organisation ihn in allen seinen Äußerungen mit dem Bewusstsein aller anderen verknüpft, ist er mit dem Fortgang des Lebens verbunden, dem er bis zum eigenen Ende zugehört. So bleibt im Sprechen und Denken eine, trotz allem, mit Anderen geteilte Aussicht auf eine Zukunft bestimmend, aus der erst der Tote als aktiver Teilnehmer ausgeschieden ist. So lange er lebt, bleibt er über die Gehalte seines Sprechens und Denkens mit allen, denen er verständlich sein kann, verbunden. Und diese Verbindung besteht – bei den Lebenden – über seinen Tod hinaus. Das prägt das Bewusstsein, in dem der Glauben gegenwärtig ist, und trägt ihn über das Lebensende des Gläubigen hinaus. So verbleibt er noch im Sterben in der Perspektive jener, die ihn im gemeinsamen Bewusstsein überdauern.

Das Erleben des Sterbens kann in jedem Einzelfall anders sein. Führt es zum Tod, nimmt der Verstorbene seine letzten Eindrücke mit sich in sein definitives Verstummen. Wir kennen es somit nur aus der Perspektive der Anderen, die aus letzten Zeichen und Worten eigentlich nur erschließen können, dass im Ausdruck des Leidens, der Abwehr oder Abkehr noch physische, psychische und soziale Momente des Ganzen gegenwärtig sind, in dem sich das Bewusstsein des Sterbenden bewegt. So bleibt auch der Horizont des Glaubens, der eine bewusste Regung des Lebens ist, dem Leben zugewandt. In der Regel werden so auch die „letzten Worte" verstanden, von denen nicht ausgeschlossen werden kann, dass sie der Sterbende im abschließenden Akt seines lebenslangen Selbstgesprächs nur zu sich selber äußert.

Mit dem Tod geht auch der Glaube verloren; aber solange er noch als eine das Leben haltende und lenkende Kraft im Bewusstsein wirksam ist, wahrt er die zum Leben gehörende Zuversicht mit Gründen, die ihn ausdrücklich mit dem ihm noch gegenwärtigen Ganzen seines Leibes und seiner Lebens verbinden. Dabei steht das im Vordergrund, was menschliches Leben überhaupt leitet: Der Wunsch, dass es nicht nur für einen selbst, sondern auch für andere ein Gewinn sein kann und vielleicht sogar im Ganzen gute Gründe für sich hat. Kurz: Es zielt, wie alles im Leben, auf das Glück im Einzelfall, auf einen günstigen Verlauf und ein Gelingen im Ganzen, wofür man früher noch den schönen Ausdruck der „Glückseligkeit" verwenden konnte.

Auf dem Evangelischen Kirchentag 2011 in Dresden wurde damit experimentiert, die aus der alltäglichen Sprache fast verschwundene „Seligkeit" ganz in den Begriff des „Glücks" zu überführen. Das wolkige Wörtchen „selig" sollte dem sozial und politisch gebräuchlichen „glücklich" weichen.[14] Angesichts der Tatsache, dass man über den Zustand und die Dauer der Seele nichts Genaues weiß,

14 Es kursierte eine „Kirchentagsübersetzung" der Seligpreisungen im Matthäus-Evangelium (5,23 ff.), die das von Luther mit „selig" übersetzte und auch von nicht-theologischen Altphilologen bis heute mit „glückselig" übertragene *makarios* nur noch als „glücklich" gelten ließ. Der Vorschlag setzte sich nicht durch, obgleich maßgebliche Redner nur von sozialen und politischen Glücksdefiziten sprachen und „selig" inzwischen als alltagssprachliches Kuriosum gelten darf. Das illustriert der Radiobeitrag „Selig oder glücklich? Ein Streifzug durchs Glücksterrain" von: Benedict 2010. – Im Folgenden deute ich an, welche Bedeutung die Unterscheidung dennoch hat und welche Rationalität ihr zukommt, selbst wenn man die wörtliche Rede von der „Unsterblichkeit" der Seele oder von der Transzendenz eines „Jenseits" vermeiden will. So sehr man auch in der Theologie auf Gegenständlichkeit und Sachhaltigkeit des Ausdrucks dringen muss, ist es doch nur vernünftig, das bereits in jeder Verständigung, vor allem aber in jeder existenziellen

schien das naheliegend. Denn wer möchte heute noch den Eindruck erwecken, er wüsste, wie sich eine Seele nach dem Tod ihres personalen Inhabers fühlt?

Man bedenke aber, dass es auch im modernen Leben eines Menschen einen guten Sinn ergibt, das Glück, von dem einer im Augenblick eines günstigen Umstands spricht, von dem Glück zu unterscheiden, das jemand im Rückblick auf sein Leben im Ganzen empfindet. Auch das, was einer seinen Nächsten und seinen Nachkommen an Wohlergehen wünscht, hat eine andere Qualität als das, was einem zuweilen auch der Zufall, ein schönes Geschenk oder eine freundliche Aufmerksamkeit bescheren kann. Das eine, das Glück des günstigen Umstands, belebt uns im alltäglichen Gang der Dinge; das andere berührt uns ganz und vermag uns in unserem Dasein zu tragen. Es ist ein Glück, das als lebensbestimmend erfahren werden kann.

Um das zum Ausdruck zu bringen, kann es auch nach dem heutigen Sprachgebrauch als höchst unzureichend empfunden werden, nur vom Selbst als dem Fokus unseres Selbstbewusstseins zu sprechen. Da sollte man nicht leichtfertig auf den uns in unserer ganzen Eigenart erfassenden Begriff der „Seele" verzichten. Denn er kann die Dauer und die Tiefe eines Glücks bezeichnen, ohne damit die grundlose Behauptung seiner metaphysischen Eigenständigkeit zu verbinden. Man braucht sich nur vorzustellen, was es für einen Menschen bedeutet, trotz allem, von der Möglichkeit eines innigen Glücks überzeugt zu sein, und man hat die Chance zu verstehen, was Glauben heißt. Und wer dies im Sinn der heute wieder geschätzten Konzeption eines gelingenden Lebens versteht, kann auch eine Idee von der Rationalität dieses Glaubens haben.

7. Glauben als ganzheitlicher Umgang mit dem Wissen. Bei der Unterscheidung von Glück und Glückseligkeit geht es nicht allein um die Perspektive individueller oder genealogischer Dauer, sondern auch um das Bewusstsein eines mit Bedacht geführten Lebens, dem das Glück immer auch im Bewusstsein einer eigenen Bemühung zuwächst. Hier liegt der Anteil der für sich selbst sorgenden „Seele", also des auf seine Eigenart bedachten Selbst, das seine personale Beachtung wünscht, aber nicht an die Überzeugung der Unsterblichkeit gebunden ist. Da es Dauer ohnehin nur als Phänomen eines zeitlich verfassten Bewusstseins gibt, ist es gänzlich unerheblich, ob man das, was es im physischen Sinn sowieso nicht geben kann (nämlich eine nach Art eines Gegenstands verfasste Seele), als etwas behauptet, dass es mit einem Mal nach dem Tod ihres Trägers geben soll. Was es aber „gibt", ist die über dem Augenblick eines Empfindens oder eines

---

Handlung in Anspruch genommen Ganze eine Lebens- und Weltzusammenhangs kenntlich zu machen. Das lässt die Rede von der „Glückseligkeit" auch heute noch als „rational" erscheinen.

Wissens hinausreichende Perspektive. Und sie wird im Glauben mit besonderer Intensität gesichert, wenn der Mensch über das Ende des eigenen Daseins hinausdenkt. Das aber gehört zur Natur seines Denkens! Es geht ihm in der existenziellen Erwartung seines eigenen Endes lediglich besonders nahe.

Gewiss: Die Tatsache des Todes berührt ihn auch beim Ableben eines ihm nahestehenden Menschen. Die Trauer kann ihn jederzeit erfassen, wenn der Tod zur Unzeit kommt, sich in dramatischer Nähe ereignet oder Kinder, Jugendliche oder andere Hoffnungsträger mit sich nimmt. In allen diesen Fällen wird die rationale Disposition des Glaubens offensichtlich: Der Gläubige springt nicht bedenkenlos aus allem heraus, was das menschliche Leben an Unglück und Elend bereithält. Er bewahrt sich seinen abwägenden Blick, bilanziert sein Dasein, kann, gerade dort, wo er auf die göttliche Gnade setzen muss, das Maß der Zeit und der Gerechtigkeit nicht außer Acht lassen, und setzt schließlich auf eine Dauer, von der er hofft, in seiner personalem Identität, also mit seinem wissenden Bewusstsein wenn nicht anwesend, so doch in Erinnerung zu bleiben.

Mehr muss zum Glauben am Lebensende (und zur Hoffnung auf ein „ewiges Leben“) nicht gesagt zu werden.[15] Mit Blick auf das Verhältnis von Rationalität und Glauben reicht es aus, wenn das selbst noch in der Grenzlage des individuellen Daseins fortwirkende Ineinander rationaler und emotionaler Faktoren erkennbar ist. Noch im äußersten Punkt unseres Wunsches nach Ruhe, Frieden und Erlösung ist die „Rationalisierung“ eines möglicherweise nur noch physischen Verlangens nach Befreiung von Qual und Schmerz derart wirksam, dass schon darin der leitende Sinn unseres personalen Daseins gewahrt bleibt, denn man möchte kein zu nichts anderem mehr fähiger Träger von Schmerzen sein.

Der Glauben unterstellt, stärkt und versichert eine Einheit von Leib, Selbst und Welt, die im Tod vermutlich völlig zerfällt. Gestützt durch das noch wache Bewusstsein, in dem Anschauung, Verstand und Vernunft dem Selbst die Chance geben, seine Einheit in der Mitteilung sach- und welthaltiger Einheiten zu wahren, wirkt der Glauben als Garant der existenziellen Verbindung von Selbst und Welt. Er bekräftigt den Zusammenhang, der im weit gefächerten Sinn unzähliger Ereignisse, Erfahrungen und Handlungen von jedem Bewusstsein benötigt wird, um nicht mit jedem neuen Eindruck im Tumult möglicher Bedeutungen unterzugehen. Damit verlöre er jede Bestimmtheit. Der Glauben, der bereits das Wissen fundiert, der es organisiert, motiviert und im Ganzen orientiert, sobald wir an die Grenzen des Wissens stoßen, ist die rationalisierende Kraft im menschlichen Wissen – weil wir dennoch leben und unter den Bedingungen unseres personalen Bewusstseins gar nicht anderes können, als nach Gründen zu handeln.

---

15 Dazu siehe vom Verf.: Gerhardt 2014a:103 f.

So wird man es vom Glauben in vielen seiner alltäglichen Bedeutungsformen sagen können. Der eine Mensch glaubt, dass es ihm gelingen kann, seinen Besitz zusammenzuhalten und er scheut die größten Strapazen nicht. Ein anderer möchte seiner Rente wegen am Leben bleiben, weil er nur so seinem Enkel den finanziellen Zuschuss zum Studium zahlen kann. Unternehmer, Künstler und Gelehrte glauben an die Vollendung ihres Werkes, durch das sie den Sinn ihrer Lebensarbeit gerechtfertigt sehen. Von dem Vater eines Freundes weiß ich, dass er fest daran glaubte, hundert Jahre alt zu werden; als das Jubiläum gefeiert war, verfielen seine Kräfte rasch; er verstarb nach wenigen Wochen. Vor allem aber sollte man an die vielen hochbetagten Paare denken, bei denen sich die Partner wechselseitig stützen, dann aber kurz hintereinander sterben, sobald einer von beiden den Anfang mit dem Ende gemacht hat.

Es ist wichtig von der Vielfalt und vom Ernst solcher Glaubensmöglichkeiten zu wissen, um das wahrhaft Alltägliche des Glaubens zu erkennen, und um sicher zu sein, dass der Glauben mit jedem menschlichen Leben einen neuen Anfang nimmt, der durch nichts in seinen Ausdrucksmöglichkeiten eingeschränkt ist. Im Vergleich dieser Glaubensformen bietet sich dann auch die Chance, die Besonderheit des religiösen Glaubens auszuzeichnen. Sein Kriterium liegt nicht in der Frömmigkeit als einer äußeren Form des Verhaltens. Auch die innere Ergriffenheit und der existenzielle Ernst, die beide gewiss von großer Bedeutung sind, sobald es um ein religiöses Bekenntnis geht, sind kein Alleinstellungsmerkmal. Denn auch die Virtuosen einer seltenen Fertigkeit, ganz gleich, ob es sich um die Beherrschung eines Musikinstruments, um den Drahtseilakt zwischen den *Twin Towers* oder den freiwilligen Dienst an Leprakranken handelt, opfern ihrer Leistung alles und setzen ihr Leben aufs Spiel. Der religiöse Glaube ist einzig durch seinen Bezug auf das Ganze des Daseins ausgezeichnet, dem sich das Individuum als Ganzes so zurechnet, dass es sich mit seinen besten Kräften als Teil dieses Ganzen begreifen kann. In dieser Verbindung von Welt und Selbst liegt das Äußerste an Sinn und Bedeutung, die dem Mensch zu begreifen möglich ist. Deshalb liegt darin der Grund von allem, was ist und was sein kann – einschließlich alles dessen, was dem Menschen selbst als bedeutungsvoll erscheint.

In dieser Auszeichnung des religiösen Glaubens ist wichtig, dass im einheitlich verstandenen Ganzen der Welt eine übergeordnete Disposition alles Geschehens anerkannt wird. Denn nur so lässt sich der überlegene Status der geglaubten Einheit annehmen, so dass man Grund hat, das Ganze als etwas Göttliches zu verehren. Das erlaubt es, um nur ein Beispiel zu nennen, der pantheistischen Nivellierung des Göttlichen zu entgehen.

Wichtig ist ferner, die in der Entsprechung von Welt und Selbst unterstellte Korrespondenz des Weltganzen mit dem individuellen Ganzen der Person. Sie macht es, trotz der damit verbundenen epistemischen Schwierigkeiten, frommen

Menschen möglich, das Göttliche selbst nach Art einer Person anzusprechen. Damit stehen dem Gebet und der Zwiesprache mit dem geglaubten Gott keine grundsätzlichen Einwände entgegen.

Der für das Problem der Rationalisierung wichtigste Aspekt liegt darin, dass der so erläuterte religiöse Glauben, nicht ohne die intellektuelle Kapazität des Gläubigen verstanden werden kann. Damit ist nicht gemeint, dass dem Glauben ein theologisches oder philosophisches Studium vorausgehen muss. Aber man braucht eine begrifflich angeleitete Vorstellung von einem Ganzen der Welt und vom Ganzen des eigenen Daseins, das in seiner Endlichkeit dem unbegrenzt erscheinenden All möglicher Ereignisse und Bedeutungen zwar gegenübersteht – ihm zugleich aber auch zugehört. Schließlich muss sich ein im religiösen Sinn gläubiger Mensch als Individuum im Verhältnis zu anderen Individuen verstehen und ein Bewusstsein von der eigenen Verantwortlichkeit haben.

Damit sind nicht alle Bedingungen des religiösen Glaubens genannt. Aber die knappe Aufzählung reicht aus, um kenntlich zu machen, dass nicht nur dem Glauben überhaupt, sondern insbesondere dem religiösen Glauben die Kraft einer Rationalisierung innewohnt, die es dem Menschen erlaubt, sich insbesondere mit seinen epistemischen Kräften auf das zu beziehen, was ihm in der Begrenzung seines Daseins als wesentlich erscheint. Rationalisierung ist die „stiptische Kraft“ des Menschen, mit deren Hilfe er sich in der Vielfalt der allererst von ihm erschlossenen unendlichen Möglichkeiten seines Daseins, selbst auf das konzentrieren kann, was ihm als wesentlich erscheint.[16] Man trifft daher den wesentlichen Punkt, wenn man den religiösen Glauben als den ganzheitlich angelegten Umgang mit dem Wissen bezeichnet. Er bringt die Vernunft zur Geltung, derer der Mensch bedarf, um Herr seines Wissens zu bleiben, ohne sich damit als Herr der Welt aufspielen zu müssen. Rationalisierung kann damit als eine wesentliche Leistung des Glaubens angesehen werden.

8. Die Rationalität des Glaubens legitimiert die Rationalität der Religion. Gesetzt, die hier lediglich extemporierten Beobachtungen treffen etwas Richtiges, wäre nicht nur für die dogmatischen und die institutionellen Formen des Glaubens, in denen das Zusammenwirken von Vernunft und gläubiger Hingabe offenkundig ist, sondern auch für die epistemisch und existenzielle Grenzlage des Todes die „Rationalisierung“ einer wie auch immer beschaffenen affektiven

16 Kant spricht von der „stiptischen Kraft der Selbsterkenntnis“, die es dem Menschen erlaubt, die „seidenen Schwingen“ der metaphysischen Welterkenntnis so zusammenzuziehen, dass er inmitten der von ihm selbst verursachten spekulativen Turbulenzen auf den Boden der empirischen Tatsachen zurückkehren und bei sich selbst zur Ruhe kommen kann. Vgl. Kant 1912:368.

Verfassung, nennen wir sie Müdigkeit, Erschöpfung, Leid, Schmerz, Schrecken, Entsetzen oder Todesangst, in einem religiösen Gefühl wahrscheinlich gemacht. Dann gäbe es Anlass zu der Vermutung, dass die Religionen, in der Form, in der sie die Zivilisierung der Menschheit in den letzten viertausend Jahren begleitet haben, nicht primär im Widerstand tätig waren. Sie haben vielmehr im Verein mit allen anderen immer auch in sich widersprüchlichen kulturellen Großmächten der Technik, der Kunst, dem Recht, der Moral und der Wissenschaft produktiv am Aufbau der Gesellschaftsformen mitgewirkt, von denen wir hoffen dass sie in der Lage sind, auch in Zukunft die Entwicklung der Menschheit zu tragen.

Die Religionen haben sich nicht nur durch Rationalisierung an verschiedene Entwicklungen angepasst, haben sie auch nicht allein in den Akten der Individualisierung, der Moralisierung, der künstlerischen Gestaltung, der Entfaltung der Gelehrsamkeit oder des sozialen Engagements entscheidend gefördert, sondern sie sind selbst Ausdruck der Selbstkultivierung der menschlichen Gattung – vorrangig durch die Rationalisierung von Gefühlen, die im Interesse der Personalisierung des Individuums, der Stärkung einer gemeinschaftlichen Sittlichkeit und (dies vor allem) der Optimierung eines Vertrauen in das Kommende, das der Mensch vorauszudenken sucht und das er durch sein Handeln gleichermaßen fördert und gefährdet.

Daraus folgt unter anderem auch, dass es keinen prinzipiellen Einwand gegen die Rationalisierung des Glaubens geben kann – es sei denn man verlangte ein Verbot der Rationalisierung des bereits Rationalisierten. Damit aber würde man nur eingestehen, dass man nicht weiß, dass Rationalisierung der relative Prozess einer Optimierung ist, für die es keine *a priori* bestehende Grenze gibt. Überdies gestände man seine Unkenntnis über den Glauben ein, der bereits in sich von einer Optimierungserwartung getragen ist. Um es in Anlehnung an Leibniz zu sagen: Man möchte in der besten aller möglichen Welten das nach Möglichkeit beste aller möglichen Leben führen.

Auch das Reden vom möglichst Besten der Welt und des Lebens ist der Logik der Rationalisierung geschuldet. Man kann es nicht vermeiden, weil der Glauben notwendig auf begrifflich erschlossene Größen setzt, die durch Einheit und Vollkommenheit gekennzeichnet sind. Sie betreffen sowohl den Selbstbegriff des Menschen wie auch seine Beziehung zu seinesgleichen und zur Welt. Hier also ist immer auch Rationalität im Spiel, die, wie man weiß, schwer von der Erwartung einer Perfektionierung zu trennen ist. Das kann den Gläubigen befremden, weil er im Ganzen Ruhe sucht und vielleicht darauf hofft, endlich auch in sich seinen Frieden zu finden.

Hier stößt der Begriff der Rationalisierung an eine theologische Grenze, die mit der im Glauben gesuchten Entsprechung zweier Ganzheiten zu tun hat. Das

Göttliche eröffnet die interne Aussicht auf die Korrespondenz des Ganzen der Welt mit dem Ganzen der Person. Mit der hier gesuchten Innigkeit eines empfunden Zusammenhangs hat der Vorgang der Rationalisierung wenig zu tun. Zunächst geht es dem Gläubigen mehr um Nähe, Gewissheit und Vertrauen sowie um das Glück einer gefundenen Einheit. Rationalisierung kann hier nur die Unruhe einer noch nicht erreichten Verbesserung bedeuten.

Wohlgemerkt: Der Begriff ist auch hier nicht gänzlich verfehlt. Denn die vergleichende und verbessernde Vernunft bleibt allemal im Spiel. Folglich wird man sich in der Aussicht auf bewusste Zustände, immer auch die Fähigkeit zur kritischen Unterscheidung wünschen. Doch die damit notwendig verbundene Sorge vor schlechten Einflüssen und ungünstigen Entwicklungen, sollte für den auf Erlösung setzenden Menschen nicht von ewiger Dauer sein. Deshalb muss er im Vertrauen darauf glauben, dass eines Tages auch die Rationalisierung ein Ende haben kann. Im „Ende aller Dinge“ kann der Anspruch auf Besserung entfallen, weil alles gut geworden ist.

References

Bellah, Robert N. 2012. *Religion in Human Evolution*. Cambridge, Mass.–London: Harvard University Press.

Benedict, Hans-Jürgen. 2010. „*Selig oder glücklich? Ein Streifzug durchs Glücksterrain.*“ In Deutschlandradio Kultur, Beitrag vom 10. Januar 2010. Online: http://www.deutschlandradiokultur.de/selig-oder-gluecklich.1124.de.html?dram:article_id=176982 (accessed December 26, 2017).

Forst, Rainer. 2003. *Toleranz im Konflikt. Geschichte, Gehalt und Gegenwart eines umstrittenen Begriffs*. Frankfurt a. M.: Suhrkamp.

Gerhardt, Volker. 2002. „Die Religion der Individualität.“ *Philosophisches Jahrbuch*, 109/2:1–16.

—. 2007. „Individualität. Individuum/Individualisierung/Institution/Universalität.“ In W. Gräb und B. Weyel (Hgg.), *Handbuch praktische Theologie*. Gütersloh: Gütersloher Verlags-Haus. 64–76.

—. 2014a. *Der Sinn des Sinns. Versuch über das Göttliche*. München: Beck.

—. 2014b. „Selbstbestimmung im Lebenszusammenhang.“ *Neue Gesellschaft, Frankfurter Hefte*, 61/9:4–8.

Hölscher, Tonio. 1998. *Öffentliche Räume in frühen griechischen Städten*. Heidelberg: Winter.

Kant, Immanuel. 1911. *Kritik der reinen Vernunft, 2. Aufl., 1787* (Kant's gesammelte Schriften. Erste Abteilung Werke = Akademie-Ausgabe, 3). II. Aufl. Berlin: Reimer (Nachdruck 1962 und 1973).

—. 1912. *Vorkritische Schriften II. 1757–1777: Träume eines Geistersehers, erläutert durch Träume der Metaphysik, 1766* (Kant's gesammelte Schriften. Erste Abteilung Werke = Akademie-Ausgabe, 2). II. Aufl. Berlin: Reimer (Nachdruck 1969).

Landwehr, Hilge, und Ursula Renz (Hgg.). 2008. *Klassische Emotionstheorien. Von Platon bis Wittgenstein*. Berlin–New York: De Gruyter.

Porete, Margareta. 1987. *Der Spiegel der einfachen Seelen. Wege der Frauenmystik.* Aus dem Altfranzösischen übertragen und mit einem Nachwort und mit Anmerkungen von Louise Gnädinger. Zürich: Topos plus.

Rohs, Peter. 2014. *Der Platz zum Glauben*, Münster: Mentis.

Sarah Stroumsa

Early Muslim and Jewish *Kalām*: The Enterprise of Reasoned Discourse

In his short bio-bibliographical book on the development of science and philosophy and their dissemination among various nations, the eleventh-century Spanish Muslim historian Ṣā'id ibn Ṣā'id al-Andalusī (d. 460/1068) observed the absence of these disciplines among the first Muslims (and by implication, among pre-Islamic Arabs):

> At the beginning of Islam, the Arabs were not interested in any of the sciences, except the art of medicine, which was practiced by some individuals and not rejected by the multitudes. Their only interest was [the study of] their language, and the knowledge of their religious rules.[1]

Similarly, regarding the Jews in antiquity, Ibn Ṣā'id remarked:

> The eighth nation, namely the Children of Israel, did not gain fame in the philosophical sciences. They were interested only in the religious sciences and the biographies of the prophets.[2]

But in the eleventh century, when Ibn Ṣā'id was writing these lines, both Jews and Muslims were already deeply immersed in the study of philosophy of various schools, as well as in the sciences. Although many learned studies have been devoted to the emergence of speculative and scientific thought under early Islam, the speedy transition from no interest and certainly no fame in the philosophical realm to the height of what has been dubbed "the Renaissance of Islam" remains, in many ways, a mystery.[3]

In the attempt to solve this mystery, modern scholarship has focused, on the one hand, on the so-called translation movement, which transmitted Greek philosophy and sciences to readers of Arabic between the late second and the fourth Islamic centuries, and, on the other hand, on the origins of Islamic dialectic theology (*Kalām*). The present paper will focus on the early development of *Kalām*, among both Muslims and Jews. In particular, it will attempt to highlight a hitherto neglected feature of early *Kalām* as we know it.

1 Ṣā'id Ibn Ṣā'id, ed. Bū 'Alwān 1985:126–127.
2 *Ibid.*:200.
3 See Mez 1922; Kraemer 1986a, 1986b.

https://doi.org/10.1515/9783110446395-013

Our rather limited knowledge of the emergence of the *Kalām* – its background, social setting, and the factors that shaped it in the earliest stages – leaves much room for speculation. By comparison, the early development of Islamic philosophy is easier to follow and its study more advanced. The role of the indigenous Greek and Syriac-speaking Christian communities, and of Pahlevi-speaking Zoroastrians, has been recognized as central to the process of transmitting the philosophical texts. Attention has also been given to the sociological background of the translation movement. In particular, the seminal study of Dimitri Gutas has analyzed the motivations – political, social, intellectual and religious – that drove the ruling elite to support not only individual translations, but a translation movement on a grand scale, grand enough to make it a game changer in the intellectual landscape of early Islam.[4]

While the steps in the transmission of the sciences and of Aristotelian philosophy – and to some extent, the steps in the transmission of Neoplatonic philosophy – can be shown to be dependent on the translation of books, the appearance of Muslim rational theology, known as *Kalām*, precedes the translation movement. The impact of Greek thought (Stoicism, Skepticism, Platonic thought as well as Aristotelian philosophy) on Muslim *Kalām* is undeniable. This is evident not merely in the general interest in speculative theology, but in details: specific ideas, structure of argumentation, terminology, as well as specific arguments and formulations. We do not know exactly how this knowledge was transmitted, as there is no evidence that any book of Greek philosophy was available in Arabic to the early *mutakallimūn*.[5]

One example may suffice here: On the basis of his study of the logic and the peculiarities of the *Kalām*, Josef van Ess pointed out that the use of terminology that might sound Aristotelian may actually reflect a very different logical system. For instance, *Kalām* texts do not use syllogistic proofs but rather resort to inference from an "indicative sign" (*dalīl*, pl. *dalāʾil*), which, according to van Ess, translates the Stoic term *sēmeion*. At times, the word *burhān*, the Arabic Aristotelian term for apodictic proof, was used with the same non-syllogistic meaning. Thus, the presence of smoke is an indicative sign for the existence of fire, and the presence of a finely written book is an indicative sign for the existence of a competent scribe. In this and other matters, van Ess pointed to the Stoics as one possible source of inspiration for the logical structure of the *Kalām*, but we have

4 Gutas 1998. On the translation movement, see also Endress 1987 and 1992; on translations from Sanskrit, see also Van Bladel 2011.
5 Van Ess (1968:3–4) suggests the Empiricist school of medicine and the medical academy in Gundēshāpūr as a possible transmission channel. See also Cook 1981:44–47, 157; Madelung 1987a.

no idea how the early *mutakallimūn* could have come by this Stoic logic.[6] Shlomo Pines, on his part, pointed to the similarity of *dalīl* to the Sanskrit term *pramāṇa*, and, while taking into consideration the parallel Stoic concepts of *sēmeion* and *kritērion*, suggested that the appearance of this term in early *Kalām* might more likely be seen as reflecting the encounters of Muslims with Buddhists.[7] But here again, in the absence of texts (and in particular, of any evidence for the translation of Indian logical works into Arabic), this suggestion remains difficult to substantiate.[8]

To be sure, the presence of converts to Islam (who could have transmitted into Arabic ideas they had read or heard in other languages) must be taken into account,[9] but the striking parallels to pre-Islamic philosophy with which the literature of *Kalām* is strewn are too numerous and too fundamental for this explanation to suffice. We find ourselves speaking of "transmission by osmosis" or through "floating ideas," which amounts to saying: We do not know.[10] The most significant factor which is mentioned in this context remains the highly developed disputation culture, which created a context where early Muslim *mutakallimūn* could have become acquainted with the legacy of these Greek schools of thought.[11]

As for the Jews, they, too, participated in this disputation culture, and by the same token would have been exposed to the same influences at the same time. Nevertheless, it has been assumed that they were exposed to these influences relatively late, through their encounters with Muslims, in the late ninth and early tenth centuries.[12] A fine-tuning of this perception has been proposed by Rina Drory, who focused on the role of the Karaites. Unlike Rabbanite Jews, who accept the authority of the talmudic tradition, the Karaites reject this tradition and in principle rely on direct access to the biblical text. Schismatic movements among the Jews seem to have proliferated in the turbulent times from the rise of Islam up to the Abbasid revolution, especially in Iraq and Iran. These movements

6 Van Ess 1970:31–32; see also Freudenthal 1996.

7 Pines 1994:187–189.

8 Van Bladel 2011:87. But see Dong, forthcoming. I am indebted to Dong Xiuyuan for allowing me to read a pre-publication draft of his paper.

9 Van Ess 1970:24, 33.

10 In a different context, see Wansbrough 1978:32. Van Ess (1968:3) suggests transmission "in a more or less underground way"; in a later article (2002:26–27) he mentions Pierre Thillet's hypothesis of "tradition diffuse" and treats it as unsatisfactory.

11 See Lazarus-Yafeh et al. 1998. On the disputation culture in late antiquity, see, e. g., Lim 1995; Cameron 2014:25–38; Walker 2006:164–190.

12 See, e. g., Guttmann 1964:54; and Van Ess 1991–1997, I:53, who relies on Sirat 1990:15 ff.

may have been the precursors of Karaism, although the Karaite movement itself was established by Daniel al-Qūmisī in tenth-century Jerusalem. Drory suggested that the Rabbanite Jews were constrained by loyalty to rigid, often stagnant traditions, which, confined as they were to the canonical rabbinic texts and literary genres, initially made their followers impermeable to the new developments in the Muslim world. By comparison, Drory argued, the split with Rabbinic Judaism left the Karaites with a literary vacuum, and their as yet non-canonized literary system gave them the necessary flexibility to look for new ways of literary expression. According to Drory, the Karaites were thus the first to adopt new literary genres which they encountered among their Muslim neighbors: systematic and to a great extent rational Bible exegesis, linguistic studies of Hebrew, philosophy and theology. According to her, it was only the tenth-century Rabbanite scholar Saadya Gaon (d. 942) who, responding to the Karaite challenge, composed in these genres, too.[13]

Drory's suggestion has the merit of introducing into the discussion the scholarly need to identify fault lines in traditional cultures that allow for new ways of thought and expression to enter and for a change of paradigm to take place, but her historical argument in this particular case is not valid. To begin with, as far as we know Karaites and Rabbanites adopted the new genres (*Kalām*, for example) around the same time, and there is no evidence whatsoever that the Karaites preceded the Rabbanites in doing so. Furthermore, Drory presents a neat line of transmission, as in a relay race where each participant transmits the torch to one and only one person. For Drory, the recourse to theology was passed from the Christians to the Muslims, from the Muslims to the Karaites, and from the Karaites to the Rabbanites. In her reconstruction, during each lap of the race, the other participants remained unaware of the ongoing process or ignored it until their own turn arrived. But religious and cultural influences in general, and perhaps in this stormy period in particular, do not work as linear developments. Rather, they are engulfed in what I have described elsewhere as whirlpools, where different influences are mixed together, working in all directions at the same time. And indeed, in the case at hand, all the available data contradict Drory's linear reconstruction.[14]

The first Jewish theological text in Arabic that is known to us was composed almost a century before Saadya. This early theological text, the *Twenty Chapters* of Dāwūd Ibn Marwān al-Muqammaṣ, was probably written in the first half of the ninth century. It thus preceded the Karaite schism, and indeed in the tenth

13 Drory 1988; 2000:127–129.
14 Stroumsa 2009:56–57.

century its influence is equally apparent in Rabbanite and Karaite texts. Furthermore, as we are informed by the tenth-century Karaite Abū Ya'qūb al-Qirqisānī, al-Muqammaṣ had converted to Christianity and studied for many years in Nisibis under the Jacobite theologian Nonnus of Nisibis (d. after 861). He then returned to Judaism and used the knowledge he had acquired in Nisibis to introduce new literary genres into Jewish thought, translating biblical exegetical texts from Syriac into Arabic, composing polemical works (also, and perhaps mostly, against Christianity) and authoring what seems to be the first Jewish theological *Summa* in Arabic. His *Twenty Chapters* is also one of the earliest extant *Kalām* works and perhaps the first Arabic theological *Summa* that we possess at all.[15] Theology was thus transmitted to Jews also directly from Christians, and not only through Muslim intermediaries. At the same time, the whirlpool effect is evident in this case as well: Al-Muqammaṣ himself records meetings with a Muslim *mutakallim*, and even the material he quotes from a Christian source is already influenced by Islam and by Muslim *Kalām*.[16]

What Is *Kalām*?

Following this brief historical survey, we can return to examine what we know of the beginning of early *Kalām*. A concise and quite accurate definition of *Kalām* is given by Ibn Khaldūn (d. 808/1406):

> This is a science that involves arguing, with logical proofs, in defence of the articles of faith, and refuting innovators who deviate in their dogmas from the early Muslims and Muslim orthodoxy.[17]

Writing in the early fifteenth century, Ibn Khaldūn has a historical perspective of almost half a millennium of *Kalām*, and he himself had some training as a *mutakallim*.[18] Although he draws on definitions given by philosophers, he pre-

---

15 Other early *Kalām* works are not *summae* but treatises devoted to one specific topic. The Ibāḍī 'Abd Allāh b. Yazīd al-Fazārī (late eighth/early ninth century) is "the earliest kalām theologian whose teaching can be comprehensively examined on the basis of his own extant works" (Madelung 2016:243). But al-Fazārī's extant theological texts are treatises on a specific topic, or answers to queries. Another equally early work is a polemical refutation of the Qadariyya, contained in its rebuttal by the Zaydī Imām Aḥmad al-Nāṣir li-Dīn Allāh (d. 322/934). I am indebted to Sabine Schmidtke and to Hassan Ansari for helping me to clarify this point.

16 See Stroumsa 1989; Al-Muqammaṣ, ed. Stroumsa 2016.

17 Ibn Khaldūn, ed. Beirut 1997:325, ed. Rosenthal 1969:348; Wolfson 1970:3–8.

18 Talbi 1986:828, col. 2.

sents *Kalām* as a *mutakallim* would see it, without animosity. According to his definition, *Kalām* is a science (*ʿilm*) rather than a mere technical craft (*ṣināʿa*). The subject matter of this science, according to Ibn Khaldūn, is the articles of faith; its tools are logical proofs, and its purpose is polemical, namely, to refute the arguments of heretics who stray from the straight and narrow path of orthodoxy.

Ibn Khaldūn's own model was the orthodox Sunnī, Ashʿarī branch of *Kalām* in which he himself was trained, but the characteristics we find in his definition are apparent already in the first *Kalām* works – both Ibāḍī and Muʿtazilī – or in citations from them going back to the eighth century. The early Muʿtazila had a strong polemical and missionary character, and its followers were sent as missionaries (*duʿāt*) across the Islamic world. Its chronological proximity to the ʿAbbāsid revolution, which also had a network of missionaries, was the main reason for Henrik Samuel Nyberg's suggestion that the Muʿtazila started as a political movement.[19] This suggestion was soon rejected by later scholarship, since the nature of the early Muʿtazila from the start was clearly and predominantly theological.[20] Nevertheless, Shlomo Pines has shown that the term *mutakallim* was also used by the early ʿAbbasid movement, to denote a spokesman who presents the arguments of his camp against the other and tries to win his opponents over. Pines also noted the close identification of the *mutakallimūn* with *aṣḥāb al-jadal*, the "Masters of controversy."[21] He therefore concluded that the *mutakallimūn* were essentially controversialists.[22] Pines's cautious reconstruction of the development of the movement deserves to be quoted:

> We would not, in my opinion, push speculation beyond the bound of plausibility if we supposed that the revolutionary Muʿtazilite discovery of the rôle of reason in discovering truth ... was due to the fact that some of the early Muʿtazilites, who represented one of the varieties of *Mutakallimūn*, directed their attention to the technique of the debates ... and in this way came to value both intuitive and discursive reason, not only as an instrument but for its own sake. Reasoning became an end in itself, and its conclusions were regarded by some as unconditionally valid, as valid as the religious beliefs and traditions.[23]

This brings us to the much-debated question of the origin of the term *kalām*. Literally, the word means "speech," and its use to denote dialectical theology is now

19 Nyberg 1913–1936:787–788, 1977:127.
20 See Stroumsa 1990.
21 See also Cook 1981:157: "The *mutakallimūn* of early Islam are the dialectical militias of warring sects, skilled representatives of their communities in the war of words."
22 Pines 1971:239–240.
23 *Ibid.*:233–234.

commonly seen as a calque. What remains less clear is: A calque of what term and from what language? The main possibilities thus far proposed are the following:[24]

(1) The origin of the term is the Greek *logos*, as in *theo-logia*, and the *mutakallim* is one who speaks about God.
(2) The origin of the term is the Greek *dialexis*, and the term *kalām* refers to the practice of disputation, or to its imitation in the structure of the written text.
(3) The origin of the term is a conflation of the two Greek terms, *logos* and *dialexis*, so that the *mutakallim* is a theologian who speaks about God, using dialectical speech.
(4) Although the term has its origin in Greek, its transmission to Arabic passed through the intermediary of Syriac translations. The Arabic *mutakallim* would then be either the equivalent of the Syriac *mᵉmallēl ʿal alāhā* (one who speaks about God, that is, a theologian) or one who uses dialectics (*mamllā*).

The search for the development of the term *Kalām* in the sense of theology cannot, however, be separated from the context in which Muslim theology itself developed.[25] In their attempt to understand the origins of *Kalām* as a distinct field of science, scholars have indeed examined not only the etymology of the term, but also the background to the emergence of the discipline. While common sense tells us that both internal and external factors must have played a role, scholars endeavor to detect the most decisive factor, the identification of which could perhaps tell us where the discipline started. Some (like Josef van Ess) put most of the weight on internal developments within Islam: the theologico-political disputations regarding the succession to Muḥammad (between Shiites, Sunnis, Khārijites, Murji'ites and others) and the fierce debates regarding issues of free will or predestination.[26] In this context, and still focusing the search within the parameters of Islam, one cannot avoid noting that one of the earliest and most divisive topics of discussion was God's speech (*kalām Allāh*), both as the creative *fiat* (*kun*) and as the revealed text, and the question of whether or not it can be considered, as the proponents of the Muʿtazila claimed, a temporal attribute of God.[27] In the other camp are those scholars who stress the formative influence on Islam of its encounter with other religions: Iranian religions with their impact on discussions of theodicy; Indian religions with their rejection of prophecy; and, perhaps most importantly, Christianity in all its versions.

---

24 See Wolfson 1970:1–2; Cook 1981:157–158; Van Ess 1966:57–59, 1970:24, 1991–1997, I:53; Frank 1988:131, n. 58; 1992:9–11; Treiger 2016:32–33.
25 Cf. Van Ess 1991–1997, I:53.
26 Van Ess 1975, 1977, 1991–1997, I:54–56.
27 Madelung 1974; Gardet 1990.

The influence of Christianity was enormous, in both content and structure. Harry Austryn Wolfson has underlined the Christian background – the discussions of the Trinity as well as of the divine Logos – to the Muslim debate on the divine attributes in general and on God's speech in particular.[28] Michael Cook, on his part, has shown the close similarity between the basic dialectical structure of *Kalām* works ("If he says: ..., we say: ...") and the "Questions and Answers" genre of late-antique Christian works. Examining an early polemical text denying free will, the *Questions against the Qadarites* ascribed to Ḥasan b. Muḥammad (d. ca. 718/100), Cook argued that its genre is "a direct and unmodified borrowing from the Syriac literature of the time."[29] For Cook, this probable Christian model for early *Kalām* works strengthens the possibility that the very term *Kalām* resulted from a conflation of the terms *theologia* and *dialexis*.[30]

Jack Tannous and Alexander Treiger have pointed out that, whereas *dialexis* and *theologia* are quite distinct in Greek, the parallel Syriac terms (*mamllā* and *m^{e}mallēl ʿal alāhā*) are rather close, and the way to their conflation in Syriac Christian circles thus also seems shorter. Treiger therefore suggests that "a plausible milieu where the Arabic term *kalām* could have been used simultaneously both for disputation and theology" might be seen among the Arabic-speaking Jacobite tribes.[31] Be that as it may, in the eighth and ninth centuries that conflation is already a fact in Arabic, and the term *kalām* is used to denote the practice of theology cast in a distinctive dialectic form.

The above-mentioned explanations of the term *kalām* are not necessarily mutually exclusive, and they are indeed often mentioned together by scholars. Whether we tilt the balance towards inner Muslim developments or towards external influences, there is no doubt that both contributed to the emergence of *Kalām* in the second/eighth century and to its shaping in the early decades after its appearance. What John Wansbrough described as the "sectarian milieu" – a term equally valid for the schismatic Christian communities and for the fractious world of early Islam – was a fertile place for doctrinal and interreligious disputations, allowing various factors to contribute simultaneously to the emergence of *Kalām* as a discipline.[32] By the same token, it seems that the term *kalām* itself also

---

28 Wolfson 1970:112–146, 205–234.
29 Cook 1981:156.
30 Cook 1980.
31 Treiger 2016:33; see also Tannous 2008.
32 Wansbrough 1978. Wansbrough's penetrating and thought-provoking book, as well as the locution he coined, have allowed others to redefine phenomena in their specific domains of research; an example is Sidney Griffith, for whom the intra-Christian texts were produced in the World of Islam in what may be called "the heresiographical milieu." See Griffith 2001:9, n.1.

reflects the different factors which may have contributed not only to the name of the discipline but also to its shaping, its practices and its concerns.

We have seen above several explanations of the term *kalām*, which together seem to cover the main concerns of the discipline and the main characteristics of its *Sitz im Leben*. Nevertheless, it is striking to find one aspect which, as far as I know, has remained practically absent from the contemporary discussions up to now. What seems to have been overlooked in the analysis is the enormous importance *mutakallimūn* gave to *kalām* in its primary sense of speech, talk, the way one speaks.[33] In the following pages, I would like to draw attention to this aspect.

Kalām as the Way One Speaks

It has already been noted that the structure and form of *Kalām* works may be their most distinctive feature, noticeable even before one grasps the author's theological position.[34] But while noting this typical, rather rigid structure, scholars have usually focused mostly on the dialectical style. We have already mentioned the structure of "if he says ..., we say ..." Another typical *Kalām* structure is the beginning of each discussion with a full taxonomy (*taqsīm* or *qisma*) of the available possibilities regarding the issue at hand. After this presentation, each possibility is examined and discarded until we are left with the remaining correct one, or until all are rejected, proving the fallacy of the question.

Beyond the external structure, however, we must also pay attention to the nature of the arguments themselves, which are often rather peculiar. As we learned from Ibn Khaldūn, the intention of the *mutakallimūn* is to argue using logical proofs, but when we examine the arguments, we often find that they amount to a scrutiny of the way we speak. People are expected to say what they mean, and therefore, in discussing a proposition with opponents (as one does in *Kalām* works), one can literally catch them by the word.

A common and widely used polemical technique in *Kalām* works is *ilzām*, an argument *ad hominem* which, starting from the opponent's own premises, develops them to show that they contradict his position, or that they contradict a commonly accepted doctrine. What remains unnoticed in modern scholarship is

---

33 Van Ess, for example, notes the early use of *kalām* in the sense of "speech," but he seems to regard this as relevant neither to the coining of the term *kalām* nor to the development of theology. See Van Ess 1970:23; and cf. *ibid.*:24 and Van Ess 1991–1997, I:51–52. See also Madelung 1987b:326; Frank 1988:131, 1992:9–11.

34 Cook 1980; Stroumsa 2003:71.

the centrality of what you *say* (as distinct from what you believe) in such an argument. By rephrasing, a person can reposition himself advantageously without having to reexamine or explain his position.

Al-Muqammaṣ is a particularly good example of this peculiar way of reasoning, not only because he is so early and because of the comprehensive character of his theological work, compared to other texts from that period, but also because of his attested biographical positioning at the crossroads between the Christian academy in Nisibis and Judaism, and thus also between philosophy (as it was used in the Christian academies) and *Kalām*. A typical example of the utmost seriousness he accords to words appears in his discussion with skeptics, where he says:

> We say to whomever claims that the world does not exist in reality: "Do you realize that the world does not exist, [or do you not realize it]?" If he says: "I do not realize it," then he is retracting his own words and invalidates his claim that the world does not exist, because he does not realize that the world does not exist. [And if he says, "I realize that the world does not exist,"] he is admitting, in spite of himself, the realization of a reality which he previously denied.[35]

The argument, or more precisely, the argumentative technique presented here is very common in early *Kalām* works in this context. In some ways, this could serve as a perfect example of the way a *mutakallim* pushes his opponent to consider in earnest what he himself had said. But one could also argue that this example does not actually prove the general centrality of speech in *Kalām* argumentation. The discussion in this particular case is about axiomatic knowledge (the awareness of the existing world, or, in a variation of this topic, the awareness of one's own self), which the *mutakallimūn* did not expect to be able to prove by syllogisms.

Other examples that do not have this shortcoming abound in the text of the *Twenty Chapters*.[36] I will quote just three.

(1) In Chapter Three, al-Muqammaṣ argues that the world is made up of self-subsistent substances and of accidents which inhere in them. This view is

---

35 Stroumsa 1989:74; Al-Muqammaṣ, ed. Stroumsa 2016:III, 2.

36 For example, *Twenty Chapters*, XII, 27, 31, where the inherently different quality of good or evil deeds is proven by the different names we use for them in our speech. Indeed, in Muslim *Kalām* this topic goes under the heading of *al-asmāʾ wa'l-aḥkām* (literally: "names and judgments"). Another example is *Twenty Chapters*, IX, 12, where, polemicizing against the Christian doctrine of the Trinity, al-Muqammaṣ juxtaposes his opponent's formulation and his beliefs and argues that the opponent uses expressions without intending their proper meaning (*innahu aṭlaqa al-lafẓ bi-lā maʿnā taḥtahu*).

fundamental to his physics, and he tries to prove it in several ways. His final proof runs as follows:

> Among the things that may prove the existence of contingent accidents is the fact that all people, both the common people and the elite, the educated and the uneducated, construct their words so as to make the various qualities of things,[37] their colors, tastes and sounds, contingent on the things themselves, whereas the things themselves are never made contingent on their qualities. We say, for example: "the heat of the fire" or "the chill of the snow," and we do not say: "the fire of the heat" or "the snow of the chill." We say: "the fire's burning" or "the snow's chilling," and we do not say: "the burning's fire" or "the chilling's snow." We say: "the Ethiopian's blackness" or "the Slav's whiteness," and we do not say "the blackness's Ethiopian" or "the whiteness's Slav." We say: "the honey's sweetness" or "the cactus's bitterness,"[38] and we do not say: "the sweetness's honey" or "the bitterness's cactus." We say: "the dog's barking," "the horse's neighing" and "the lion's roar," and we do not say: "the barking's dog," "the neighing's horse" or "the roar's lion." There are many such examples among things that [in our speech], are made contingent on others, and whose subsistence is in other than themselves. This is the best proof for the existence of accidents and for the futility of the claims of those who deny them. Praise be to God.[39]

There is no attempt here to demonstrate the physical structure of the world; this whole lengthy proof focuses on what we say (*mā naqūl*) and specifically on the common way to use the construct state in Arabic.

(2) Chapter Nine of the *Twenty Chapters* is dedicated to the divine attributes. Al-Muqammaṣ argues in it that, although both scripture and common sense oblige us to use certain attributes of God, these attributes are not additional eternal entities but are identical with God's essence; God is living by His essence, knowing by His essence, etc. In this, al-Muqammaṣ's position is identical to that adopted by the early Muʿtazilites, and in particular by Abū al-Hudhayl al-ʿAllāf (d. ca. 226/840–842 or 234/849). Al-Muqammaṣ explains:

> We say that the light of the sun is shining; it is not shining by virtue of another light, but rather it is the sun which is shining by virtue of the light. We say that the fragrance of musk is sweet-smelling, not by virtue of another fragrance, but rather it is the musk that is sweet-smelling by virtue of the fragrance. We say that the eye sees, meaning not that the eye sees by virtue of another eye, but rather that it is the human being who sees by virtue of the

37 Literally: "the potentialities and the actions of things," i.e., their potential and actual qualities.

38 The same example is used by Al-Jāḥiẓ, ed. Hārūn 1943:V, b8 (and see Al-Muqammas, ed. Stroumsa 2016:VII, 9).

39 Al-Muqammas, ed. Stroumsa 2016:III, 16; Stroumsa 1989:84–85.

eye. We say that the tongue articulates, meaning not that it articulates by virtue of another tongue, but rather that it is the human being who articulates by virtue of the tongue.[40]

This paragraph is part of the discussion of divine attributes, and at the same time a polemical discussion with the Christians regarding the Trinity and Christology. The Christian context of the Arabic discussion of the attributes has been analyzed in detail and is very relevant in the case of al-Muqammaṣ, who in this paragraph obviously employs metaphors used by Christians.[41] What is striking here is the focal point of the argument: Al-Muqammaṣ's use of parallels is not poetic or mystical in character and is not intended to impress the reader by the force of its metaphors. He clearly intends to present a rational argument, but this argument is not based on a logical syllogism. Even his use of the parallel is not what we would expect. He does not bring the examples of the sun, the eye or musk to demonstrate a possible link between a power or a phenomenon and its source; it is not the physical world in which he is interested. The thrust of his argument is that we all *say* something, and we all know intuitively what we *mean* when we say it. This is the argument from common sense, i. e., from the sense we commonly give to our speech.

(3) Chapter Twelve, which is devoted to theodicy and free will, includes a section on the evaluation of human acts. In this context, al-Muqammaṣ recounts a debate that he conducted in Damascus with a certain Shabīb al-Baṣrī. Al-Muqammaṣ gleefully reports how he made fun of Shabīb; and yet he describes his opponent with respect, saying that he was "one of the best-known ascetics of his community, and among the leading sages of his period."[42] Georges Vajda suggested that this Muslim *mutakallim* was Shabīb b. Shayba al-Baṣrī (d. 161/778), an identification which, if correct, would confirm the earlier dating for al-Muqammaṣ. According to al-Muqammaṣ, Shabīb denied the reality of evil, saying: "The term 'bad' is only a word (*lafẓ*), an utterance (*dhikr*) used to indicate suffering, and suffering is nothing but good." At the end of the discussion, al-Muqammaṣ summarizes his own argument, saying:

If both those who give you [something] and those who steal from you do only good, either to you or to themselves, assertions that people commonly make (*qawl al-nās*), such as: "He has done wrong" or "He behaved well" ... become meaningless, and it is also meaningless to speak of sentiments of hatred and love, enmity and friendship. ... It is also meaningless to

40 Al-Muqammas, ed. Stroumsa 2016:IX, 17; Stroumsa 1989:196–197.
41 On the Christian background of the discussion of attributes in Islam, see Wolfson 1970:112–146, 205–234; Wansbrough 1978:114.
42 Al-Muqammas, ed. Stroumsa 2016:XII, 28; Stroumsa 1989:248.

speak of truthful or deceitful utterances (*fī'l-lafẓ*), or, for that matter, of true or false sayings (*fī'l-kalām*).[43]

The two opponents in this debate are educated people; al-Muqammaṣ's work shows him to have had some training in Aristotelian logic (as was the custom in the Christian education system in the Syriac academies), and Shabīb was reputed for his high moral standards and ascetic tendencies. The difference between their opinions is significant, and, given their education, we might have expected them to discuss the issue at hand, namely, the short and long-term outcomes of human deeds, as an ethical, practical or soteriological issue. Instead, the discussion between these two *mutakallimūn* remains on the level of the meaning of the spoken word.

In most of these examples, al-Muqammaṣ refers to human speech as *qawl* or *lafẓ*, but in at least one place he actually uses the term *kalām*. In Chapter Ten, which is dedicated to a refutation of Christology, Al-Muqammaṣ draws attention to the meaning of the verb "to beget." According to him, begetting denotes temporality, which applies only to bodies and therefore contradicts the eternal nature of God. In closing his disputation about Jesus' Sonship, al-Muqammaṣ says: "The Christians find this disputation (*kalām*) very difficult."[44] The word *kalām* here probably refers to the whole polemical refutation of Jesus' Sonship, and not just to his last argument.[45]

I have focused on the examples in the work of al-Muqammaṣ, where this phenomenon is particularly striking, but examples abound in other *Kalām* works. Another early example is Abū Rabīʿ Ibn al-Layth's letter to the Byzantine Emperor Constantine, cited by Ibn Abī Ṭāhir Ṭayfūr (d. 280/893) in his *Kitāb al-Manthūr wa'l-manẓūm*. Ibn al-Layth's polemical strategy, like that of al-Muqammaṣ, focuses on the conventional usage of language (*mā tajrī al-aqāwīl bi-hi*, or *mā tajrī bi-hi alsin al-ʿibād*) and on the generally agreed meaning of words.[46] In his polemic against the Christian doctrine of the Sonship of Jesus, he argues that the Christians' usage of the verb "to beget" contradicts its normal usage in their own speech (*mā ijtamaʿat ʿalay-hi al-Naṣārā wa-dhahabat ilay-hi bi-him al-maʿānī min tashqīq al-kalām wa-taṣrīf al-kutub*).[47] This fascination with speech was clearly an

43 Al-Muqammas, ed. Stroumsa 2016:XII, 31; Stroumsa 1989:250.
44 Al-Muqammas, ed. Stroumsa 2016:X, 16; Stroumsa 1989:217.
45 Cf. Stroumsa 1989:216.
46 See Ibn al-Layth, ed. al-Rifāʿī 1927, II:193, 222; Wakelnig, forthcoming. I am indebted to Elvira Wakelnig for drawing my attention to this text and for allowing me access to her article before its publication. On Ibn Abī Ṭayfūr see Toorawa 2005.
47 See Ibn al-Layth, ed. al-Rifāʿī 1927, II:221–222.

important aspect of the early *Kalām*, and it quite likely also contributed to fixing the name of the discipline as *ʿilm al-kalām*. At times, this obsessive preoccupation with the spoken word may seem pedantic. But if we examine it in the context of the contemporary scholarly mood, we may form a less harsh view.

As noted by Ibn Ṣāʿid al-Andalusī in the passage with which I began, "at the beginning of Islam" the study of the Arabic language was prominent. It was central to what the Muslims called "the sciences of the Qurʾān," and to what Drory has described as "the scriptural cluster" – those disciplines that developed because they were crucial for the study of the divine message. Arabic lexicography and the study of Arabic syntax proved indispensable to the development of Qurʾānic exegesis, as well as to the development of legal reasoning based on the Qurʾān.

The prominent place given to language emerged also in the early encounters with Greek philosophy. A case in point is the famous debate that took place in Baghdad in 320/932 between the young grammarian (and theologian) Abū Saʿīd al-Sīrāfī (d. 369/979) and the Nestorian Christian Abū Bishr Mattā ibn Yūnus (d. ca. 328/940), a translator of philosophical texts,[48] about the relative merits of logic and grammar as tools for distinguishing truth from falsehood. Abū Bishr Mattā presented logic as "a linguistic instrument (*āla min ālāt al-kalām*), by which one can distinguish correct speech (*ṣaḥīḥ al-kalām*) from incorrect, and unsound meaning (*maʿnā*) from sound, just as one uses a yardstick."[49] Al-Sīrāfī retorted that "correct speech (*ṣaḥīḥ al-kalām*) is recognized by its well-ordered structure and by its acknowledged syntax (*iʿrāb*) when we are speaking in Arabic (*idha natakallamu biʾl-ʿarabiyya*), whereas the distinction between correct and incorrect meaning is made by common sense (*ʿaql*)." Logic, he said, was invented by a Greek, who set it up according to the language of the Greeks and in their conventional terminology; there is no reason in the world why it should also compel the Turks or the Indians, the Persians or the Arabs. Al-Sīrāfī continues to berate Abū Bishr:

> You are not actually inviting us to learn the science of logic, but rather to learn the Greek language, a language which you yourself do not know, and whose usage disappeared a long time ago ... So you translate from Syriac; but what would you say about the changed

48 Al-Tawḥīdī, ed. Amīn and al-Zayn 1939–1944, I:108–128; Mahdi 1970:50–81. The story of the debate is also mentioned briefly in Ibn al-Qifṭī, ed. Müller and Lippert 1903:323. On the relevance of this debate to both "sacred" and "profane" knowledge, and on the linguistic aspect of philosophy, see: Heck 2002:2–3 and note 5, as well as p. 20.

49 *Mīzān*, literally: "balance"; see: al-Tawḥīdī, ed. Amīn and al-Zayn 1939–1944, I:108.

> meaning in the translation from one language – Greek – to another – Syriac, and then to yet another one, Arabic?[50]

Muhsin Mahdi, who has analyzed this anecdote in detail, assumed that al-Sīrāfī, an able polemicist, detected the ambiguity of the term *kalām* in his interlocutor's definition of logic and exploited it in his response, by distinguishing between "speech as language and speech as the realm of the intelligible ideas."[51] That is why he demanded that Abū Bishr present his claim in a language that everyone could understand. This interpretation, however, overlooks the fact that al-Sīrāfī was not only a grammarian and a polemicist, but that he had also been trained as a theologian, and that his polemical technique relied on his own epistemology. As is well known, the *mutakallimūn* used the term *ʿaql* not to denote the intellect as the Aristotelian philosophers understood it, but rather as common sense, and that is indeed how al-Sīrāfī uses the term in this passage. In the same way, it seems to me that al-Sīrāfī's presentation of the term *kalām* as the commonly spoken language was not merely a polemical ploy but rather reflected his own concern as a *mutakallim*. The debate between Abū Bishr Mattā and al-Sīrāfī revolves around a topic that lay at the heart of the discourse culture: Are its building blocks syntactical, or are they logical? For al-Sīrāfī and the *mutakallimūn*, the commonly spoken Arabic language became part of the logical system, and *kalām* – not God's speech, but everyday human language – was its main instrument. In this context, we can see how the meaning of what one says becomes all-important.

The *Kalām* as Others See It

An interesting perspective on the success of the *Kalām* system can be gained from observations made by its opponents on all sides. For the traditionalists, the *mutakallimūn*'s fascination with rational speech was wholly misplaced; the only speech that mattered was *kalām Allāh*, God's uncreated speech. This is particularly obvious in the western Islamic world, in al-Andalus. In the eighth century, Muʿtazilī missionaries had been sent to North Africa, but the mission lost its

50 Al-Tawḥīdī, ed. Amīn and al-Zayn 1939–1944, I:110–111. A similar criticism was expressed against another famous translator, Ḥunayn ibn Isḥāq, who, as a result, disappeared from Baghdad for a couple of years and returned sporting a peculiar hairdo and citing Homer in Greek. Presumably, Ḥunayn took the criticism to heart and crossed the border to Byzantium to perfect his knowledge of Greek. See Strohmaier 1980:196; Ibn Abī Uṣaybiʿa, ed. Riḍā, n. d.:258.
51 Mahdi 1970:64.

strength at the Straits of Gibraltar, and the Muʿtazila as a movement did not gain a foothold in the Iberian peninsula.[52] Nevertheless, the anxiety of the dominant Mālikī orthodoxy regarding rational thought seems to have focused disproportionately on *Kalām*, perhaps even more so than on philosophy.

The first notable philosopher in al-Andalus, Muḥammad ibn Masarra, was a Neoplatonist philosopher whose father is said to have traveled to the East and to have had some Muʿtazilī connections. Very little of the father's purported interest in the Muʿtazila is reflected in the Neoplatonic mystical philosophy of the son. Ibn Masarra died in 318/931, and some twenty years after his death, Caliph ʿAbd al-Raḥmān III began to persecute those who were said to have been his disciples. The main reason for this wave of belated persecution of the Masarrians and for subsequent ones was the growing challenge of the Fāṭimid caliphate in North Africa. The suspected affinity of the Fāṭimid, Ismāʿīlī, Neoplatonic, "*bāṭinī*" philosophy with the mystical philosophy of Ibn Masarra, also known as Bāṭinism, was probably at the root of the Caliph's concern.[53] Interestingly, however, the accusations against the Masarrians seem to have been directed against the effigy of Muʿtazilite rationalism at least as much as against the Masarrian mystical approach. In one of the anti-Masarrian edicts, we find the following startling declaration:

> By [supplying us with] clearly-stated rules of conduct, God has spared us the toil of thinking.[54]

A similar aversion to *Kalām*, its disputation culture and its rules of the game is reflected in a famous conversation between two western Mālikī scholars, recorded by al-Ḥumaydī. The Andalusī scholar Ibn Saʿdī, who resided in Qayrawān, recounted his experience of two sessions of *Kalām* inter-confessional debate (*majlis*) that he had witnessed in Baghdad. Ibn Saʿdī had found the inclusion of infidels and heretics as equal participants in the debate, and the rules of disputation – using rational arguments and avoiding arguments from the Qurʾān and *Ḥadīth* – too offensive to bear, and had left both meetings before the actual discussion began. Predictably, perhaps, his Qayrawānī interlocutor, the Mālikī scholar Abū Muḥammad b. Abī Zayd, was also appalled by the procedure of the *Kalām* meeting.[55]

---

52 Van Ess 1991–1997, IV:272–273; Stroumsa 2014.
53 Ibn Ḥayyān, ed. Chalmeta 1979:20 ff; Cruz-Hernández 1981, 1986; Fierro 2004:133–135, 2005:131; Safran 2013:72–73; Stroumsa 2014:87.
54 "Wa-kafānā bi-wāḍiḥ al-manāhij muʾnat al-fikra." Ibn Ḥayyān, ed. Chalmeta 1979:26, 14.
55 Al-Ḥumaydī, ed. al-Ṭanjī 1952:101–102, No. 185; Cook 2007.

Although Arabic philosophical literature from the Orient had reached Islamic Spain and contributed to the development of philosophy there, Andalusian philosophy developed in quite different ways from its counterpart in the Orient. There is more than one reason for this separate development. But, among the contributing factors, it would be interesting to examine the effect of the presence – or absence – of *Kalām* in the vicinity of the emerging Andalusian philosophy.

Also interesting to note is the fact that, despite the difference between Andalusian and Oriental philosophers, they appear to have been united by their aversion to *Kalām*. For al-Fārābī, the *mutakallimūn* were mere propagandists who cynically used their tools of seemingly rational argument to prove their religion and defend it.[56] For Ibn Rushd, what the *mutakallimūn* presented to the multitudes was not solid rational argumentation but rather a simulacrum of rationality. Their claims were on the one hand far from the truth, and on the other hand enough to confuse the simple people, who were unable to understand them.[57] Particularly biting are the evaluations of *Kalām* by two consecutive heads of the Baghdad school of philosophy, the Jacobite Christian Yaḥyā b. ʿAdī (d. 974) and his student, the Muslim philosopher Abū Sulaymān al-Sijistānī *al-manṭiqī* ("the Logician," d. ca. 375/985). Their descriptions of the *mutakallimūn* at work are also relevant for the suggestion adduced here regarding the meaning of the term *kalām*. Endeavoring to define the difference between *mutakallimūn* and philosophers, al-Sijistānī remarks:

> It is obvious for any discerning, intelligent and understanding person, that their method [i.e., that of the *mutakallimūn*] is based on measuring one word against another (*makāyil al-lafẓ bi'l-lafẓ*) and on responding to one thing by weighing another thing against it, either by pushing in some rational evidence, or without such evidence whatsoever.

After elaborating this point at length, he moves on to quote Yaḥyā b. ʿAdī:

> I wonder about our colleagues, who, when we meet at the *Majlis*, say: "We are those who speak (*mutakallimūn*), and we are the masters of speech (*arbāb al-kalām*); speech is our thing (*al-kalām lanā*), with us it increased and was disseminated, became sound and well-known." As if other people do not speak, or do not master speech! Perhaps the *mutakallimūn* consider [the others] to be deaf and dumb! Would you, people, say regarding the jurist and the linguist, the physician and the engineer, the logician, astronomer, physicist, metaphysicist or the Sufi, that all these people do not speak?[58]

---

56 Al-Fārābī, ed. Amīn 1949:107–113.

57 Averroës, ed. Butterworth 2001:16–17, 26–27.

58 See al-Tawḥīdī, ed. al-Sandūbī 1929:224 (*muqābasa* 48).

For both these philosophers, the *mutakallimūn* clearly have false pretensions. But it is also clear from their description that they perceive the *mutakallimūn* as those for whom everyday speech – the way one speaks, the words one uses – is the main instrument of both thinking and arguing. In this (notwithstanding their sarcasm and exaggeration) they seem to reflect something of the *mutakallimūn*'s self-perception, at least in the first generations of *Kalām*.

Conclusion: *Kalām* as Reasoned Speech

As mentioned above, the early *mutakallimūn* seem to have been exposed to Indian, Iranian and Greek influences, although this influence was probably not anchored in texts. They encountered Christians, dualists and Buddhists and held disputations with them, and they debated, sometimes fiercely, with each other. But this polemical drive is not enough to account for the sustained, durable and wholesale introduction of reason to the Arabic world by the early *mutakallimūn*, and particularly the Muʿtazilites; a forceful and growing quest for rationality for its own sake seem to have played a major part in this process.

Notwithstanding the derision of the philosophers, one must appreciate the enormous role that the *mutakallimūn* played in legitimizing and standardizing the recourse to reason in intellectual argumentation. The rarity of statements of the kind found in the above-mentioned anti-Masarrian edict, which delegitimize reason altogether, is largely attributable to the rational enterprise of the *Kalām* and testifies to its relative success. This enterprise often came under attack by the orthodoxy and was consequently restricted, qualified or modified, but it was not shelved.

Within the Jewish community, the success of *Kalām* in introducing rational, reasoned discourse was even more extensive than among the Muslims. Al-Muqammaṣ was followed by towering theologians like Saadya (d. 942), who brought rational theology into the heart of the Rabbanite academies and legitimized it; after them, the necessity of presenting a rational argument was no longer questioned. The same happened on the Karaite side, with al-Qirqisānī and others like him. The drive and the success of the *mutakallimūn* were certainly powered by a scientific urge: Reason was perceived as a legitimate vehicle of truth. But, perhaps more importantly, what we discern in the work of both Jewish and Muslim *mutakallimūn* is their commitment to what they regarded as reasoned discourse.

We mentioned above the puzzle of "transmission by osmosis" and our abiding inability, in the absence of translated texts, to account for the presence in early *Kalām* of certain traits of specific pre-Islamic philosophical schools, like the

Stoics. The material presented here does not solve this puzzle, but it draws attention to a central feature of the early *Kalām* that may help to explain its distinct, non-Aristotelian development.

Typically, the *mutakallimūn* constructed dialectical, dialogical discussions: "they say ...; we answer ..." It is thus not surprising to find a *mutakallim* like al-Muqammaṣ repeatedly attempting to catch his opponent contradicting himself or admitting something that he had not intended to admit. One may discern in the texts discussed above a fascination with the structure of reasoned speech and, even more narrowly, with the conventional signification of words; we can say, following the philosopher John Austin, that the early *mutakallimūn* tried to show "how to do things with words." What serves as a yardstick here is not syllogistic logic, but rather logic as an expression of *logos* in the primary sense of speech, the logic of the discourse. In the early days of *Kalām*, before the translated texts became available, focusing on the discourse – one's own as well as that of one's opponent – may have seemed a particularly fruitful way to approach debated subjects, while the demand for reasoned discourse kept the debate on a rational track.

References

Averroës, *Decisive Treatise & Epistle Dedicatory*, ed. and transl. by Charles E. Butterworth. 2001. Provo, Utah: Brigham Young University Press.

Cameron, Averil. 2014. *Dialoguing in Late Antiquity.* Cambridge, Mass.: Harvard University Press.

Cook, Michael Allan. 1980. "The Origins of Kalām." *Bulletin of the School of Oriental and African Studies*, 43:32–43.

—. 1981. *Early Muslim Dogma: A Source-Critical Study.* Cambridge: Cambridge University Press.

—. 2007. "Ibn Saʿdī on Truth-Blindness." *Jerusalem Studies in Arabic and Islam*, 33:169–178.

Cruz-Hernández, Miguel. 1981, 1986. "La persecución anti-masarrī durante el reinado de ʿAbd al-Raḥmān al-Nāṣir li-dīn Allāh segun Ibn Ḥayyān." *Al-Qanṭara*, 2:51–67; 3:482–483.

Dong Xiuyuan. Forthcoming. "The Presence of Buddhist Thought in Kalām Literature." *Philosophy East and West.*

Drory, Rina. 1988. *The Emergence of Jewish-Arabic Literary Contacts at the Beginning of the Tenth Century* (Literature, Meaning, Culture, 17). Publications of the Porter Institute for Poetics & Semiotics. Tel-Aviv: Tel-Aviv University. (Hebrew)

—. 2000. *Models and Contacts: Arabic Literature and Its Impact on Medieval Jewish Culture*. Leiden: Brill.

Endress, Gerhard. 1987. "Die wissenschaftliche Literatur." In Helmut Gätje (ed.), *Grundriss der arabischen Philologie*, II: *Literatur*. Wiesbaden: Ludwig Reichert Verlag. 400–506.

—. 1992. "Die wissenschaftliche Literatur." In Wolfdietrich Fischer (ed.), *Grundriss der arabischen Philologie*, III: *Supplement.* Wiesbaden: Ludwig Reichert Verlag. 3–152.

Al-Fārābī, Abū Naṣr. *Iḥṣāʾ al-ʿUlūm*, ed. ʿUthmān Amīn. 1949. Cairo: Dār al-Fikr al-ʿArabī.

Fierro, Maribel. 2004. "La Politica religiosa de ʿAbd al-Raḥmān III (r. 300/912–350/961)." *Al-Qanṭara*, 25:119–156.
—. 2005. *ʿAbd al-Raḥmān III: The First Cordoban Caliph*. Oxford: Oneworld.
Frank, Richard. 1988. "Al-Ashʿarī's *Kitāb al-Ḥathth ʿalā l-Baḥth*." *Mélanges de l'Institut Dominicain d'études Orientales du Caire*, 18:83–152. (Reprinted in idem, *Texts and Studies on the Development and History of Kalām*, II, ed. Dimitri Gutas. 2007. Aldershot: Ashgate.)
—. 1992. "The Science of Kalām." *Arabic Sciences and Philosophy*, 2:7–37. (Reprinted in idem, *Texts and Studies on the Development and History of Kalām*, III, ed. Dimitri Gutas. 2008. Aldershot: Ashgate.)
Freudenthal, Gad. 1996. "Stoic Physics in the Writings of R. Saadia Ga'on Al-Fayyumi and Its Aftermath in Medieval Jewish Mysticism." *Arabic Science and Philosophy*, 6:113–136.
Gardet, Louis. 1990. "Kalām." *Encyclopaedia of Islam*[2], IV. Leiden: Brill. 468–471.
Griffith, Sidney. 2001. "'Melkites,' 'Jacobites' and the Christological Controversies in Arabic in Third/Ninth-Century Syria." In David Thomas (ed.), *Syrian Christians under Islam: The First Thousand Years*. Leiden: Brill. 9–55.
Gutas, Dimitri. 1998. *Greek Thought, Arabic Culture: The Graeco-Arabic Translation Movement in Baghdad and Early ʿAbbasid Society (2nd–4th/8th–10th centuries)*. London–New York: Routledge.
Guttmann, Julius. 1964. *Philosophies of Judaism*. English transl. by David W. Silverman. Garden City, NY: Doubleday.
Heck, Paul L. 2002. *The Construction of Knowledge in Islamic Civilization: Qudāma b. Jaʿfar and his Kitāb al-Kharāj wa-ṣināʿat al-kitāba*. Leiden–Boston–Köln: Brill.
Al-Ḥumaydī, Muḥammad b. Futūḥ. *Jadhwat al-Muqtabis fī Taʾrīkh ʿUlamāʾ al-Andalus*, ed. M.T. al-Ṭanjī. 1952. Cairo: Dār al-Kitāb al-Miṣrī.
Ibn Abī Uṣaybiʿa. *ʿUyūn al-Anbāʾ fī Ṭabaqāt al-aṭibbāʾ*, ed. Nizār Riḍā. n. d. Beirut: Dār Maktabat al-ḥayāt.
Ibn Ḥayyān, Abū Marwān Ḥayyān ibn Khalaf. *Al-Muqtabas [V]*, ed. Pedro Chalmeta Gendrón. 1979. Madrid: Instituto Hispano-Árabe de Cultura.
Ibn Khaldūn. *The Muqaddimah: An Introduction to History*, English transl. by Franz Rosenthal. 1969. Princeton: Princeton University Press.
—. *Muqaddima*. 1997. Beirut: Dār al-Fikr al-ʿArabī.
Ibn al-Layth. *Risālat Abī l-Rabīʿ Muḥammad ibn al-Layth allatī katabahā li-l-Rashīd ilā Qusṭanṭīn malik al-Rūm*. In *ʿAṣr al-Maʾmūn*, ed. Aḥmad Farīd al-Rifāʿī. 1927. Cairo: Maṭbaʿat dār al-kutub al-miṣriyya. II:188–236.
Ibn al-Qifṭī. *Taʾrīkh al-ḥukamāʾ*, ed. A. Müller and J. Lippert. 1903. Leipzig: Dieterich'sche.
Al-Jāḥiẓ, Abū ʿUthmān ʿAmr ibn Baḥr. *Kitāb al-Ḥayawān*, ed. ʿAbd al-Salām Muḥammad Hārūn. 1943. Cairo: Maktabat al-Bābī al-Ḥalabī.
Kraemer, Joel L. 1986a. *Humanism in the Renaissance of Islam: The Cultural Revival during the Buyid Age*. Leiden: Brill.
—. 1986b. *Philosophy in the Renaissance of Islam: Abu Sulaiman al-Sijistani and His Circle*. Leiden: Brill.
Lazarus-Yafeh, Hava, Mark R. Cohen, Sasson Somekh and Sidney H. Griffith (eds.). 1998. *The Majlis: Interreligious Encounters in Medieval Islam*. Wiesbaden: O. Harrassowitz.
Lim, Richard. 1995. *Public Disputation, Power, and Social Order in Late Antiquity*. Berkeley: University of California Press.

Madelung, Wilferd. 1974. "The Origins of the Controversy Concerning the Creation of the Koran." In J. M. Barral (ed.), *Orientalia Hispanica sive studia F.M. Pareja octogenario dicata*, I: *Arabica-Islamica*. Leiden: Brill. 504–525.

—. 1987a. "Nachkoranische religiöse Literatur des Islam: Vorbemerkung." In Helmut Gätje (ed.), *Grundriss der arabischen Philologie*, II: *Literatur*. Wiesbaden: Ludwig Reichert Verlag. 299.

—. 1987b. "Der Kalām." In Helmut Gätje (ed.), *Grundriss der arabischen Philologie*, II: *Literatur*. Wiesbaden: Ludwig Reichert Verlag. 326–337.

—. 2016. "Early Ibāḍī Theology." In Sabine Schmidtke (ed.), *Oxford Handbook of Islamic Theology*. Oxford: Oxford University Press. 242–251.

Mahdi, Muḥsin. 1970. "Language and Logic in Classical Islam." In Gustav E. von Grunebaum (ed.), *Logic in Classical Islamic Culture* (Giorgio Della Vida Biennial Conference). Wiesbaden: O. Harrassowitz. 50–81.

Mez, Adam. 1922. *Die Renaissance des Islams*. Heidelberg: C. Winter. Reprinted Hildesheim 1968. English translation: *The Renaissance of Islam*, transl. by Salahuddin Khuda Bukhsh and D.S. Margoliouth. 1937. London: Luzac.

Al-Muqammaṣ. *Twenty Chapters*, ed. and English transl. by Sarah Stroumsa. 2016. Provo, Utah: Brigham Young University Press.

Nyberg, Henrik Samuel. 1913–1936. "Muʿtazila." *Encyclopaedia of Islam*[1], VI. Leiden: Brill.

—. 1977. "ʿAmr Ibn ʿUbaid et Ibn al-Rawendi, deux réprouvés." In Robert Brunschvig and Gustav E. von Grunebaum (eds.), *Classicisme et déclin culturel dans l'histoire de l'islam: Actes du symposium international d'histoire de la civilisation musulmane*. Paris: Maisonneuve et Larose. 125–139.

Pines, Shlomo. 1971. "A Note on an Early Meaning of the Term *Mutakallim*." *Israel Oriental Studies*, 1:224–250. Reprinted in Sarah Stroumsa (ed.), *Studies in the History of Arabic Philosophy: The Collected Works of Shlomo Pines*, III. Jerusalem–Leiden: Magnes. 1996. 62–78.

—. 1994. "A Study of the Impact of Indian, Mainly Buddhist, Thought on Some Aspects of Kalām Doctrines." *Jerusalem Studies in Arabic and Islam*, 17:182–203.

Safran, Janina M. 2013. *Defining Boundaries in al-Andalus: Muslims, Christians and Jews in Islamic Iberia*. Ithaca–London: Cornell University Press.

Ṣāʿid Ibn Ṣāʿid al-Andalusī. *Ṭabaqāt al-Umam*, ed. Ḥ. Bū ʿAlwān. 1985. Beirut: Dār al-ṭalīʿa.

Sirat, Colette. 1990. *A History of Jewish Philosophy in the Middle Ages*. Cambridge: Cambridge University Press.

Strohmaier, Gotthard. 1980. "Homer in Bagdad." *Byzantinoslavica*, 41:196–200.

Stroumsa, Sarah. 1989. *Dāwūd ibn Marwān al-Muqammiṣ's* Twenty Chapters (*ʿIshrūn Maqāla*). Leiden: Brill.

—. 1990. "The Beginnings of the Muʿtazila Reconsidered." *Jerusalem Studies in Arabic and Islam*, 13:265–293.

—. 2003. "Saadya and Jewish Kalam." In D. H. Frank and O. Leaman (eds.), *The Cambridge Companion to Medieval Jewish Philosophy*. Cambridge: Cambridge University Press. 71–90.

—. 2009. "The Muslim Context of Medieval Jewish Philosophy." In Steven Nadler and Tamar Rudavsky (eds.), *The Cambridge History of Jewish Philosophy: From Antiquity through the Seventeenth Century*. Cambridge: Cambridge University Press. 39–59.

—. 2014. "The Muʿtazila in al-Andalus: The Footprints of a Phantom." *Intellectual History of the Islamicate World*, 2:80–100.

Talbi, Muḥammad. 1986. "Ibn Khaldūn." *Encyclopaedia of Islam*², III. Leiden: Brill. 825–831.
Tannous, Jack. 2008. "Between Christology and Kalām? The Life and Letters of George, Bishop of the Arab Tribes." In George Antun Kiraz (ed.), *Malphono w-Rabo d-Malphone: Studies in Honor of Sebastian P. Brock*. Piscataway, N.J.: Gorgias. 671–716.
Al-Tawḥīdī, ʿAlī b. Muḥammad Abū Ḥayyān. *Al-Muqābasāt*, ed. Ḥasan al-Sandūbī. 1929. Cairo: al-Maktaba al-tijāriyya al-kubrā.
—. *Al-Imtāʿ waʾl-muʾānasa*, ed. Aḥmad Amīn and Aḥmad al-Zayn. 1939–1944. Cairo: Lajnat al-ta ʾlīf.
Toorawa, Shawkat M. 2005. *Ibn Abī Tayfūr and Arabic Writerly Culture: A Ninth-Century Bookman in Baghdad*. London: Routledge.
Treiger, Alexander. 2016. "Origins of Kalām." In Sabine Schmidtke (ed.), *Oxford Handbook of Islamic Theology*. Oxford: Oxford University Press. 27–43.
Van Bladel, Kevin. 2011. "The Bactrian Background of the Barmakids." In A. Akasoy, C. Burnett and R. Yoeli-Tlalim (eds.), *Islam and Tibet: Interactions along the Musk Routes*. London: Ashgate. 43–88.
Van Ess, Josef. 1966. *Die Erkenntnislehre des ʿAḍudaddīn al-Īcī: Übersetzung und Kommentar des ersten Buches seiner Mawāqif*. Wiesbaden: Franz Steiner.
—. 1968. "Skepticism in Islamic Religious Thought." *Al-Abḥāth*, 21:1–18.
—. 1970. "The Logical Structure of Islamic Theology." In Gustav E. von Grunebaum (ed.), *Logic in Classical Islamic Culture* (Giorgio Della Vida Biennial Conference). Wiesbaden: O. Harrassowitz. 21–50.
—. 1975. "The Beginnings of Islamic Theology." In John Emery Murdoch and Edyth Dudley Sylla (eds.), *The Cultural Context of Medieval Learning: Proceedings of the First International Colloquium on Philosophy, Science and Theology in the Middle Ages – September 1973*. Dordrecht–Boston: D. Reidel. 87–111.
—. 1977. *Anfänge muslimischer Theologie: Zwei antiqadaritische Traktate aus dem ersten Jahrhundert der Hiǧra*. Beirut–Wiesbaden: Franz Steiner.
—. 1991–1997. *Theologie und Gesellschaft im 2. und 3. Jahrhundert Hidschra: Eine Geschichte des religiösen Denkens im frühen Islam*. I–VI. Berlin: De Gruyter.
—. 2002. "60 Years After: Shlomo Pines's *Beiträge* and Half a Century of Research on Atomism in Islamic Theology." *Proceedings of the Israel Academy of Sciences and Humanities*, 8:19–41.
Walker, Joel Thomas. 2006. *The Legend of Mar Qardagh: Narrative and Christian Heroism in Late Antique Iraq*. Berkeley: University of California Press.
Wakelnig, Elvira. Forthcoming. "Muḥammad ibn al-Layṯ's Letter to the Byzantine Emperor."
Wansbrough, John. 1978. *The Sectarian Milieu: Content and Composition of Islamic Salvation History*. Oxford: Oxford University Press.
Wolfson, Harry Austryn. 1970. *The Philosophy of the Kalam*. Cambridge, Mass.: Harvard University Press.

Acknowledgement

I wish to express my warm thanks to Sabine Schmidtke and Alexander Treiger for their insightful comments on drafts of this paper.

Livnat Holtzman and Miriam Ovadia

On Divine Aboveness (*al-Fawqiyya*): The Development of Rationalized Ḥadīth-Based Argumentations in Islamic Theology

Introduction

Abū Bakr ibn Isḥāq ibn Khuzayma al-Sulamī al-Nīsābūrī (d. 311/924, at the age of eighty-nine) was one of the most prominent Sunnī traditionists – transmitters of Ḥadīth[1] – in ninth-century Nīshāpūr. An indication of his prominence is the lengthy entry dedicated to him by the prolific traditionist and historian Shams al-Dīn al-Dhahabī (d. ca. 748/1348) in his *Siyar Aʿlām al-Nubalāʾ*,[2] in which Ibn Khuzayma is depicted as a pious and charitable traditionist with a legendary memory, who was committed to a scholarly investigation of the Ḥadīth and other related fields of knowledge.[3] Ibn Khuzayma did not restrict himself to the mere transmission of the Prophetic legacy, but also strove to define the borderlines of traditionalism. As such, he was a vociferous opponent of speculative theology (*kalām*).[4]

A resident of stormy Nīshāpūr, in which theological controversies among the Sunnī traditionalists, the Muʿtazilites, the Shīʿites and the corporealist Karrāmites were frequent,[5] Ibn Khuzayma regarded *kalām* as a potentially lethal threat to the welfare of Muslim society. Apart from declaring his strictest adherence to the Qurʾān and the Ḥadīth on many occasions, Ibn Khuzayma – like many a zealous

1 In this article, we use the noun "traditionist" and its plural form to denote scholars who were fundamentally Ḥadīth transmitters (*muḥaddith*, pl. *muḥaddithūn*), while the noun "traditionalist" and its plural form are reserved for scholars whose main body of theological teachings relied on the Ḥadīth but who were not necessarily Ḥadīth transmitters. The adjective "traditionalistic" denotes teachings, arguments and works that voice the worldview of the traditionalists. See Abrahamov 1998:ix–x; 2014.

2 Al-Dhahabī, ed. al-Arnāʾūṭ et al. 1985, 14:365–383. Al-Dhahabī affiliates Ibn Khuzayma with *al-ṭabaqa^tu al-sābiʿ^ta ʿashrat^a*, "the seventeenth class of notables." Half a page, on average, is devoted to the lion's share of these notables' entries in *Siyar Aʿlām al-Nubalāʾ*. Only the massive forty-page entry on the controversial mystic al-Ḥallāj (d. 309/922) exceeds Ibn Khuzayma's entry. *Ibid.*, 14:313–354.

3 *Ibid.*, 14:372.

4 *Ibid.*, 14:377.

5 Madelung 1988:188.

https://doi.org/10.1515/9783110446395-014

traditionist before him – proposed the use of a theological concept as a means of appraising an individual's loyalty to Muslim society. According to his peers, he used to say: "Whoever refuses to affirm that God sits on His throne above His seven heavens is a heretic. It is lawful to spill his blood, and his property is regarded as booty."[6] One of Ibn Khuzayma's disciples testified that, in addition to urging execution of the heretic, Ibn Khuzayma suggested that his body be thrown on the local dunghill, "so that the Muslims who are devoted to their faith will not suffer from the stench of his corpse."[7]

Interestingly enough, the sentence that Ibn Khuzayma regarded as the ultimate "litmus test" to differentiate heretics from believers does not appear verbatim either in the Qur'ān or in the Ḥadīth. To be sure, the Qur'ān refers to "the Lord of Mercy, established on the throne" (*Al-Raḥmān*^{u} *ʿalā ʾl-ʿarsh*^{i} *ʾstawā*, Q. 20:5),[8] and several Qur'ānic verses place God "above" His creatures (*rabbahum min fawqihim*, Q. 16:50).[9] Several Prophetic traditions, too, indicate that God is enthroned,[10] while others indicate that God resides or is situated above the seventh heaven.[11] However, the formula "God sits on His throne above His seven heavens" (*Allāh*^{u} *ʿalā ʿarshih*^{i} *qad*^{i} *ʾstawā fawq*^{a} *sab*^{ʿi} *samāwātih*^{i}) does not appear in the Ḥadīth material. Although a unique *ḥadīth* states that God is situated simultaneously "above His heavens" (*fawq*^{a} *samāwātih*^{i}) and on his throne,[12] it does not mention the number seven. This specific *ḥadīth*, like many other theological *ḥadīth*s, found its way into marginal Ḥadīth compilations, probably because of the dubious creditability of one of its transmitters.[13] Through these compilations, it merged into the mainstream traditionalistic curriculum.

In later generations, the theological concept promoted by Ibn Khuzayma was labeled *fawqiyyat al-Rabb*, "God's aboveness" (henceforth: *fawqiyya*), or *al-ʿulūw*, "altitude" or "sublimity." Based on the prepositions *fawq*^{a} and *ʿalā* ("above" and

---

6 Al-Dhahabī, ed. al-Arnāʾūṭ et al. 1985, 14:373.
7 Al-Ḥākim al-Nīsābūrī, ed. al-Salūm 2003:285–286.
8 Parallel verses are Q. 7:54, 32:4 and 11:7. The English versions of the Qur'ānic verses quoted in this article are taken from *Qur'an*, ed. Abdel Haleem 2008.
9 Abdel Haleem (*Qur'an* 2008) renders Q. 6:18 and 6:61, which state that God is *al-qāhir*^{u} *fawq*^{a} *ʿibādih*^{i}, as figures of speech: "God is the Supreme Master over His creatures."
10 Al-Ājurrī, ed. Mu'assasat al-Rayyān 2000:303, 306 (nos. 656–659, 666); Ibn Khuzayma, ed. al-Shahwān 1988:241–247 (nos. 148–152).
11 Al-Ājurrī, *ibid.*:305–306 (nos. 663–665); Ibn Khuzayma, *ibid.*:234–237 (no. 144).
12 Al-Ājurrī, *ibid.*:306 (no. 667); Ibn Khuzayma, *ibid.*:239–240 (no. 147).
13 Al-Albānī, ed. Beirut–Damascus 1980, 1:252–253.

"on"),[14] this traditionalistic concept, which appears in the divine scriptures, attributes a spatial relation to God's existence. In Ibn Khuzayma's most mature theological treatise (in the guise of a Ḥadīth compilation), *Kitāb al-Tawḥīd*, he states: "Following what God has told us, we believe that our creator is established **on** His throne.[15] We dare not change the words of God. We never utter a creed other than the creed that was transmitted to us."[16] In theological Ḥadīth compilations of this kind, the theme of God's aboveness is juxtaposed to chapters on the divine attributes (*ṣifāt Allāh*) and, more specifically, to chapters presenting *ḥadīth*s that expand on the anthropomorphic descriptions of God as they appear in the Qur'ān. In addition to the topic of God's aboveness, the theological Ḥadīth compilations present the themes of His throne (*ʿarsh*) and His directionality (*jiha*).

Two questions arise from the case of Ibn Khuzayma and his statement that "God sits on His throne above His seven heavens." The first is: On what basis did Ibn Khuzayma formulate this assertion? Obviously, he combined the formulae appearing in the Qur'ān and in two different sets of *ḥadīth*s to produce his much-improved and catchy *ʿaqīda*, a brief creed or article of faith.[17] Ibn Khuzayma had no need to explain the rationale behind this technique, which was frequently employed by the traditionists. It enabled them to expand the fixed boundaries of the traditionalistic curriculum, to detour around the exact wording of the texts, to which they were highly committed, and, in a way, to articulate their own views rather than confining themselves to the mere recitation of Qur'ānic verses and *ḥadīth*s.[18] In the generation after Ibn Khuzayma, the Baghdadian traditionist Abū Bakr al-Ājurrī (d. 360/971) developed the same formula as Ibn Khuzayma's and explained why the combination of *ḥadīth*s is permissible: "These *ḥadīth*s are compatible in their content, and they actually verify one another. All of them prove what we say, that God is on His throne, above His heavens."[19] In short, combin-

---

14 These prepositions have several different meanings in Arabic, depending on the verb they follow.

15 The verb *istawā*, used in Q. 20:6: *al-Raḥmānu ʿalā 'l-ʿarsh^{i} 'stawā*, has several possible meanings in English, including "established Himself," "situated upon," or simply "sat on." Different theological meanings and implications might be inferred from each of these English phrases; for example, "to establish oneself/itself" might express a more transcendent meaning, whereas "to sit" might allude to a human-like attribute of God. In our discussions of the interpretation of the verses in which *istawā* appears, we have chosen what seems to be the most appropriate English rendering according to the context.

16 Ibn Khuzayma, ed. al-Shahwān 1988:233.

17 For the *ḥadīth*s that Ibn Khuzayma relied on when formulating his *ʿaqīda*, see *ibid.*:265–290.

18 All the traditionalistic creeds are, in a way, products of the same technique. An accessible compilation of creeds is Watt 1994.

19 Al-Ājurrī, ed. Mu'assasat al-Rayyān 2000:307.

ing apparently non-contradictory texts gave the medieval traditionists a certain degree of flexibility when discussing theological matters.[20]

The second and more important question that arises from the case of Ibn Khuzayma and his brief creed is: Why did Ibn Khuzayma assert "God sits on His throne above His seven heavens" as an irrevocable postulate? God's aboveness was one of the most popular themes in the traditionalists' highly theatrical public disputes (*munāẓarāt*) with the Muʿtazilites and the corporealist Karrāmites; held frequently in tenth-century Nīshāpūr,[21] these disputes provided entertainment for scholars and laymen alike. By formulating his creed, Ibn Khuzayma supplied his fellow traditionalists with the ultimate weapon to use in these disputes. He also gave the lay admirers of the Nīshāpūri traditionalists a slogan to yell in the streets. Indeed, in *Kitāb al-Tawḥīd*, Ibn Khuzayma clarified that his efforts in formulating this article of faith arose as part of the polemics with the Muʿtazila, or, as he called them, the Muʿaṭṭila.[22]

Four centuries after Ibn Khuzayma, his creed and the concept of *fawqiyya* were reexamined by the traditionalists of Mamluk Cairo and Damascus and once again became a bone of contention. The intellectually dense environments of fourteenth-century Cairo and Damascus were fertile breeding grounds for theological controversies. One that particularly attracted the public's attention was conducted between Taqī al-Dīn Aḥmad ibn Taymiyya (d. 728/1328) and his rivals, mainly the Shāfiʿites, most of whom were zealous advocates of the Rāziyyan form of Ashʿarite *kalām*.

A major charge against Ibn Taymiyya in the Damascus trials of 705/1306, one upon which he elaborated in his defense, was his commitment to the literal concept of God's aboveness.[23] The traditionalists of the Mamluk period, well acquainted with the writings of their predecessors, were in a position to provide a full-scale presentation of the traditionalistic set of arguments on God's aboveness. As a result, the theological writings of Ibn Taymiyya and other scholars of

20 Abrahamov 2014.
21 Al-Dhahabī, ed. al-Arnāʾūṭ et al. 1985, 14:369–382.
22 Ibn Khuzayma, ed. al-Shahwān 1988:273. The derogatory name Muʿaṭṭila means "the group that denies the divine attributes by practicing *taʿṭīl*." *Taʿṭīl* is the negating of God's attributes or the divesting of God's essence from His attributes. In Ibn Khuzayma's time, the Muʿaṭṭila were the Muʿtazilites; in Ibn Taymiyya's time, they were the Ashʿarites. Notwithstanding the accusation applied by this designation, the "Muʿaṭṭila" – be they Muʿtazilites or Ashʿarites – did not negate the entire bulk of attributes. Rather, they negated all forms of anthropomorphism. See van Ess 2000:343–344.
23 Jackson 1994:71–73.

the period include their own dogmas stemming from the elaborate arguments developed by their predecessors over the course of four centuries.

This article follows milestones in the development, from the ninth to fourteenth centuries, of the arsenal of arguments on God's aboveness, His throne and His directionality. Although God's aboveness is but one component of the theological debate on God's attributes, this theme drew the attention of the entire spectrum of scholars. Its centrality is demonstrated in the writings of the traditionalists, but theologians of strong rationalistic tendencies, too, notwithstanding their fundamental approach of criticizing and even discrediting theological *ḥadīth*s, did not ignore the ultra-traditionalistic texts drawn from the Ḥadīth material. And so, even as the traditionalists gladly adopted kalāmic vehicles to defend their tenets, the rationalists were equally informed of the traditionalistic curriculum and in fact were well read in this material. George Makdisi has convincingly shown throughout his oeuvre that there were no clear-cut boundaries between the early traditionalist and rationalist intelligentsias: Both shared the same education; their discussions often overlapped; and both were intimately familiar with the transmitted sources. As Makdisi puts it:

> In the eleventh century, the study of rationalist theology (*kalām*) had no place as such in the institutions of learning ... Law (*fiqh* and *uṣūl al-fiqh*), not rationalist *kalām*, was in the honor as the supreme subject of study, supported by the study of the Qurʾān, the traditions of the Prophet, and the Arabic grammar and literature ... The traditional sciences thus achieved a prestige similar to that of the legal sciences. *Kalām* however found no patron to endow it with such institutions of learning.[24]

The present article, inspired by Makdisi's scholarship, aims to examine further this diffusion of ideas between the two sharply distinguished poles of Islamic theology through the lens of the concept of *fawqiyya*. The first part presents different topoi of God's aboveness as reflected in the Ḥadīth material and outlines the didactic narrative that flourished in the ultra-traditionalistic literature. The second part presents the rationalistic concepts of God's supposed location and directionality, which were mainly based on Qurʾānic verses and kalāmic doctrines. The debates within the rationalistic circles took place in parallel to the activities of the traditionalists and hence triggered and enriched the discussions. The third part of the article concentrates on Ashʿarite theologians who drew upon the Ḥadīth literature in conceptualizing a set of arguments, at once semi-traditionalistic and semi-rationalistic, that blended rationalistic ideas and methods into traditionalism. The

24 Makdisi 1966:83–84. In fact, this remark applies to a longer period, roughly from the tenth century onward. For further elaboration, see Makdisi 1981a:228–238; 1981b:301–302.

fourth and final part of the article sheds light on the prominent trend in the later, more developed traditionalistic views, as reflected in the writings of authors from the Mamluk period. These authors made a substantial contribution to the theological debate.

As far as we know, western research has not hitherto provided a systematic survey of the theological concept of God's aboveness in Islamic literature,[25] let alone examined various views on this topic. By tracing the development of the concept of *fawqiyya*, we aim to reveal landmarks in the intellectual evolution of a theological concept that has its roots in the Ḥadīth literature and to place these landmarks in a historical context, in the hope of providing a preliminary outline for further discussion.

The Basic Traditionalistic Approaches to the Ḥadīth Material

It was the Ḥadīth, rather than the Qur'ān, that best served the proponents of the concept of God's aboveness. The teachings of the Prophet Muḥammad were often the starting point of the discussions of *al-fawqiyya*, although the relevant Ḥadīth accounts were not always equally received among Muslim scholars of the various schools of thought. The *ḥadīth*s on God's aboveness appeared frequently in theological treatises on the divine attributes, and they indeed constituted the ultra-traditionalistic narrative on this topic. It seems that the traditionalists from the ninth to the eleventh centuries were more interested in compiling these *ḥadīth*s than with constructing elaborate arguments based on them. Instead, they used these *ḥadīth*s for several purposes and functions. The *ḥadīth*s served them as vital textual evidence for affirming (*ithbāt*) God's attribute of aboveness; as the ultimate weapon in their polemics with the rationalists; and as the raw material for constructing and reconstructing creeds, as illustrated by the above-mentioned case of Ibn Khuzayma.

Most of the *ḥadīth*s used by theologians as unequivocal evidence for God's aboveness were tagged by the Ḥadīth experts as dubious and weak (*ḍaʿīf*). Nevertheless, some found their way into the canonical Ḥadīth compilations. Unlike the Islamic law experts, theologians rarely viewed the dubious credibility of the *ḥadīth*s they used in their discussions as problematic. On the contrary: By affirming the veracity of these *ḥadīth*s and incorporating them into their traditional-

---

25 The entry "Samāʾ" (Heinen 1995) in *EI*², which contains several points of interface with our discussion, is an exception. It provides an accurate, albeit schematic description of the traditionalistic and rationalistic perceptions of the cosmos and God's place in or outside it.

istic narrative, the traditionalists effectively detoured around the question of these texts' credibility and ignored the problems their content might have raised. The traditionalistic criticism remained within the limits of *ʿilm al-jarḥ wa'l-taʿdīl* (evaluation of the credibility of Ḥadīth transmitters);[26] only later did traditionalists articulate harsh criticism of the use of dubious *ḥadīths* in theological discussions.[27]

There are diverse *ḥadīths* that, in one way or another, express a spatial dimension to God's existence, by describing His exact location or literally pointing in His direction. All of these *ḥadīths* provide elaborate cosmologies embedded in frame-narratives that present dialogues between the Prophet and his companions. Some of these frame-narratives are exceptionally detailed and vivid, such as the following passage, known as "the *ḥadīth* of the mountain goats" (*ḥadīth al-awʿāl*):

> Al-ʿAbbās ibn ʿAbd al-Muṭṭalib [d. 32/652, the paternal uncle of the Prophet Muḥammad] once recounted that he was sitting together with a group of people near al-Baṭḥā' [a small creek in Mecca] in the company of the Messenger of God. Suddenly a cloud passed by in the sky, and they all raised their heads to look at it. The Messenger of God said: "Do you know what this is?" They replied: "A cloud." ... Then he said: "Do you know the distance between the heaven and the earth?" They replied: "No, we do not know." The Prophet said: "The distance between the earth and the heaven above is seventy-one, seventy-two or seventy-three years." He then continued to calculate the distance between the heavens until he counted seven heavens. Then he said: "Above the seventh heaven there is a sea, which is as deep as the distance between two heavens. Above the sea, there are eight mountain goats. The distance between each goat's hoofs and knees is like the distance between two heavens. On their backs lies the throne, which is as high as the distance between two heavens. And God is above all these."[28]

The following cosmological *ḥadīth* is often mentioned as an interpretation of the verse: "The angels will be on all sides of it and on that Day [i.e., doomsday] eight of them will bear the throne of your Lord above them" (Q. 69:17). The *ḥadīth* reflects the teachings of the *tābiʿī* Qur'ān commentator al-Ḍaḥḥāk ibn Muzāḥim (d. 105/723). Apart from further developing the brief Qur'ānic reference to the carriers of the throne, it provides details of their physical stature and location:

---

26 Brown 2009:86–87.

27 A few theologians were criticized for their use of dubious and even forged *ḥadīths*. The most famous was Abū Yaʿlā (d. 458/1066), who was harshly criticized by Ibn al-Jawzī (d. 597/1201). See Holtzman 2010:187–191.

28 Ibn Khuzayma, ed. al-Shahwān 1988:234–237; Al-Ājurrī, ed. Mu'assasat al-Rayyān 2000:305–306. The editions of both sources contain detailed footnotes indicating where the *ḥadīths* appear in the canonical Ḥadīth compilations.

> Al-Ḍaḥḥāk said: "Some say: eight lines of angels, whose number no one knows except for God. Others say: eight angels, whose heads are near the throne in the seventh heaven, and their legs are in the nether earth. They have horns, which are similar to the horns of mountain goats. [The distance] between the base of the horn and its tip is five hundred years."[29]

"The *ḥadīth* of descent" (*ḥadīth al-nuzūl*) seems to imply God's aboveness, in that it depicts Him going downward to the earthly world. Several versions of this *ḥadīth* can be found, with slight differences among them; however, they all feature a description of God's descent to the lowest heaven:

> The Prophet said: "God exalted descends every night to the first heaven [*al-samā' al-ūlā*] before the final third of the night, and asks: 'Who calls for Me [in prayer] that I may answer? Who is in need of something that I may grant? Who is asking for My forgiveness, so that I forgive him?'"[30]

The Prophet Muḥammad's reply in another *ḥadīth* once again reflects the idea of God's locus above His creation. The message is amplified by a gesture made by the Prophet at the end of the narrative, demonstrating to his audience the spatial relationship between God and the creation.[31]

> A Bedouin came to the Messenger of God and said: "O Messenger of God, we are exhausted, our children are starving, the camels died, our resources are exhausted, and our sheep perished. Do pray to God on our behalf, and ask Him to give us rain. We ask you to make intercession for us to God, and we ask God to make intercession for us to you!" The Messenger of God replied: "Woe unto you! Do you understand what you are saying?" Then he kept praising the Lord, until [the impression of his actions] was clearly manifested on the faces of his companions. Then he said: "Woe unto you! God should never be asked to make intercession to one of His creatures, for God is greater than that. Do you know what God is? God is on top of [*ʿalā*] His throne, His throne is on top of His heavens, and His heavens are on top of His earth, like this" – he said, as his fingers formed a dome – "and under Him, it [i.e., the throne] makes the same sound as the moaning of a new saddle beneath its rider's [weight]."[32]

---

29 Al-Suyūṭī, ed. al-Turkī 2003, 14:282.

30 Ibn Khuzayma, ed. al-Shahwān 1988:316; Al-Ājurrī, ed. Muʾassasat al-Rayyān 2000:321. One of the best-known alternative versions of this *ḥadīth* reads: "God exalted descends towards the lowest sky [*al-samā' al-dunyā*] every Friday night, and asks: 'Will I pardon the one who repents? Will I forgive the one who asks for My forgiveness? Will I answer the one who calls [for Me]?'" Al-Juwaynī, ed. Mūsā and ʿAbd al-Ḥamīd 1950:161. For a French translation and references to other Ḥadīth compilations and theological treatises, see Gimaret 1997:90–102.

31 On the topic of hand-gestures accompanying the transmission of the anthropomorphic *ḥadīths*, see Holtzman 2010:173–184; 2011.

32 Ibn Khuzayma, ed. al-Shahwān 1988:239–240; Al-Ājurrī, ed. Muʾassasat al-Rayyān 2000:306.

A *ḥadīth* frequently quoted in the discussions of the traditionalists teaches its readers that acknowledging God's aboveness is a natural trait of the true believer; hence, it does not need any other proof. This lesson is reflected in a dialogue between the Prophet Muḥammad and his followers. The teacher of this lesson is one of the lowest members of early Islamic society, a female slave:

> [It was transmitted on behalf of] Abū Hurayra [d. 61/681], who said: A man brought his female slave, who was a foreigner, to the Messenger of God and asked: "Should I free this slave? Is she a believer?" The Messenger of God asked her: "Where is God?" and she pointed at the sky. The Messenger of God asked her: "And who am I?" and she pointed at the Messenger of God and at the sky. She meant to say "You are the Messenger of God." Then the Messenger of God said: "Set her free, for she is a believer."[33]

How did the traditionalists use these *ḥadīth*s? In most cases, they simply quoted them. In *Kitāb al-Ibāna*, Abu 'l-Ḥasan al-Ashʿarī (d. 324/935) quoted three different versions of *ḥadīth al-nuzūl* and one of the *ḥadīth* of the female slave[34] as part of his argument for God's aboveness. Al-Ashʿarī did not discuss the content of these *ḥadīth*s; however, he did discuss the relevant Qurʾānic verses that served as a starting point for his rationalistic arguments. Later theologians, such as Ibn Khuzayma and Abū Bakr al-Ājurrī, used the Ḥadīth materials as the building blocks of their traditionalistic narrative. Their motivation seems to have been mostly educational: Seeking to construct a reasonable narrative on God's aboveness for their students, they explained the material and elucidated obscure points without delving too much into the content of the texts.

Ibn Khuzayma, for example, considered several versions of "the *ḥadīth* of the mountain goats,"[35] the authenticity of which he of course accepted. Nevertheless, he was concerned about the apparent contradiction between ʿAbbās ibn ʿAbd al-Muṭṭalib's version and a parallel version attributed to the *ṣaḥābī* ʿAbd Allāh ibn Masʿūd (d. 32/652–3), in which the distance between the earth and the lowest heaven is given as five hundred years.[36] As we saw above, the basic unit of measurement in ʿAbbās's version is that of seventy-one, seventy-two or seventy-three years.[37] Ibn Khuzayma considered the typical inquisitive student, whom he names "one of the seekers of knowledge" (*baʿḍ muqtabisī 'l-ʿilm*). This student,

For a translation into French and references to other Ḥadīth compilations and theological treatises, see Gimaret 1997:76–77.

33 Ibn Khuzayma, ed. al-Shahwān 1988:284–285.

34 Al-Ashʿarī, ed. Beirut n. d.:35; 36–37.

35 Ibn Khuzayma, ed. al-Shahwān 1988:231–250.

36 *Ibid.*:242–245.

37 *Ibid.*:235.

says Ibn Khuzayma, may wrongly perceive the two versions as contradictory. However, the student should consider that a journey's duration will differ according to one's vehicle; it will take longer on the back of a work-camel or work-horse than on the back of a riding-camel or race-horse, not to mention the difference between hiking and riding a mule or donkey![38] Therefore, concludes Ibn Khuzayma, it is impossible to claim on this basis that these two *ḥadīth*s, or any others for that matter, are contradictory. Interestingly, it does not seem to have occurred to Ibn Khuzayma either to check these *ḥadīth*s' *isnād*s (chains of transmission) or to mention that ʿAbbās's version was a Prophetic *ḥadīth* (*ḥadīth nabawī*), while Ibn Masʿūd's version reflected the latter's own teachings. As noted, theological *ḥadīth*s were treated differently than *ḥadīth*s on legal matters and were accepted without scrutiny of their *isnād*s.[39] Thus, Ibn Masʿūd's version was also attributed to the second generation of Qurʾān commentators, like al-Ḍaḥḥāk, without any credit being given to Ibn Masʿūd.[40]

Another predominant technique of the traditionalists was to provide brief summaries following each group of *ḥadīth*s.[41] These often concluded with doctrinal declarations emphasizing the substantial moral benefits to be gained from memorizing the *ḥadīth*s without inquiring into their content. Abū Bakr al-Ājurrī, for example, considered the *ḥadīth*s on God's aboveness as reliable medicine against the temptations of the devil, such as singing, dancing and other amusements.[42] The basic traditionalistic approach to these and other theological *ḥadīth*s was first and foremost an educational one. The traditionalists circulated the material while suppressing any possibility for inquisitive activities in the classroom. By the end of the tenth century, this material was an integral part of the traditionalistic curriculum.

---

38 *Ibid.*:250.

39 Brown 2009:173–183.

40 Shākir, ed. al-Bāz 2005, 3:19 (commentary to Q. 32:4–6).

41 Ibn Khuzayma, ed. al-Shahwān 1988:241; Al-Ājurrī, ed. Muʾassasat al-Rayyān 2000:307. Insights on the concept of divine aboveness by several influential scholars are interwoven into their biographies in al-Dhahabī's monumental *Tārīkh al-islām*. Thus, the following statement is ascribed to Aḥmad ibn Ḥanbal (d. 241/855): "Our Lord, blessed and exalted, is on the throne [*ʿalā ʾl-ʿarsh*] with no limit and no description [*bi-lā ḥadd*^{in} *wa-lā ṣifa*^{tin}], *bi-lā ṣifa*^{tin} meaning 'without ascribing modality [*kayfiyya*] or describing [*waṣf*].'" Similarly, when asked by his contemporary Ibn al-Mubārak (d. 181/797), "How do we recognize our Lord?" Ibn Ḥanbal replied: "He is in the seventh heaven on His throne." Al-Dhahabī, ed. ʿAbd al-Salām 1990–2000, 18:87–88, 22:238.

42 Al-Ājurrī, ed. Muʾassasat al-Rayyān 2000:31.

The traditionalistic convention (amounting to an "unofficial edict") of *bi-lā kayfa* (do not inquire), which prohibited discussing the content of these *ḥadīths*,[43] gradually crumbled when the traditionalists were forced to confront the attacks of their rationalistic opponents, alongside the emergence of the semi-traditionalistic discourse of the Ashʿarites. The *ḥadīths* became stimulants to the theological debates on God's attribute of aboveness and formed the infrastructure of the manifold range of arguments from both the traditionalistic and the rationalistic sides. Although it is difficult to generalize unequivocally and say that all Islamic schools of thought were preoccupied with *ḥadīths*, these *ḥadīths* were most definitely one of the prime scriptural sources nourishing the intellectual discussion on the attribute of God's aboveness.

Rationalistic Views Detached from Ḥadīth Material

That God's pure abstractedness and transcendence is the basic stance of Islamic rationalism is almost an axiom that needs no further proof. This stance is clearly articulated in the opening passage of Abu 'l-Ḥasan al-Ashʿarī's chapter, in his *Maqālāt al-Islāmiyyin*, on the Muʿtazilite concept of God's absolute uniqueness (*tawḥīd*; also: monotheism):

> The Muʿtazilites unanimously agreed that God is one ... He is no body ... and therefore has no directions: He has no right hand or left hand, before or behind, above or beneath. He is not confined by space.[44]

This stance, albeit not verbatim, was later adopted by the Ashʿarites.[45] Like Islamic traditionalism, Islamic rationalism was a weave of numerous and varied voices.[46] It is tempting to generalize the rationalistic approaches to God as simply advocating pure abstractedness and transcendence; however, that is only one side of the coin. How should we, for instance, define the corporealistic views that

---

43 *Bi-lā kayfa*: literally "without asking how," refers to a prohibition against inquiring into the nature of the divine attributes, including the anthropomorphic expressions for God in the Qurʾān and the Ḥadīth. Abrahamov 1995:365–366.

44 Al-Ashʿarī, ed. Ritter 1963:155. This is our translation of the passage; cf. Arberry 2008:23. For a summary of this passage, see Gimaret 1993:789.

45 Al-Shahrastānī, ed. Guillaume 2009:97.

46 We follow Abrahamov's definition of rationalism as "the tendency to consider reason the principle device or one of the principle devices to reach the truth in religion, and the preference of reason to revelation and tradition in dealing with some theological matters" (Abrahamov 1998:ix). This definition corresponds with al-Rāzī's *al-Qānūn al-Kullī* (Al-Rāzī, ed. al-Saqā 1986:220–221).

did not draw upon the Ḥadīth, and which their proponents endeavored to verify using kalāmic methods?

One of the fundamentals of Islamic rationalism was that God could not be limited to one place (*lā yakūn*^{u} *fī makān*^{in} *dūn*^{a} *makān*^{in}). From this principle emerged two dogmas: that God existed everywhere (*annah*^{u} *fī kull*^{i} *makān*^{in} *ḥāll*^{un}),[47] and that He was infinite (*lā nihāya*^{ta} *lah*^{u}).[48] Neither dogma necessarily entailed God's transcendence or abstractedness. In fact, unidentified corporealists claimed that "God is a body. He is everywhere, [although] He surpasses all places. Furthermore, He is infinite, and His surface (*masāḥa*) exceeds the surface of the entire universe, because He is bigger than everything."[49] This stance, which has no roots in the scriptures and is based on pure speculation, was totally unacceptable to the Muʿtazilites, who ruled out the possibility of God's corporeality.[50]

For the purpose of our discussion, suffice it to say that the spectrum of Islamic rationalism was wide. In the discussions of God's aboveness, as recorded or reconstructed mainly by Ashʿarite authors, two rationalistic trends emerged: the Mujassima – the corporealists – whose rationalized views on God's corporeality resembled the Stoic ideas of the early Christian theologians,[51] and the Muʿtazila, the adherents of God's absolute transcendence and incorporeality, whose views emerged as a response to, among others, those of the traditionalists, on the one hand, and the corporealists, on the other. The well-rationalized views of the corporealists, whether they were purely scholastic or merely applied scholastic hermeneutics to the scriptures, required equally well-rationalized reactions, and these came mainly from the Muʿtazilites (and later, as we hope to demonstrate, from the Ashʿarites). The transcendental stance was contrasted with the views of the Mujassima as early as the formative phase of the Muʿtazilite school. At the dawn of his career as a *mutakallim*, the illustrious Baṣran Muʿtazilite Abu 'l-Hudhayl (d. ca. 226/840–842 or 234/849) conducted stormy debates with the Shīʿite-Rāfiḍite *mutakallim* Hishām ibn al-Ḥakam (d. 179/795–796), presented in

---

47 The idea that God is everywhere was attributed to al-Jahm ibn Ṣafwān (d.128/746), the alleged founder of the Jahmiyya, an early and unidentified Islamic sect. Al-Dhahabī depicted him as "the deviating *mutakallim* and the head of the sect of al-Jahmiyya. ... He denied God's attributes; thereby he argued for His transcendence. ... He also argued that God is not on the throne, but everywhere [*fī kull*^{i} *makān*^{in}]." Al-Dhahabī, ed. ʿAbd al-Salām 1990–2000, 8:65–66.

48 Al-Ashʿarī, ed. Ritter 1963:210. Cf. Ibn Ḥazm, ed. Naṣr and ʿUmayra 1996, 2:287.

49 Al-Ashʿarī, ed. Ritter 1963:208. For the connection between the discussion of God's omnipresence and the notion of the beatific vision (*ru'yat Allāh*), see van Ess 1990–1997, 4:414–415.

50 (Pseudo-)ʿAbd al-Jabbār, ed. ʿUthmān 1996:217.

51 The best-known Mujassima were the Karrāmiyya, seen by modern scholars as aggressive traditionalists. For the resemblance between their teachings and those of the Stoics, see Zysow 2014.

the sources as the most notorious archetype of a corporealist. Abu 'l-Hudhayl and Hishām met during a pilgrimage to Mecca. According to Abu 'l-Hudhayl, Hishām declared that God was a three-dimensional body, because only bodies have existence. Abu 'l-Hudhayl pointed to Mount Abū Qubays on the eastern outskirts of Mecca and asked Hishām which was greater, "your god or this mountain?" Hishām responded that the mountain was bigger than God.[52] Abu 'l-Hudhayl's response to Hishām was not recorded; however, the concise formula of the Mu'tazilite concept of *tawḥīd*, as quoted above, would have sufficed.

It seems that the Mu'tazilite (and later the Ash'arite) views on God's aboveness were molded and defined partly in response to corporealistic views and were not merely a result of independent speculation, whether based on contemplating Qur'ānic verses or on adopting a Neo-Platonic *via negativa*.[53] At least, this is the impression obtained from reading the sources: The Mu'tazilite views on *tawḥīd* are clearer against the backdrop of corporealistic views. Interpreting Q. 6:18 ("He is the Supreme Master over His creatures" – *wa-huw^a 'l-qāhir^u fawq^a 'ibādih^i*), Jār Allāh al-Zamakhsharī (d. 538/1144) states that *fawq^a 'ibādih^i* is an illustration (*taṣwīr*) of God's mightiness and power. Al-Zamakhsharī here conveys the Mu'tazilite figurative interpretation (*ta'wīl*) of every corporeal feature attributed to God as a metaphor (*majāz*). Then, following the Baṣran Mu'tazilite tradition, al-Zamakhsharī states that God is indeed a "thing" or "entity" (*shay'*), as this term encompasses everything that the human brain grasps and conceptualizes, with the following reservation: "Yet, God is a 'thing' unlike other things. This is the same as saying: He is the object of knowledge unlike other objects of knowledge." His final remark, "Yet, it is not true that He is a body unlike other bodies," sounds like the last word in a dispute between the Mu'tazilites and the Mujassima.[54]

The Mu'tazilite reaction to the corporealists is cited in (pseudo-)'Abd al-Jabbār's (d. 415/1025) discussion of God's corporeality, part of which is relevant to our discussion.[55] 'Abd al-Jabbār mentions a prominent sophistic argument developed by the corporealists while contemplating "the Lord of Mercy, established on the throne" (*Al-Raḥmān^u 'alā 'l-'arsh^i 'stawā*; Q. 20:5): "Establishing," *al-istiwā'*, meant standing, getting up and rising, actions that could be applied only to bodies, which necessarily entailed that God was a body.[56] 'Abd al-Jabbār attacks

52 Al-Ash'arī, ed. Ritter 1963:32.
53 Arberry 2008:23.
54 Al-Zamakhsharī, ed. al-Mawjūd and Mu'awwaḍ 1998, 6:330–331.
55 (Pseudo-)'Abd al-Jabbār, ed. 'Uthmān 1996:225–226. The true author of *Sharḥ al-Uṣūl al-Khamsa* was the Zaydite Mu'tazilite Mānkdīm Shashdīv (d. 425/1034).
56 *Ibid.*:226.

this corporealist view using a *qisma*[57]-type argument. He first claims that, on scriptural evidence, we must assume God to be just (*ʿadl*) and wise. However, the epithet "just" can be applied only to Him who is in need of none (self-sufficient, *ghanī*). Because a body by definition cannot be in need of none, God cannot be a body. Secondly, ʿAbd al-Jabbār claims that God knows Himself (*ʿālim*[an] *li-dhātih*[i]). A body cannot be described as knowing itself; therefore, God is not a body. God's sitting on the throne, then, cannot be referred to as limited to a specific physical place, because God is no body. It must therefore be interpreted figuratively as denoting God's rule (*istīlāʾ*) over the world.[58]

Al-Ashʿarī, in a chapter devoted to the notion of *al-fawqiyya* in his *Maqālāt al-Islāmiyyin*, presents further rationalistic arguments used by the corporealists. Al-Ashʿarī detected several tendencies within the group that he labeled as the Mujassima. The most prominent theologian he quotes in this context is Hishām ibn al-Ḥakam, who, perceiving God as a body (*jism*) with well-defined dimensions (although unlike the human body, for Hishām was anti-anthropomorphist),[59] described Him as being "in one place and not another" ([*huw*[a]] *fī makān*[in] *dun*[a] *makān*[in]), hence, a definite body.[60] At first, according to Hishām, God was in no place, but then He created a place, which is the throne, and that is His place;[61] He is physically connected (*mumāss*) to the throne, and "the throne contains Him and limits Him."[62]

If we take al-Ashʿarī's description at face value, Hishām's views appear to have stirred discussions among the Shiʿite-Rāfiḍites. While Hishām's immediate followers claimed that God is physically connected to the throne, "does not exceed the throne, and the throne does not exceed Him," other Rāfiḍites claimed that "God sits on His throne without touching it. Do not inquire [*bi-lā kayfa*, i. e., into the nature of the sitting]!"[63] A group of anonymous corporealists who did not share Hishām's naïve views that God can be tasted, smelled and touched nevertheless affirmed His physical position on His throne,[64] and this led to a discussion of where God is situated. While Hishām claimed that God is in one place and not another (and hence in one direction and not another), other corporealists claimed that God's "surface" (*misāḥa*) is infinite, and therefore He extends in "all six direc-

---

57 For *qisma* and its basic structure in *kalāmic* logic, see van Ess 1970:40–42.
58 (Pseudo-)ʿAbd al-Jabbār, ed. ʿUthmān 1996:226–227.
59 Madelung 1971:497.
60 Al-Ashʿarī, ed. Ritter 1963:207.
61 *Ibid.*:32.
62 *Ibid.*:210.
63 *Ibid.*:33–34.
64 *Ibid.*:208.

tions: right, left, front, back, above [*al-fawq*] and below [*al-taḥt*]."[65] Because they were formulated as mere rationalistic speculations rather than as textually based claims, these and other corporealistic views served as a lodestone for Muʿtazilite reactions.

As for the Muʿtazilites' approach to the question of God's aboveness, their polemics with the traditionalists are unfortunately difficult to trace. Primarily, the Muʿtazilites were concerned with the hermeneutic method to be applied to the anthropomorphic verses in the Qurʾān, to which they applied their hallmark figurative approach. They were less interested in the validity of other textual evidence, mainly because of their tendency toward wholesale rejection of the theological *ḥadīth*s.[66] However, for the sake of their argument with the traditionalists, they were willing to consider and examine the Ḥadīth material on the way to discrediting it.[67] They were prepared to accept the anthropomorphic *ḥadīth*s only in the event that an applicable figurative explanation of the problematic description of God was provided.[68]

An illuminating example is the Muʿtazilite refutation of *ḥadīth al-nuzūl*. The Muʿtazilites claimed that God could not go down to the lowest heaven every night, because His descent contradicted His being everywhere, as may be understood from two Qurʾānic verses: "There is no secret conversation between three people where He is not the fourth, nor between five where He is not the sixth, nor between less or more than that without Him being with them, wherever they may be [*illā huw*^a^ *maʿahum ayn*^a^ *mā kānū*]" (Q. 58:7); and "It is He who is God in heaven and God on earth" (Q. 43:84).[69] According to al-Ashʿarī, the Muʿtazilites understood the precept that God is everywhere either figuratively, meaning that God rules every place (*mudabbir*^un^ *li-kull*^i^ *makān*^in^),[70] or as meaning that God never ceases to exist. However, some Muʿtazilites understood God's omnipresence literally: God supervises all places, while His entity (*dhāt*) is present in all of them.[71]

The Muʿtazilites famously preferred to interpret *istawā* in Q. 20:5, i.e., "sits" or "is established," as *istawlā*, "dominates" or "rules."[72] However, there were variations to the basic Muʿtazilite approach. Zuhayr al-Atharī (dates unknown),

---

65 *Ibid.*:209.

66 A good summary of the overall Muʿtazilite approach to Ḥadīth is Brown 2014:36–37.

67 The Muʿtazilites referred to these *ḥadīth*s as *khurāfāt*, prolix fables. See Ibn Ḥazm, ed. Naṣr and ʿUmayra 1996, 2:291.

68 Holtzman 2011.

69 Ibn Qutayba, ed. al-Aṣfar 1999:393; Ibn Ḥazm, ed. Naṣr and ʿUmayra 1996, 2:58–59.

70 Al-Ashʿarī, ed. Ritter 1963:212.

71 *Ibid.*:212.

72 *Ibid.*:211.

a *mutakallim* whose affinity to the Muʿtazila was rather obscure, combined the Muʿtazilite view that "God is everywhere" with the ultra-traditionalistic view that God sits on His throne and will be seen by the believers in the afterlife, "without asking how." Apparently, Zuhayr believed in the essential presence of God in concrete places. "On the Day of Resurrection," he claimed, "there will be no place devoid of His presence."[73]

In conclusion, the rationalistic approaches to the concept of God's aboveness cannot be understood properly without also considering the corporealists. Notwithstanding the somewhat vague descriptions of them in the heresiographical sources, the corporealists were prominent actors in the arena of Islamic theology. The most conspicuous corporealistic force was that of the Karrāmiyya, who were active in Nīshāpūr and other parts of the eastern Islamic world. In most cases, the abovementioned variants of corporealistic views can be traced back to known Karrāmite *mutakallimūn*, starting with the eponymous Abū ʿAbd Allāh Muḥammad ibn Karrām (d. 255/869).[74]

The Wider Horizons of the Receptive Traditionalistic Heritage

We can broaden our understanding of the corporealistic approach of the Karrāmites by reading al-Dhahabī's description of a public debate between the Ashʿarite theologian Muḥammad ibn al-Ḥasan ibn Fūrak (d. 406/1015) and the Turkish sultan Maḥmūd ibn Subuktikīn (r. 388–421/998–1030),[75] a zealous adherent of the Karrāmite doctrine. According to al-Dhahabī, Ibn Fūrak said to the sultan: "It is impermissible to ascribe aboveness to God, for this compels one to ascribe belowness [*taḥtiyya*] to Him, too.[76] If it is conceivable to think that one has aboveness, it is equally conceivable to think that he has belowness." The sultan responded: "I did not describe Him to you so that you could contradict me by using your kalāmic witticism. It is He who described Himself." Defeated in the

73 *Ibid.*:215, 299; van Ess 1990–1997, 2:738–742.
74 The relevant chapter on the Karrāmiyya in al-Shahrastānī's *Milal* summarizes the variants of Karrāmite views (which incidentally contains the formula *bi-lā kayfa*): al-Shahrastānī, ed. Muḥammad 1992, 1:99–105. Another important source for Karrāmite views is al-Baghdādī, ed. Khashin n. d.:190. For further sources on the Karrāmiyya, see Zysow 2014.
75 In Turkish: Sebüktegin. He was the first fully independent sultan of the Turkish Ghaznavid dynasty in Persia and India. See Bosworth 2014; Al-Dhahabī, ed. ʿAbd al-Salām 1990–2000, 29:69.
76 This is a typical *ilzām* argument; see van Ess 1970:25–26, and further below, in the chapter on the later traditionalists.

debate, Ibn Fūrak felt so bad, writes al-Dhahabī, that he died instantly out of frustration.[77]

As suggested earlier, the rationalistic argumentations on God's transcendent aboveness were shaped, among other factors, in response to rationalized corporealistic views. The efforts invested by the Ashʿarites in refuting the corporealistic worldview – as illustrated by the anecdote about Ibn Fūrak and the sultan – were systematic and conspicuous, especially in eleventh-century Nīshāpūr, which was the capital of Ashʿarite *kalām*. Ibn Fūrak and his old classmate from Baghdād, Abū Isḥāq Ibrāhīm ibn Muḥammad al-Isfarāyīnī (d. 418/1027), imported Ashʿarite *kalām* to the city. They actively propagated *kalām* in the *madrasa*s that the governor of Nīshāpūr built especially for them, and the city's educated elite – mainly Shāfiʿites – enthusiastically embraced the Ashʿarite teachings.

The corporealistic Karrāmites comprised the majority of Nīshāpūr's lower class.[78] With the sultan's outspoken encouragement, their corporealistic views were audibly present in the Nīshāpūri public sphere, as again illustrated by an anecdote about Abū Isḥāq al-Isfarāyīnī's resounding victory in a debate with an anonymous Karrāmite in the sultan's court. The Karrāmite asked Abū Isḥāq al-Isfarāyīnī whether it was possible that God was on His throne and that the throne was the place of God (*makān lahu*). Patiently refuting the Karrāmite's position, Al-Isfarāyīnī theatrically spread his arms and, placing one palm over the other, said: "This is how a thing is above another thing." Unlike his palms, he explained, God could not be particularized (*mukhaṣṣaṣ*), because every particular thing (*makhṣūṣ*) is physically limited, and what is limited cannot be a god. In this case, al-Isfarāyīnī won the debate, and the Karrāmites, unable to answer his winning argument, gathered around him in a threatening sort of way until the sultan himself pushed them aside. When the vizier, whose name was Abu 'l-ʿAbbās al-Isfarāyīnī, entered the court, the frustrated sultan exclaimed: "Where have you been? Your townsman hit the god of the Karrāmites on his head!"[79]

Like the Muʿtazilites, the Ashʿarites used the device of rationalistic argumentation to refute the corporealistic views. A typical example of the use of rationalistic argumentation stemming from a Muʿtazilite origin appears in Abu 'l-Muẓaffar al-Isfarāyīnī's (d. 471/1079) *al-Tabṣīr fī al-Dīn*.[80] In the context of his effort to refute the doctrines of various heretical sects, among which the Karrāmites took center stage, Abu 'l-Muẓaffar al-Isfarāyīnī enumerates the components of the lat-

77 Al-Dhahabī, ed. ʿAbd al-Salām 1990–2000, 29:68–69, 73.
78 Bosworth 1973:165–166; Bulliet 1973:76–77.
79 Al-Isfarāyīnī, ed. al-Ḥūt 1983:112.
80 Not much is known about this scholar. *Ibid.*:9–10.

ter's worldview: God has a body (*jism*). His body has one borderline (*ḥadd wāḥid*) between one side of His body and the throne, while His other sides (*al-jawānib al-ukhar*) are unlimited. This concept enabled the Karrāmites to claim that God either physically touches or is in contact with His throne (*mumāss lil-ʿarsh*), and that the throne is His place (*makān*). Abu 'l-Muẓaffar al-Isfarāyīnī declares that ascribing the quality of end or limit (*nihāya*) to God is absurd.[81] In *al-Tabṣīr fī al-Dīn*, al-Isfarāyīnī for the most part prefers linguistic arguments leading to figurative interpretations similar to those of the Muʿtazilites. For example, contemplating the meaning of God's sitting on the throne, al-Isfarāyīnī opines that the prepositions "on" (*ʿalā*) and "to" (*ilā*) are in fact interchangeable. Thus, the verse "the Lord of Mercy, established on [*istawā ʿalā*] the throne" (Q. 20:5) may be read "Lord of Mercy, turning to [*istawā ilā*] the throne." Al-Isfarāyīnī uses Q. 41:11 as clear-cut evidence for this interpretation: "Then He turned to [*istawā ilā*] the sky, which was smoke." Accordingly, he determines that *istawā ʿalā 'l-ʿarsh* should be taken as a figure of speech denoting God's rule and not as referring to a specific physical throne.[82]

In the same vein, the prominent Ashʿarite theologian and historian ʿAbd al-Karīm al-Shahrastānī (d. 548/1153) dedicated a lengthy chapter in his *kalām* manual *Nihāyat al-Aqdām fī ʿIlm al-Kalām* to refuting the arguments for anthropomorphism (*tashbīh*). Like Abu 'l-Muẓaffar al-Isfarāyīnī, al-Shahrastānī was a resident of Khurāsān and was intimately familiar with "heretical" views, of which the notion of God's spatial dimension was one. He was appalled by the idea, advanced by the Karrāmites, that God resides in a place and has directionality. His basic argument was straightforward and simple: It is inconceivable to think that God is subject to change (*qābil lil-aʿrāḍ*) and that changes occur in Him (*maḥall lil-ḥawādith*). From this fundamental principle ensued several declarations that echoed the Muʿtazilite stance: God is neither substance (*jawhar*) nor body (*jism*) nor accident (*ʿaraḍ*). He is neither in a place (*lā fī makān*) nor in time (*lā fī zamān*).[83] Were God limited in time and space or oriented in a specific direction (*mukhtaṣṣ*^{an} *bi-jiha*^{tin}), He would have been created (i.e., not a god).[84]

Al-Shahrastānī directs his sophistic arrows at the Karrāmites and at two other unidentified groups, "The People of Images" (*aṣḥāb al-ṣuwar*) and "The People of Direction" (*aṣḥāb al-jiha*). These groups, claims al-Shahrastānī, believe that God is indeed a substance and a body and that "His direction is above" (*bi-jihat*^{i}

---

81 *Ibid.*:111–112, 120–121.

82 *Ibid.*:157–159.

83 Al-Shahrastānī, ed. Guillaume 2009:97. See the summary in Gardet 1960:410–411.

84 Al-Shahrastānī, *ibid.*:99.

'l-fawq).[85] Al-Shahrastānī's adversaries cite the Qur'ānic verses (Q. 6:18; 57:4; 50:16; 2:186) that imply God's directionality or aboveness, and they claim that even more Qur'ānic verses indicate God's closeness to His creation. Al-Shahrastānī provides a psychological description of their invalid notions:

> In general, anyone who imagines that God exists in a place, and insists that He has some kind of direction, that He is separated from this world by a separation of great finite length or of great infinite length ... merely fantasizes. God's existence is not in a place.[86]

This is the official Ashʿarite position on God's aboveness: He cannot be described in terms of place and direction. Ibn Fūrak's and Abū Isḥāq al-Isfarāyīnī's assertions in the debates with the Karrāmites relied on this postulate.

Further elaboration of this approach may be found in Ibn Fūrak's surviving theological treatise, *Mushkil al-Ḥadīth* (the Book of ambiguous *ḥadīths*). Discussing the female-slave *ḥadīth*, which he considers a problematic text in need of further clarification, Ibn Fūrak declares:

> When we say that God is above His creatures, we do not mean aboveness in terms of place [*fawqiyyat al-makān*]. We do not mean that He is above places and looks down at them. We do claim that "above" carries two meanings: The first is that He is "Supreme Master over His creatures" [*al-qāhir*^{u} *fawq*^{a} *ʿibādih*^{i}; Q. 6:18, 61] ... the second is that He is detached from any attribution and description.[87]

In this case, Ibn Fūrak applies the hermeneutical device of *ta'wīl* to the ambiguous female-slave *ḥadīth*, aiming to sterilize and even eliminate the scene depicted in this *ḥadīth*, probably with the intention of averting his readers from pointing their fingers to the sky and claiming that God was there. God's aboveness, according to Ibn Fūrak, is purely metaphorical.

As established Ashʿarites, Ibn Fūrak, Abū Isḥāq al-Isfarāyīnī, Abu 'l-Muẓaffar al-Isfarāyīnī and al-Shahrastānī represent the scholastic phase of later Sunnism. However, strong lines of rationalistic argumentation existed already in earlier generations. Ibn Qutayba's (d. 276/889) *Ta'wīl Mukhtalif al-Ḥadīth*, which preceded the Ashʿarite discourse by several decades, was intended as a guide for traditionalists in distress, but in essence the work, far from traditionalistic in spirit, was a reservoir of rationalistic arguments against the Ḥadīth material. Ibn Qutayba puts his best efforts into defending pure traditionalism by constructing rather sophis-

85 *Ibid.*:97–98.
86 *Ibid.*:106.
87 Ibn Fūrak, ed. Gimaret 2003:81.

ticated arguments, with the purpose of refuting those who negate the teachings of the Ḥadīth.

For example, Ibn Qutayba tries to reconcile *ḥadīth al-nuzūl*, which implies that God is situated in one location and then moves to another, with a handful of Qur'ānic verses that state that God is everywhere,[88] as the Mu'tazilites claim, based on Q. 58:7 and Q. 43:84. Ibn Qutayba responds that the Qur'ānic phrase "He is with them wherever they may be" (*huwa ma'ahum ayna mā kānū*, Q. 58:7) signifies "He knows what they are up to."[89] How can anyone claim that God is physically everywhere when Q. 20:5 asserts that He is established on His throne?[90] Were He not above, the prayers and the good deeds of the believers would not have gone up to him, as the Qur'ān (Q. 35:10) explicitly declares.[91] However, Ibn Qutayba saw God's aboveness not as a spatial relation, a physical attribute or an essential position (*ḥulūl*), but as a figure of speech. The words of God to Moses, as they appear in the *ḥadīth* attributed to Wahb ibn Munabbih (d. ca. 106–118/725–737), are such figures of speech. The saying "God is above you, in front of you, behind you, encompasses you, and is nearer to you than your own soul" means that He knows you better than you know yourself.[92]

Similarly to Ibn Qutayba's approach, the Ash'arites embraced the traditionalistic discourse and – on the basis of the Ḥadīth – constructed a semi-rationalistic method of argumentation for their theological debates. One of the most illuminating examples of such rationalization of the traditionalistic material appears in Abu 'l-Ḥasan al-Ash'arī's discussion in *Kitāb al-Ibāna* of the concept of God sitting on the throne. Al-Ash'arī viewed his theological treatise as a traditionalistic manifesto. His aim in writing it was to confirm the credo of "the People of Truth and Sunna" (*ahl al-ḥaqq wa'l-sunna*).[93] The references in *al-Ibāna* to the teachings of Aḥmad ibn Ḥanbal (d. 241/855) and other pillars of traditionalism attest to this intention. However, *al-Ibāna* also systematically combines rationalistic arguments with the textual evidence of the Qur'ān and the Ḥadīth.

An example of the apparently simplistic presentation of traditionalistic axioms is al-Ash'arī's interpretation of Q. 67:16, "Are you sure that He who is in Heaven will not make the earth swallow you up with a violent shudder?" Here al-Ash'arī has two goals: (1) to determine that the throne is above all heavens; and

88 Ibn Qutayba, ed. al-Aṣfar 1999:393–394.
89 *Ibid.*:393
90 *Ibid.*:394. Ibn Qutayba interprets *istawlā* as *istaqarra*.
91 *Ibid.*
92 *Ibid.*:398.
93 Al-Ash'arī, ed. Beirut n. d.:33.

(2) to determine that God's specific location is the throne, which is the highest possible point in the universe. Without further explaining his line of thought or disclosing his sources, al-Ashʿarī presents, with much conviction, the following cosmology:

> Above the heavens is the throne. This is why the Qur'ān states: "Are you sure that He who is in Heaven ...?" The meaning of the verse is that He sits on the throne which is above the heavens. All that is above is heaven, and the throne is on top of all heavens. Although the Qur'ān says "heaven" [*al-samā'*], it actually means "all heavens" [*jamīʿ al-samawāt*], and not just one heaven. In particular, it means the throne, which is above the heavens.[94]

The proof that al-Ashʿarī provides for this axiom echoes the *ḥadīth* of the female slave:

> We see that all Muslims raise their hands towards the sky when they pray, because God sits on His throne, which is above the heavens. Were God not on the throne, they would not have raised their hands towards the throne. Furthermore, they do not lower their hands to the ground when they pray.[95]

Indeed, the *ḥadīth* of the female slave closes al-Ashʿarī's discussion of God sitting on the throne.[96]

However, al-Ashʿarī possessed a variety of rationalistic arguments *par excellence*, and he used them to prove that God was situated at the highest possible point, and not just everywhere. In the following example, we clearly observe al-Ashʿarī's processes of logical deduction:

> The Muʿtazila, Ḥarūriyya and Jahmiyya claimed that God was everywhere. This claim forced them to admit that God resided in Mary's womb, in dunghills [*ḥushūsh*] and in empty spaces [*akhliya*]. This contradicts the tenets of our religion, and God is above and beyond what they claim! This is the answer they should be given: If God does not sit on His throne alone, as all the scholars, Ḥadīth transmitters and teachers say, then He is everywhere. Therefore, He is under the earth, above which there are heavens. If He is under the earth, and the earth is above Him, and the heavens are above the earth, then you are forced to say that God is underneath, under the lowest possible point [*taḥtᵃ 'l-taḥt*], and all the things are above Him, whereas He is above the highest point possible [*fawqᵃ 'l-fawq*] and all the things are under Him. What you say entails that He is under things that He is above, and above things that He is under. This is a contradictory absurdity. God is above and beyond the lies you fabricate about Him.[97]

---

94 *Ibid.*
95 *Ibid.*
96 *Ibid.*:36–37.
97 *Ibid.*:34.

Both al-Ashʿarī and Ibn Fūrak applied rationalistic devices to the Ḥadīth materials, yet they arrived at different and in fact opposing conclusions: Whereas Ibn Fūrak saw *al-fawqiyya* as a metaphor for God's omnipotence, al-Ashʿarī saw it as the only direction appropriate for God, a necessary outcome derived from the most basic religious convictions.

The Ashʿarites approached the theological Ḥadīth material from several different angles. One arose from their effort to estimate the value of the material as evidence, using vocabulary adapted from the field of legal theory.[98] A *ḥadīth* yielded probable knowledge (*ẓann*, presumption) or absolute certainty (*yaqīn*), depending on the number of its earliest narrators: One transmitted by at least ten narrators (*ḥadīth mutawātir*) was viewed as *yaqīn*, while one transmitted by less than five narrators (*ḥadīth al-āḥād*) was tagged as *ẓann*.[99] Thus, the Ashʿarite theologian Imām al-Ḥaramayn Abu 'l-Maʿālī al-Juwaynī (d. 478/1085) considered the number of the original narrators of *ḥadīth al-nuzūl*, marking as his rivals the ultra-traditionalists, who (as noted in the first part of this article) accepted the entire bulk of the theological Ḥadīth material without applying any device of classification and selection. As a *ḥādīth al-āḥad*, claimed, al-Juwaynī, *ḥadīth al-nuzūl* did not lead to certain knowledge.[100]

Al-Juwaynī was not unique in showing interest in the credibility of the Ḥadīth material, but Ashʿarite scholars with limited knowledge of the Ḥadīth did not bother themselves with such questions. To prove that God has no directionality, for example, Abu 'l-Muẓaffar al-Isfarāyīnī cited a *ḥadīth* attributed to the Prophet, according to which an angel who had descended from heaven met with an angel who had ascended from the seventh (lowest) earth. They asked one another: "Where did you come from?" Each replied: "From God." In Abu 'l-Muẓaffar al-Isfarāyīnī's opinion, this proved that God was unlimited and infinite, since the entire universe submitted to His governance, power and knowledge.[101] Though it was not uncommon in theological treatises for a *ḥadīth* to be quoted without giving a chain of transmitters, the reason Abu 'l-Muẓaffar al-Isfarāyīnī did not do so is that this *ḥadīth* was fabricated. It was one of the few *ḥadīth*s used by the Muʿtazilites in their polemics with the traditionalists to reject God's descent and directionality. One of its versions appears in a polemical treatise against the Muʿtazila composed by the Ḥanbalite ʿUthmān ibn Saʿīd al-Dārimī (d. 280/894),

---

98 Brown 2009:178–179.

99 *Ibid.*:104–105.

100 Al-Juwaynī, ed. Mūsā and ʿAbd al-Ḥamīd 1950:160–162.

101 Al-Isfarāyīnī, ed. al-Ḥūt 1983:157–159.

who declared that this *ḥadīth* was invoked by scholars who lacked sufficient knowledge of the sources.[102]

As indicated earlier, the later Ashʿarites preferred figurative interpretations of the Ḥadīth material. Al-Juwaynī, for example, argued that the descent of God described in *ḥadīth al-nuzūl* must be interpreted figuratively as the action of God in granting favors to His worshippers.[103] As with Ibn Fūrak before him, al-Juwaynī's rationalistic approach was put to the test. A zealous traditionalist (not a corporealist) asked him about Q. 20:5: "The Lord of Mercy, established on the throne." Al-Juwaynī found it difficult to interpret the verse, and at some point he started mumbling. The traditionalist defied him:

> Do explain to us what you meant! Do you have a kalāmic trick up your sleeve? A pious man raises his face upward before he starts praying. He turns neither to the right nor to the left, only above [*fawq*]. Do you have some kind of trick to release us from this endless discussion of above and beneath?

This embarrassing incident distressed al-Juwaynī and stirred the atmosphere in the mosque: His rival started to cry, and the entire crowd in the mosque cried with him.[104] This anecdote illustrates the image of the Ashʿarites as an aloof scholarly elite. Al-Juwaynī's fault was not merely doctrinal; it was also socio-cultural: By refusing to ascribe aboveness to God, he hurt the feelings of his traditionalistic opponent and of the crowd in the mosque.

A complete assimilation of the Muʿtazilite doctrine of God's transcendence into the Ashʿarite discourse is demonstrated in the later Ashʿarite theologian Fakhr al-Dīn al-Rāzī's (d. 606/1210) *Asās al-taqdīs*. Al-Rāzī's fundamental conviction was that God's nature was transcendent, above any kind of corporeality, spatiality or directionality (*munazzah*^{un} *ʿan*^{i} *'l-jismiyya*^{ti} *wa'l-ḥayyiz*^{i} *wa'l-jiha*^{ti}),[105] a view he supported through his reading of the Qurʾānic evidence (*dalāʾil samʿiyya*).

For example, al-Rāzī analyzes God's statement in Q. 2:186 that He is near (*fa-innī qarīb*^{un}), a verse revealed, as he points out, to the Prophet Muḥammad. The Prophet was asked whether the Lord is close to His believers, so that they can whisper to Him, or far, so that they must call to Him out loud. After analyzing this problem, al-Rāzī concludes: "If God indeed were in the heaven or on the throne, it would have been incorrect to believe that He was close to His worshipers."[106] If

102 Al-Dārimī, ed. al-Badr 1985:84–86.
103 Al-Juwaynī, ed. Mūsā and ʿAbd al-Ḥamīd. 1950:162.
104 Al-Dhahabī, ed. ʿAbd al-Salām 1990–2000, 2:238.
105 Al-Rāzī, ed. al-Saqā 1986:30.
106 *Ibid.*:41.

the direction of aboveness were ascribed to God (*law kān*^{a} *taʿālā fī jihat*^{i} *fawq*^{in}), al-Rāzī goes on to explain, He would have been the sky (*al-samāʾ*) itself – an absurd conclusion, since the sky is created. Al-Rāzī unfolds two arguments to support this assertion. First, the Arabic word for sky, *samāʾ*, is derived from the root *s. m.w*, whose general meaning is to be elevated or above something. This is the conventional usage of *s. m.w* in the Qurʾān.[107] Therefore, following both linguistic and Qurʾānic usage, anything that is described as elevated and high should correctly be referred to as sky. Second, from a logical perspective, were God situated above a heavenly throne, the denizens of the throne (*sukkān al-ʿarsh*) would see the end of the divine entity (*nihāyat*^{a} *dhāt*^{i} *Allāh*^{i} *taʿālā*), just as the earth's denizens (*sukkān al-arḍ*) see the sky. In other words, they would see the divine essence as the sky (*kān*^{a} *dhātuhu ka'l-samāʾ*^{i} *li-sukkān*^{i} *'l-ʿarsh*^{i}), which is a created entity. Thus, the notion of God physically sitting on the throne is absurd.[108] Consequently, al-Rāzī concludes, God cannot be described as having the directionality of aboveness.[109]

Noticeable in al-Rāzī's proof is his exclusive derivation of scriptural evidence from the Qurʾān and his neglect of the Ḥadīth, enabling him to build a logical structure that is detached from the detailed pictures of the Ḥadīth. This hermeneutical methodology enabled al-Rāzī to pass over the traditionalistic formula of *bi-lā kayfa* and develop an independent interpretation – his own *taʾwīl*.

The creativity demonstrated by the Ashʿarites in their readings of the Qurʾān was not limited to advanced hermeneutics. They were also greatly inspired by certain notions drawn from the Greco-Islamic scientific heritage. An astonishing argument about God's aboveness appears in *Risāla fī Ithbāt al-Istiwāʾ wa'l-Fawqiyya*, a treatise that conveys the tenets of Ashʿarite theology with a peppery touch of independent rationalistic argument. The author, ʿAbd Allāh ibn Yusūf al-Juwaynī (d. 438/1047), was the father of the above-mentioned Imām al-Ḥaramayn al-Juwaynī. In the introduction to his treatise, ʿAbd Allāh al-Juwaynī declares his aim to provide an accurate explanation – one that will serve as a warning against the pitfalls of figurative interpretation and anthropomorphism – for God's aboveness and sitting on the throne.[110] To that end, he adduces a pseudo-scientific explanation that, by his own avowal, he found in the writings of the astronomers – though he unfortunately does not specify the titles or authors of

---

107 For example, "He sends hail down from [such] mountains in the sky" (*wa-yunazzil*^{u} *min*^{a} *'l-samāʾ*^{i}, Q. 24:43) and "We send down pure water from the sky" (*wa-anzalnā min*^{a} *'l-samāʾ*^{i} *māʾ*^{an} *ṭahūr*^{an}, Q. 25:48).

108 Al-Rāzī, ed. al-Saqā 1986:42.

109 *Ibid.*:43.

110 Al-Juwaynī, ed. Ḥaqqī 1998:32.

these works – which he supplemented using evidence drawn from the Qur'ān.[111] Using geometrical calculations, the astronomers had discovered that the globe was situated precisely in the middle of the sky, "like a watermelon inside another watermelon." Therefore, the lowest point in the world is actually the center of the globe, and it is called "below" (*taḥt*); anything beneath that thus cannot be called "below," but only "above" (*fawq*). A body going upward (*ilā jihat*ⁱ *'l-fawq*ⁱ) either goes up to the sky or passes through the center of the world.[112] Accordingly, the heavens wrap around the earth and are always on top. If this perplexing assertion is correct regarding a body (*jism*) such as the heavens, then it is surely correct regarding God, "nothing is like Him" (Q. 42:11). Aboveness and being above every existent is an essential attribute of Him (*dhātī lahu*).[113]

Al-Juwaynī the father concludes his rationalistic explanation with a traditionalistic statement, according to which aboveness is the quality that befits God, and we should not ask how He is above (*bi-lā takyīf*).[114] The interesting point, of course, is this author's acquaintance with spherical geometry. His description of the lack of orientation and the irrelevance of directions like "up" and "down" in spherical bodies is quite surprising, even in the context of Ashʿarite theology.[115]

The Later Traditionalists and Their Rationalized Approach to the Ḥadīth Material

Theological controversies between traditionalists (mainly the Ḥanbalites) and rationalists (mainly the Ashʿarites) comprised the lion's share of intellectual activity in the scholarly circles of fourteenth-century Damascus. These controversies were not purely theological; they were also shaped by political and personal inter-

111 *Ibid.*:81.

112 *Ibid.*:82. The Muslim world became acquainted with the notion that the earth is spherical in the wake of the massive translation movement of classical Greek writings in the second/eighth–third/ninth centuries. After the Islamic conquests, other early sources on astronomy reached the Muslims from Persia and India. Muslim writings on astronomy mainly conveyed Ptolemaic astronomy, according to which the earth was the center of a planetary system. Another influential classical Greek science that penetrated Islamic scientific thought was spherical astronomy, which postulates spherical bodies revolving in circles around the stable earth. By and large, this adheres to the Aristotelian astronomical model. Ragep 2014.

113 Al-Juwaynī, ed. Ḥaqqī 1998:83.

114 *Ibid.*

115 A similar discussion appears in al-Shahrastānī, who also claims that because the earth is a spherical body there is no absolute up (*fawq*) or down (*taḥt*). What is up for one standing at the north pole is down for one standing at the south pole. Al-Shahrastānī, ed. Guillaume 2009:107.

ests.[116] As noted above, the highly documented trials of Ibn Taymiyya in Damascus provide us with a rare glimpse into the nature of the theological debate on God's aboveness. The theological discussions of Ibn Taymiyya and his devoted disciple Shams al-Dīn Muḥammad ibn Qayyim al-Jawziyya (d. 751/1350) on this topic, which they based on the writings of their traditionalistic predecessors and on the rationalized discourse of the Ashʿarites, represent a new form of traditionalism that does not hesitate to profess its credo in a rationalistic language.

The intellectual efforts of Ibn Taymiyya and Ibn Qayyim al-Jawziyya in this regard must be placed in the context of the writings of their colleagues, the later traditionalists of Damascus and Cairo. Their townsman Shams al-Dīn al-Dhahabī[117] was also the author of *Kitāb al-ʿArsh*, a treatise on God's aboveness, throne and directionality. A typical traditionalistic creed, *Kitāb al-ʿArsh* endeavors to affirm God's aboveness and sitting on His throne by way of massive citations of the relevant Ḥadīth material. Complying with traditionalistic writing conventions, it begins with Qurʾānic verses and then cites the Ḥadīth material "chronologically" or "hierarchically" – first the sayings of the Prophet and then those of his companions (*al-ṣaḥāba*), their followers (*al-tābiʿūn*) and a few generations of their disciples (*tābiʿū al-tābiʿīn*). Finally, it cites scholars of later generations, including both traditionalists such as Ibn Khuzayma and Abū Bakr al-Ājurrī[118] and rationalistic Ashʿarites such as Ibn Fūrak and Imām al-Ḥaramayn al-Juwaynī.[119] Al-Dhahabī also dedicates a lengthy chapter to al-Ashʿarī, and he even sifts through Ibn Qutayba's *Taʾwīl Mukhtalif al-Ḥadīth*, selecting and then citing his more traditionalistic sayings.[120] The quantity of citations from the Ashʿarite literature in *Kitāb al-ʿArsh* indicates the extent of the infiltration of rationalistic ideas into traditionalistic discourse, although al-Dhahabī was careful not to cite sayings that did not correspond with his ultra-traditionalistic point of view. Any mention in *Kitāb al-ʿArsh* of the figurative interpretations deployed by the Muʿtazilites and the Ashʿarites is intended to highlight a contradictory statement by one of the traditionalistic scholars.[121] Al-Dhahabī, it seems, did not allow any advanced

---

116 Holtzman 2009:209–211, 220; Bori and Holtzman 2010:17–22; Jackson 1994:41–43.

117 Al-Dhahabī supported Ibn Taymiyya and Ibn Qayyim al-Jawziyya in their struggle with the Shāfiʿite scholastic elite and the Mamlūk authorities (Irwin 2003:23–24). In a short biographical entry dedicated to Ibn Qayyim al-Jawziyya, al-Dhahabī testifies that he was Ibn Qayyim al-Jawziyya's classmate in their youth, when they studied Ḥadīth together (Al-Dhahabī, ed. al-Hīla 1988:269).

118 Al-Dhahabī, ed. al-Tamīmī 2003, 2:277–278, 309–311.

119 *Ibid.*, 2:339, 362–364.

120 *Ibid.*, 2:291–303, 269–277.

121 *Ibid.*, 2:315–318.

reading of the Qurʾānic text and adhered to the literal meaning of the anthropomorphic verses and other "ambiguous" texts (*mutashābihāt*, i. e., the Qurʾānic verses which are not to be interpreted, as opposed to *muḥkamāt*).

Notwithstanding al-Dhahabī's admirable efforts in constructing an encyclopedic work on the topic of God's aboveness, he produced a standard, conventional text. His independent additions to the citations he adduces consist of scant biographical details and brief notices on the scholarly merit of the cited authorities, without any deeper delving into the theological arguments.[122] Al-Dhahabī's work could have served as a useful tool for further discussion, and his contemporaries, such as Ibn Qayyim al-Jawziyya, may have used it as a bibliographical aid.[123]

A colleague of Al-Dhahabī, the renowned historian ʿImād al-Dīn Ismaʿīl Ibn Kathīr (d. 774/1373), an adherent of the Taymiyyan school,[124] belonged to the elite group of the traditionalists in Mamluk Damascus.[125] Ibn Kathīr addressed the topic of God's aboveness and throne in his monumental *al-Bidāya wa'l-Nihāya fī al-Tārīkh*. Here, too, he relied on quoting Qurʾānic verses and *ḥadiths* without explaining them.[126] This fairly crude method of massive citations evidently represented the curriculum of mainstream traditionalism. It is almost impossible to detect the authors' own views on the subject, because they rarely expressed them. Earlier generations of traditionalists, such as Ibn Khuzayma, seem to have had much more leeway in professing their views. Both Ibn Kathīr and al-Dhahabī were well acquainted with the bold intellectual efforts of Ibn Taymiyya and Ibn Qayyim al-Jawziyya, but, unlike the latter, they perpetuated a rigid form of puristic traditionalism. As scholars of Ḥadīth, they preferred to focus on the Ḥadīth.

By contrast, the constant engagement of Ibn Taymiyya and Ibn Qayyim al-Jawziyya with the Damscene milieu, both its educated elite and its laymen, taught them the necessity of expanding the boundaries of the discussion beyond the borders of the standard traditionalistic discourse. They were prepared to go beyond the simplistic *bi-lā kayfa* and offer elaborate answers to the questions of the educated non-scholarly elite about issues that stimulated the imagination. Thus, Ibn Taymiyya responded with great care and consideration to a set of questions from an anonymous inquirer, who asked him about the heavenly throne and its cosmological qualities (Is it round? What substance surrounds it?), and

122 *Ibid.*, 1:399, 413–416. See the analysis of the editor, Muḥammad al-Tamīmī.
123 *Ibid.*, 2:323, note 3.
124 Laoust 1971.
125 Irwin 2003:24.
126 See, for instance, his chapter "On the [verses] dealing with the creation of the throne [*al-ʿarsh*] and the stool [*al-kursī*]"; Ibn Kathīr, ed. al-Turkī 2003, 1:15–18.

about its place in the cosmos (Is it located in the ninth orbit, *falak*?). These questions reflect some acquaintance with the writings of the philosophers.[127] Ibn Taymiyya was further asked why the quality of aboveness was ascribed to God and His throne. His answer appears in a short epistle entitled *al-ʿArshiyya*.[128]

Ibn Taymiyya begins by clarifying that there is neither rational proof (*dalīl ʿaqlī*) nor scriptural evidence (*dalīl sharʿī*) to sustain the philosophers' claim that the throne is situated in the ninth orbit of the cosmos, or indeed that the cosmos consists of only nine orbits.[129] He thus attacks the scholarship found in ʿAbd Allāh al-Juwaynī's discussion of the cosmos and the earth. According to Ibn Taymiyya, the combination of the Greco-Arab scientific heritage of the philosophers with poor and inadequate knowledge of the Ḥadīth material leads to grave errors. He even offers a humorous description of the erroneous process, involving constant shifts of position that led these scholars to determine that the throne was situated in the ninth orbit.[130]

Ibn Taymiyya counsels his readers to abide by the sacred texts, but his final answer does not rely on them. Although he quotes several verses about the heavenly throne – for example, "It is He who created the heavens and the earth in six days; His throne extends over the water" (Q. 11:7) – his categorical answer is: "The reports [*akhbār*] indicate that the throne is separated [*bāʾin*] from all the other created things."[131] This is Ibn Taymiyya's variation on the traditionalistic stance articulated by traditionists from the ninth century onward in response to the Muʿtazilite concept of God's omnipresence.[132] Ibn Taymiyya could have said other things about the throne and supported them with solid textual evidence from the Qurʾān and the Ḥadīth. However, as a deliberate rhetorical strategy, he leaves his sources obscure and chooses to quote the most rationalistic view of the earlier traditionalists, namely, that the throne is entirely separated from the universe.

Another example of Ibn Taymiyya's approach is found in *al-Akmaliyya*, a bulky epistle responding to dozens of questions addressed to him on various theological issues. In one section, in which he systematically analyzes *ḥadīth al-nuzūl*,

127 Examplary Hellenistic works on the subject are Plato's *Timaeus* and Aristotle's *De Caelo*. Of special influence on Islamic astronomy were the works of the great second-century Greek astronomer Claudius Ptolemy. Ragep 2014.
128 Ibn Taymiyya, ed. Cairo 1966, 1:261–265.
129 *Ibid.*, 1:261. For Ibn Sīnā's interpretation of the throne as the ninth orbit, see Abdul-Raof 2012:229.
130 Ibn Taymiyya, ed. Cairo 1966, 1:261–264.
131 *Ibid.*, 1:264.
132 See. e. g., al-Dhahabī, ed. al-Tamīmī 2003, 2:247.

he again responds to a set of questions that were detached from the traditionalistic discourse. He was asked how it is possible for God to descend to the earth every night, when night arrives at different times in different countries, so that God must remain on earth all the time. Ibn Taymiyya's answer is divided into two parts. First, in the Qurʾān God attributes to himself both transitive and intransitive actions (*al-afʿāl al-mutaʿaddiya wa'l-lāzima*). Intransitive actions, such as descent (*nuzūl*), require a preposition. So, linguistically, there is no problem in stating that God descends to the lower heaven. However, stresses Ibn Taymiyya, the divine descent is strictly unlike the descent of the human body from a higher point to a lower one. As with God's other attributes, such as His being situated in Heaven or sitting on the throne, God's descent to the lowest heaven cannot be likened to the descent of His creatures, "because a quality belongs to the object it describes, and an action belongs to its agent." Since "nothing is like Him" (Q. 42:11), God's action cannot be compared to those of created human beings.[133] Elsewhere, Ibn Taymiyya explains that technically it is possible for God's descent to occur in several places simultaneously: He comes close to some people and not to others because "the descent is unlike the physical descent of human bodies."[134]

Ibn Qayyim al-Jawziyya followed the lines drawn by his master Ibn Taymiyya, combining traditionalistic and rationalistic narratives. His early theological work *Ijtimāʿ al-Juyūsh al-Islāmiyya*, which fits nicely within the traditionalistic discourse, is a collection of numerous citations from the Qurʾān, the Ḥadīth and the sayings of the early and later traditionists, resembling al-Dhahabī's *Kitāb al-ʿArsh*. It serves as a companion to Ibn Qayyim al-Jawziyya's later work of dialectics, *al-Ṣawāʿiq al-Mursala ʿalā 'l-Jahmiyya wa'l-Muʿaṭṭila*,[135] and its simple method of argumentation established the infrastructure for the latter work, which is more sophisticated and developed.[136] Together, these two works deliver a polemical line of thought that reflects the debate against the rationalistic claims regareding the attributes of God, including His aboveness. Delving into Ibn Qayyim al-Jawziyya's stance is especially worthwhile in this context, in that he provides a systematic presentation of the Taymiyyan view on God's aboveness, using various argumentative devices.

---

133 Ibn Taymiyya, ed. al-Jazzār and Anwar al-Bāz 1998, 5:195–197.

134 *Ibid.*, 5:285. This answer appears in *al-Risāla al-Madaniyya*, *ibid.*, 6:211–225.

135 Literally: "The Unleashed Thunderbolts Directed against the Jahmiyya and the Muʿaṭṭila." The Muʿaṭṭila and Jahmiyya are, respectively, the Muʿtazilite and Ashʿarite schools (see above, notes 22 and 47). Ḥanbalite scholars often referred to their adversaries as "Jahmiyya," and so did Ibn Taymiyya and Ibn Qayyim al-Jawziyya with regard to the rationalist Ashʿarite school and other rival groups. Watt 1965.

136 Holtzman 2009:214–215, 217; Krawietz 2006:31.

In *Ijtimāʿ al-Juyūsh*, most of Ibn Qayyim al-Jawziyya's references to divine aboveness appear in the last section, "The Refutation of the apostates and the deniers of the divine attributes" (*al-radd ʿalā al-malāḥida wa'l-muʿaṭṭila*).[137] Ibn Qayyim al-Jawziyya quotes often from *Kitāb Maʿrifat al-Ḥadīth*, a manual of traditionalistic theology (*uṣūl al-dīn*, the principles of religion) by the Shāfiʿite Ḥadīth scholar and traditionalistic theologian Ibn al-Ṣalāḥ Abū ʿAmr ʿUthmān al-Shahrazūrī (d. 643/1245).[138] The following passage, heavily reliant on Ibn al-Ṣalāḥ, illustrates Ibn Qayyim al-Jawziyya's traditionalistic treatment of the topic of God's aboveness, and also his "copy-paste" composition strategy, drawing upon the Qurʾān, the Ḥadīth and the teachings of the early and later traditionists – in this case, the *tābiʿī* traditionist ʿAbd Allāh ibn al-Mubārak (d. 181/797) and the ninth-century Nīshāpūrī traditionist Ibn Khuzayma:

> Among His attributes, blessed and exalted is He, are His aboveness and His sitting on His throne by His own essence [*bi-dhātihⁱ*], as He described Himself in His book and as He is described in the words of His Prophet, peace be upon him, without asking how [*bi-lā kayfa*]. ... Then he [Ibn al-Ṣalāḥ] said that the scholars of the Islamic community and the renowned Imāms among the ancients and past generations had no disagreement concerning God's sitting on His throne and the fact that His throne was above the seven heavens. Ibn al-Ṣalāḥ then mentioned the saying attributed to ʿAbd Allāh ibn al-Mubārak: "we know for a fact that our Lord is above His seven heavens on His throne separated from His creation [*bāʾin min khalqihⁱ*]." [Ibn al-Ṣalāḥ] moved on to the words of Ibn Khuzayma: "Whoever refuses to affirm that God sits on His throne above His seven heavens is a heretic."[139]

Besides its obvious usage of Ḥadīth accounts, this passage combines two eminent yet not purely traditionalistic features. The first is its invocation of the *bi-lā kayfa* formula, which in the context may be understood to mean "without ascribing any modality to the attribute of aboveness." It thus connotes a more refined meaning than the literal sense of refraining from any kind of comments or interpretation, representing Ibn Qayyim al-Jawziyya's loyalty to the nuanced reading of the divine attributes articulated by Ibn Taymiyya in, for instance, his *al-ʿAqīda al-Wāsiṭiyya*.[140] The second feature is the declaration of God being "separated

---

137 Ibn Qayyim al-Jawziyya, ed. al-Muʿtaq 1988, 2:95.

138 Ibn Qayyim al-Jawziyya (*ibid.*, 2:183) refers to Ibn al-Ṣalāḥ as one of the leading scholars of the Shāfiʿites. The work has several titles: *Kitāb Maʿrifat Anwāʿ ʿIlm al-Ḥadīth*, *Muḳaddimāt Ibn al-Ṣalāḥ fī ʿUlūm al-Ḥadīth* and *ʿUlūm al-Ḥadīth* (see Robson 1971). The book has survived and was translated into English (Dickinson 2006), accompanied by a comprehensive introduction by the translator.

139 Ibn Qayyim al-Jawziyya, ed. al-Muʿtaq 1988, 2:183–184.

140 *Al-ʿAqīda al-Wāsiṭiyya* is one of the prominent creeds authored by Ibn Taymiyya, one to

from His creation," an advanced traditionalistic concept not drawn from Qur'ānic terminology. Ibn Qayyim al-Jawziyya uses the term *bā'in* to articulate the complete transcendence of God and eliminate any suspicion of anthropomorphism.[141] As we have seen, Ibn Taymiyya, too, used *bā'in* to indicate God's presence above the seventh heaven, not "everywhere," as the Muʿtazilites claimed. Ibn Qayyim al-Jawziyya thus alludes to a complex approach while hiding it under heavy layers of citations.

In a different section of *Ijtimāʿ al-Juyūsh*, Ibn Qayyim al-Jawziyya demonstrates a more intricate understanding of the concept of divine aboveness, as he turns to the "sayings of the later philosophers and the early wise men" (*al-falāsifa 'l-mutaqaddimīn wa'l-ḥukamā' 'l-awwaliyyin*). He quotes verbatim, almost without alteration or omission, from *al-Kashf ʿan Manāhij al-Adilla fī ʿAqā'id al-Milla*, by the illustrious philosopher Abu 'l-Walīd Ibn Rushd (Averroes, d. 595/1198).[142] In this treatise, which systematically refutes the opinions of Islamic theologians from across the spectrum, Ibn Rushd harshly criticizes the figurative interpretations of the Muʿtazilites and the later Ashʿarites,[143] using the same selection of Qur'ānic verses and *ḥadīth*s adduced by the traditionalistic authors,[144] such as *ḥadīth al-nuzūl*.[145] In his chapter about the divine attributes, and more specifically in a section about the divine directionality (*jiha*), Ibn Rushd claims that the people of *shariʿa* – i.e., the traditionalists – who affirm God's attribute of aboveness, which rests upon the literal meanings of the expressions in the

---

which he referred often during his trials in Cairo and Damascus. Most relevant to the divine attributes and the abovementioned passage from *Ijtimāʿ al-Juyūsh* is his statement: "Belief in God includes the belief in the attributes that God used in order to describe Himself in the Qur'ān and the attributes that His messenger Muḥammad used in order to describe Him, without any distortion of meaning [*taḥrīf*], denying [*taʿṭīl*], ascribing modality [*takyīf*], or comparing [*tamthīl*]." Ibn Taymiyya, ed. Laoust 1986:1; Jackson 1994:49–51.

141 This idea also appears in the polemical treatise *al-Radd ʿalā 'l-Zanādiqa wa'l-Jahmiyya*, ascribed to Aḥmad ibn Ḥanbal, in which the author attacks the Jahmiyya for arguing that "He is in everything, not contiguous, nor separated" (*ghayr mumās li-shay' wa-lā mubāyin minh*ᵘ). See Seale 1964:120–121. See also Abū Jaʿfar al-Ṭabarī's (d. 310/923) treatment of this issue in his interpretation of Q. 17:79: Al-Ṭabarī, ed. al-Turkī 2001, 15:51–52.

142 Ibn Rushd challenged the Ashʿarite, Muʿtazilite and traditionalistic conceptions of God's attributes and accused the respective schools of using superficial methods. As an alternative, Ibn Rushd revived the peripatetic Aristotelian tradition in Islam. Only in the thirteenth century did Ashʿarite scholars such as Fakhr al-Dīn al-Rāzī and Sayf al-Dīn al-Āmidī (d. 631/1233) substantially develop the Ashʿarite arguments, spurring a revival of Ashʿarite thought and its flourishing for a period. Özervarli 2010:78–79.

143 Ibn Rushd, ed. al-Jābirī 1998:123–124, 149–150. See also Abrahamov 1995:377–378, note 48.

144 Ibn Rushd, *ibid.*:145.

145 *Ibid.*:140.

scriptures (*ẓawāhir al-sharʿ*), are better than the Muʿtazilites and Ashʿarites who deny it. Unfortunately, he laments, the use of figurative interpretation (*taʾwīl*) is widespread among the Muslims. The textual evidence undoubtedly indicates that God is in heaven, along with His angels. The rationalistic approach denies God's aboveness for fear of ascribing to Him a physical place (*makān*), which might lead to affirming His corporeality (*jismiyya*). However, says Ibn Rushd, this is entirely erroneous, for God's aboveness does not require His corporeality. In fact, the common perception of many people that "whatever exists is a body, and whatever does not exist is not a body" (*huwa mawjūdun huwa jismun, lā mawjūdun laysa bi-jismin*) is false. God exists and He is not a body, and where He is, is not a place.[146] The definition of a place is that a body can be in it.[147] The surface of the last sphere of the world (*saṭḥu ākhiri ajsāmi ʾl-ʿālami*) is no place, because a body cannot be there. God is therefore in no place, and He is not a body; however, He has directionality (*jiha*).[148]

While Ibn Rushd proved this last conviction using the Aristotelian theory of place,[149] what interested Ibn Qayyim al-Jawziyya was the concluding remark in Ibn Rushd's philosophical defense of the concept of God's aboveness:

> According to the opinions of the ancients and the past generations, and according to [the teachings] of bygone religions, this "location" [*mawḍiʿ*, where God exists] is the abode of the spiritual beings, by which they meant God and the angels. This "location" is not a place [*laysa bi-makānin*], and time does not hold possession of it. Everything which is confined to the [dimensions] of place and time is doomed to perdition ... I have clarified for you that confirming [the divine] directionality is obligatory according to the religious laws and human reason.[150]

Ibn Qayyim al-Jawziyya's observation on this statement by Ibn Rushd reads as though it were followed by an exclamation mark: "These are the very words of the philosopher of Islam, who was better acquainted with the teachings of the philosophers, more privy to their content and more accurate in citing them than Ibn Sīnā."[151] Ibn Qayyim al-Jawziyya's eagerness to conscript even elements of Islamic philosophical thought in his quest to confirm God's aboveness is striking, especially in a traditionally framed work like *Ijtimāʿ al-Juyūsh*. It marks a shift in

---

146 Ibn Qayyim al-Jawziyya, ed. al-Muʿtaq 1988, 2:324; Ibn Rushd, ed. al-Jābirī 1998:146.
147 Ibn Rushd, *ibid.*:146; this sentence is omitted by Ibn Qayyim al-Jawziyya.
148 Ibn Qayyim al-Jawziyya, ed. al-Muʿtaq 1988, 2:324; Ibn Rushd, *ibid.*:146.
149 Arnaldez 1971, 3:914.
150 Ibn Qayyim al-Jawziyya, ed. al-Muʿtaq 1988, 2:324–325; Ibn Rushd, ed. al-Jābirī 1998:147.
151 Ibn Qayyim al-Jawziyya, *ibid.*, 2:325–326.

the development of Islamic traditionalism: This is not the puristic traditionalism of al-Dhahabī, but a much subtler form of traditionalism that embraces portions of the philosophical teachings that comply with its worldview.

Ibn Qayyim al-Jawziyya's view on the essentiality of the attribute of aboveness, meaning that God is really above, is further elaborated in *al-Ṣawāʿiq al-Mursala*.[152] This later, large-scale and more mature work expresses the author's coherent critique of the Muʿtazilites and the Ashʿarites, and in particular of their readings of the anthropomorphic expressions in the Qurʾān.[153] In the course of his concise and highly organized discussion, Ibn Qayyim al-Jawziyya examines the rationalistic reading strategy of *taʾwīl*, and more specifically the device of *majāz* (metaphor, assigning any non-literal meaning to the text), and systematically refutes them.[154] He adopts Ibn Taymiyya's basic analysis, according to which the division of the language into *ḥaqīqa* (literal meaning) and *majāz* (non-literal interpreted meaning) is alien to the ancient – and hence authentic – science of Arabic grammar.[155] In Ibn Qayyim al-Jawziyya's mind, there was no obligatory theoretical basis to the *majāz* concept. All of God's attributes were to be understood in the sense of *ḥaqīqa*, because they denoted an essential reality; God's aboveness must be understood in the traditional, essential meaning of "He *is* literally situated above all."

Ibn Qayyim al-Jawziyya's discussion of the divine attribute of aboveness in *al-Ṣawāʿiq* is based on two fundamentals: the literal and essential meaning of

---

152 *Al-Ṣawāʿiq* is best read alongside its popular abridgement (*Mukhtaṣar*) by Ibn al-Mawṣilī (ed. al-ʿAlawī 2004). Preacher (*khaṭīb*) of the Grand Mosque in Damascus and a prosperous bookseller, Ibn al-Mawṣilī (d. 774/1372) had in his possession the full version of *al-Ṣawaʿiq*. His abridgement is considered reliable, and it contains missing and crucial portions of *al-Ṣawaʿiq* that were lost. Qadhi 2010:137.

153 For the monograph's main outline, see Qadhi 2010; Krawietz 2006:31.

154 For Ibn Qayyim al-Jawziyya's discussion of *taʾwīl* and *majāz* in *al-Ṣawāʿiq al-Mursala*, see Ovadia (Ben-Moshe) 2012:38–55, 67–81. He discusses *taʾwīl* in *al-Ṣawāʿiq*, ed. al-Dakhīl Allāh 1998, 1:175–398 and 2:399–631. The separate discussion of the negation of *majāz* appears in the refutation of one of the rationalistic fundamentals, found only in the abridgement: Ibn al-Mawṣilī, ed. al-ʿAlawī 2004, 2:690–706. For Ibn Qayyim al-Jawziyya's linguistic contribution and the development of the idea of *majāz*, see Belhaj 2010.

155 In this Ibn Qayyim al-Jawziyya seems to have relied heavily on Ibn Taymiyya's *Kitāb al-Īmān*. For the concept of *majāz* as articulated there, see Heinrichs 1984:115–118, which includes a translation of several passages in *Kitāb al-Īmān*. Ibn Qayyim al-Jawziyya's claim that *majāz* was developed by the rationalistic Muʿtazilite School in the third/ninth century to address the anthropomorphic texts is corroborated by several studies of Muʿtazilite texts: Modarressi 1986; Versteegh 1993; Gleave 2012:22–23, 146; and Vishanoff 2011:194. These studies do not address Ibn Qayyim al-Jawziyya's thought.

God's attributes, and their perfection.[156] He again opens his systematic investigation of the attribute of aboveness with numerous citations of Qurʾānic verses and *ḥadīths*. As a starting point, he emphasizes the importance of the customary use of the preposition "above" (*fawq*^{a}) in Arabic. Against the Ashʿarite understanding of God's aboveness as a metaphor for God's superiority and great strength, Ibn Qayyim al-Jawziyya claims that the Arabic language does not allow for such a figurative interpretation of divine aboveness:

> The literal and essential meaning of aboveness [*ḥaqīqat al-fawqiyya*] is that a thing is higher than other things. However, the Jahmiyya[157] falsely claim that it is a metaphor [*majāz*] for a superiority of status and strength, as is customarily said: Gold is above silver [*al-dhahab*^{u} *fawq*^{a} *'l-fiḍḍa*^{ti}, i.e., in value], and: the Emir is above his deputy [*wa'l-amīr*^{u} *fawq*^{a} *nāʾibih*^{i}, i.e., in rank]. Even if this were true with regard to God, denying the essentiality of His aboveness and forcing an interpretation according to the *majāz* on the word *fawqiyya* is wrong. ... When the speaker says: "gold is above silver," the context [*al-siyāq*] and the conventions of the language lead to the understanding of two things: that they are both in the same place [*makān*], and that they are different in their status [*makāna*]. Thus, the discourse [*al-khiṭāb*] refers to what the listener knows and what is not ambiguous for him. Is there a similar linguistic convention regarding God's aboveness, which takes into consideration such an understanding of the listener? ... Linguistic conventions [*ʿahd*], human instincts [*fiṭar*], human minds [*ʿuqūl*], religious law [*sharāʾiʿ*] and all of God's revealed books oppose [the use of *majāz*]. God Himself [*bi-dhātih*^{i}; by His own essence] is above the world. The discourse about His aboveness emanates from what is firmly established in the human instincts, the human mind and the books of revelation.[158]

The linguistic convention according to which the word *fawq*^{a}, "above," is a preposition in Arabic provides the basic argument that allows Ibn Qayyim al-Jawziyya to invalidate the rationalistic argument for a figurative understanding of God's aboveness. Ibn Qayyim al-Jawziyya expresses the traditionalistic view that God is above the world, and yet this passage provides a splendid example of the distinctive approach, shared by both Ibn Qayyim al-Jawziyya and Ibn Taymiyya, of combining rationalistic argumentations with the sacred texts.[159] Ibn Qayyim al-Jawziyya employs the scholastic devices of kalāmic speculative theology for the purpose of negating the kalāmic worldview. This is not a standard traditionalistic method of argumentation but an advanced technique practiced only by Ibn Taymiyya. Compared to *Ijtimāʿ al-Juyūsh* and to the writings of the traditionalists

---

156 Ibn al-Mawṣilī, ed. al-ʿAlawī 2004, 3:1060–1100.
157 On the Jahmiyya, see above, notes 47 and 137.
158 Ibn al-Mawṣilī, ed. al-ʿAlawī 2004, 3:1061–1062.
159 For Ibn Taymiyya's approach, see Abrahamov 1992:257, 260–267.

surveyed in this article, *al-Ṣawāʿiq* represents a quantum leap forward towards rationalized Ḥadīth-based argumentation.

Stressing the principle he had previously established regarding the correct and logical use of common figures of speech, Ibn Qayyim al-Jawziyya goes on to point out that ascribing allegorical meaning to God's attribute of aboveness is simply unreasonable, in that it is incommensurate with any familiar conventions of speech. A verse from classical Arabic poetry is adduced to bolster this claim:

> Had this *majāz* been declared with respect to God, it would have been repugnant. *Majāz* can be used only with respect to two [things] that have a similar or close status, when one of them is better than the other. When the two [things] are by no means close to one another, [using *majāz*] is incorrect. Therefore, it is absolutely repugnant to say: A piece of jewelry is above an onion skin. If you say this, every reasonable person will laugh because of the tremendous contrast between these two [things]. The contrast between the Creator and His creation is far more tremendous, as the poem goes: "Why, don't you know that a sword loses its value / when [its seller] says: 'This sword is sharper than a stick'?"[160]

Taking his critique yet another step forward, Ibn Qayyim al-Jawziyya objects to the extensive application of *majāz* to all the Qurʾānic verses referring to God's aboveness:

> Neither in the Qurʾān nor in the Ḥadīth is God praised for being better than His throne [*al-ʿarsh*]. Neither in the Qurʾān nor in the Ḥadīth is it stated that His status is above the status of the throne, and that He is better than the heavens, the throne or the footstool [*kursī*]. Such [an expression] appears in the Qurʾān only as an answer to whoever worshipped other gods with Him and made them the associates of God in His rule. God clarified that He is better than those gods, when He said: "Who is better? God, or those they set up as partners with Him?" (Q. 27:59) "Would many diverse gods be better than God the One?" (Q. 12:39) However, nowhere in the Qurʾān does He commence His speech by praising Himself as being better than the heavens, the throne or the footstool. It is incorrect to link this example to these verses. What is appropriate when arguing with an opponent (i. e., the idol-worshippers) and defying the opponent's repugnant arguments is totally inappropriate in a different context. Using *ilzām*-argumentation, by which one forces the opponent to accept your conclusive argument, is totally inappropriate in a different context. Only a complete ignoramus will deny this.[161]

Interestingly enough, here Ibn Qayyim al-Jawziyya agrees with the rationalistic view that, in some cases, God's attribute of aboveness can be interpreted figura-

---

160 Ibn al-Mawṣilī, ed. al-ʿAlawī 2004, 3:1062. We were unable to identify the source of the verse.
161 *Ibid.*, 3:1062–1063.

tively as a supremacy of status. Nonetheless, in his opinion, such a use of *majāz* is permitted only within the framework of theological debate. In addition, Ibn Qayyim al-Jawziyya demonstrates his familiarity with the terminology of *kalām* by mentioning one of the most significant tools of the theological debate, namely, the *ilzām* method of argumentation. *Ilzām* is aimed to compel an ideological opponent to confess an opinion expressing an absurdity, a heretical view or a contradiction of his own claims, by deducing it from his initial point of departure.[162] By so invoking it, Ibn Qayyim al-Jawziyya – to a degree – embraces the rationalistic methodology.

After exhausting the Qur'ānic materials, Ibn Qayyim al-Jawziyya adds dozens of *ḥadīth*s to his cumulative evidence. He seemingly deploys every *ḥadīth* within reach to prove God's essential and physical aboveness. Like his traditionalistic predecessors, he pays less attention to the credibility of the Ḥadīth transmitters, treating all of them as equally binding.[163] His deployment of "the *ḥadīth* of the mountain goats," with its particularized depictions, demonstrates Ibn Qayyim al-Jawziyya's argumentation against *majāz*. After quoting the *ḥadīth*, with its seas, heavens, mountain goats and heavenly throne, Ibn Qayyim al-Jawziyya exclaims:

> Please consider the concept of aboveness as it appears in the wording of this *ḥadīth*. Is there in its content any intention to express a superiority of status [*fawqiyyat*ᵘ *'l-rutba*ᵗⁱ]?[164]

The final section of Ibn Qayyim al-Jawziyya's refutation of God's metaphorical aboveness illustrates the distinctiveness of his own voice. His speculative argumentation runs as follows: God's aboveness is one of His attributes of perfection (*ṣifat kamāl*). As the Creator of all beings, God is the most perfect essence; hence, only attributes that express absolute perfection with no hint of deficiency (*naqṣ*) can be ascribed to Him, and so, as the sole source of perfection, God is necessarily more perfect than His creation. Consequently, God's attributes are more perfect than those of the creatures He created. Several attributes that do not denote perfection in the creatures denote perfection in God. Their absence would necessarily entail imperfection in God. Thus, God necessarily sees and hears perfectly; otherwise, He would have been considered essentially "unsee-

---

162 See above, note 77.
163 Noteworthy are sections (*wujūh*) 10–13 of Ibn Qayyim al-Jawziyya's discussion, which contain an enormous number of citations, most of them drawn from the six canonical Ḥadīth collections (*al-nuṣūṣ al-shar'iyya*). Ibn al-Mawṣilī, ed. al-ʿAlawī 2004, 3:1064–1085.
164 *Ibid.* Ibn Qayyim al-Jawziyya also cites the *ḥadīth* of the mountain goats in *Ijtimāʿ al-Juyūsh* (ed. al-Muʿtaq 1988, 2:232).

ing" or "unhearing."[165] Ibn Qayyim al-Jawziyya uses this concept, which is rooted in Taymiyyan thought,[166] to affirm his view that God's ultimate aboveness, i. e., the fact that He is essentially above His creation, necessarily entails His absolute perfection:

> Were God not described by the aboveness of His entity [*bi-fawqiyyat*ⁱ *'l-dhāt*ⁱ] in addition to His existence through Himself [*qā'im*ᵘⁿ *bi-nafsih*ⁱ] and His aloofness from the world, He would have been described by the opposite attribute, because the recipient of an attribute [*al-qābil*ᵘ *li'l-shay'*ⁱ] must possess either an attribute or its opposite. The opposite of "aboveness" is "belowness" [*sufūl*], and it is a completely reprehensible attribute, because it is the abode of Iblīs and his soldiers. ... Altitude and aboveness are attributes of perfection [with regard to God]. They do not imply deficiency or ascribe anything inappropriate that one should be very careful not to say about Him. They do not contradict the Qur'ān, the Sunna or the consensus of the Islamic community. Therefore, negating their literal meaning is a false deed.[167]

Ibn Qayyim al-Jawziyya claims in this passage that his theology is identical to that of the traditionalists; however, his weave of arguments, in this case as in others, is imbued with rationalism. Ibn Qayyim al-Jawziyya's method is to rationalize the ultra-traditionalistic view of God's aboveness by deploying every argument he can access, from the linguistic terminology of the Muʿtazilites, which echoes in the above passage, to the teachings of Ibn Rushd.

Further Observations and Concluding Remarks

Nearly four centuries separate Ibn Khuzayma's *Kitāb al-Tawḥīd* and Ibn Qayyim al-Jawziyya's *Ijtimāʿ al-Juyūsh*, and over that period Islamic traditionalism came to embody many ideas. Ibn Khuzayma's simplistic and straightforward understanding of the Ḥadīth material does not resemble Ibn Qayyim al-Jawziyya's willingness to embrace the rationalized arguments of Ibn Rushd; nevertheless, both scholars wished to reach the same outcome, namely, to establish that God's aboveness, directionality and sitting on His throne are elements of the irrefutable Islamic creed. When Ibn Khuzayma's *Kitāb al-Tawḥīd* is juxtaposed to Shams al-Dīn al-Dhahabī's *Risalāt al-ʿArsh*, the tenth-century Ibn Khuzayma seems more

---

165 Ibn al-Mawṣilī, ed. al-ʿAlawī 2004, 3:1094.
166 Ibn Taymiyya develops this idea in his *al-Akmaliyya*, which is discussed in Hoover 2007:62–67. For God's laughter as an attribute of perfection according to Ibn Taymiyya, see Holtzman 2010:194–199.
167 Ibn al-Mawṣilī, ed. al-ʿAlawī 2004, 3:1094.

daring than the fourteenth-century al-Dhahabī. In turn, Ibn Qayyim al-Jawziyya's *Ijtimāʿ al-Juyūsh* contains rather unexpected notions when compared with Ibn Khuzayma's *Kitāb al-Tawḥīd* and Shams al-Dīn al-Dhahabī's *Risalāt al-ʿArsh*. Still, there is a common thread to all three works: As products of Islamic traditionalism, they all unequivocally affirm God's aboveness by deploying a massive number of citations from the mainstream traditionalistic curriculum. Ibn Khuzayma and al-Dhahabī's waterproof traditionalism did not allow the penetration of ideas alien to the Ḥadīth material, while Ibn Qayyim al-Jawziyya's eclecticism to a degree reconciled rationalistic ideas with hard-core traditionalism.

Below the surface of Islamic traditionalism flowed undercurrents that subverted the comprehensive demand that the sacred texts of the Qurʾān or the Ḥadīth be accepted "without inquiring into the nature of the divine attributes," or rather, "without asking how" (*bi-lā kayfa*). First, people kept on asking questions. Ibn Taymiyya's and Ibn Qayyim al-Jawziyya's nuanced descriptions of God's aboveness were addressed to a sophisticated audience, which was not satisfied with the simplicity of the older traditionalistic arguments but was simultaneously unwilling to reject the old doctrines, as the later Ashʿarites did. The impression given by Ibn Taymiyya's response and Ibn Qayyim al-Jawziyya's treatises is that this audience had a certain degree of familiarity with philosophy, geography, geometry and rationalistic theology. This familiarity encouraged curiosity, and curiosity encouraged questions.

Second, in fourteenth-century Damascus even an ultra-traditionalist like al-Dhahabī could not approve of the rigid approach of the early traditionalists. In *Siyar Aʿlām al-Nubalāʾ*, after citing Ibn Khuzayma's call to kill the heretic who does not affirm God's aboveness, al-Dhahabī remarks:

> He who affirms that [God sits on His throne above His seven heavens] because he believes in the Qurʾān and the Prophetic Ḥadīth, and because he entrusts the meaning of these texts to God and His Prophet, and because he does not go into the figurative interpretation [*taʾwīl*], is the truly obedient Muslim. He who rejects this [article of faith], because he is not familiar with what the Qurʾān and the Ḥadīth say, is simply negligent [in matters of faith]. However, God forgives him, because God does not oblige every Muslim to remember by heart what is written in the scriptures. But he who denies [the veracity of this article of faith] when he is familiar with what the scriptures say, and does not follow in the footsteps of the ancients and past generations, and presents sophistic argumentations regarding the sacred texts – his matter is entrusted to God. We ask for God's protection from misguidance and false convictions![168]

---

168 Al-Dhahabī, ed. Al-Arnāʾūṭ et al. 1985, 14:373–374.

Al-Dhahabī, one of the most esteemed traditionists of his generation, here shows understanding for laymen whose education in dogmatic matters is lacking, while demonstrating no compassion for the sophisticated theologians who dare argue about the content of the scriptures. Though his intention in this passage is to criticize the place occupied by Rāziyyan thought in the hearts of the Damascene ruling elite, he shows unexpected tolerance, to the point of diminishing the importance of the concept, in remarking that "Even though what Ibn Khuzayma said [i. e., that the denier of God's aboveness should be executed] was true, his words were blunt and intolerable in the eyes of most of the scholars of later generations."[169]

Al-Dhahabī's pragmatic approach was shaped by politico-theological factors, particularly the Damascene Ashʿarites' embrace of Fakhr al-Dīn al-Rāzī's doctrine against God's essential aboveness and directionality (as demonstrated in the trials of Ibn Taymiyya). Obviously, one could not call for the execution of the entire Ashʿarite school in Damascus. Only idealists like Ibn Taymiyya and Ibn Qayyim al-Jawziyya felt compelled to confront the later Ashʿarite concept of God's aboveness; pragmatists like al-Dhahabī preferred to remain backstage and advance their ultra-traditionalistic worldview simply by teaching the Ḥadīth material or writing Ḥadīth compilations, rather than by means of public theological debates. Moreover, who could actually say what God's aboveness meant, when the traditionalistic arena was teeming with all kinds of notions about God's exact place, whether in the universe or outside of it?

As the selection of scholarly views and approaches on God's aboveness discussed above has shown, there was a gradual and systematic process of exchange of ideas between the ultra-traditionalists and the rationalists. These ideas, seriously and meticulously examined in different circles, transcended the boundaries of "traditionalism" and "rationalism"; rationalistic ideas were mirrored in the traditionalistic discourse, and vice versa. Just as the various rationalistic theologians made their inquiries into the divine aboveness, an idea drawn directly from the Qur'ān and the Ḥadīth, the traditionalistic theologians absorbed a number of rationalistic concepts and modes of argumentation and integrated them into their own discourse. The diffusion of ideas was not unidirectional; however, it seems that the party that was more willing to absorb new ideas was the traditionalistic one.

Ibn Khuzayma's simplistic traditionalism was nothing like the complex traditionalism of scholars of the Mamluk period, who were well read in the writings of their rationalistic predecessors. Even an ultra-traditionalist like Ibn Qayyim al-Jawziyya was attracted in his youth to the charms of Ashʿarite *kalām*.[170] Another

---

169 *Ibid.*, 14:374.
170 Holtzman 2009:209.

case in point is the gradual shift of Jalāl al-Dīn al-Suyūṭī (d. 911/1505) from adopting some of the kalāmic hermeneutical devices to neglecting them altogether. This Shāfiʿite polymath was forty-nine when he completed his *al-Durr al-Manthūr fī al-Tafsīr bi'l-Maʾthūr*, a massive Qurʾān commentary that relies solely on Ḥadīth material,[171] leaving no room for personal observations of the commentator.[172] However, in the earliest stages of his scholarly career, al-Suyūṭī had willingly adopted *majāz* and applied it to some of the divine attributes. In his manual on Qurʾānic sciences, *al-Itqān fī ʿUlūm al-Qurʾān*, which he authored at the age of thirty-four, he claimed that God's aboveness is "aboveness without direction" (*al-ʿulūw^u min ghayr^i jihat^in*) and does not denote "a physical place" (*al-ʿulūw^u al-makānī*).[173] In completing his part in the *Tafsīr al-Jalālayn* at age twenty-one, al-Suyūṭī's use of *majāz* was even more ubiquitous:

> Q. 6:61 "He is the Supreme Master [*wa-huw^a 'l-qāhir^u*]," meaning, He is superior [*mustaʿliyy^an*] over His servants ...[174]
> Q. 16:50 "They fear," meaning the angels, ... "their Lord above them," meaning the state of their Lord, which is higher than their [state] in superiority [*ʿāliyy^an ʿalayhim bi'l-qahr^i*] ...[175]

Al-Suyūṭī's strictly traditionalistic approach at the peak of his scholarly career did not lead him to repudiate his earlier works, although he had obviously embraced the Ashʿarite *majāz* in them. In his autobiography, al-Suyūṭī mentions *al-Itqān* as the most prominent and widely distributed of his works.[176] Al-Suyūṭī's case reflects the ease with which rationalistic argumentations flourished in the traditionalistic arena, and with which these apparently conflicting approaches could coexist in a single author's intellectual heritage.

In this article, we have shown that the real "litmus paper" testing the diffusion of ideas between Islamic traditionalistic stances and rationalistic ones (and vice versa) in the debates about God's aboveness, throne and directionality was the contestants' perception of the Ḥadīth material. The rationalists – both Muʿtazilites and Karrāmites – were familiar with this material; however, they used it rather selectively and unsystematically. Whether they supported the notion of

171 On the chronology of al-Suyūṭī's works, see Nuna 2014:14.
172 For the connection between *al-Durr al-Manthūr* and the views of Ibn Taymiyya on Qurʾānic exegesis, see Saleh 2010.
173 Al-Suyūṭī, ed. Ibrāhīm 1974, 3:22. Al-Suyūṭī refers to the verses: "He is the Supreme Master over [i.e., above] His subjects" (Q. 6:61), and "they fear their Lord above them" (Q. 16:50).
174 Al-Maḥallī and Al-Suyūṭī, ed. al-Marʿashlī 1999:135.
175 *Ibid.*:272.
176 Nuna 2014:22.

God's aboveness (the Karrāmites), or negated it completely (the Muʿtazilites), they were more interested in kalāmic argumentations. The Muʿtazilites, with their outspoken contempt for the *ḥadīth*s that presented elaborate cosmologies, focused on refining their ability to read the relevant Qurʾānic verses and rarely bothered with the Ḥadīth material. As for the Ashʿarites, they applied their advanced reading methodology to the Ḥadīth material, employing the same method of *majāz* that they used for the anthropomorphic verses in the Qurʾān. However, the Ḥadīth did not take center stage in their discussions, and the Ashʿarites did not develop a methodology for evaluating its content. The case of Imām al-Ḥaramayn al-Juwaynī, who checked the credibility of the Ḥadīth material while promoting his views against God's aboveness, is rather exceptional. Most of the Ashʿarites neglected the Ḥadīth material and occupied themselves with developing their scholastic argumentation. In this respect, Abu ʾl-Ḥasan al-Ashʿarī, who was well read in the Ḥadīth material and addressed it seriously, appears to be more a traditionalist than a rationalist.

The traditionalists, or the ultra-traditionalists, are the most interesting party in this scenario. In the ninth and tenth centuries, they allowed the penetration of weak *ḥadīth*s into their curriculum. They also allowed a certain degree of flexibility in discussing the contents of these *ḥadīth*s, although "without asking how," and they of course used them as raw material for new creeds. In the fourteenth century, the former weak *ḥadīth*s became a legitimate part of the traditionalistic curriculum. Zealous Ḥadīth scholars like al-Dhahabī and al-Suyūṭī (in the last phase of his career) concentrated on compiling the numerous Ḥadīth versions, but they dared not discuss the material or even paraphrase it. Traditionalists like Ibn Taymiyya and Ibn Qayyim al-Jawziyya represent a completely different approach: They examined the content of these *ḥadīth*s, discussed them and based their credo on them, while employing a rationalistic terminology. Most of all, both Ibn Taymiyya and Ibn Qayyim al-Jawziyya applied an advanced reading methodology to the texts, at least whenever this methodology was deemed feasible. The traditionalists were a strong group whose voice was heard in many venues and who established a firm base of support by spreading the knowledge of Ḥadīth among laymen.

In an atmosphere of Ḥadīth learning, the Ashʿarites, with their limited knowledge of the material, their vocabulary of logical argumentation and their insistence on negating God's aboveness, seemed remote and detached, both from their traditionalistic peers and from the general religious atmosphere. The scholarship of the Ashʿarites clashed with the natural religious feeling of the society in which they lived. The debate over God's aboveness is one example of this clash. Against the backdrop of the cold relationship between the Ashʿarites and the laymen, the ultra-traditionalists freely developed their rationalized Ḥadīth-based argumentations.

References

Primary Sources

(Pseudo-)ʿAbd al-Jabbār ibn Aḥmad (d. 415/1024). *Sharḥ al-Uṣūl al-Khamsa*, ed. ʿAbd al-Karīm ʿUthmān. 1416/1996. Cairo: Maktabat Wahba.

Al-Ājurrī, Abū Bakr Muḥammad ibn al-Ḥusayn ibn ʿAbd Allāh (d. 360/971). *Kitāb al-Sharīʿa*, ed. Muʾassasat al-Rayyān editorial board. 1421/2000. Beirut: Muʾassasat al-Rayyān.

Al-Albānī, Muḥammad Nāṣir al-Dīn (d. 1419/1999). *Kitāb al-Sunna lil-Ḥāfiẓ Abī Bakr ʿAmr ibn Abī ʿĀṣim al-Ḍaḥḥāk ibn Mukhallad al-Shaybānī* [d. 287/900] *wa-Maʿahu Ẓilāl al-Janna fī Takhrīj al-Sunna*. 1400/1980. Beirut–Damascus: al-Maktab al-Islāmī.

Al-Ashʿarī, Abu ʾl-Ḥasan ʿAlī ibn Ismāʿīl (d. 324/935). *Al-Ibāna ʿan Uṣūl al-Diyāna*. n. d. Beirut: Dār Ibn Zaydūn.

—.*Kitāb Maqālāt al-Islāmiyyin wa-'Khtilāf al-Muṣallīn*, ed. Hellmut Ritter. 1382/1963. Wiesbaden: Franz Steiner Verlg GMBH.

Al-Baghdādī, Abū Manṣūr ʿAbd al-Qāhir ibn Ṭāhir ibn Muḥammad (d. 429/1037). *Al-Farq bayna al-Firaq wa-Bayān al-Firqa al-Nājiya Minhum*, ed. Muḥammad ʿUthmān al-Khashin. n. d. Cairo: Maktabat Ibn Sīnā.

Al-Dārimī, ʿUthmān ibn Saʿīd (d. between 280–282/894–895). *Al-Radd ʿalā al-Jahmiyya*, ed. Badr al-BaDr. 1405/1985. Kuwait: al-Dār al-Salafiyya.

Al-Dhahabī, Shams al-Dīn Muḥammad ibn Aḥmad ibn ʿUthmān (d. ca. 748/1348). *Siyar Aʿlām al-Nubalāʾ*, ed. Shuʿayb al-Arnāʾūṭ et al. 1405/1985. Beirut: Muʾassasat al-Risāla.

—. *Al-Muʿjam al-Mukhtaṣṣ bi'l-Muḥaddithīn*, ed. Muḥammad al-Ḥabīb al-Hīla. 1408/1988. Taʾif: Maktabat al-Ṣiddīq.

—. *Tārīkh al-Islām wa-Ṭabaqāt 'l-Mashāhīr wa'l-Aʿlām*, ed. ʿUmar ʿAbd al-Salām Tadmurī. 1410–1421/1990–2000. Beirut: Dār al-Kitāb al-ʿArabī.

—. *Kitāb al-ʿArsh*, ed. Muḥammad ibn Khalīfa ibn ʿAlī al-Tamīmī. 1424/2003. Medina: ʿImādat al-Baḥth al-ʿIlmī bil-Jāmiʿa al-Islāmiyya.

Al-Ḥākim al-Nīsābūrī, Abū ʿAbd Allāh Muḥammad ibn ʿAbd Allāh (d. 405/1014). *Maʿrifat ʿUlūm al-Ḥadīth wa-Kamiyyat Ajnāsihi*, ed. Aḥmad ibn Fāris al-Salūm. 1424/2003. Beirut: Dār Ibn Ḥazm.

Ibn Fūrak, Abū Bakr Muḥammad ibn 'l-Ḥasan (d. 406/1015). *Mushkil al-Ḥadīth wa-Bayānuhu*, ed. with comments by Daniel Gimaret. 2003. Damascus: Institut Francais d'etudes arabes de Damas.

Ibn Ḥazm, Abū Muḥammad ʿAlī ibn Aḥmad ibn Saʿīd (d. 456/1064). *Al-Faṣl fī al-Milal wa'l-Ahwāʾ wa'l-Niḥal*, ed. Muḥammad Ibrāhīm Naṣr and ʿAbd al-Raḥmān ʿUmayra. 1416/1996. Beirut: Dār al-Jīl.

Ibn Kathīr, ʿImād al-Dīn Abū al-Fidāʾ Ismaʿīl (d. 774/1373). *Al-Bidāya wa'l-Nihāya fī al-Tārīkh*, ed. ʿAbd Allāh ibn ʿAbd al-Muḥsin al-Turkī. 1424/2003. [Cairo]: Dār Hajar li'l-Ṭibāʿa wa'l-Nashr wa'l-Tawzīʿ wa'l-Iʿlān.

Ibn Khuzayma, Abū Bakr Muḥammad ibn Isḥāq (d. 311/935). *Kitāb al-Tawḥīd wa-Ithbāt Ṣifāt al-Rabb ʿAzza wa-Jalla*, ed. ʿAbd al-ʿAzīz ibn Ibrāhīm al-Shahwān. 1408/1988. Riyadh: Dār al-Rushd.

Ibn al-Mawṣilī, Shams al-Dīn Abū ʿAbd Allāh Muḥammad ibn Muḥammad (d. 774/1372). *Mukhtaṣar al-Ṣawāʿiq al-Mursala ʿalā al-Jahmiyya wa'l-Muʿaṭṭila*, ed. Al-Ḥasan ibn ʿAbd al-Raḥman al-ʿAlawī. 2004. Riyadh: Aḍwāʾ al-Salaf.

Ibn Qayyim al-Jawziyya Shams al-Dīn ibn Abī Bakr Muḥammad (d. 751/1350). *Ijtimāʿ al-Juyūsh al-Islāmiyya ʿalā Ghazw al-Muʿaṭṭila wa'l-Jahmiyya*, ed. ʿAwwād ʿAbd Allāh Muḥammad al-Muʿtaq. 1408/1988. Riyadh: Maṭābiʿ al-Farazdaq al-Tijāriyya.
—. *Al-Ṣawāʿiq al-Mursala ʿalā al-Jahmiyya wa'l-Muʿaṭṭila*, ed. ʿAlī al-Dakhīl Allah. 1418/1998. Riyadh: Dār al-ʿĀṣima.
Ibn Qutayba, Abū Muḥammad ʿAbd Allāh ibn Muslim ibn Qutayba (d. 276/889). *Ta'wīl Mukhtalif al-Ḥadīth*, ed. Muḥammad Muḥyī al-Dīn al-Aṣfar. 1419/1999. Beirut–Dha: al-Maktab al-Islāmī–Mu'assasat al-Ishrāq.
Ibn Rushd, Abu 'l-Walīd Muḥammad ibn Aḥmad (d. 595/1198). *Al-Kashf ʿan Manāhij al-Adilla fī ʿAqā'id al-Milla* (Silsilat al-Turāth al-Falsafī al-ʿArabī: Mu'allafāt Ibn Rushd, 2), ed. Muḥammad ʿĀbid al-Jābirī. 1998. Beirut: Markaz Dirāsāt al-Waḥda al-ʿArabiyya.
Ibn Taymiyya, Taqī 'l-Dīn Abū 'l-ʿAbbās Aḥmad ibn ʿAbd 'l-Ḥalīm (d. 728/1328). *Majmūʿat al-Rasā'il al-Kubrā*. 1385/1966. Cairo: Maktabat wa-Maṭbaʿat Muḥammad ʿAlī Ṣubayḥ-wa-Awlādihi.
—. *Al-ʿAqīda al-Wāsiṭiyya*, ed. Henri Laoust, *La profession de foi d'Ibn Taymiyya: Texte, traduction et commentaire de la Wāsiṭiyya*. 1986. Paris: Geuther.
—. *Majmūʿat al-Fatāwā li-Shaykh al-Islām Taqī al-Dīn Aḥmad Ibn Taymīyah al-Ḥarrānī*, ed. ʿĀmir al-Jazzār and Anwar al-Bāz. 1419/1998. Riyadh–al-Mansura: Dār al-Wafā'–Maktabat al-ʿAbīkān.
Al-Isfarāyīnī, Abu 'l-Muẓaffar (d. 471/1079). *Al-Tabṣīr fī al-Dīn wa-Tamyīz al-Firqa al-Nājiya ʿan al-Firaq al-Hālikīn*, ed. Kamāl Yūsuf al-Ḥūt. 1403/1983. Beirut: ʿĀlam al-Kutub.
Al-Juwaynī, Abū Muḥammad ʿAbd Allāh ibn Yūsuf (d. 438/1047). *Risāla fī Ithbāt al-Istiwā' wa'l-Fawqiyya*, ed. Aḥmad Maʿādh ibn ʿUlwān Ḥaqqī. 1419/1998. Riyadh: Dār Ṭuwayq lil-Nashr wa'l-Tawzīʿ.
Al-Juwaynī, Imām al-Ḥaramayn (d. 478/1085). *Kitāb al-Irshād ilā Qawāṭiʿ al-Adilla fī Uṣūl al-Iʿtiqād*, ed. Muḥammad Yūsuf Mūsā and ʿAlī ʿAbd al-Munʿim ʿAbd al-Ḥamīd. 1369/1950. Cairo: Maktabat al-Khangī.
Al-Maḥallī, Jalāl al-Dīn Muḥammad ibn Aḥmad (d. 864/1459), and al-Suyūṭī, Jalāl al-Dīn ʿAbd al-Raḥmān ibn Abī Bakr (d. 911/1505). *Tafsīr al-Jalālayn fi-Hāmishi al-Qur'ān al-Karīm*, ed. Muḥammad ʿAbd al-Raḥmān al-Marʿashlī. 1460/1999. Beirut: Dār Iḥyā' al-Turāth al-ʿArabī.
The Qur'an, English transl. by M.A.S. Abdel Haleem (Oxford World's Classics). 2008. New York: Oxford University Press.
Al-Rāzī, Abū ʿAbdullah Muḥammad ibn ʿUmar Fakhr 'l-Dīn (d. 606/1209). *Asās al-Taqdīs*, ed. Aḥmad Ḥijāzī al-Saqā. 1406/1986. Cairo: Maktabat al-Kulliyyāt al-Azhariyya.
Al-Shahrastānī, Abu 'l-Fatḥ Muḥammad ʿAbd al-Karīm (d. 548/1153). *Al-Milal wa'l-Niḥal*, ed. Aḥmad Fahmī Muḥammad. 1413/1992. Beirut: Dār al-Kutub al-ʿIlmiyya.
—. *Kitāb Nihāyat al-Aqdām fī ʿIlm al-Kalām*, ed. Alfred Guillaume. 1430/2009. Cairo: Maktabat al-Thaqāfa al-Dīniyya.
Shākir, Aḥmad. *ʿUmdat al-Tafsīr ʿan al-Ḥāfiẓ Ibn Kathīr: Mukhtaṣar Tafsīr al-Qur'ān al-ʿAẓīm*, ed. Anwar al-Bāz. 1426/2005. Mansura: Dār al-Wafā'.
Al-Suyūṭī, Jalāl al-Dīn ʿAbd al-Raḥmān ibn Abī Bakr (d. 911/1505). *Al-Itqān fī ʿUlūm al-Qur'ān*, ed. Muḥammad Abū al-Faḍl Ibrāhīm. 4 vols. 1394/1974. [Cairo]: al-Hay'a al-Miṣriyya al-ʿĀmma lil-Kitāb.
—. *Al-Durr al-Manthūr fī al-Tafsīr bi'l-Ma'thūr*, ed. ʿAbd Allāh ibn ʿAbd al-Muḥsin al-Turkī. 1424/2003. Cairo: Markaz Hajar li'l-Buḥūth wa'l-Dirāsāt 'l-ʿArabiyya wa'l-Islāmiyya.

Al-Ṭabarī, Abū Jaʿfar Muḥammad ibn Jarīr (d. 310/923). *Tafsīr al-Ṭabarī Jāmiʿ al-Bayān ʿan Ta'wīl Āy al-Qur'ān*, ed. ʿAbd Allāh ibn ʿAbd al-Muḥsin al-Turkī. 1422/2001. Giza: Hagar lil-Ṭibāʿa wa'l-Nashr wa'l-Tawzīʿ.
Al-Zamakhsharī, Jār Allāh Abu 'l-Qāsim Maḥmūd ibn ʿUmar (d. 538/1144). *Al-Kashshāf ʿan Ḥaqā'iq Ghawāmiḍ al-Tanzīl wa-ʿUyūn al-Aqāwīl*, ed. ʿĀdil Aḥmad ʿAbd al-Mawjūd and ʿAlī Muḥammad Muʿawwaḍ. 1418/1998. Riyadh: Maktabat al-ʿAbīkān.

Secondary Sources

Abdul-Raof, Hussein. 2012. *Theological Approaches to Qur'anic Exegesis: A Practical Comparative-Contrastive Analysis*. New York: Routledge.
Abrahamov, Binyamin. 1992. "Ibn Taymiyya on the Agreement of Reason with Tradition." *The Muslim World*, 82/3–4:256–273.
—. 1995. "The *Bi-lā Kayfa* Doctrine and Its Foundations in Islamic Theology." *Arabica*, 42/1–3:365–379.
—. 1998. *Islamic Theology: Traditionalism and Rationalism*. Edinburgh: Edinburgh University Press.
—. 2014. "Scripturalist and Traditionalist Theology." In Sabine Schmidtke (ed.), *The Oxford Handbook of Islamic Theology*. Oxford: Oxford University Press. At: www.oxfordhandbooks.com/view/10.1093/oxfordhb/9780199696703.001.0001/oxfordhb-9780199696703-e-025?rskey=iYjGUy&result=1.
Arberry, A.J. 2008 [1957]. *Revelation and Reason in Islam*. Oxon–New York: Routledge.
Arnaldez, R. 1971. "Ibn Rushd." *EI²*, 3:909–920. At: http://dx.doi.org/10.1163/1573-3912_islam_COM_0340.
Belhaj, Abdessamad. 2010. "Ibn Qayyim al-Ǧawziyyah et sa contribution à la rhétorique arabe." In Bori and Holtzman 2010:151–160.
Bori, Caterina, and Livnat Holtzman (eds.). 2010. *A Scholar in the Shadow: Essays in the Legal and Theological Thought of Ibn Qayyim al-Ǧawziyyah* (Oriente Moderno, 90/1). Rome: C.A. Nallino.
Bosworth, Edmund C. 1973. *The Ghaznavids: Their Empire in Afghanistan and Eastern Iran 994–1040*. Beirut: Librairie du Liban.
—. 2014. "Maḥmūd ibn Sebüktegin." *Encyclopaedia Iranica*. At: www.iranicaonline.org/articles/mahmud-b-sebuktegin.
Brown, Jonathan A.C. 2009. *Ḥadīth: Muhammad's Legacy in the Medieval and Modern World*. Oxford: Oneworld.
—. 2014. *Misquoting Muhammad: The Challenge and Choices of Interpreting the Prophet's Legacy*. London: Oneworld.
Bulliet, Richard W. 1973. "The Political-Religious History of Nīshāpūr in the Eleventh Century." In D.S. Richards (ed.), *Islamic Civilisation 950–1150: A Colloquium Published under the Auspices of the Near Eastern History Group Oxford*. Oxford: Bruno Cassiers. 71–91.
Dickinson, Eerik. 2006. *An Introduction to the Science of the Ḥadīth: Kitab Maʿrifat anwāʿ ʿilm al-ḥadīth* [by Ibn al-Ṣalāḥ Abū ʿAmr ʿUthmān al-Shahrazūrī]. Reading, UK: Garnet Publications.

van Ess, Joseph. 1970. "The Logical Structure of Islamic Theology." In G.E. von Grünebaum (ed.), *Logic in Classical Islamic Culture: The First Giorgio Levi Della Vida Biennial Conference*. Wiesbaden: Harrassowitz. 21–50.

—. 1990–1997. *Theologie und Gesellschaft im 2. und 3. Jahrhundert Hidschra*. Berlin–New York: De Gruyter.

—. 2000. "Tashbīh wa-Tanzīh." *EI*², 10:341–344. At: http://dx.doi.org/10.1163/1573-3912_islam_COM_1190.

Gardet, Louis. 1960. "Allāh." *EI*², 1:1–417. At: http://dx.doi.org/10.1163/1573-3912_islam_COM_0047.

Gimaret, Daniel. 1993. "Muʿtazila." *EI*², 7:783–793. At: http://dx.doi.org/10.1163/1573-3912_islam_COM_0822.

—. 1997. *Dieu à l'image de l'homme: Les anthropomorphismes de la sunna et leur interprétation par les théologiens*. Paris: Les Éditions du Cerf.

Gleave, Robert. 2012. *Islam and Literalism: Literal Meaning and Interpretation in Islamic Legal Theory*. Edinburgh: Edinburgh University Press.

Heinrichs, Wolfhart. 1984. "On the Genesis of the *Ḥaqīqa-Majāz* Dichotomy." *Studia Islamica*, 59:111–140.

Heinen, Anton M. 1995. "Samāʾ." *EI*², 8:1014–1017. At: http://dx.doi.org/10.1163/1573-3912_islam_COM_0991.

Holtzman, Livnat. 2009. "Ibn Qayyim al-Jawziyya (1292–1350)." In Joseph E. Lowry and Devin Stewart (eds.), *Essays in Arabic Literary Biography 1350–1850*. Wiesbaden: Harrassowitz. 201–222.

—. 2010. "'Does God Really Laugh?': Appropriate and Inappropriate Descriptions of God in Islamic Traditionalist Theology." In A. Classen (ed.), *Laughter in the Middle Ages and Early Modern Times*. Berlin: De Gruyter. 165–200.

—. 2011. "Anthropomorphism." In Kate Fleet, Gudrun Krämer, Denis Matringe, John Nawas, Everett Rowson (eds.), *Encyclopaedia of Islam: THREE*. At: http://dx.doi.org/10.1163/1573-3912_ei3_COM_23759.

Hoover, Jon. 2007. *Ibn Taymiyya's Theodicy of Perpetual Optimism*. Leiden–Boston: Brill.

Irwin, Robert. 2003. "Mamluk Literature." *Mamlūk Studies Review*, 7/1:1–29.

Jackson, Sherman A. 1994. "Ibn Taymiyyah on Trial in Damascus." *Journal of Semitic Studies*, 39/1:41–85.

Krawietz, Birgit. 2006. "Ibn Qayyim al-Jawzīyah: His Life and Works." *Mamlūk Studies Review*, 10/2:19–64.

Laoust, Henri. 1971. "Ibn Kathīr." *EI*², 3:817–818. At: http://dx.doi.org/10.1163/1573-3912_islam_SIM_3237.

Madelung, Wilfred. 1971. "Hishām b. al-Ḥakam." *EI*², 3:496–498. At: http://dx.doi.org/10.1163/1573-3912_islam_SIM_2906.

—. 1988. *Religious Trends in Early Islamic Iran*. Albany: SUNY Press.

Makdisi, George. 1966. "Remarks on Traditionalism in Islamic Religious History." In Carl Leiden (ed.), *The Conflict of Traditionalism and Modernism in the Muslim Middle East: From Papers Delivered March 29–31, 1965*. Austin, TX: University of Texas. 77–87.

—. 1981a. "Hanbalite Islam." In Merlin Swartz (ed.), *Studies on Islam*. New York: Oxford University Press, 216–274.

—. 1981b. *The Rise of Colleges: Institutions of Learning in Islam and the West*. Edinburgh: Edinburgh University Press. Modarressi, Hossein. 1986. "Some Recent Analyses of the

Concept of Majāz in Islamic Jurisprudence." *Journal of the American Oriental Society*, 106/4:787–791.
Nuna, Liron. 2014. "Jalāl al-Dīn al-Suyūṭī (d. 911/1505) and the Anthropomorphic Expressions in the Qurʾān: Methodology and Hermeneutical Approaches." MA Thesis, Bar-Ilan University. Hebrew.
Ovadia (Ben-Moshe), Miriam. 2012. "Ibn Qayyim al-Jawziyya's Hermeneutical Approach to God's Attributes and the Anthropomorphic Expressions in the Qurʾān and the Ḥadīth Literature." MA Thesis, Bar-Ilan University. Hebrew.
Özervarli, M. Sait. 2010. "The Quranic Rational Theology of Ibn Taymiyya and His Criticism of the Mutakallimūn." In Yossef Rapoport and Shahab Ahmed (eds.), *Ibn Taymiyya and His Times*. Karachi: Oxford University Press. 78–100.
Qadhi, Yassir. 2010. "'The Unleashed Thunderbolts' of Ibn Qayyim al-Jawziyya: An Introductory Essay." In Bori and Holtzman 2010:135–149.
Ragep, F. Jamil. 2014. "Astronomy." In Kate Fleet, Gudrun Krämer, Denis Matringe, John Nawas, Everett Rowson (eds.), *Encyclopaedia of Islam: THREE*. At: http://dx.doi.org/10.1163/1573-3912_ei3_COM_22652.
Robson, James. 1971. "Ibn al-Ṣalāḥ." *EI*², 3:927. At: http://dx.doi.org/10.1163/1573-3912_islam_SIM_3353.
Saleh Walid A. 2010. "Ibn Taymiyya and the Rise of Radical Hermeneutics: An Analysis of an Introduction to the Foundations of Qurʾānic Exegesis." In Yossef Rapoport and Shahab Ahmed (eds.), *Ibn Taymiyya and His Times*. Karachi: Oxford: University Press. 123–162.
Seale, Morris S. 1964. *Muslim Theology: A Study of Origins with Reference to the Church Fathers*. London: Luzac.
Versteegh, Kess. 1993. *Arabic Grammar and Qurʾānic Exegesis in Early Islam*. Leiden: Brill.
Vishanoff, David R. 2011. *The Formation of Islamic Hermeneutics: How Sunni Legal Theorists Imagined a Revealed Law*. Ann Arbor: American Oriental Society.
Watt, William Montgomery. 1965. "Djahmiyya." *EI*², 2:388. At: http://dx.doi.org/10.1163/1573-3912_islam_COM_0176.
—. 1994. *Islamic Creeds: A Selection*. Edinburgh: Edinburgh University Press.
Zysow, Aaron. 2014. "Karrāmiyya." In Sabine Schmidtke (ed.), *The Oxford Handbook of Islamic Theology*. Oxford: Oxford University Press. At: http://www.oxfordhandbooks.com/view/10.1093/oxfordhb/9780199696703.001.0001/oxfordhb-9780199696703-e-29?rskey=eqjPeH&result=1.

Acknowledgement

Livnat Holtzman is Chair of the Department of Arabic at Bar-Ilan University, Ramat Gan. Miriam Ovadia is a doctoral candidate in the Berlin Graduate School Muslim Cultures and Societies, Freie Universität Berlin. This research was supported by the Israel Science Foundation (ISF grant no. 79/10).

Binyamin Abrahamov

Rationality and Rationalism in Islamic Mysticism: The Case of Ibn al-ʿArabī

At first sight, the terms rationality and rationalism seem to contradict the various definitions of mysticism. Rationalism uses logical tools to demonstrate ideas such as God's existence and unity without referring to scripture, while rationality means to prove logically what was written in the Quran or in Muhammad's sayings. In our context, rationality can serve as a device for proving ramifications of mystical ideas or the relationships between spiritual elements, previously demonstrated by sacred texts or by other kinds of revelation. Indeed, I incorporate various types of rationality in our discussion, including examination of an issue from several perspectives[1] and reaching logical conclusions on the basis of available data.[2] Thus, reason occupies the second place in dealing with mystical issues. In contradistinction to rationality, rationalism may be the first device used to found mystical notions or issues related to them. In the present paper, rationalism is not understood as in the eighteenth and nineteenth centuries, when it was considered the sole device to be used in establishing human values, both spiritual and material. In the Islamic context, reason is not given priority in all spheres, but only in some, such as proving God's existence and unity.[3] An approach similar to modern rationalism was shared by some Muslim philosophers, such as al-Kindī (d. 867), al-Fārābī (d. 950) and Ibn Sīnā (d. 1037), who believed that reason (*ʿaql*) without revelation was sufficient to understand the realities of things and the absolute truth.[4]

In the present article, I analyze the place of rationality and rationalism in Islamic mysticism by focusing on the mystical thought of Ibn al-ʿArabī. I include philosophical and theological ideas in the discussion only insofar as they are rational, and not, as is sometimes the case, the outcome not of rational thinking but of unquestioning acceptance. Often, however, philosophical conclusions,

1 Al-Qayṣarī 1962:1035.

2 For example, if the world's infinite phenomena reflect God's names, it follows that God's names are infinite. While general notions regarding reason and revelation are not our concern here, one should bear in mind the question of whether a religion based on scriptures can escape rational thinking. Note, for example, the exegesis of sacred texts.

3 Abrahamov 1998:ix–x.

4 Chittick 1981:89.

https://doi.org/10.1515/9783110446395-015

such as the impossibility of referring to God by any human name or attribute, seem to me the result of reasoning.[5] Thus, the theory of emanation adopted by some Sufis can be deemed a rational solution to the logical question of how a purely spiritual entity (God) is able to create and make contact with the material world.[6] Hence, emanation may be viewed as a logical philosophical theory. Notably, many Sufis were acquainted with philosophy, and many philosophers were also mystics.[7] The same is true of Muslim theologians.[8]

Having considered the terms we are using and their application, I shall begin by examining the place of rationality and rationalism in Islamic mysticism prior to Ibn al-ʿArabī. The Sufis' attitude toward reason (rational thinking) underwent a change in the twelfth century. This leads me to divide into two periods the era that stretches from the first great masters of Sufism, in the ninth century, to Ibn al-ʿArabī (d. 1240). The first period, up to al-Ghazālī (d. 1111), is characterized by the absence of rationality and rationalism in the Sufi context. If rationality existed in this period, it did not have an impact on mysticism. For example, we might have expected the *Kitāb māhiyyat al-ʿaql* (The Book on the essence of the intellect), by the mystic and theologian al-Muḥāsibī (d. 857), to contain discussions of the connection between one's intellect and mysticism, but it does not. Al-Muḥāsibī's main concern was to improve human morality. He expressed some ideas based on Muʿtazilite thought, such as the role of reason in attaining knowledge of God and the knowledge of the benefits and damages caused by human acts. However, these notions play no role in his mystical path, which is mainly discussed in his *Kitāb al-riʿāya li-ḥuqūq allāh* (The Book of keeping what God deserves).[9]

The concept of reason or rational thinking is also absent from discussions of the Sufi mystical stations (*maqāmāt*) in the works of al-Kharrāz (d. 899 or 900), al-Sarrāj (d. 988), al-Kalābādhī (d. 990 or 994), al-Makkī (d. 996) and al-Qushayrī (d. 1072). Theological notions like those characterizing Ashʿarite Kalām do appear in the mystical manuals of these scholars, but those notions do not influence their

5 Cf. Akasoy 2011:233, who discusses the question of whether or not the indescribability of God can be considered in the context of philosophy.
6 Netton 2003:255–256.
7 Chittick 1981:87.
8 On Sufism and theology, see Shihadeh 2007 (and for a review of this book see Abrahamov 2009b). On the proximity of Sufism and Ashʿarism as expressed in the adherence of the former to rational ways of interpretation in, for example, the use of figures of speech in understanding anthropomorphic phrases, see Nguyen 2012:220–222, 228–229, 232–233.
9 Abrahamov 2015:36.

mystical ideas. Reason neither supports a given mystical doctrine nor explains it.[10]

In fact, these early Sufi manuals express clear opposition to reason. Al-Hujwīrī (d. ca. 1071), in *Kashf al-maḥjūb* (The Revelation of the veiled), asserts that Sufism is based on the traditions (*akhbār*) of the Shaykhs, and reason has no place in it.[11] He rejects the suggestion that reason may lead to real knowledge of God, arguing that if reason were the basis of that knowledge, then every reasoning person would know God, which is not the case.[12] According to al-Hujwīrī, only three Sufis – Abū ʿAlī al-Daqqāq (d.1015 or 1021), Abū Sahl al-Ṣuʿlūkī and his father – thought that gnosis (divine knowledge directly reaching the mystic) begins with demonstration, though it ends with intuitive (necessary) knowledge, and he rejects their view.[13] Another figure, al-Tirmidhī (d. between 905 and 910), who must be regarded as a theosophist rather than a Sufi, held that reason is the first step toward achieving illumination.[14] In sum, most of the early Sufis displayed a negative attitude toward reason as a device for establishing and explaining their mystical theories.

The second period begins with al-Ghazālī, whose predilection for reason may be explained at least partly by his adherence to a philosophical theology.[15] In *Mishkāt al-anwār*, a conspicuously mystical treatise, Al-Ghazālī devotes a number of pages to the value of the intellect; all existents, he claims, can be investigated by the intellect, and its judgment, when not disturbed by fantasy and imagination, is flawless.[16] Moreover, the intellect leads one to perfection, which he defines as knowledge of things as they really are. Indeed, humanity was brought into existence for the sake of the intellect.[17]

Al-Ghazālī considers the mystical sciences, whether practical or metaphysical, among the rational sciences. This does not mean that he prefers the way of rational investigation to the way of revelation for the purpose of attaining the truth. It seems, rather, that he holds to both ways, while strongly inclining to the rational way.[18]

---

10 *Ibid.*:36–37.
11 Al-Hujwīrī, ed. Nicholson 2000:176.
12 *Ibid.*:268–269.
13 *Ibid.*:272–273; Abrahamov 2015:37–38.
14 Abrahamov 2015:38.
15 Griffel 2009.
16 Al-Ghazālī, ed. Buchman 1998:5–9.
17 Al-Ghazālī, ed. Dunya 1965:196, 210, 331.
18 Abrahamov 2010:7–9.

Al-Ghazālī's inclination toward rational thinking is also attested in two other fields. First, his theory of causality in his mystical writings is clearly rational, although without forsaking God's role. In this context, he emphasizes the world's rational structure and hence the need to understand the world through rational principles.[19] Second, he holds that our love for God is based on our intellectual endeavors. Inasmuch as an individual's knowledge of the world's phenomena increases, so does his love for God. This process, which is reminiscent of the *eros* motif, is never-ending and continues even in the world to come.[20]

Finally, al-Ghazālī's attitude toward the syllogism is the best proof of his rational approach to all facets of Islam. In *Kitāb al-tafakkur* (The Book of syllogistic thinking), in his *Iḥyā' 'ulūm al-dīn* (The Revivification of the sciences of religion), he states plainly that syllogistic reasoning is the foundation of mysticism in both theory and practice. To safeguard the religious element, he insists that the syllogistic procedure sometimes occurs through divine light cast on a prophet's heart, but generally it is the outcome of study. In fact, all that he says in the *Iḥyā'*, including his discussion of the interpretation of qur'ānic verses, is based on syllogism. Thus, every notion not found in the Qur'ān or the tradition is built on reason. His rationalism in this context is clear. For those who cannot think in this way, God bestowed the sacred text and the traditions. Such elitism is a revolution in Islamic religious thought.[21]

Ibn al-'Arabī's approach must be discussed against this background of rationality and rationalism in Islamic mysticism. The Great Master declared that the structure of the universe is rational, founded as it is upon the immanent rationalizing principle of the Logos or First Intellect. Since the Logos contains the ideas that represent all the phenomena in the cosmos, the whole cosmos is structured along rational lines.[22]

I begin my discussion of Ibn al-'Arabī by presenting the essentials of his thought. In his view, God is the only real entity, and the cosmos is the reflection of God's names and attributes, which are not spiritual entities inhering in God's essence but relationships between Him and His self-manifestations.[23] God's essence cannot be known; however, from the perspective of His attributes, His essence and the cosmos constitute one entity that can be known. Ibn al-'Arabī is fond of the method of examining issues from different perspectives. Thus, God,

---

19 Abrahamov 1988:75–98.

20 Abrahamov 2003:42–86.

21 Abrahamov 2015:43–44.

22 Affifi 1939:67–69; Abrahamov 2007, II:9.

23 Ibn al-'Arabī, ed. Affifi 2002: Chap. 4.

from a rational perspective, is transcendent, while from an imaginational perspective He is immanent.[24] And, because the cosmos is God's manifestation, all religions within it are equal, but from the terrestrial perspective each religion has its own merits and advantages. The oneness of existence (*waḥdat al-wujūd*), a term used not by Ibn al-ʿArabī himself but by his commentators, applies to Being when considered from the perspective of God's essence, which includes His attributes. Thus, God's Unity is absolute from the perspective of His essence but multifaceted from the perspective of the cosmos.[25] God's various names (= attributes) are arranged in hierarchical order, but in relation to God's essence they are equal. Further elucidation of Ibn al-ʿArabī's thought in this regard would go beyond the scope of this article, but I shall return to an element of it further on.

I now turn to the issues of what can be attained using reason; philosophical and theological notions adopted by Ibn al-ʿArabī; the characteristics of the intellect, its weakness and the superiority of revelation; and contradictions in our author's approach to reason.

Reason is an indispensable tool in Ibn al-ʿArabī's *Weltanschauung*, as may be demonstrated by referring to the theological principles for which he holds the intellect responsible. Thus, knowledge of God's existence (*al-ʿilm bi-wujūd allāh*) is achieved by reason, either discursively or, in Ibn al-ʿArabī's view, in the preferable way of immediate necessary knowledge.[26] However, knowledge of God (*al-ʿilm bi-allāh*) is attained only by revelation.[27] God's transcendence, one of the foundations of Ibn al-ʿArabī's thought, is also known only through the intellect.[28] Since reason is the device for attaining knowledge of these two matters, Ibn al-ʿArabī can be regarded in this respect as an adherent of rationalism, although God's existence and transcendence is attested in the Qurʾān.[29] That is because, from a logical perspective, knowledge of God's existence must precede knowledge of the Qurʾān. To prove God's existence, Ibn al-ʿArabī also uses the argument from design in its teleological sense, although without adducing qurʾānic verses to this effect.[30]

---

24 From one perspective the cosmos is creation, but from another it is the real. *Ibid.*:112.
25 *Ibid.*: Chaps. 22, 25.
26 Chittick 1989:234.
27 Ibn al-ʿArabī, ed. Hyderabad 1948, II:2.
28 Ibn al-ʿArabī, ed. Beirut 1999, I:145, III:244–245, IV:18; idem, ed. Affifi 2002:181 (the beginning of Chap. 22). From the epistemological point of view, there is no possibility of knowing God's essence, because the contingent entity, that is, the human being, cannot know the essence that is necessary by virtue of itself. Idem, ed. Hyderabad 1948, II:3.
29 "There is nothing like God." Qurʾān 42:11.
30 Ibn al-ʿArabī, ed. ʿAbd al-Fattāḥ 2001–2004, IV:293–294.

The tool for arriving at the knowledge that the world has a cause is the syllogism, which is the philosopher's best way to prove ideas. Everything that comes into being (*ḥādith*), explains Ibn al-ʿArabī, has a cause; the cosmos came into being, and therefore the cosmos has a cause. Ibn al-ʿArabī justifies his use of this device on the basis of its employment in establishing the law that prohibits drinking intoxicating liquids. That syllogism runs as follows: (1) Every intoxicating (*muskir*) substance is prohibited (*ḥarām*); (2) wine made from dates (*nabīdh*) is intoxicating; and so (3) this wine is prohibited. As in the theological case, the conclusion of the syllogism (*hukm*) – the prohibition – is more general than its cause (*ʿilla*) – preventing intoxication – because the prohibition may have other causes.[31] His use of the syllogism and its conditions shows Ibn al-ʿArabī's familiarity with philosophy, a subject to which I shall return.

Concerning the use of syllogism or analogy (*qiyās*) in legislation, however, Ibn al-ʿArabī expresses an equivocal approach. On the one hand, he justifies the use of this device, for if its use is allowable in establishing the fundamentals of religion, all the more so may it be employed to elucidate the branches (*furūʿ*) that stem from these roots, that is, the specific laws.[32] But, on the other hand, he informs the reader that he abstains from using *qiyās*, because this implies addition to the existing laws.[33] Thus, while he personally prefers the practical approach rooted in the tradition, which states that God wishes to release the Muslims from any additional burden in matters of the law, he admits that, objectively, the use of this tool is permitted.

Two other theological notions invoked by Ibn al-ʿArabī, although they are affirmed in the Qur'ān, reveal his rationalism, for he views them as principles that may be proven by reason. The first derives from the notion of God's transcendence and teaches the incomparability of God to the creation. The second is the belief that God is one, which is proven by the speculative way of Kalām. Here our author states that the teaching of the Qur'ān[34] corresponds to this rational proof.[35]

31 Ibn al-ʿArabī, ed. Beirut 1999, I:260–261.
32 *Ibid.*, III:245.
33 *Ibid.*:247.
34 Qur'ān 21:22.
35 Ibn al-ʿArabī, ed. Beirut 1999, III:434. The proof from assumed mutual prevention (*dalīl al-tamānuʿ*) demonstrates that if divinity were divided between two gods, each would lack a part of divinity, and whoever lacks a part of divinity cannot be God. This proof appears in Kalām literature in different versions. Abrahamov 1990:190–192, n. 89.

Reason leads one to knowledge not only of God's existence, transcendence, incomparability and unity, but also of God's attributes and names,[36] which Ibn al-ʿArabī divides into two categories. The first are the names reason alone perceives, applies to God and, by them, designates Him, while the second class of names would not have been accepted had religion not delivered them to humanity.[37] Reason also establishes the relationship between God's attributes and their hierarchy. For example, it is inconceivable that God's will should precede God's knowledge, for God cannot will what He does not know. Likewise, God's power follows His will.[38] Refuting the Ashʿarite theory that the divine attributes inhere in God's essence, our author insists that they are relationships between God's essence and cosmic phenomena.[39]

Does Ibn al-ʿArabī espouse rationalism or rationality? The answer to this question is complicated. He states explicitly that the obligation to engage rational thinking on theological matters derives from the Qurʾān (7:184–185), and he even sets out the order of attaining theological knowledge by way of reason: (1) demonstrating God's existence; (2) establishing His unity; (3) knowing His attributes; and (4) verifying the Prophet's message. Because the intellect must ascertain the Prophet's message, which includes the first three religious fundamentals indicated above, the intellect becomes the highest arbiter of religion. Add to this our author's statement that "Had one of these foundations been ruined, religions would have been annulled," and we can safely say that Ibn al-ʿArabī, perhaps without realizing it, goes in the direction of rationalism.[40] Elsewhere, he emphatically states: "religion can be proven only by the intellect [*al-sharʿ lā yuthbatu illā biʾl-ʿaql*]; otherwise, everyone would have said regarding the real (God) whatever he wishes, that is, things that reason finds absurd or not."[41] Syllogism appears in his writings as the two arms of a balance of meanings, which symbolize the syllogism's two premises. This balance, also called logic, judges everything, be it action, rank, state or station.

36 By attribute, I mean a faculty or activity of God. Thus, God is named the Creator because of His act of creation. Muslim theologians discussed the relationships between God's essence and attributes.

37 Ibn al-ʿArabī, ed. Beirut 1999, III:229.

38 Ibn al-ʿArabī, ed. Beirut 2000, I:299–300.

39 Chittick 1989:5, 35.

40 Ibn al-ʿArabī, ed. Beirut 1999, III:244–245; Abrahamov 2007, II:11–12. For the priority of reason in Kalām, see Heer 1993.

41 Ibn al-ʿArabī, ed. Beirut 1999, IV:440.

The intellect (*ʿaql*) not only endows humans with the ability to know things as they really are,[42] such knowledge being the aim of the philosophers, but also serves as a device to improve and elevate human morality. Its name derives from the verb *ʿaqala*, to bind or confine, or from the noun *ʿiqāl*, a rope for tying a camel's legs. Thus, *ʿaql* is what restrains a person from committing unlawful acts. Ibn al-ʿArabī regards the intelligent person (*ʿāqil*) as one whose intellect leads him to virtue – in contradistinction to the many people affiliated with formal religion who are dominated by their desires.[43]

In *Tahdhīb al-akhlāq* (The Refinement of character), Ibn al-ʿArabī states that the perfection of one's virtues is attained, *inter alia*, through knowledge of the essences of things, their causes and effects. Although he does not mention the intellect explicitly, it is undoubtedly implied here, because the whole course of the discussion is philosophical, citing no qurʾānic verses or traditions.[44]

Another proof of the significance Ibn al-ʿArabī ascribes to the intellect is the notion that it preserves religion. He sees a person's life as being founded upon three basic elements: intellect, religion and truth. The intellect preserves religion, and religion preserves truth. "Whoever claims to be a religious person without using his intellect, his claim is not valid, for God obliges only intelligent people to carry out precepts, not insane persons or children."[45] Here Ibn al-ʿArabī creates a synthesis between the three indispensable elements: reason, religion and mysticism (represented by the term *ḥaqīqa* – truth). Although truth is given the highest position, the whole hierarchy depends on reason, which guards religion. In like manner, Ibn al-ʿArabī declares that truth without religion is not valid.[46]

The esteem in which he holds the intellect, as a necessary ingredient of religion, explains Ibn al-ʿArabī's opposition to blindly following authorities or books (*taqlīd*). He plainly states: "If you are a scholar [*ʿālim*], the law forbids you [*ḥarām ʿalayka*] to act contrary to your rational proof. [Furthermore,] the law forbids you to blindly follow others, when you are able to attain a proof. And in the case that you are not in such a position and have to blindly follow a certain school ... you should take the counsel of the scholars of the Qurʾān and the Sunna [the tradition]."[47]

---

42 *Ibid.*, V:369.

43 *Ibid.*, VI:59.

44 Ibn al-ʿArabī, ed. ʿAbd al-Fattāḥ 2001–2004, I:60–61

45 Ibn al-ʿArabī, ed. Beirut 1999, VIII:199.

46 *Ibid.* Ibn al-ʿArabī's idea is reminiscent of Gilson's remark: "True mysticism is never found without some theology, and sound theology always seeks the support of some philosophy" (Gilson 1937:36).

47 Ibn al-ʿArabī, ed. Beirut 1999, VIII:299.

Reason is a necessary condition not only for the subsistence of religion, but also for human behavior in the absence of revelation. Very probably following the Muʿtazilite teaching on human knowledge of moral principles, Ibn al-ʿArabī asserts that whoever does not receive the Islamic call should carry out the moral laws established by reason, such as that of thanking one's benefactor (*shukr al-munʿim*).[48]

Apart from the contexts in which Ibn al-ʿArabī explicitly mentions the intellect and its functions, or what can be achieved by the intellect, he also develops ideas that can undoubtedly be called rational, even if he himself does not characterize them as such. Thus, establishing relativity is the outcome of a rational procedure. Ibn al-ʿArabī devotes much space to explaining the Sufi stations (*maqāmāt*), which constitute the Sufi way (*ṭarīqa*). However, almost every station has an opposite one, called "abandoning the station" (*tark al-maqām*). The rationale of adding this opposite station lies in establishing the highest human value, namely, proximity to God, for which the mystic ought to exert all his effort. In relation to this highest end, all other stations serve as a means. Measuring every station by the criterion of the highest value is a rational act, just as establishing relationships and making comparisons derive from rational considerations.[49]

Yet another essential ingredient of Ibn al-ʿArabī's theory is his aforementioned propensity to examine issues from different perspectives. Although he does not declare this a fundamental principle, the formula "from this perspective" recurs often in his writings. Thus, considering the cosmos from the rational perspective leads one to the idea of God's transcendence, while examining it from the perspective of imagination leads one to believe in God's immanence. Furthermore, we can gauge the real from the perspective of His names or from that of His essence (*dhāt*). The real can be known from the first perspective, but not from the second.[50] Without doubt, considering things from different perspectives is a rational act.

Similarly, reaching conclusions from premises is an activity of reason. For example, from the premise that a human being cannot know himself, Ibn al-ʿArabī concludes that humans are unable to know their God, because if one could know himself, he would know his Lord.[51] To take another example, if the cosmos is God's self-manifestation, then there is no difference between all the phenomena

48 *Ibid*., IV:369. Frank 1971:5–18; Reinhart 1995.

49 Abrahamov 2010:23–46.

50 Ibn al-ʿArabī, ed. Affifi 2002:48, 103, 109, 139; ed. Hyderabad 1948, II:5.

51 Ibn al-ʿArabī, ed. Hyderabad 1948, II:24.

of the world. Hence, from this perspective, all religions are equal.[52] However, from the perspective of this world, religions differ from each other.

Ibn al-ʿArabī was very fond of using definitions, which of course is an act of reasoning. In his view, the basis of defining lies in differentiating (*tafriqa*) between things. As he says: "The foundation of all things is differentiation."[53] Needless to say, that definition paves the way for the creation of universals.

I disagree with Franz Rosenthal's statement that Ibn al-ʿArabī "probably had no fixed system in mind, certainly no system that was in the least 'philosophical.'"[54] In my view, Ibn al-ʿArabī's system of thought is based on a fundamental premise that can be summed up in his own words: "Know that existence is one, having an external [aspect], which is the cosmos, and an internal [aspect], which is the names [of God]."[55] His mystical philosophy depends on this premise, and many ramifications are logically deduced from it.

The use of reason is one of Ibn al-ʿArabī's five interpretative devices for understanding the Qurʾān. The full list includes: (1) simple logical arguments; (2) the first meanings of the words; (3) play with the etymology of the words; (4) paraphrasing of verses; and (5) creating a whole picture through adding verses from different *sūras*. Although the last four tools of interpretation also sometimes involve the use of reason, I focus on the first because it is the most salient with regard to Ibn al-ʿArabī's evaluation, at least partially and in certain contexts, as a rational thinker.

Apart from engaging in rational debates with other theological schools, mainly the Ashʿarites,[56] Ibn al-ʿArabī uses simple logical arguments to support his theories. One of them is the theory of the fixed entities (*aʿyān thābita*).[57] Like Plato's ideas, these are the spiritual forms of all the phenomena in the cosmos, which inhere in God's thought and come into being when God bestows existence on them. Qurʾān 16:40 teaches how God creates things: "When We will a thing [to be], We only say to it 'be' and it comes into being." If God says to a thing "be," deduces our author, then the thing must already exist; otherwise it could not be addressed. This demonstrates that the thing had existed in God's knowledge before its concrete existence; it is a fixed entity that comes into worldly being after God says to it "be."[58]

---

52 Ibn al-ʿArabī, ed. Beirut 1999, III:319.
53 *Ibid.*, IV:220; see Bashier 2001:25.
54 Rosenthal 1988:6.
55 Ibn al-ʿArabī, ed. ʿAbd al-Fattāḥ 2001–2004, I:410; ed. Hyderabad 1948, I:9.
56 Ibn al-ʿArabī, ed. Beirut 1999, I:73.
57 Chittick 1989: 83–84; 1998:389, n. 9.
58 Ibn al-ʿArabī, ed. Beirut 1999, I:77; ed. Affifi 2002:115–116.

Although, as noted, Ibn al-ʿArabī employs other tools of qurʾānic interpretation, often leading to fantastic notions that are remote from the plain meaning,[59] his use of rational arguments to explain qurʾānic verses shows that he regards every interpretative tool as legitimate in justifying his ideas, and the logical way is no exception.

Philosophical and rational theological notions are an indispensable part of Ibn al-ʿArabī's mystical thought, in both the cosmological and the terrestrial domains. In the present context, I shall not attempt to reconcile Ibn al-ʿArabī's theory of God's self-manifestation, according to which God says to things "be" and so directly creates the cosmos, and his cosmological ideas, according to which the Logos is the first creation and is responsible for creation.[60] Be that as it may, Ibn al-ʿArabī's cosmology bears the imprint of the Neoplatonist teachings of *Rasāʾil ikhwān al-ṣafāʾ*,[61] notwithstanding his denial of any such philosophical influence. In the context of writing on primordial matter (hyle, *hayūlā*), he declares: "We are not those who relate the philosophers' views on a certain issue, nor the views of others. In the present book [*Futūḥāt*] and in all our books we only provide that which revelation bestows on us and what the Real dictates to us; this is the way of the people [the Sufis]."[62]

The philosophical terms "contingent" or "possible" (*mumkin*), "necessary" (*wājib*) and "impossible" (*mumtaniʿ*, *muḥāl*), too, are indispensable to Ibn al-ʿArabī's thought. By their means, he concludes that God is a necessary existent by virtue of His essence (*wājib al-wujūd bi-dhātihi*).[63]

Ibn al-ʿArabī knows Aristotle's rules of definition and states that God cannot be defined, because a definition comprises genus (*jins*) and differentia (*faṣl*), both of which are inconceivable in relation to the Real.[64] His perception of time as a function of motion also derives from Aristotle.[65] He even answers the question raised by Aristotle as to whether time is an existent or nonexistent (*Physics* 216b31). In Ibn al-ʿArabī's view, time has no concrete existence but is a relationship in the mind, having neither existence nor nonexistence.[66]

In Aristotelian fashion, our author asserts that nonexistence is pure evil, while existence is pure good. And, echoing Aristotle's view, he expresses the

59 The chapter on Nūḥ in the *Fuṣūṣ* is an excellent example of this kind of interpretation.
60 Affifi 1939: Chap. 2.
61 Ibn al-ʿArabī, ed. Beirut 1999, I:144, IV:92, VI:5–6; Affifi 1939:185–188.
62 Ibn al-ʿArabī, ed. Beirut 1999, IV:92; see also ed. Affifi 2002:48.
63 Ibn al-ʿArabī, ed. Beirut 1999, I:194, 294.
64 *Ibid.*:294.
65 *Ibid.*, II:17, III:83.
66 Rosenthal 1988:29–30.

notion that from one, only one can emerge. Thus, "the real is one, and only one comes out of Him."[67] Concerning Aristotle's ten categories, they all apply, in Ibn al-ʿArabī's thought, to the terrestrial aspect; however, from the point of view of the real there are only two categories: the agent (*fāʿil*), that is, the real, and the recipient of action (*munfaʿil*), that is, the cosmos and all its phenomena.[68] "In sum," asserts Rosenthal, "we may fairly say that Aristotelian logic was unquestionably accepted by Ibn al-ʿArabī up to the point where his metaphysical presuppositions take over."[69] This summation also applies to ethics, politics and medicine.[70]

Just as our author was acquainted with the teachings of the philosophers, he was also very well versed in the notions of the speculative theologians (*mutakallimūn*). Sometimes he accepts their ideas as they are, while in other instances he bases himself on a kalāmic notion but adapts it to his own purposes. The theory of atoms and accidents is a good example of this approach. Basically, Ibn al-ʿArabī agrees with the theory that deems the atoms to be equal particles, devoid of qualities, and the accidents to be their properties or forms. When atoms are joined, they constitute a body with its forms. According to the Ashʿarite theological school, the accidents do not endure but are always recreated, so that the whole world is continuously being recreated.[71] Elsewhere, however, contrary to the Ashʿarite approach, Ibn al-ʿArabī proves logically that the atoms are also constantly being recreated.[72] They are the substrate of the property of joining, and in this they are like the accidents and hence continuously recreated.

Ibn al-ʿArabī rejects another Ashʿarite notion that does not coincide with his theory of the fixed entities, relating to the status of the nonexistent. According to the Ashʿarites, the nonexistent is not a thing. However, Ibn al-ʿArabī, loyal to his theory of the fixed entities from which concrete things emerge, considers the fixed entities relative nonexistents that can be actualized.[73] On this issue, our author adopts the Muʿtazilite approach.

Accepting the Ashʿarite theory of acquisition of one's acts (*kasb*),[74] our author states that although the human being feels that he is free to act, all his actions are created by God. He holds this theory in its Ghazalian version, as sum-

---

67 Ibn al-ʿArabī, ed. ʿAbd al-Fattāḥ 2001–2004, I:394.

68 Ibn al-ʿArabī, ed. Nyberg 1919:21–27.

69 Rosenthal 1988:23.

70 *Ibid.*:23–28. For the theory of the four humors, see his *Tahdhīb al-akhlāq*, in Ibn al-ʿArabī, ed. Beirut 2000, I:80–82.

71 Ibn al-ʿArabī, ed. Beirut 1999, III:310. On this theory, see Pines 1997.

72 Ibn al-ʿArabī, ed. Affifi 2002:155–156, 188.

73 Ibn al-ʿArabī, ed. Beirut 1999, V:69; Abrahamov 1990:184, n. 24.

74 For acquisition, see Abrahamov 2008; 1989:210–221.

marized by the formula “the human being is compelled in his choosing” (*majbūr fī ikhtiyārihi*).[75]

We have already shown that Ibn al-ʿArabī adopts the logical proof of God’s unity. In dealing with God’s attributes he also holds a kalāmic theory that views the attributes as names. He rejects the kalāmic theory of negative attributes, because these do not praise God, and he denies the notion that the attributes inhere in God, because this infringes upon His unity, and because there is none like Him (Qurʾān 42:11).[76] Furthermore, had the attributes been additional entities to His essence, meaning that God is God only through them, He would have been an effect of them (*maʿlūl bihā*), and God is the effect of His own essence; were He the effect of other causes, that would mean that He needs others, which is absurd where God is concerned.[77]

Like other Mutakallimūn, Ibn al-ʿArabī, as we have already seen, states that God’s basic attributes are arranged logically. Thus, God’s life is the condition of His attribute of knowledge, His knowledge serves as the condition of His will, and His power is conditioned by His will.[78] Ibn al-ʿArabī did not invent this arrangement, but that he uses it again shows his inclination toward reason.

I would like now to consider Ibn al-ʿArabī’s characterization of rational thinking, his raising of revelation above reason, and some contradictions in his writings about reason and revelation. The most salient feature of reason, in Ibn al-ʿArabī’s view, is that it sometimes hits the target and sometimes misses. Our author takes care not to ascribe errors to reason in every case; however, he argues that one cannot know whether reason is right or wrong, and in one place he says that it is more often wrong than right. Contrary to knowledge attained by “unveiling” (*kashf*), the knowledge received by reason is open to doubt, perplexity and criticism regarding the ways that reason is used.[79]

In *Kitāb al-yaqīn* (The Book of certainty), the weakness of the intellect is said to derive from the basis on which it acts, namely, the objects of sensual perception. This kind of perception often misleads people and causes them to err. Thus, one cannot know God’s essence, because there is no correspondence between God and His creatures; God is totally different from the cosmos.[80] This is an

75 Ibn al-ʿArabī, ed. Beirut 1999, VI:12.
76 *Ibid.*, V:220–221; Abrahamov 1990:184, n. 24.
77 Ibn al-ʿArabī, ed. ʿAbd al-Fattāḥ 2001–2004, IV:179.
78 *Ibid.*, I:199.
79 Ibn al-ʿArabī, ed. Beirut 1999, III:447–448, IV:337.
80 *Ibid.*, I:147–148.

example of how reason may be used to prove its own inadequacy for dealing with some basic questions.[81]

Furthermore, the "people of unveiling and certainty" (*ahl al-kashf wa'l-yaqīn*) experience phenomena that contradict sensory perception, such as inanimate things speaking. Another phenomenon that makes people mistrust reason is that beliefs based on reason, though once considered certain, may change. Hence, the objects of rational thinking are unreliable. Moreover, theological schools such as the Ashʿarites and the Muʿtazilites, which base their doctrines on reason, do not agree with each other on crucial issues in religion, such as free will and predestination. Summing up his approach to reason, Ibn al-ʿArabī states that most people have no certain knowledge.[82] These arguments against reason are not new in Islamic theological literature, and one can find them in the attacks of the traditionalists against the rationalists.[83]

Elsewhere, Ibn al-ʿArabī explains why the nature of the intellect is such. In principle, the intellect is a pure entity, and so the knowledge it attains intuitively is always right. However, in most cases the intellect's thinking suffers impediments, causing it to miss its target. God is responsible for these obstacles, which include a cover upon the intellect that prevents it from knowing the truth.[84]

This idea of obstacles to the intellect likely has some connection with the notion of the intellect's twofold nature: It is both active and passive, on the one hand conceiving logical proofs and on the other a tablet upon which divine information is imprinted.[85] I assume that this notion is relevant to the definition of the qur'ānic term *ummī*[86] as one who is bereft of any knowledge received by reason. Such a person is best qualified to receive revelation, which is beyond rational perception. Ibn al-ʿArabī brings the example of al-Ghazālī, who tried to receive revelation after studying the sciences but failed time and again.[87]

Ibn al-ʿArabī does not reject the role of the intellect in knowing God. However, in light of the intellect's weakness, he states that the highest way to know God is the science of revelation and that the science based on reason is beneath it (*aʿlā al-ṭuruq ilā al-ʿilm bi-allāh ʿilm al-tajalliyāt wa-dūnahā ʿilm al-naẓar*). Thus, reason

---

81 Gilson 1937:34–35.
82 Ibn al-ʿArabī, ed. ʿAbd al-Fattāḥ 2001–2004, IV:48–51.
83 Abrahamov 1998: Chap. 3.
84 Ibn al-ʿArabī, ed. Beirut 1999, IV:330.
85 *Ibid.*, V:11; Abrahamov 2007, I:15–16.
86 According to the usual exegesis of the Qur'ān, an *ummī* is illiterate. This label was attributed to the Prophet to magnify the miracle of his revelation, but it can also designate one who does not know the sacred texts or one of the gentiles. Geoffroy 2012; Gunther 2006.
87 Ibn al-ʿArabī, ed. Beirut 1999, IV:409–410; Abrahamov 2009a:113–115.

also plays a role, albeit inferior to revelation, in providing knowledge of God. Ibn al-ʿArabī exhibits a negative attitude toward reason in his poetics as well, saying that one should beware of using rational thinking.[88]

However, Ibn al-ʿArabī is not consistent in his approach to the relationship between reason and revelation and their roles in knowing God. In chapter 421 of the *Futūḥāt*, he places reason, witnessing and reception of revelation on the same level, claiming that none of these tools can enable a person to attain "the true aspect of the divine knowledge" (*al-wajh al-ṣaḥīḥ fī'l-ʿilm al-ilāhī*). Using these three devices to know God can only induce a state of pure perplexity; instead, our author recommends the device of God's announcement (*iʿlām ilāhī*) of this knowledge to humans.[89] Elsewhere, he says that one attains true knowledge only through witnessing and mystical experience; all other devices offer only conjecture.[90]

In dealing above with syllogism, I mentioned analogy (*qiyās*) and Ibn al-ʿArabī's equivocal attitude toward it. Another inconsistency occurs in our author's discussion of *qiyās* in matters of legislation. *Qiyās* is one of the four basic foundations of the creation of laws (the other three being Qur'ān, Sunna and *ijmā* ʿ – consensus). In the absence of an existing judgment concerning a certain issue, the legislator uses *ijtihād* (effort); that is, he employs these elements, or some of them, to reach a legal conclusion. Analogy is an important part of *ijtihād*, and Ibn al-ʿArabī, in *Fuṣūṣ*, seems to advocate the use of this rational device.[91] Elsewhere, however, he states explicitly that *qiyās* is legitimate only when a revelation of the Prophet confirms the validity of a certain analogy.[92] Did Ibn al-ʿArabī change his mind in *Fuṣūṣ*, his last treatise, to espouse an approach that relies on revelation alone?

Now, if, in Ibn al-ʿArabī's view, God's essence cannot absolutely be known, while His existence, unity and attributes and the relationships between them are known by reason, what does he mean by "the true aspect of the divine knowledge"? Moreover, his above-mentioned negative attitude toward perplexity becomes positive in chapter 430 of the same book, where he says explicitly that "coming to perplexity as regards God means the essence of coming to God."[93]

88 Ibn al-ʿArabī, ed. Cairo 1855:104, 153–154; McAuley 2012:137–138.
89 Ibn al-ʿArabī, ed. Beirut 1999, VII:45. Our author may be referring to an explicit announcement like the Qur'ān.
90 Ibn al-ʿArabī, ed. Affifi 2002:173.
91 *Ibid.*:135.
92 Ibn al-ʿArabī, ed. Beirut 1999, VI:65; Abrahamov 2007, II:17–18.
93 Ibn al-ʿArabī, ed. Beirut 1999, VII:62.

The solution to this inconsistency seems to lie in Ibn al-ʿArabī's statement regarding the nature of the intellect as having active and passive aspects. By virtue of the former, the intellect produces rational proofs to attain knowledge, while by virtue of the latter, it receives what God bestows on it. In its active aspect, the intellect is limited and cannot perceive things as they really are.[94] It seems that in speaking of the superiority of the imagination to reason,[95] Ibn al-ʿArabī is referring to the intellect in its first aspect.

Nevertheless, there remain inconsistencies that seem unresolvable. For example, Ibn al-ʿArabī claims that the world is structured in a logical way, and hence one can understand the world using one's intellect. However, when speaking of the twofold nature of the divine, transcendent and immanent, the intellect is said to understand only the transcendent aspect, not the immanent one, which is perceived by imagination. Thus, the intellect perceives only part of the whole of existence.

Be that as it may, examining Ibn al-ʿArabī's treatises discloses something about his integrity. For example, there is a debate in the Kalām as to whether one accident can inhere in another, or only in a substrate.[96] The specific question refers to ʿĪsā (Jesus), whose oppressors "certainly did not kill him" (Qurʾān 4:157). Here an assumed killing is qualified by certainty (*yaqīn*), whereas we know, says Ibn al-ʿArabī, that accidents do not inhere in other accidents. He concludes: "In our opinion, this is one of the issues that rationally cause perplexity (*min maḥārāt al-ʿuqūl*) and that one cannot definitely settle; some of us deem [the inherence of one accident in another] absurd, and some of them deem it possible."[97]

Notwithstanding these inconsistencies, Ibn al-ʿArabī's attitude toward the use of reason is fairly clear. Reason has some crucial advantages in proving God's existence, unity, transcendence, attributes and the relationships between them. Regarding these themes, Ibn al-ʿArabī's rationalism is evident. Moreover, he puts reason in the position of a judge who verifies prophecy and hence the sacred texts

---

94 Ibn al-ʿArabī, ed. Hyderabad 1948, I:3; *Kitāb al-waṣāya*, in Ibn al-ʿArabī 1948, II:2–3; Abrahamov 2007, II:10; Ibn al-ʿArabī, ed. Affifi 2002:122, 133, 208, 210. There are some parallels between the kabbalist Moses Cordovero's (d. 1570) teachings and Ibn al-ʿArabī's, such as: rational discussion of God's *sefirot* (God's aspects or attributes) and their relationship to His essence; the limitation and weakness of the intellect; that the intellect cannot serve as a device for attaining mystical knowledge; and the use of philosophical terms such as contingent, necessary, etc. See Ben-Shlomo 1965:32, 34, 36, 37, 38.

95 Ibn al-ʿArabī, ed. Affifi 2002:181.

96 Pines 1997:28–31. For example, one accident that inheres in another is endurance, because it is the accident that endures, not the substrate in which it inheres.

97 Ibn al-ʿArabī, ed. Beirut 1999, III:308. The referents of "us" and "them" are unclear to me.

without which religion cannot exist. In this last respect, and in his interpretation of the Qur'ān, he shows his rationality.

However, in his view, one cannot know the innermost secrets of God and things as they really are by reason alone. Only revelation can impart this, through the second aspect of the intellect, which is the ability to receive divine disclosure directly.

A cursory examination of the teachings of four scholars[98] who succeeded Ibn al-ʿArabī and formed the foundations of what may be called his school[99] generally shows the same ambivalent attitude toward rational thinking, albeit with slight modifications, attesting to Ibn al-ʿArabī's impact on later generations. His influence on the Sufis extends to the present day.[100]

References

Abrahamov, Binyamin. 1988. "Al-Ghazālī's Theory of Causality." *Studia Islamica*, 67:75–98.

—. 1989. "A Re-examination of Al-Ashʿarī's Theory of *Kasb* according to *Kitāb al-Lumaʿ*." *Journal of the Royal Asiatic Society*, 2:210–221.

—. 1990. *Al-Ḳāsim ibn Ibrāhīm on the Proof of God's Existence: Kitāb al-Dalīl al-Kabīr*. Leiden: Brill.

—. 1998. *Islamic Theology: Traditionalism and Rationalism*. Edinburgh: Edinburgh University Press.

—. 2003. *Divine Love in Islamic Mysticism: The Teachings of al-Ghazālī and al-Dabbāgh*. London–New York: RoutledgeCurzon.

—. 2007. "Ibn al-ʿArabī's Theory of Knowledge." *Journal of the Muhyiddin Ibn ʿArabi Society*, 41:1–29, 42:1–22.

—. 2008. "Acquisition." *Encyclopedia of Islam*³. At: http://dx.doi.org/10.1163/1573-3912_ei3_COM_26299.

—. 2009a. "Ibn al-ʿArabī's Attitude toward al-Ghazālī." In Y.T. Langermann (ed.), *Avicenna and His Legacy: A Golden Age of Science and Philosophy*. Turnhout: Brepols. 101–115.

—. 2009b. Review of Ayman Shihadeh, *Sufism and Theology*. *Jerusalem Studies in Arabic and Islam*, 36:553–563

—. 2010. "Abandoning the Station (*tark al-maqām*), as Reflecting Ibn al-ʿArabī's Principle of Relativity." *Journal of the Muhyiddin Ibn ʿArabī Society*, 47:23–46.

—. 2015. "Al-Ghazali and the Rationalization of Sufism." In Georges Tamer (ed.), *The Proceedings of Islam and Rationality: The Impact of al-Ghazālī*. Leiden: Brill. 35–48.

Affifi, Abū al-ʿAlā. 1939. *Mystical Philosophy: The Mystical Philosophy of Muhyid Dīn-Ibnul ʿArabī*. Cambridge: Cambridge University Press.

98 These are al-Qūnawī (d. 1274), Ibn al-ʿArabī's son-in-law and his the first important disciple and interpreter, al-Jandī (d. 1291), al-Kāshānī (d. between 1329 and 1336) and al-Qayṣarī (d. 1350). All four scholars were connected to one another by master–disciple relationships.

99 Chittick 1996.

100 Al-Baghdādī 1986. Al-Baghdādī (d. 1995) was the Shaykh of the Qādiriyya order in Israel.

Akasoy, Anna. 2011. "What is Philosophical Sufism?" In P. Adamson (ed.), *In the Age of Averroes: Arabic Philosophy in the Sixth/Twelfth Century*. London: Warburg Institute. 229–249.
al-Baghdādī, Muḥammad Hāshim. 1986. *Dustūr al-walāya wa-marāqī al-ʿināya*. Amman.
Bashier, Salman. 2001. "The Standpoint of Plato and Ibn ʿArabī on Skepticism." *Journal of the Muhyiddin Ibn ʿArabi Society*, 30:19–34.
Ben-Shlomo, Joseph. 1965. *The Mystical Theology of Moses Cordovero*. Jerusalem: Bialik Institute. Hebrew.
Chittick, William. 1981. "Mysticism versus Philosophy in Earlier Islamic History: The Al-Ṭūsī, Al-Qūnawī Correspondence." *Religious Studies*, 17:87–104.
—. 1989. *The Sufi Path of Knowledge*. New York: SUNY.
—. 1996. "The School of Ibn ʿArabī." In Seyyed Hossein Nasr and Oliver Leaman (eds.), *History of Islamic Philosophy*, I. London–New York: Routledge. 510–523.
—. 1998. *The Self-Disclosure of God: Principles of Ibn al-ʿArabī's Cosmology*. New York: SUNY.
Frank, Richard. 1971. "Several Fundamental Assumptions of the Baṣra School of the Muʿtazila." *Studia Islamica*, 33:5–18.
Geoffroy, E. 2012. "Ummī." *Encyclopedia of Islam*[2]. At: http://dx.doi.org/10.1163/1573-3912_islam_SIM_7726.
Al-Ghazālī. *Mīzān al-ʿamal*, ed. Sulayman Dunya. 1965. Cairo.
—. *Mishkāt al-anwār (The Niche of Lights): A Parallel English-Arabic Text*, English transl., introduction and notes by David Buchman. 1998. Provo, Utah: Brigham Young University Press.
Gilson, Etienne. 1937. *The Unity of Philosophical Experience*. New York: Charles Scribner's Sons.
Griffel, Frank. 2009. *Al-Ghazālī's Philosophical Theology*. Oxford: Oxford University Press.
Gunther, S. 2006. "Ummī." In Jane Dammen McAuliffe (ed.), *Encyclopaedia of the Qurʾān*, V. Leiden: Brill. 399–403.
Heer, Nicholas. 1993. "The Priority of Reason in the Interpretation of Scripture: Ibn Taymiyyah and the Mutakallimūn." In Mustansir Mir (ed., with J.E. Fossum), *Literary Heritage of Classical Islam: Arabic and Islamic Studies in Honor of James A. Bellamy*. Princeton: Princeton University Press. 181–195.
Al-Hujwīrī. *Kashf al-Maḥjūb of al-Hujwīrī: "The Revelation of the Veiled" – An Early Persian Treatise on Sufism*, English transl. from the Persian by Reynold A. Nicholson. 2000 [1911]. London: Gibb Memorial Trust.
Ibn al-ʿArabī. *Dīwān Ibn al-ʿArabī*. 1855. Cairo: Būlāq.
—. *Kitāb inshāʾ al-dawāʾir*, ed. Henrik Samuel Nyberg. 1919. In Nyberg, *Kleinere Schriften des Ibn al-ʿArabī*. Leiden: Brill.
—. *Rasāʾil ibn al-ʿarabī*. 1948. Hyderabad.
—. *Al-Futūḥāt al-makkiyya*. 1999. Beirut: Dār al-Kutub al-Ilmiyya.
—. *Majmūʿat rasāʾil ibn al-ʿarabī*, I–III. 2000. Beirut: Dār al-Maḥajja al-Bayḍāʾ.
—. *Rasāʾil Ibn ʿArabī*, I–IV, ed. Saʿīd ʿAbd al-Fattāḥ. 2001–2004. Beirut: Muʾassasat al-Intishār al-ʿArabī.
—. *Fuṣūṣ al-ḥikam*, ed. Abū al-ʿalāʾ ʿAffifi. 2002 [1946]. Beirut: Dār al-Kitāb al-ʿArabī.
McAuley, Denis. 2012. *Ibn ʿArabī's Mystical Poetics*. Oxford: Oxford University Press.
Netton, Ian. 2003. "The Neoplatonic Substrate of Suhrawardī's Philosophy of Illumination: *Falsafa* as *Taṣawwuf*." In L. Lewisohn (ed.), *The Heritage of Sufism*, II: *The Legacy of Medieval Sufism (1150–1500)*. Oxford: Oneworld.

Nguyen, Martin. 2012. *Sufi Master and Qur'an Scholar: Abū'l-Qāsim Al-Qushayrī and the Laṭā'if Al-Ishārāt*. Oxford: Oxford University Press.
Pines, Shlomo. 1997 [1936]. *Studies in Islamic Atomism*. English transl. by M. Schwarz, ed. T. Langermann. Jerusalem: The Magnes Press.
Al-Qayṣarī, Dāwud. 1962. *Sharḥ fuṣūṣ al-ḥikam*. Qom.
Reinhart, Kevin. 1995. *Before Revelation: The Boundaries of Muslim Moral Thought*. New York: SUNY.
Rosenthal, Franz. 1988. "Ibn ʿArabī between 'Philosophy' and 'Mysticism.'" *Oriens*, 31:1–35.
Shihadeh, Ayman. 2007. *Sufism and Theology*. Edinburgh: Edinburgh University Press.

Yohanan Friedmann

Quasi-Rational and Anti-Rational Elements in Radical Muslim Thought: The Case of Abū al-Aʿlā Mawdūdī

The rich theological literature of classical Islam reflects a great variety of views concerning the place of reason in determining religious truth and correct belief. In his *Islamic Theology: Traditionalism and Rationalism*,[1] Binyamin Abrahamov has provided an illuminating and richly documented survey of the struggle between traditionalism and rationalism in the history of Islamic thought. He has shown that there is no pure rationalism in Islamic theology, because even thinkers who are closest to rationalism believe in divine revelation; but pure traditionalism is to be found in the attitudes of Islamic scholars who do not use reason to prove the existence of God or to determine the articles of faith. Abrahamov has also shown that a wide spectrum of essentially traditionalist scholars use rational arguments in a variety of ways. The purpose of this article is to investigate the place of Abū al-Aʿlā Mawdūdī on the spectrum of Muslim attitudes toward rationalism.

Abū al-Aʿlā Mawdūdī (1903–1979) is one of the most influential thinkers in modern Islam. Many of his works have been translated from the original Urdu into Arabic, English and other languages, and he seems to have influenced radical Arab Muslim thinkers such as Sayyid Quṭb, the chief ideologue of the Muslim Brethren, and others.[2] His lifetime spans the last decades of British rule in India and the first thirty years of Pakistan's independence. He had an intensive career, first as a journalist and later, between 1941 and 1972, as the leader of Pakistan's Jamāʿat-i islāmī ("Islamic group") party, which he established and brought to political prominence despite the small number of registered members. Especially noteworthy is the party's struggle during the drafting of Pakistan's constitution, in which it focused on the inclusion of as many Islamic elements as possible in the preamble, known as the "Objectives Resolution."[3] With the help of other religious leaders, Mawdūdī succeeded in introducing into this foundational document a clause specifying that "sovereignty over the entire universe belongs to God Almighty alone," though God has delegated authority to the State of Pakistan "to be exercised within the limits prescribed by Him." The description of the State

1 Abrahamov 1998.
2 See Sivan 1985:passim; and Euben 1999:68.
3 This document was adopted on February 25, 1949.

https://doi.org/10.1515/9783110446395-016

of Pakistan in a subsequent clause as "sovereign and independent" seemingly creates a joint sovereignty of God and the State of Pakistan, reflecting a compromise reached after a struggle between the various political forces involved in the constitution-drafting process.[4] The idea of God's sovereignty on earth has since become a hallmark of the political thought of many radical groups in contemporary Islam.[5]

The political involvement of Mawdūdī and his party has been the subject of extensive research.[6] Until recently, much less attention had been paid to Mawdūdī's thought system, which occupies the lion's share of his writings. This imbalance has now largely been redressed by the seminal work of Jan-Peter Hartung.[7] The purpose of the present paper is to make a further contribution in this regard.

Mawdūdī wrote several articles in Urdu addressing the question of rationality or rationalism. Most of these were originally published in the 1930s in *Tarjumān al-Qur'ān*, a journal he edited. Copies of this journal are very difficult to come by, but numerous articles originally published there were republished in three collections of Mawdūdī's writings, *Tafhīmāt* (1940), *Tanqīḥāt* (1939) and *Rasā'il o Masā'il* (2006–2010),[8] and in the form of separate pamphlets. Some of these articles relate directly to the issue of rationality and rationalism, while in others, though these terms appear in their titles, the relevant conclusions are only implied and to a certain extent are a matter of interpretation.

As he explains in "Islam Is a Scientific and Rational Religion" ("Islām ēk 'ilmī awr 'aqlī madhhab," 1936),[9] Mawdūdī's basic premise is that rationality and a scientific approach are the hallmarks of Islam. In his view, not all religions are of this type. Some religions came into being as a result of a "high flight of the imagination" (*mukhayyal kī buland parwāzī*) and appeal to the "human adoration of miracles" (*insān kī u'jūba pasandī*), while others are "born of the desires of the soul" (*khwāhishāt awr ahwā'-i nafs*) and appeal to the human senses. Both of these types make use of the intellect and of "scientific capabilities" (*'aql awr isti'dād-i 'ilmī*), but only as tools. The intellect is not their "mover," and they do not appeal to it; rational conclusions are not their purpose (p. 34). Mawdūdī offers

4 See Binder 1961:passim; Hartung 2014:227–228; Nasr 1994:123–126.
5 For this concept as it appears among contemporary Muslim radical groups, see Lav 2012:passim.
6 The last major monograph on the Jamā'at-i Islāmī is Nasr 1994. On the involvement of the Jamā'a in the process of drafting the constitution, see Binder 1961.
7 Hartung 2014.
8 Mawdūdī 1968a, 1939, 2006–2010.
9 Mawdūdī 1936b:34–35.

no examples of these two types, but the first likely refers to religions with a substantial element of myth, such as the Hindu religious traditions or the religions of ancient Greece. It is much more difficult to guess what he means by religions "born of the desires of the soul." In all events, Mawdūdī considers Islam to be a substantially different type of religion.

Of divine origin, "born of pure knowledge"[10] (*khāliṣ ʿilm se paydā huʾā hay*), Islam, according to Mawdūdī, appeals to the intellect, and its purpose is to extricate man from the darkness of ignorance into the light of knowledge (*ʿilm kī rawshnī*; pp. 34–35). It is a quintessentially scientific and rational religion (*sarāsar ʿilmī awr ʿaqlī madhhab*), which cannot be observed properly without knowledge (*ʿilm*) and intellect (*ʿaql*), because a Muslim needs understanding (*tafaqquh*) and reflection (*tadabbur*) on each step of his spiritual life. Without understanding, belief cannot be stable (pp. 36–37).[11] Mawdūdī gives much weight to the Qurʾānic verses according to which God gave the prophets "the book and the wisdom" (*al-kitāb wa al-ḥikma*).[12] This "wisdom," he explains, is "the understanding of religion, the light of knowledge (or science), the light of intelligence, the capability to reflect and the aptitude to understand" (*dīn kī samajh, ʿilm kī rawshnī, baṣīrat kā nūr, tadabbur kī ṣalāḥiyyat awr tafaqquh kī qābiliyyat*, p. 37).[13] In his view, one may reasonably infer, rational analysis will necessarily lead to the conclusion that Islam is the true religion.

Another article with a promising title for the investigation of our topic is "Rational Proof of the Muḥammadan Prophethood" ("Nubuwwat-i Muḥammadī kā ʿaqlī thubūt," 1937). At the outset, Mawdūdī invites the reader to go back 1,400 years and consider the dismal conditions that prevailed in the Arabian peninsula in the sixth century CE. Arabia was close to such civilizational centers as the Byzantine and Persian empires, but it was completely isolated from them. Superstition and desolation, ignorance and immorality reigned supreme. Revolting cusṭoms were widespread, such as female infanticide, prostitution, naked

---

10 The word *ʿilm* can also be translated as "science." The semantic multivalence of this word enabled numerous modern Muslim thinkers to assert the essential compatibility of Islam with science.

11 *Tafaqquh* and *tadabbur* are enjoined in numerous verses of the Qurʾān, the assumption being that understanding and reflection will necessarily lead to the acceptance of Islam.

12 See Qurʾān 2:129, 3:48, 4:53 and elsewhere.

13 Classical commentators adduce various explanations of the term *ḥikma*. Some understand it as the *sunna* of the Prophet; others as "knowing religion, understanding it and following it" (*al-maʿrifa bi-ʾl-dīn wa al-fiqh fī al-dīn wa al-ittibāʿ lahu*) or as "(use of) intelligence in religion" (*al-ʿaql fī al-dīn*). Ṭabarī prefers "knowledge of divine laws" (*al-ʿilm bi-aḥkām Allāh*), which is far from the primary meaning. See Ṭabarī 1954, I:557–558 (on Qurʾān 2:129).

circumambulation of the Kaʿba and sons marrying their own stepmothers after the death of their fathers. The Arabs practiced idolatry and worshiped spirits and stars. There was no way to acquire even the most elementary education (pp. 239–240). Students of Islam will recognize Mawdūdī's portrayal as a faithful reflection of early Muslim descriptions of and attitudes toward the society and lifestyle of pre-Islamic Arabia.[14]

Muḥammad was born into this environment. Following a description of the Prophet's exemplary morals and integrity, Mawdūdī concentrates mainly on his achievements. In the twenty-two years of his prophetic career, he peacefully subdued the bellicose and uncivilized tribes that inhabited Arabia's 120,000 square miles of desert, inducing them to abandon superstition (*wahmiyyat*), "miracle worship" (*ʿajāʾib parastī*) and monasticism (*rahbāniyyat*) and embrace rationalism (*ʿaqliyyat*), due regard for reality (*ḥaqīqat pasandī*) and "pious worldliness" (*muttaqiyāna dunyā dārī*). In a world that demanded "concrete miracles" (*maḥsūs muʿjizē*), he developed a taste for "rational miracles" (*ʿaqlī muʿjizē*) – a strange collocation which probably refers to miracles that "address the mind," so to speak, such as the dogma of the inimitability of the Qurʾān. He moved the Arabs from the path of speculation to the path of rationality (*taʿaqqul*), thinking (*tafakkur*), observation (*mushāhada*) and research (*taḥqīq*), creating a scientific spirit out of the power of religion and true religion out of the scientific spirit (*madhab kī ṭāqat sē dunyā mēñ scientific [i]spirit awr scientific [i]spirit sē ṣaḥīḥ madhabiyyat paydā kī*). Against all odds, he became a world-class leader (pp. 249–250).[15]

The article certainly declares Islam to be a rational religion, but, notwithstanding its title's promise, it includes no explicit or "rational proof of the Muḥammadan prophethood." The implicit argument seems to be that Muḥammad's achievements were so monumental and were accomplished against such great obstacles that the only "rational" way to explain them is to assume that he acted as a divine messenger.

Another relevant article, "The Decision of the Intellect" (*ʿAql kā fayṣala*, 1933), takes the form of a parable on how people understand the working of electricity. If both the power plant that generates it and the cables that deliver it are in public view, the phenomenon of electricity elicits no amazement. People know the location of the plant, the people who work there and the engineers who supervise their work. But suppose all this was hidden. People would not know how elec-

---

14 This attitude toward the Jāhiliyya is presented succinctly in the speech attributed to Jaʿfar b. Abī Ṭālib in Ibn Hishām's description of the encounter between the Muslim emigrants to Abyssinia and the Abyssinian king (*al-Najāshī*). See Ibn Hishām 1990 I:265–266.

15 Similar arguments are provided in Mawdūdī 2000 I:272–274 (on Qurʾān 10:16).

tricity works, and, perplexed, they would offer a variety of explanations. Some would say that light bulbs shine and ceiling fans revolve by themselves, without any external force to power them. Others would get tired of thinking and say: "Our intellect is not able to reach the bottom of this mystery" (*hamārī ʿaql is ṭilasm kī kunh tak nahīñ pohonch saktī*, p. 10).

Now suppose, writes Mawdūdī, that a man should appear in the course of these disputes, declaring that he has knowledge that is unavailable to anybody else. He tells the people about hidden wires and an invisible power plant run by engineers who are subject to "a great engineer" whose knowledge and ability make the system work. The people declare him insane, expel him from his home, and beat him up – but he stands his ground. Then more people come – by the thousands – all saying the same thing. All are declared insane, but they persist. All of them are honest people whose righteousness is acknowledged even by their opponents.

The dispute between the two parties is now presented to "the court of the sound intellect" (*ʿaql-i salīm kī ʿadālat*). In its judicial capacity, the intellect needs to understand the position of the two parties and rule in favor of one of them. It has no independent means of ascertaining the reality (*amr-i wāqiʿī*). It can only consider the arguments of the two parties and decide whose are right.

What are the considerations to be taken into account by our court? It seems that the opponents of the person who claims to have a solution to the mystery have disparate views and do not agree on a single point. They do not claim to have information that is unavailable to others. They are uncertain about their ideas and beliefs. Their views change with age, intelligence and experience. Their only argument is that their rivals have not shown them the hidden cables or the power plant (pp. 12–13).

The people who claim to understand the mystery are different. They are united in their views.[16] They unanimously maintain that they have means to acquire information that is unavailable to the common people. None of them claims that his views are based on analogy or conjecture; they claim, rather, to have a special relationship with the "engineer," whose workers came to them and took them on a guided tour of the (power) plant. None of them changes his views even minimally over his entire lifetime. They live a pure life, free of deception and upright in all their deeds, making it unlikely that they would lie in this particular matter. They have no personal interest in the question at hand. On the contrary: They have suffered for their views; some have been tortured or even killed. Yet none

16 For unanimity of opinion as a proof of truth in Islamic theology, see Abrahamov 1998:20–21.

has withdrawn his claims, even to save his life. They are all wise people of sound intelligence (*salīm al-ʿaql*; pp. 13–14).

After considering both views, the court rules in favor of the second group. One rational argument is offered in support of this ruling: It is not logical to assume that the electrical appliances somehow operate by themselves, because when there is no movement in the ceiling fans, there is also no light in the bulbs, so that both would seem to have the same source of power. The other arguments are of a different nature. Clearly influenced by the Muslim idea of consensus (*ijmāʿ*) and the belief in its infallibility, the court gives much weight to the unanimity of the second group, the moral qualities of its members, the stability of their views and their self-assurance. Nevertheless, Mawdūdī maintains that despite its importance, the verdict of the court is not sufficient in itself to create belief; one also needs *wijdān*, the inner voice that puts an end to all manner of doubt. Clearly, the "great engineer" is God; the person who came to tell the people about Him is the Prophet Muḥammad; and the members of the second group are the Muslims. However, Mawdūdī nowhere mentions this explicitly.

These are some examples of Mawdūdī's ways of arguing for Islam as a rational religion. But in what sense does he use this term? In the three articles surveyed so far, we learn that Islam was born of pure knowledge, that a Muslim must employ understanding and reflection at all times, and that God revealed to mankind not only divine books of law, but also wisdom. The article about Muḥammad's prophethood contrasts the uncivilized environment into which the prophet was born with his extraordinary achievements. Mawdūdī speaks of rationalism in several places in the article, but he gives few details. The thrust of the argument seems to be that since one cannot understand Muḥammad's extraordinary achievements otherwise, one must assume that they were accomplished with divine help; in other words, the claim that Muḥammad was the messenger of God is based on a rational inference of sorts. In the electricity parable, "the court of the sound intellect" decides in favor of Islam more on the basis of the moral character and unanimity of the Muslims than on the basis of rational arguments. All three articles imply that if people only used their intellect, they would necessarily become convinced of the truth of Islam. This is well in line with the Qurʾānic argumentation according to which the Arab contemporaries of Muḥammad, if they only employed their intellect, would necessarily be convinced that Islam is the true religion. In dozens of verses, the Qurʾān asks the opponents of the Prophet: "Do you not understand?" – implying that if only they used their faculty of understanding, they would necessarily believe in what the Prophet has to say.[17] If we

17 See, e. g., Qurʾān 6:32: "The present life is naught but a sport and a diversion; surely the Last

call Mawdūdī a rationalist, it is in this traditional Muslim sense that Islam is the necessary outcome of rational considerations.

Mawdūdī's approach is completely different when dealing with the question of how a Muslim should act after he has embraced Islam, or rather, after rational analysis has convinced him of Islam's truth. His response is evident in two articles published in Urdu in 1934 and 1936, both entitled "The Deception of Rationalism" (*ʿAqliyyat kā farēb*).[18] On the one hand, these articles attack modern Western civilization by denying its rationalism; on the other, they explain why rationalism cannot be the Muslims' guide in choosing their way of life.

According to Mawdūdī, Western civilization, which has its supporters in the East, is morally corrupt. It is led by "heretical leaders who do not believe in the laws of God and do not obey Him" (*al-zuʿamāʾ al-malāḥida alladhīna lā yuʾminūna bi-sharāʾiʿ Allāh wa lā yaʾbahūna bi-ṭāʿatihi*).[19] Mawdūdī's attack on Darwinism is instructive in this regard. He maintains that the westerners who developed science since the Renaissance period made up their minds to eliminate "any supernatural entity" (*fawq al-fiṭrat dhāt*) from "the workshop of being." Thus, every educated person should know the difference between theory and fact, but, in order to deny God's creation, the West has treated Darwinism, which is nothing but theory, as if it were a proven fact.[20]

As Mawdūdī writes in *al-Islām wa al-Madaniyya al-Ḥadītha* (1978), Western civilization is based on three principles: secularism (*ʿalmāniyya*), nationalism (*qawmiyya*) and democracy (*dīmuqrāṭiyya*). Secularism aimed to exclude religion from the public sphere, but it resulted in the ascendancy of leaders who had no place for religion even in their private lives. Nationalism gave a central place to the interests of the nation, even if they involve aggression, iniquity and other crimes that are unforgivable in religious and moral terms. Democracy has its positive traits, in that it prevents any single group from imposing its will on the population, but the rule of the majority and its legislative power are not a guarantee against injustice and evil (pp. 9–17). Assuming that God's creation of the universe is a matter of general consensus, Mawdūdī declares that to restrict Him to the private sphere and exclude Him from the public sphere is repugnant to the intellect. It is illogical to say that every individual accepts the necessity of

---

Abode is better for those who are godfearing. What, do you not understand?" (English transl. Arberry 1955). Cf. Hartung 2014:87.

18 Mawdūdī 1934, 1936a. Tārik 2003 translates *ʿAqliyyat kā farēb* as "The finitude of rationalism," which does not convey the pungent meaning of the original Urdu title.

19 Mawdūdī 1978:7.

20 Mawdūdī 1968b:349–350.

obeying God in private, but when these same individuals come together to form a society, they reject Him. What kind of intellect would worship a God who has removed His authority from our lives? Mawdūdī can speak thus because he does not countenance the possibility that some people do not believe in God at all (pp. 20–21). Furthermore, a man who has been freed – presumably from the restraints of divine laws – becomes "a prisoner of the desires of his soul" (*ṣāra asīr ahwā' al-nafs*); "intoxicated with egoism" (*akhīdh nashwat al-anāniyya*), he is seated on the "throne of deification" (*'arsh al-ta'līh*). In Mawdūdī's view, the tyranny of an individual ruler is no worse than this type of popular "tyranny" (p. 29). He does not envision the possibility that a secular system of moral values could replace the religious one. Once the religious value system has been removed, man does whatever he likes.

Having proved in this manner, to his own satisfaction, the deficiencies of Western civilization, Mawdūdī attempts to undermine the Western claim of rationality. According to his understanding, Western modernity (*nash'a jadīda*) is a rebellion against intellect and nature. It has abandoned "intellectual guidance, rational inference and natural conscience" (*'aqlī hidāyāt awr manṭiqī istidlāl awr fiṭrī wijdān*), turning instead to materialism (*mādda parastī*) and viewing everything that cannot be measured or weighed as baseless. Mawdūdī does not seem to take into account the possibility of observing nature and submitting the results to rational analysis. He accuses Western civilization of reliance on the senses and of becoming enslaved to the desires and necessities of the human body and soul (*khwāhishāt kī ghulāmī awr muṭālabāt-i nafs o jasad*), to the extent that all other things are considered superstitious and archaic (*wahm parastī awr daqyānūsiyyat*). Here Mawdūdī reflects the longstanding Islamic conception of the soul (*nafs*) as the site of base instincts, bidding evil and seeking illicit pleasures, so that it must be overcome and subdued before a believer can attain true religiosity.[21] In Mawdūdī's thinking, human desires and aspirations, which might be seen as positive traits in other civilizations, bear a pejorative tinge.[22]

Mawdūdī thus levels against Western civilization the charge that it has abandoned rationalism – a charge that can easily also be directed against Muslims who have acquired a Western, mainly British, education. Mawdūdī accuses them of an inability to define the nature of a question and then decide upon the appropriate rational deductive method for solving it. Despite appearances to the contrary, these people's thinking deviates from rationalism (*unkā dhihn 'aqliyyat sē munḥarif hōtā hay*). This is especially prominent in questions concerning religion.

---

21 See Qur'ān 12:53, and Ṣūfī treatises such as Sulamī 1976.

22 Mawdūdī 1939b:84–85.

The following passage illustrates some surprising definitions of what rationalism means:

> Speak to a British-educated man about a religious question. In order to test his intellectual quality, first make him acknowledge that he is a Muslim. Then present him with a single *sharʿī* ruling, explain it and give him proof. He will immediately shake his shoulders and say in a pompous, rationality-admiring style (*ʿaql parastāna andāz*): "This is *mullā*-talk (*mullāʾiyyat*); bring me a rational proof. If you do not have rationally acceptable proofs (*maʿqūlāt*), but only traditional ones (*manqūlāt*), I cannot believe you." After only a few sentences, the secret will be revealed that this man has not been touched by even a passing puff of rationalism. After years of study and education, this wretch does not know what are the rational requisites for seeking a proof and what is the correct position of someone who seeks a proof. Rationally [speaking], from the point of view of Islam, a person can be either a Muslim or an infidel. If he is a Muslim, this means that he has surrendered to God and to the Prophet as the prophet of God. It also means that he accepts that if God's Prophet communicated a certain law from God, he will obey it without asking "how and why." He has no right to require a rational proof for each individual [Islamic] law. As a Muslim, he has only to ascertain whether the Messenger of God promulgated a certain law or not. If the law is proven by a traditional proof, he must obey it immediately. He can seek a rational proof in order to attain repose of the heart (*iṭmiʾnān-i qalb*) and further insight. But until then [i.e., until he finds a rational proof], he must bow his head, obey orders and consider the traditional proof as [sufficient] proof for acquiescence. If [rational] proof is not forthcoming, or repose of the heart is not attained and he [therefore] refuses to obey, the basic meaning of this is rejecting the authority or sovereignty (*ḥākimiyyat*) of God and the Prophet. It is tantamount to infidelity – though at the outset this man declared himself a Muslim.[23]

The obligation to obey the leadership without looking for proofs is related to Mawdūdī's perception of Islam. It is of course very common to define Islam as a religion (*madhhab, dīn*). In the common understanding, writes Mawdūdī, religion is nothing more than a conglomerate of beliefs, rituals and customs, and it should therefore be a private matter (*private muʿāmāla*). People embrace the beliefs they like, and some of the more enthusiastic also propagate them and try to convince others of their truth. However, in Mawdūdī view, as expressed in this context, Islam is not (only) a religion, but (also) an "international revolutionary party" (*bayna al-aqwāmī inqilābī jamāʿat*) that aims to transform the global social order.[24] It is thus first and foremost an organization, and so organizational rules apply to it. No organization can exist without its members' obedience. No government could exist if each citizen were to seek rational proofs for every decision and refuse obedience until he gets it. No army could exist if each soldier were to seek

---

23 *Ibid*:87.
24 Mawdūdī 1968c:77.

the reasons for every one of the general's orders and make his obedience contingent upon the "repose of his heart" (*iṭmi'nān-i qalb*) – upon being fully satisfied of the order's rationality. The obligation to obey is essential for the functioning of any organization and is based on sound intelligence.[25]

This does not mean that Islam rejects rationality. Rationality is used to convince humanity of the existence of Allah as the only God and of the status of Muḥammad as His prophet. Whoever is not convinced by these rational arguments is not forced to embrace Islam; in this case, no Islamic law will be applicable to him. But after he does embrace Islam, he must obey without questioning.

> Belief and proof-seeking, which is a condition of consent and obedience, contradict each other, and their conjunction goes manifestly against sound intelligence. Whoever is a believer cannot demand proof because of his nature; and he who demands proof is not a believer. "It is not for any believer, man or woman, when God and His Messenger have decreed a matter, to have the choice in the affair."

> Īmān awr aysī ṭalab-i ḥujjat jō taslīm o iṭā'at kē li'ē sharṭ hō bāham mutanāqiź hayñ awr in dōnōñ kā ijtimā' ṣarīḥ 'aql-i salīm kē khilāf hay; jō mu'min hay wuh is ḥaythiyyat sē ṭālib-i ḥujjat nahīñ hō saktā awr jō aysā ṭālib-i ḥujjat hay wuh mu'min nahīñ hō saktā.[26]

As an example of unacceptable attitudes that are common among Muslims, Mawdūdī quotes a few passages from an article by a Muslim who wrote of his impressions as a tourist in China and Japan.[27] The tourist speaks of the joyous and prosperous people of China and Japan, adding sarcastically that "this is the advanced condition of the nation that knows neither religion not God" (*yih hay is qawm kī taraqqī kā ḥāl jō na madhhab kō jāntī hay awr na khudā kō*). He mentions their consumption of pork and says that its prohibition in the Qur'ān, probably a result of some special conditions in Arabia, needs to be relaxed. He gives a non-*shar'ī* definiton of Islam as "performance of good deeds" (*iḥsān*) and declares that the Muslims will make progress only if they break the fetters of the *sharī'a*.[28]

How did Islam reach a situation in which such unacceptable questioning of divine laws came into being? Mawdūdī maintains that this is related to the educational path of many contemporary Indian Muslims. Born into a Muslim society and household, their acceptance of Islam in childhood is natural; they come to believe in it by force of circumstance, intuitively and without intellectual accept-

25 *Ibid.*
26 Mawdūdī 1939b:89, quoting Qur'ān 33:36.
27 Mawdūdī names the tourist as Greg White, apparently an Englishman who embraced Islam. No details of the publication are given.
28 Mawdūdī 1939a:73–74.

ance (*iźṭirārī awr ghayr shu'ūrī Islām*). Before this type of Islam can be transformed by means of learning and education into a faith embraced by choice, intellectually internalized (*ikhtiyārī awr shu'ūrī islām*) and put into practice – before they become "true" Muslims – they are sent to British schools and colleges, where the nurturing of their mental and intellectual faculties (*quwā-yi dhihnī o fikrī*) is totally un-Islamic. Their minds are swamped by the principles of Western civilization, to the extent that they start looking at everything from the Western viewpoint and lose their ability to break loose from the domination (*istīlā'*) of "westernism" (*maghribiyyat*). Their rationalism (*'aqliyyat*), learned from the West, becomes "Frankish" (*firangī*). Their intellect, consequently, is not their own, and their criticism (*tanqīd*) is not free: They take Western principles as the criteria by which non-Western things are to be judged, but those principles themselves are above criticism. Such people graduate from college and start their working lives with their hearts and minds as distant from each other as East and West (*un kē dil o dimāgh mayñ bu'd al-mashriqayn wāqi' hō chukā hay*): Their hearts are Muslim, but their minds are not. They stay among Muslims; their transactions are with Muslims; but their thinking and understanding are cast in a Western mold, with no connection to Islam. They start criticizing everything Muslim on the basis of Western criteria and argue that Islamic principles and Muslim practices that do not conform to these criteria must be changed.[29]

On the basis of this survey, we may say that Mawdūdī developed two different approaches to rationalism. In speaking of Islam as a rational religion, he maintains that people who use their intellect will necessarily reach the conclusion that Islam is the true religion. For him, rationalism is a strategy for converting people to Islam rather than a guide for human life in general. It is a rationalism designed to reach a foregone conclusion; since the conclusion is correct, this use of rationalism is desirable and useful. However, once a person embraces Islam on the basis of "rational" analysis, rationalism is no longer needed and even dangerous. It could make obedience to Islamic commandments and to the decrees of Muslim rulers contingent upon rational deliberations, which may lead to undesirable conclusions and interfere with the functionality of Islam.[30] Rationality has done its duty and must go. A movement that considers itself a revolutionary avant-garde, intent on changing the world's social and political system on the basis of divine law, cannot afford the luxury of rational debates that might impede its progress.

29 Mawdūdī 1939a:74–75. On the general theme of opposition among radical Muslim groups to adopting Western values, see Cook 2014:389–393.
30 Mawdūdī 1939b:91.

References

Abrahamov, Binyamin. 1998. *Islamic Theology: Traditionalism and Rationalism*. Edinburgh: Edinburgh University Press.
Arberry, Arthur J. 1955. *The Koran Interpreted*. London–New York: Allen & Unwin–Macmillan.
Binder, Leonard. 1961. *Religion and Politics in Pakistan*. Berkeley–Los Angeles: University of California Press.
Cook, Michael. 2014. *Ancient Religions, Modern Politics: The Islamic Case in Comparative Perspective*. Princeton: Princeton University Press.
Euben, Roxanne L. 1999. *Enemy in the Mirror: Islamic Fundamentalism and the Limits of Modern Rationalism*. Princeton: Princeton University Press.
Hartung, Jan-Peter. 2014. *A System of Life: Mawdūdī and the Ideologisation of Islam*. New York: Oxford University Press.
Ibn Hishām, ʿAbd al-Malik. 1990. *al-Sīra al-Nabawiyya*. Beirut: Dār al-Khayr.
Tārik, Jān. 2003. "Mawdūdī's Critique of the Secular Mind." *The Muslim World*, 93:503–519.
Lav, Daniel. 2012. *Radical Islam and the Revival of Medieval Theology*. Cambridge, UK: Cambridge University Press.
Mawdūdī, Abu al-Aʿlā. 1933. "ʿAql kā fayṣala." In Mawdūdī 1968, I:9–17.
—. 1934. "ʿAqliyyat kā farēb I." In Mawdūdī 1939:72–83.
—. 1936a. "ʿAqliyyat kā farēb II." In Mawdūdī 1939:84–92.
—. 1936b. "Islām ēk ʿilmī awr ʿaqlī madhhab." In Mawdūdī 1968a, I:34–45.
—. 1937. "Nubuwwat-i Muḥammadī kā ʿaqlī thubūt." In Mawdūdī 1968, I:238–255.
—. 1939 (reprinted 1959). *Tanqīḥāt*. Rāmpūr: Maktaba-yi Jamāʿat-i Islāmī-yi Hind.
—. 1968a (1940). *Tafhīmāt: Baʿź Maʿrakat al-Ārā Masāʾil-i Islāmī kī Tashrīḥ o Tawźīḥ*, I–II. Lahore: Islamic Publications Limited.
—. 1968b (1944). "Dārwin kā naẓariyya-yi irtiqā." In Mawdūdī 1968a, II:348–359.
—. 1968c. "Jihād fī sabīl Allāh." In Mawdūdī 1940, I:74–97.
—. 1978. *al-Islām wa al-Madaniyya al-Ḥadītha*. Cairo: Dār al-anṣār.
—. 2000. *Tafhīm al-Qurʾān*. New Delhi: Markazī Maktaba-yi Islāmī Publishers.
—. 2006–2010. *Rasāʾil o Masāʾil*, I–IV. Lahore: Islamic Publications.
Nasr, Seyyed Wali Reza. 1994. *The Vanguard of the Islamic Revolution: The Jamāʿat-i Islāmī of Pakistan*. Berkeley–Los Angeles: University of California Press.
Sivan, Emmanuel. 1985. *Radical Islam: Medieval Theology and Modern Politics*. New Haven–London: Yale University Press.
Sulamī, Abū ʿAbd al-Raḥmān. 1976. *Jawāmiʿ ʿUyūb al-Nafs wa Mudāwātuhā*, ed. Etan Kohlberg. Jerusalem: Jerusalem Academic Press.
Ṭabarī, Muḥammad b. Jarīr. 1954. *Jāmiʿ al-Bayān ʿan Taʾwīl Āy al-Qurʾān*. Cairo: Maṭbaʿat al-Bābī al-Ḥalabī.

Contributors to This Volume

Binyamin Abrahamov
Department of Arabic, Bar-Ilan University

Yohanan Friedmann
Institute of Asian and African Studies, The Hebrew University of Jerusalem, and Department of Middle Eastern and Islamic Studies, Shalem College, Jerusalem

Simon Gerber
Berlin-Brandenburgische Akademie der Wissenschaften

Volker Gerhardt
Institute of Philosophy, Humboldt University of Berlin

Livnat Holtzman
Department of Arabic, Bar-Ilan University

Moshe Idel
Department of Jewish Thought, The Hebrew University of Jerusalem

Aryeh Kofsky
Department of Israel Studies, University of Haifa

Christoph Markschies
Faculty of Theology, Humboldt University of Berlin

Yonatan Moss
Department of Comparative Religion, The Hebrew University of Jerusalem

Maren R. Niehoff
Department of Jewish Thought, The Hebrew University of Jerusalem

Miriam Ovadia
Doctoral candidate, Berlin Graduate School Muslim Cultures and Societies, Freie Universität Berlin

Serge Ruzer
Department of Comparative Religion, The Hebrew University of Jerusalem

Shaul Shaked
Department of Islamic and Middle Eastern Studies, The Hebrew University of Jerusalem

Moshe Sluhovsky
Department of History, The Hebrew University of Jerusalem

https://doi.org/10.1515/9783110446395-017

Sarah Stroumsa
Department of Arabic Language and Literature and Department of Jewish Thought, The Hebrew University of Jerusalem

Johannes Zachhuber
Faculty of Theology and Religion, University of Oxford

Index

Places

Abū Qubays, Mount 236
Abyssinia 292 n.14
Africa (Afrika) 184
Al-Andalus 47 f., 216 f.
Alexandria 2, 24–39, 63 f., 103, 105 n.10, 115
Antioch 110, 115
Arabia 291 f., 298
Asia (Asien) 181, 184
Asia Minor (Kleinasien) 181
Athens 23
Baghdad 18 n.37, 215–218, 226, 240
al-Baṭḥāʾ 230
Berlin 2 f., 146
Bethzatha 78
Byzantine Empire 291
Byzantium 216 n.50
Caesarea 64, 68
Cairo 227, 249, 254 n.140
Central Europe 58
Chalcedon 103 f.
China 298
Constantinople 104
Damascus 213, 227, 248–250, 254 n.140, 256 n.152, 261 f.
Dresden 194
Dublin 160
Edessa 74
Egypt 48, 103
Ephesus 104 n.4, 112
Europe (Europa) 47, 58, 127 f., 137, 157, 184
France 152
Germany (Deutschland) 58, 152, 181
Gibraltar, Straits of 217
Greece (Griechenland) 22, 181 n.3, 291
Iberian Peninsula 217
India 14, 239 n.75, 248 n.112, 289
Iran 8, 204
Iraq 204
Israel (Land of Israel) 34, 286 n.100
Italy 152
Japan 298
Jerusalem 2, 64, 205
Jordan River 79
Khorasan (Khurāsān) 18 n.37, 241
Loretto 152
Mecca 230, 236
Nazareth 152
Nisibis 206, 211
Nīshāpūr 224, 227, 239 f.
North Africa (Nordafrika) 181 n.3, 216 f.
North America (Nordamerika) 184
North Pole 248 n.115
Orient 1, 218
Pakistan 289 f.
Palestine 152
Paris 135
Persia 239 n.75, 248 n.112
Persian Empire 291
Portugal 152
Princeton 2
Provence 48
Prussia 162
Qayrawān 217
Rome 22 f., 26, 31–39, 137, 152
Safed 49, 55
Sinai 103
South America (Südamerika) 184
South Pole 248 n.115
Spain 47 f., 152, 218
Syria 152
St. Catherine's Monastery 103
Tübingen 65, 167
Western Europe (Westeuropa) 181
Zurich 65

https://doi.org/10.1515/9783110446395-018

Names

A

Abaelard 159
ʿAbbās ibn ʿAbd al-Muṭṭalib 230–233
ʿAbd al-Jabbār 236 f.
ʿAbd al-Raḥmān III, Caliph 217
ʿAbdīšōʿ 7
Abrahamov, Binyamin 289
Abū al-Hudhayl al-ʿAllāf 212, 235 f.
Abū Bishr Mattā ibn Yūnus 215
Abū Hurayra 232
Abū Yaʿlā 230 n.27
Abulafia, Abraham 52–54
Ādurbād ī Ēmēdān 8
Agrippa, Heinrich Cornelius 135
Aḥmad al-Nāṣir li-Dīn Allāh 206
al-Ājurrī, Abū Bakr 226, 232 f., 249
Albertus Magnus 183 n.6
Alemanno, Yohanan 54 n.29
Alfonso X Sabio (the Wise) 48
Allen, Pauline 106
Ammonius Saccas 64
Anastasius of Sinai 103–110, 113 f., 122
Andreas of Samosata 107 n.18
Anselm of Canterbury 165, 190 n.10
Aphrahat 74, 83 n.41, 87 n.61, 88
Apion 34
Apollinarius of Laodicea 82 n.39, 85 f., 110 n.33, 112 f., 122 n.76
Aristeas 25
Aristobulus 24 f.
Aristotle (Aristoteles) 132, 160, 162, 178, 251 n.127, 280 f.
al-Ashʿarī, Abu ʿl-Ḥasan 232, 234, 237 f., 243–245, 249
Athanasius 111
al-Atharī, Zuhayr 238 f.
Augustine (Augustinus) 22 n.3, 24, 94, 132, 190 n.11
Austin, J.L. 54, 220
Averroes – see Ibn Rushd

B

Bacon, Francis 132
Basil of Caesarea 104, 106, 115–120
al-Baṣrī, Shabīb ibn Shayba 213 f.
Baur, Ferdinand Christian 162, 167, 171, 173 f.
Benedict XIV, Pope 136
Berner, Ulrich 65
Biel, Gabriel 133
Bonhoeffer, Dietrich 183 n.7

C

Carlebach, Joseph 183 n.7
Cascardi, Anthony J. 127 n.2
Chrysippus 32
Chrysostom, John 106, 117 f.
Cicero 22 n.3, 32, 35, 37, 133
Clark, Stuart 128, 139
Cleanthes 37 f.
Clement of Alexandria 2, 23, 63
Cohen, Hermann 58
Constantine, Emperor 214
Cook, Michael 209
Cordovero, Moses 55–58, 285 n.94
Crouzel, Henri 65–67
Cyril of Alexandria 104–106, 115 f., 119 f.

D

al-Ḍaḥḥāk ibn Muzāḥim 230 f., 233
al-Daqqāq, Abū ʿAlī 272
al-Dārimī, ʿUthmān ibn Saʿīd 245
Darwin, Charles 192 n.13
Daston, Lorraine 137
Della Porta, Giambattista 135
Delp, Alfred 183 n.7
Delrio, Martin 135
Descartes, René 129, 132–134, 139 f.
al-Dhahabī, Shams al-Dīn 224, 233 n.41, 235 n.47, 239 f., 249 f., 252, 256, 260–262., 264
Diodore of Tarsus 74 f., 81 f., 84
Dioscorus of Alexandria 104
Drory, Rina 204 f., 215
Duns Scotus, John 132
Dupré, Louis 127 n.2

E

Eckhart, Meister 183 n.6, 190 n.11
Ephrem the Syrian 75

Euclid 135
Eudorus 29
Eusebius of Caesarea 24, 87
Eusebius of Emesa 74
Euthyphron 180 n.2

F
al-Fārābī 218, 270
de Faye, Eugène 66 f.
al-Fazārī, ʿAbd Allāh b. Yazīd 206
Felix of Rome 110 n.33
Festinger, Leon 108
Fichte, Johann Gottlieb 163, 192
Flavian of Constantinople 104 f., 107 n.18
Foucault, Michel 140, 141 n.46
Freud, Sigmund 21, 108

G
Gaius Caligula 25, 34
Gerson, Jean 136, 140
Gethmann, Carl Friedrich 1, 63
al-Ghazālī 271–273, 283
Gray, Patrick 109 f., 114, 115 n.56
Gregory of Nazianzen 104, 113, 115 f., 119 f.
Gregory of Nyssa 115, 119 f.
Gregory of Nystazon 103–105
Gregory of Rimini 133
Gregory the Wonderworker (Gregor Thaumaturgus) 68, 110–113, 122 n.76
Gutas, Dimitri 203

H
Halevi, Yehuda 48
Harnack, Adolf von 66 f., 173
Hartung, Jan-Peter 290
Ḥasan b. Muḥammad 209
Hegel, Georg Wilhelm Friedrich 163, 166, 169, 178, 192
Heraclitus 22
Herodot 181
Hildegard von Bingen 190 n.11
Hishām ibn al-Ḥakam 235–237
Homer 21–23, 26, 28 f., 39, 216 n.50
Horace 34
al-Hujwīrī 272
al-Ḥumaydī 217
Humboldt, Wilhelm von 183 n.5
Ḥunayn ibn Isḥāq 216 n.50
Hypatius 112

I
Ibn Abī Ṭāhir Ṭayfūr 214
Ibn Abī Zayd, Abū Muḥammad 217
Ibn al-ʿArabī 270–286
Ibn Dawud, Abraham 48
Ibn Ezra, Abraham 48 f.
Ibn Ezra, Moshe 48
Ibn Fūrak, Muḥammad ibn al-Ḥasan 239 f. 242, 245 f., 249
Ibn Gabbai, Meir 58 n.42
Ibn Gabirol, Shlomo (Abicebrol) 48, 51
Ibn Ḥanbal, Aḥmad 233 n.41, 243, 254 n.141
Ibn Hishām, ʿAbd al-Malik 292 n.14
Ibn al-Jawzī 230 n.27
Ibn Karrām, Abū ʿAbd Allāh Muḥammad 239
Ibn Kathīr, ʿImād al-Dīn Ismaʿīl 250
Ibn Khaldūn 206 f., 210
Ibn Khuzayma 224–227, 229–233, 249 f., 253, 260–262
Ibn Latif, Isaac 51
Ibn al-Layth, Abū Rabīʿ 214
Ibn Masarra, Muḥammad 217
Ibn Masʿūd, ʿAbd Allāh 232 f.
Ibn al-Mawṣilī 256 n.152
Ibn al-Mubārak, Abd Allāh 233 n.41, 253
Ibn Munabbih, Wahb 243
Ibn al-Muqaffaʿ 7, 8 n.5
Ibn Qayyim al-Jawziyya, Shams al-Dīn Muḥammad 249 f., 252–262, 264
Ibn al-Qifṭī 215 n.48
Ibn Qutayba 242 f., 249
Ibn Rushd, Abu ʾl-Walīd (Averroes) 218, 254 f., 260
Ibn Saʿdī 217
Ibn Ṣāʿid al-Andalusī, Ṣāʿid 202, 215
Ibn Sīnā 251 n.129, 255, 270
Ibn Subuktikīn, Maḥmūd (Sebüktegin) 239
Ibn Taymiyya, Taqī al-Dīn Aḥmad 227, 249–254, 256 f., 260–264

Irenaeus of Lyons 63, 68, 87
Isaac of Acre 51
al-Isfarāyīnī, Abu 'l-ʿAbbās 240
al-Isfarāyīnī, Abū Isḥāq ibn Muḥammad 240, 242
al-Isfarāyīnī, Abu 'l-Muẓaffar 240–242, 245
Ivins, William M. Jr. 128

J
Jacob ben Sheshet 51
Jacobi, Friedrich Heinrich 150 n.26, 151
Jaʿfar b. Abī Ṭālib 292 n.4
Jahm ibn Ṣafwān 235 n.47
al-Jandī 286 n.98
Jay, Martin 128, 132
Jesus 23, 76–80, 83, 86–98, 103, 112, 113 n.49, 148–150, 168, 214, 285
John the Baptist 79 f.
John of Scythopolis 111 n.42
John of Zyga 103–105
Joseph ben Shalom Ashkenazi 54 n.29
Josephus 34
Julian of Halicarnassus 112 f., 120
Julius of Rome 110 n.33, 111
Justin Martyr 23, 25, 63, 87
Justinian, Emperor 111
al-Juwaynī, ʿAbd Allāh ibn Yusūf 247 f., 251
al-Juwaynī, Imām al-Ḥaramayn Abu 'l-Maʿālī 245–247, 249, 264

K
al-Kalābādhī 271
Kant, Immanuel 150 n.26, 178, 183 n.5, 192, 198 n.16
al-Kāshānī 286, n.98
Kepler, Johannes 132
al-Kharrāz 271
Kieckhefer, Richard 128
Kierkegaard, Søren 190 n.11
al-Kindī 270

L
Lambertini, Prospero 136 f.
Lavater, Ludwig 138
Leibniz, Gottfried Wilhem 178, 199
Leibowitz, Yeshayahu 58
Leo of Rome 104, 107 n.18
Leontius of Byzantium 75, 111 n.42
Leontius of Jerusalem 108 n.22, 111 n.42, 115 n.59
Lessing, Gotthold Ephraim 161
Lévi, Israël 15 n.29
Luhmann, Niklas 178
Luther, Martin 179, 194 n.14

M
Mahdi, Muḥsin 216
Maimonides 33, 48, 53, 58
Makdisi, George 228
al-Makkī 271
Mānkdīm Shashdīv 236
Mardān-Farrox 8, 16, 18 n.37
Mawdūdī, Abū al-Aʿlā 289–299
Mendelssohn, Moses 58
Merton, Robert 127 n.2
Mill, John Stuart 183 n.5
Moltke, Helmuth James von 183 n.7
Moses 24, 27, 35, 51, 148, 243
al-Mubārak, ʿAbd Allāh ibn 233 n.41, 253
Muḥammad (the Prophet) 148, 208, 229–232, 246, 254 n.149, 270, 292, 294, 298
al-Muḥāsibī 271
al-Muqammaṣ, Dāwūd Ibn Marwān (Muqammis) 33 n.22, 205 f., 211–214, 219 f.

N
Nestorius 112
Newman, John Henry 158 n.8, 160
Nonnus of Nisibis 206
Nyberg, Henrik Samuel 207

O
Oresme, Nicole 132, 134
Origen of Alexandria (Origenes) 2, 63–71, 83 n.42, 87, 159 n.10

P
Pannenberg, Wolfhart 160
Pascal, Blaise 190 n.11

Paul, St. 23, 38, 63, 69 f., 80, 83, 86, 106 f., 130, 133, 172
Paul of Samosata 119
Pena, Jean 135
Peter of Callinicum 110, 114–122
Petronius 34
Phillips, Adam 103, 122
Philo of Alexandria 21–39, 45
Philolaus 29
Philoponus, John 159 n.10
Philoxenus of Mabbug 80 n.30
Pines, Shlomo 204, 207
Plato 22 f., 27–31, 35, 39, 67, 180 n.2, 251 n.127, 279
Pope, Alexander 49
Popkin, Richard 139
Posidonius 35
Ptolemy, Claudius 251 n.127

Q
Qardagh, Mar 7
al-Qāsim b. Ibrāhīm 7, 8 n.5
al-Qayṣarī 286
al-Qirqisānī, Abū Yaʿqūb 206
al-Qūmisī, Daniel 205
al-Qūnawī 286 n.98
al-Qushayrī 271
Quṭb, Sayyid 289

R
al-Rāzī, Fakhr al-Din 234 n.46, 246 f., 254 n.142, 262
Ritschl, Albrecht 162, 173 f.
Rosenthal, Franz 279, 281
Rufinus of Aquileia 68
Rufus, John 105 n.8

S
Saadya Gaon 18 n.37, 33, 205, 219
Sarasin, Philipp 65, 67, 70
al-Sarrāj 271
Schäfer, Peter 2
Schelling, Wilhelm Joseph 170 f.
Schleiermacher, Friedrich Daniel Ernst 146–154, 160, 162–166, 168–170, 172–174, 192
Schmidtke, Sabine 2
Scholem, Gershom 59
Searle, John 54
Sebuktegin – see Ibn Subuktikīn
Seneca 35, 37 f.
Severus of Antioch 105 nn.10 and 12, 110–116, 120–122
al-Shahrastānī, ʿAbd al-Karīm 241 f.
al-Shahrazūrī, Ibn al-Ṣalāḥ Abū ʿAmr ʿUthmān 253
al-Sijistānī, Abū Sulaymān 218
al-Sīrāfī, Abū Saʿīd 215 f.
Sokrates 183 n.5
Spinoza, Baruch 132, 150 n.26
Strauss, David Friedrich 162, 168–174
al-Ṣuʿlūkī, Abū Sahl 272
al-Suyūṭī, Jalāl al-Dīn 263 f.

T
Tacitus 34
Tannous, Jack 209
Teresa, Saint, of Avila 135
Tertullian 24
Theodore of Mopsuestia 74–98
Theodoret of Cyrrhus 75 n.10
Theodosius of Alexandria 103, 115–120
Thillet, Pierre 204 n.10
Thomas Aquinas 135, 160, 164, 178
al-Tirmidhī 272
Treiger, Alexander 209
Troeltsch, Ernst 171

V
Vajda, Georges 213
van Ess, Josef 203 f., 208, 210 n.33
Varro 22–24
Viberg, Åke 129
Virgil 133
Vogt, Hermann Josef 65, 67

W
Wansbrough, John 209
Weber, Max 1–3, 63 n.2, 108, 127 n.2, 156, 158 nn.6 and 7, 175
Whittaker, John 29 f.
William of Ockham 132 f., 160
Wolfson, Harry Austryn 209

www.ingramcontent.com/pod-product-compliance
Lightning Source LLC
Chambersburg PA
CBHW031758220426
43662CB00007B/446
* 9 7 8 3 1 1 0 7 3 6 5 9 5 *